The Incomplete Child

Disability
Studies in
Education

Susan L. Gabel and Scot Danforth
General Editors

Vol. 6

PETER LANG
New York • Washington, D.C./Baltimore • Bern
Frankfurt am Main • Berlin • Brussels • Vienna • Oxford

SCOT DANFORTH

The Incomplete Child

An Intellectual History of Learning Disabilities

PETER LANG
New York • Washington, D.C./Baltimore • Bern
Frankfurt am Main • Berlin • Brussels • Vienna • Oxford

KH

Library of Congress Cataloging-in-Publication Data

Danforth, Scot.
The incomplete child: an intellectual history of learning disabilities / Scot Danforth.
p. cm. — (Disability studies in education; v. 8)
Includes bibliographical references and index.
1. Learning disabilities—History. I. Title.
RJ506.L4D36   618.92'85889—dc22   2009000751
ISBN 978-1-4331-0171-7 (hardcover)
ISBN 978-1-4331-0170-0 (paperback)
ISSN 1548-7210

Bibliographic information published by **Die Deutsche Bibliothek**.
Die Deutsche Bibliothek lists this publication in the "Deutsche
Nationalbibliografie"; detailed bibliographic data is available
on the Internet at http://dnb.ddb.de/.

The artist's permission to reproduce the cover image is gratefully acknowledged.

The paper in this book meets the guidelines for permanence and durability
of the Committee on Production Guidelines for Book Longevity
of the Council of Library Resources.

Printed in the United States of America

12/10/10

This book is dedicated to James L. Paul, William C. Rhodes, and George W. Danforth, Sr., three men who taught me with great patience and wisdom.

Table OF Contents

Acknowledgments

I wish to thank the helpful staff members at the Archives Research Center, University of Illinois, for providing assistance with the Samuel A. Kirk Papers. I am also thankful for the assistance provided by the staff at the Archival Services and University of Northern Colorado, James A. Michener Library, in arranging my access to the Newell C. Kephart Special Collection.

I am grateful for the support of my friend Susan Gabel, who graciously reviewed the entire manuscript.

Finally, I thank the capable editorial and production teams at Peter Lang, who have worked so hard to produce this book.

CHAPTER ONE

Introduction

OF CORRIDORS AND CANYONS

In 1929, a graduate student in psychology at the University of Chicago met each night with a 10-year-old boy in the doorway of a bathroom of an Oak Forest (Illinois) institution for delinquent children. Samuel A. Kirk was working in the hospital ward, caring for and playing with the children in the evening hours. He found that a boy was unable to read, a less-than-surprising discovery among a population of mental defectives. Kirk began tutoring the youngster after all the other children had gone to bed. The two sat on the cold tile floor, under a small light in the corridor, whispering so as not to be caught by the staff nurses. There, in the least auspicious surroundings possible, the young man who later would be viewed as the father of the field of learning disabilities first encountered a child who could not read.[1]

This instructional moment would seem to be almost pure in its simplicity, an example of the kind of undistilled and genuine experience described by novelist Walker Percy in his account of Spanish explorer García López de Cárdenas discovering the Grand Canyon. In his well-known essay "The Loss of the Creature," Percy theorizes that when the sixteenth-century Spaniard first stumbled upon the Grand Canyon, it was possible for him to directly appreciate the natural phenomenon. The explorer's initial experience of the canyon had an authenticity that is no longer available to the millions of modern tourists who now visit the site. In modern life, authoritative cultural knowledge and many artifacts of expertise are often accumulated around an object of interest such that the object itself is obscured. The result is that one experiences an organized and standardized package rather than the raw, unadorned thing itself.

> Why is it almost impossible to gaze directly at the Grand Canyon under those circumstances and see it for what it is as one picks up a strange object from one's back yard and gazes directly at it? It is impossible because the Grand Canyon, the thing that it is, has been appropriated by the symbolic complex which has already been formed in the sightseer's mind. Seeing the canyon under approved circumstance is seeing the symbolic complex head on. The thing is no longer the thing as confronted by the Spaniard; it is rather that which has already been formulated by picture postcards, geography book, tourist folders, and the words *Grand Canyon*.[2]

The tourist who visits the Grand Canyon engages an array of culturally prescribed meanings, a symbolic formulation about what the canyon is, its significance, and how it appears to a visitor. Percy notes that the tourist who travels to the Grand Canyon appraises the quality of his visit based on a comparison of his experience to what he believes such a trip should look and feel like. The features of the symbolic complex that conceal the canyon from authentic experience dominate the tourist's mode of appreciation, rendering the canyon itself hidden.

Sitting alone on the floor with a child struggling to learn, communicating in hushed tones to preserve secrecy, neither supported nor fettered by the authorized curriculum and instructional procedures of the classroom, the young Kirk faced the pedagogical challenge in the raw. Stripped of all educational accoutrements, teacher met student in pure encounter, in innocence uncluttered by the theoretical trappings of educational research or the regimented traditions of the typical school. It was Kirk's first attempt at solving the puzzle that would frame his entire career. He tried to figure out what the child actually needed and what the teacher could effectively provide.

The educational and psychological literature available to an enthusiastic graduate student avidly seeking expertise on how to provide a program of remedial reading was slim. Kirk read what he could, including physician James Hinshelwood's studies of word-blindness,[3] psychologist Marion Monroe's application of new educational measurement techniques to the problem of reading defects,[4] and Grace Fernald's use of kinesthetic methods of instruction.[5] Still Kirk proceeded without substantial guidance that actually applied to the situation. In 1929, there was little scientific information on reading disabilities to organize and direct the instructor's thinking. Kirk was left with whatever ideas he could muster from within the actual experience of teaching the child.

It would be difficult to believe that Kirk was operating in a vacuum of cultural or authoritative knowledge. Despite the lack of useful knowledge available to inform his teaching, he was far from conceptually naked in his first pedagogical encounter at the Illinois institution for the feebleminded. His understanding of the non-reading child—although practically underfunded, given the immense challenge of developing a program of educational treatment—was derived from an existing symbolic complex. Like nearly all of his colleagues in the fields of psychology and medicine who would contribute to the understanding of learning disability in later decades, Kirk began his career working with children with mental retardation in institutional settings. He was fully steeped in the then-current scheme of educational and psychological notions about mental deficiency. His thinking about children who fail to learn began with a symbolic complex concerning the mentally retarded child.

FEEBLEMINDEDNESS AS SYMBOLIC COMPLEX

As reading researcher Marion Monroe observed in 1932, psychology and education had two primary explanations for children who did not learn under typical instructional circumstances. They were "either lazy or stupid."[6] Or as Alfred Binet had put it, "the teacher and the parent must incriminate either the child's intelligence or his character."[7] Some children of adequate intelligence simply lacked the proper motivation, attitude, or moral character to succeed in school. Other children were mentally deficient, feebleminded, operating with a substandard intellectual capacity that failed to garner basic educational concepts and skills.

The cultural meaning of mental deficiency at that time was greatly guided by the popularization of American intelligence tests. Lewis Terman of Stanford University and Henry H. Goddard at the Vineland Training School were among the earliest American producers and most influential proponents of English-language versions of Alfred Binet's original test. The French ministry of education had asked Binet to develop an instrument to identify students who were failing in school and needed some form of special education. Between 1905 and 1911, Binet published three versions of his intelligence scale. Unlike Binet, however, both Terman and Goddard viewed their tests as more than rough and handy ways to find children needing extra assistance. Both thought that their tests tapped into the essence of individual thinking capacity, the very power of a person's mind. Although John Dewey objected to this notion of individual intelligence as being contrary to democratic values, he had to admit that it fell neatly within an American brand of individualism that construed personal achievements of wealth, success, and social standing as expressions of individual constitution and character.[8] To Terman and Goddard, intelligence was a unitary, innate intellectual trait that remained unchanged over time and greatly dictated the course of a person's economic and social career. The vertical scale of status and wealth within society was a strong reflection of an underlying hierarchy of innate intellectual prowess across the population.[9]

If the developers of the new intelligence tests framed mental capacity as an inherited trait, it was eugenic science that loaded feeblemindedness with negative cultural meaning.[10] The most prominent example was Henry H. Goddard's 1912 study of the Kallikak family. The Kallikaks served as a professional and popular parable of eugenics, appearing in eleven printings over three decades and elevating Goddard to international fame.[11]

Beginning with a young woman named Deborah who was institutionalized at the Vineland Training School in New Jersey, Goddard traced mental defect along the branches of her family tree. He viewed his Kallikak study as "a natural experiment in heredity,"[12] a large-scale attempt to dramatically illustrate the popular eugenics belief that mental defect was passed down through generations by Mendel's laws of inheritance. Through a reconstruction of Deborah's family ancestry, Goddard found that, some six generations prior, a man of normal intelligence named Martin Kallikak, Jr., had fathered children with two women, one feebleminded and one normal. That presented Goddard with two distinct ancestral lines for the purposes of comparison, "one characterized by thoroughly good, respectable, normal citizenship, with almost no exceptions; the other being equally characterized by mental defect in every generation."[13] Of the 480 descendants on the defective half of the Kallikak family tree, Goddard identified 143 as feebleminded, only 46 clearly normal, and the rest either unknown or suspected of mental deficiency. In his analysis, reports of poverty, sexual license, and alcoholism were frequently interpreted as evidence of the weak-minded, defective type.[14] Goddard concluded: "Feeblemindedness is inherited and transmitted as surely as any other character."[15]

More striking, though, was Goddard's rhetoric of moralistic panic. His portrait of the Kallikaks sounded an urgent eugenic alarm that the feebleminded constituted "a distinct menace to society"[16] that must be addressed through institutional segregation and sterilization. His generational story of Deborah and her family was a starkly powerful melodrama that summarily reduced a wide variety of social ills—prostitution, alcoholism, unemployment, poverty, sexual perversion, and criminality—to the biological constitution of a single evil character. Weaving together sensational narratives and blunt statistics, he created a matinee spectacle that conflated societal ill and psychological defect within an identifiable culprit.

> These (morons) divide according to temperament into two groups, those who are
> phlegmatic, sluggish, indolent, simply lie down and would starve to death, if some

one did not help them. When they come to the attention of our charitable organizations, they are picked up and sent to the almshouse, if they cannot be made to work.
The other type is the nervous excitable kind who try to make a living, and not being
able to do it by a fair day's work and honest wages, attempt to succeed through dis-
honest methods. "Fraud is the force of weak natures." These become the criminal
type.[17]

Goddard estimated that one half of all criminals residing in prisons in the United
States were feebleminded. Prostitution and alcoholism could greatly be explained
as the folly of feebleminded persons lacking moral judgment and self-control.
Poverty and urban slums were social expressions of intellectual defect, loathsome
displays of the individual stain.

Goddard's esteemed colleagues Edgar Doll and Wallace Wallin, scientific
men of a more restrained and circumspect nature, also described mental deficiency
through the eugenic lexicon of racial betterment. Doll, a leading psychologist in
the field of mental deficiency who conducted his research with Goddard at the
Vineland Training School, viewed the mentally defective as a lesser sort of creature altogether, a mammalian type developed and then abandoned by evolution at
a stage somewhat less than fully human.

> Comparative psychologists have studied the learning of the paramecium, others
> have studied the adaptive reactions of the earthworm, while still others are inter-
> ested in the perceptual adaptations of the chimpanzee. In the idiot we have a level of
> behavior which bridges the gap between the highest animals and the lowest human
> species.[18]

This opinion greatly mirrored Charles Darwin's own view of feeblemindedness as
an evolutionary link between beasts and humans.[19]

Wallace Wallin was a scrupulous empiricist who analyzed every thesis in the
light of available scientific evidence. His principle message was the need for a more
rigorous science of diagnosis in order to properly place children in special classes
and schools.[20] After conducting a thorough review of prior research, he supported
a somewhat restrained version of Goddard's social menace thesis.

> All students of social problems will at least concede that feebleminded is *one* of the
> fundamental causes of our numerous social ills. It is a prolific source of poverty, desti-
> tution, all kinds of crime against property and persons, alcoholism, social immorality,
> illegitimacy, and of prolific and degenerate progeny.[21]

A full third of Wallin's 1924 text on the education of handicapped children was
devoted to a comprehensive discussion of all data and arguments concerning "the
social menace of the feebleminded."[22] His recommended solution to the problem

involved a complete eugenics program consisting of preventing "the marriage of the biologically unfit"[23] (through laws outlawing marriage for the feebleminded), authorizing euthanasia or "painless extermination,"[24] and enforcing sterilization of identified feebleminded persons.

"The ultimate objective should be to prevent or eradicate the condition, for the feebleminded…constitute a racial liability."[25] Wallin called euthanasia "an economical, expeditious, and practicable means of ridding society of defective strains."[26] Sterilization was a "beneficent operation for all those who are clearly feebleminded."[27] On both measures, however, Wallin griped that the public was too "sentimental"[28] to take the necessary eradication steps. "It is a waste of effort to advocate euthanasia at the present time. Society will not tolerate execution of defectives who have not committed a capital offense."[29] Similarly, even if forced sterilization laws could be passed in all states, "there is little likelihood that they will be enforced."[30]

Education and colonization were generally viewed as the most pragmatic forms of public defense against the social menace of the feebleminded. Incarceration in institutions was widely recommended for children of the lower grades of intellect, the idiots and imbeciles who were consistently viewed by researchers and school districts as "a menace to other pupils" who "should be cared for in public institutions."[31] Segregation was necessary to safeguard against the moral damage that a defective would wreak upon society. For children of the upper grades of intelligence, often called morons, many public schools and state training schools provided educational programs aimed at preparing them for lower-level industrial vocations and inculcating proper moral attitudes and social habits.[32] The feebleminded tended to fill the lower rungs of the socioeconomic ladder. The question for education was whether they could be adequately prepared, in relation to moral habits and basic labor skills, to hold down jobs and escape delinquent activity. In order to avoid becoming an economic burden, a moral blight, and a social hardship to the normal population, morons of a docile attitude might be trained to fill "the ranks of unskilled labor" that readily awaited them in the industrial economy.[33]

SPECIAL EDUCATION FOR FEEBLEMINDED CHILDREN

Wallin and Doll served on an Ohio committee organized to plan special education programs in the public schools. The committee's 1925 report described the preventative purpose of schooling mental defectives.

It is a recognized fact that the early training of the mentally deficient child, in many instances, determines whether he is to become a stable, law-abiding, even self-supporting citizen, or a menace to his community and a financial burden to his state.[34]

In order to "establish such habits as may be valuable to the child in the social and industrial world,"[35] the committee recommended that Ohio schools offer a curriculum limited to less than half academic instruction in the most rudimentary form; "numbers, simple writing, drawing, fundamentals of reading."[36] The greater part of instruction should be devoted to manual arts, vocational preparation, and moral training. "Health habits, courtesy, regularity of attendance, punctuality, obedience, self-control, stability, and cooperation should be stressed."[37]

A survey of the special education program in the public schools of Trenton, New Jersey, completed by a committee chaired by Doll, recommended a decrease in academic instruction because of the defectives' "inaptitude for academic school work except when such work is of the most concrete and routine character."[38] Even the highest grades of feebleminded students might reach only fourth-grade level academic work. Instruction should instead focus on preparation for the social roles and employment activities potentially available to them. "Training in domestic activities" should prepare girls to "work in their own homes as housekeepers, in other homes as maids or servants, or in restaurants or other commercial establishments."[39] For "the manually minded boy,"[40] instruction should emphasize vocational skills necessary for "industrial adjustment,"[41] especially project work with wood and metal. The ability to accept and operate effectively within a limited range of social roles at the lower rungs of the economic system was not only viewed as the most positive educational outcome but was also understood to serve as a deterrent to the development of "antagonistic social attitudes" and "delinquent tendencies."[42]

Perhaps the most popular account of the special education of feebleminded children was Meta Anderson's description of the Newark (New Jersey) program that she supervised. In contrast to the sweeping scientific statements of Goddard, Wallin, and Doll, Anderson's 1917 book offered a humble guide to other educators based on her own experiences. She provided frank, practical advice and detailed discussions of many aspects of educational programming for these students. In terms of academic skills, the defective child, in her experience, was "retarded three years or more"[43] in comparison to his classmates. More often than not, he was a boy living in "the ghetto," where a dearth of income and intelligence united in a crude social environment. The students

know the roughest kind of talk. They defend themselves from their brothers and sisters and companions, and even from their fathers, by fighting. It is enlightening to watch the children and even the adults of the slums at play. They often amuse themselves by banging each other on the back, by tripping each other, and in various not gentle ways. It is their idea of fun.[44]

Anderson advised teachers to understand why such children, coming from primitive families and communities, cannot "act in accordance with the teacher's ideals and standards."[45]

Given the mental and cultural limitations of the students, Anderson counseled educators to devise a curriculum that downplayed academics in favor of moral and vocational goals.

> The following subjects should be included in the course of study for the classes of defectives: habits of personal cleanliness, sense training, manual training, physical training, vocational and industrial training, gardening, academic work, [and] speech training.[46]

In the Introduction to Anderson's book, Goddard wholeheartedly praised the author for her pragmatic approach to teaching mentally defective children. She set aside "will-o-the-wisp" dreams "that the end of the work shall be to make these children normal" in order to "train them to do some simple thing which will be useful."[47] Preparation for social utility consisted primarily of training in habits of moral behavior and, if possible, the skills of a very basic form of manual labor.

Ironically, as the leading experts in the field of the education of mentally defective children presented practical advice on all manner of pedagogical detail, such as diagnostic procedures, classroom placement, and curriculum, they also declared the evident futility of even attempting to educate this population. Goddard described efforts to educate high-grade defectives in the most profoundly reluctant terms.

> A child once feebleminded is never made normal. A very, very small percentage of them can be trained to eke out a miserable existence, perhaps supporting themselves; but it is probably cruel to require even that of them.[48]

He advised the public schools of New York City to try to convince parents of the feebleminded that colonies and institutions were attractive and joyful places so that they would choose for their children incarceration over living at home and attending the public schools. He also proposed that child labor laws be modified so as to not apply to mentally retarded children so that they could leave school for employment as early as possible.

Meta Anderson, after carefully delivering one hundred pages of her hard-earned wisdom drawn from her years of working closely with mentally deficient students, concluded her book by throwing her hands up in despair.

> This discussion has treated the education of the true defective, not of the backward or the borderline case. It has been contended that the borderline and backward cases are the only ones to whom it is worthwhile to give special education. This is undoubtedly

true. However every school system has a large number of defectives attending the regular schools. Most authorities say that two per cent of the school population is feebleminded. These children must be taken care of. Each and every true defective cannot be expelled from the school and left to roam the streets.[49]

Almost as an afterthought, Anderson noted that the education of the defective child was of really no use. If a teacher somehow had some success in teaching such a child, then that student must not be a "true defective." If he actually learned and grew, that was evidence of intellectual potential. Only a backward or border-line case would have actual potential, some underlying mental assets that might expand and progress when subjected to instruction. The truly defective child was educationally hopeless.

When President Hoover organized the 1930 White House Conference on Child Health and Protection, with a significant list of expert-loaded subcommit-tees devoted to studying the education and well-being of handicapped children, it marked a renewed professional and governmental attitude toward special educa-tion. The conference reports were filled with fresh optimism. The resulting "Bill of Rights for the Handicapped Child" mixed a mature commitment to improving the education and lives of disabled children with a maudlin promise of "a life on which his handicap casts no shadow." The high-profile meetings were buoyant with hope. Yet the Committee on Problems of Mental Deficiency[50] laced their description of mental retardation with the ideological language of eugenic racism. The feebleminded were portrayed as a dangerous class prone to chronic unemploy-ment, dependency on charitable institutions, and criminal behavior.

The optimism offered by the committee was in the nature of a surprising solution. Programs of educational and vocational training, as primary methods of "social control," had proved to be more successful in setting the feebleminded on paths of decency than Goddard, Doll, or anyone else had predicted.

> We know that they need specialized and differentiated training; we have some knowledge of the types of industries and occupations that can be taught successfully to the various groups at the various age levels; and many more persons of low intel-ligence can be diverted into channels of social usefulness if we act on our present knowledge, incomplete though it undoubtedly is.[51]

When combined with practices of institutional segregation and selective steriliza-tion, as well as careful programs of community supervision of deinstitutionalized parolees, school-based training could effectively diminish the harm that the fee-bleminded inflicted on America's communities.

Even when packaged within the almost mandated sanguinity of the 1930 White House Conference, the early twentieth-century account of the educational potential of mentally deficient children was a tale of virtually impenetrable incompetence. To the extent that schooling opportunities were provided to these children, standard practice set aside typical academic pursuits in favor of training in functional skills such as hygiene care and simple forms of manual labor.[52] Reading was widely understood to be not only beyond the intellectual potential of the mentally deficient child but quite unnecessary given the child's meager life prospects.[53]

Sam Kirk's efforts in 1929 to provide remedial reading instruction to his first student were immersed in the thick symbolic complex that fashioned the mentally retardated child as wholly incapable and unworthy of serious academic instruction. No wonder the instructional sessions took place on the sly, for he was teaching the undeniably unteachable.

AN ODD ASSUMPTION

The history of the science of learning disabilities involved multiple efforts to locate intellectual potential among children generally viewed as having none. Such efforts re-theorized the capacities of *some* mentally defective children in a more positive light. Possibilities for growth and advancement were culled from the human pool of deficiency. The result was the very forthright celebration of hidden potential now reclaimed, of overlooked and undervalued children now elevated through focused instruction. At the underside, unnoticed but still resounding, was the quiet rededication of the destitute quality of those children left behind. Some would be—indeed, only those that could be—saved. And some would be, especially after the sweeping pass of optimistic educators searching for concealed abilities, left behind as more truly defective than before.

But it all began most assuredly not with thoughts of leaving the most severely impaired behind but with grand ideas about the chances of learning and growth among educationally forlorn cases. Kirk's actions demonstrated his belief that a mentally defective child living in an institution could learn to read to a significant degree. In a defective human being that, by authoritative definition and common sense, lacked useful potential to learn, Kirk assumed that a proper instructional approach could find and tap into unacknowledged intellectual assets. His naiveté or optimism was rewarded, as the boy made substantial progress in reading under his tutelage.

Sam Kirk was not alone in this odd assumption. Soon after his first pedagogical experience in the corridor shadows of the boy's ward, countercurrents to the dominant narrative of educational hopelessness erupted at two American scientific sites. The Wayne County Training School in Northville, Michigan, and the

Iowa Child Welfare Research Station in Iowa City, research centers that would become the scientific proving grounds for future leaders in the learning disabilities movement, launched investigations of the educational potential of persons who ostensibly had none. Prior to World War II, the Iowa Station and the Wayne School research programs crafted the two primary approaches to the diagnostic identification and educational cultivation of intellectual potential among mentally defective children.

The Iowa Station researchers greatly embraced the American psychometric invention of a unitary concept of mental power, as measured by the IQ test. Their novel proposal was that a mind's general level of functioning could be dramatically raised through early education. The Wayne School drew extensively from the European medical science of aphasiology to frame the mind as multifaceted rather than singular in nature. Learning failures frequently involved specific brain dysfunctions occurring in some degree of isolation from the remaining and ample capacities of the mind. What these psychological research centers shared was a theoretical and practical assumption about the existence of hidden or untapped learning potential within the defective child. In doing so, each presupposed the profound ability of physicians, psychologists, and educators to locate cases of previously undetected intellectual capacity and provide instructional treatment for normalization.

MIND AS MULTIPLE: THE WAYNE SCHOOL

In 1929, Wayne School research director Thorleif G. "Ted" Hegge initiated the clinical study of reading difficulties of feebleminded children with an emphasis on developing instructional practices for successful remediation. Hegge was an unusual psychologist who believed that all children with IQs above 60 could learn to read, and that many more with even lower scores had reading potential. Working closely with his assistant Sam Kirk, by then a new Ph.D. graduate from the University of Michigan, he focused on the development of a pedagogical treatment for reading defect among this population.[54] In the late 1930s, Hegge was joined by Alfred A. Strauss, Heinz Werner, and Laura Lehtinen—a physician, a psychologist, and an educator respectively—who dramatically extended the pursuit of unacknowledged learning potential through a new concept of undiagnosed brain injury among the Wayne School children. While Hegge was the originator and the leadership force behind Wayne School's conceptual orientation to human potential and child learning difficulties, German neurologist Alfred Strauss became the intellectual source of the school's adaptation of medical aphasiology to the learning problems of children.

Strauss had been trained in the European study of aphasia, a medical science that viewed the human mind as consisting of somewhat compartmentalized areas of capability. Aphasia researchers had traced various forms of language loss to disease, injury, or congenital defect within the brain. A mind fully capable and a person completely competent could, with the sudden inflammation of brain tissue due to fever or illness, lose the ability to speak, read, or understand spoken language.[55] In 1895, James Hinshelwood described a case of word-blindness, a very specific type of aphasia involving an inability to read, in a 55-year-old "man of intelligence and education."[56] The patient "was greatly startled to find that one morning in his own house that he could not read."[57] No other mental capacities were lost, only his reading skills. Hinshelwood concluded that word-blindness was "an isolated condition...the pathological condition of a special faculty" of language utilization in which the remaining mental abilities continued undisturbed. The patient was intellectually normal, still as smart as ever, but functionally and neurologically incomplete.

W. Pringle Morgan, in 1896, identified a case of a seventeen-year-old boy with word-blindness. He described his patient as "bright and intelligent...in no way inferior to others his age."[58] The mental disorder was highly specific and limited to reading activities.

> He says that he is fond of arithmetic, and has no difficulty with it, but that printed or written words "have no meaning to him," and my examination of him quite convinces me that he is correct in that opinion.[59]

Brain activities involving mathematics were untouched by the malady that targeted only the ability to comprehend printed words.

The medical science of aphasia was a knowledge tradition that studied the distinct anomalies of mental incompetence taking place within otherwise functioning minds. Intellectual activities were understood as multiple and parallel, involving numerous distinct abilities that could operate at greatly varied levels of practical effectiveness. Trained in the European aphasiology that variegated human intellectual potential into numerous areas of distinct capacities, Strauss viewed childhood learning failure not as a sign of total mental defect, or as a blight on psychological potential, but as an indication of discrete dysfunction within otherwise capable brains.

RAISING MINDS UP: THE IOWA STATION

In Iowa City, by the late 1930s, Beth Wellman, Harold Skeels, and George D. Stoddard had established the Iowa Child Welfare Research Station as the brightest beacon of American environmentalist thought. They formulated the foremost response to the Terman and Goddard thesis of human intelligence as an inherited and static constitutional trait. The Iowa Station research team proclaimed the groundbreaking thesis that minds grow, that intelligence—especially the still-developing capacity of young children—improves under the influence of educational stimulation.[60]

The self-conscious importance as well as the lofty benevolence of the environmentalist proposal was best stated by Newell C. Kephart, a doctoral student who studied under Stoddard and Skeels, worked closely with Strauss, and later became a leading learning disabilities researcher: "We have the enviable task of changing human liabilities into human assets."[61] The exalted notion that school environments could greatly influence, or even mold, young minds offered the fields of psychology and education an opportunity no smaller and no meeker than the total renovation of incompetence into competence, the purposeful elevation of mental deficients to the status of the normal or even greater. There is perhaps no notion more simultaneously humane and arrogant, optimistic and haughty, than the proposition that one can modify the power and capability of another person's mind, thereby elevating a human being to a higher terrain of dignity and accomplishment. This was the golden ring that awaited psychologists and educators, or at least those willing to embrace the environmental theory of intelligence, those wanting to have a lasting impact on children and families. It was undoubtedly an overwhelmingly appealing mission.

Harold Skeels and Beth Wellman, colleagues at the Iowa Station, occupied very different roles in the building and communication of that environmental message. Wellman was the stalwart and steady researcher trudging forward on the long road of empirical discovery. She worked meticulously with mounds of data from the Iowa Station preschool to demonstrate measured differences between the mental growth of children who attended preschool and those who did not. Throughout much of the 1930s, Wellman carefully tracked comparative groups of children with varied levels of preschool attendance. She found that the more preschool education a child received the higher his IQ in subsequent years.[62] Her research foreshadowed and supported the development of Head Start programs decades later, but she was under-celebrated for her scientific work. Perhaps because Wellman was a woman in a field of psychological science dominated by men, she was not the lauded star of the Iowa Station or the environmental movement.

Quite accidentally, Harold Skeels was the star. In the midst of his rather mundane work of administering intelligence tests to children, he stumbled upon a remarkable phenomenon and crafted the story that became the archetypal narrative of the environmental movement. It was the strange story of two mentally defective toddlers cared for by similarly deficient women residents at an Iowa state institution for the feebleminded. In less than two years of care, the children's IQ levels rose to normal levels.[63] It was the ultimate underdog, comeback kid, down-trodden rise up and the home team wins it in the bottom of the ninth story that both Hollywood and American psychology loved. It was a heart-wrenching saga of two parentless, unloved babies turned away by an orphanage because of their mental handicap. Sent to the desolate institution, they found the tender love of women who themselves had been cast away by society, adult defectives incarcerated by the State. The union of improbable mothers and rejected toddlers produced a miracle. In Iowa, in America's earnest heartland, defectiveness was cured. The Iowa Station's thesis professed that early stimulation influenced mental development, but no one had imagined a less likely group of characters to play the role of early educators. Even the stimulation provided by those lacking intelligence could grow normal minds! The two children, healed of mental deficiency, were subsequently adopted by normal families.[64] Skeels and his moving story of youngsters rescued from the throes of defectiveness would become the uplifting wind to the sails of generations of American psychologists and special educators.[65]

LEARNING DISABILITY AS SYMBOLIC COMPLEX

If today in the United States a young graduate student were to sit face to face with a 10-year-old boy who could not read, and to tutor the child, one can be certain that the term "learning disability" would be raised as a possible interpretation of the case. Kirk was teaching a child who, at first glance from our current perspective, would fit the general parameters of the well-known condition. He was clearly achieving far below his age and grade level in the area of reading. Undoubtedly further investigation involving multiple professionals and a number of psychometric and educational instruments would be required for a complete diagnosis. If this situation were set in current time, the graduate student would not only be struggling to figure out how to teach a non-reading youngster but also contending with a rich repository of psychological and neurological concepts, a vast scientific lexicon of learning disability that has accumulated over many decades of research and practice. He would need to confront, in Walker Percy's terms, the densely formulated symbolic complex in order to even begin to understand and teach the child.

Many researchers and practitioners in the field of learning disabilities would claim that appropriating and utilizing that complex greatly facilitates the goal of teaching the non-learning child. The symbolic complex of learning disability is a constellation of scientifically generated concepts, terms, and practices that yield an improved understanding of the child and his needs. Comprehending the

10-year-old struggling reader through the current science of learning disabilities is roughly parallel to understanding a person with dangerously high levels of blood sugar in terms of a medical science of diabetes. It is a lens that clarifies the situation and better allows helpful professionals to take effective action.

Critics of the field of learning disabilities would counter that the theoretical and empirical basis for the disorder is often a scientifically flawed distraction from the reality of the situation. Over the past three decades, the American public schools have misused the category of learning disability as a jargon-heavy, seemingly authoritative way of blaming individual students for the instructional and organizational shortcomings of the public schools. Rather than serving as a pathway to helpful treatment and support, the learning disability diagnosis has become a stigmatized ticket to an isolated classroom or school where the educational recipe consists of low academic expectations, an overrepresentation of students of color and those from low-income families, and decreased chances of high school graduation.

Regardless of where one stands on the validity of the science of learning disability, the work of many researchers who built the very concepts that frame our understanding of this condition and the diagnosed population matters deeply. Current efforts in the American public schools around learning disabilities utilize a series of notions whose origins and development remain greatly unexamined. Even most teachers who are prepared to teach students with identified learning disabilities know the science of learning disabilities only in an abridged and reduced form, a textbook depiction that often provides static, decontextualized lists of psychoeducational characteristics. The frequent result is a two-dimensional cutout character—the generic, multiply-flawed, learning-disabled child—a reified stereotype of who a child with a learning disability is as well as what that crudely crafted character cannot do. Often stripped away from such stale accounts is the richness, complexity, and contradiction of the long historical path involving many researchers attempting, within their own varied conceptions of the practice of a human science, to understand and then provide treatment for learning and behavioral difficulties of childhood. What is missing from researchers' understanding of the usual lists of learning disability characteristics is a serious appreciation of the variegated grounds of intellectual labor that fed and simultaneously undermined the construction of those very lists.

EXPLORING HISTORY

This is a book about how ideas about children and learning were gathered and fashioned into the late twentieth-century American notion called the learning disability. This is a story about how researchers from the fields of medicine, psychology, and education gradually built a new theoretical complex that was publically proclaimed by Kirk in a conference presentation in 1963 and established in federal special education policy with the passage of Learning Disabilities Education Act of 1969 (P.L. 91–230) and the Education of Handicapped Children Act of 1975 (P.L. 94–142).[66] It is an exploration of how the ideas and scientific practices of multiple disciplines were marshaled toward new understandings of children, and how those new understandings contributed to what became by the late 1960s the learning disability. Today 2.9 million American schoolchildren—4.3% of all public school students—are identified as having learning disabilities.[67] The goal of this book is to illuminate the multiple strands of scientific work that contributed to the founding of that specific way of understanding the learning difficulties of millions of American students.

The scientific development of the learning disability is not a wholly new topic, but it has received surprisingly little attention from historians. I began this project by turning to the important scholarship of James Carrier[68] and Barry Franklin.[69] Each has provided necessary insight into the history of the field of learning disabilities. Broadly speaking, the central focus for these researchers has been the examination of learning disabilities within twentieth-century American social and institutional life. Franklin explores the terrain of public school reform that occurred in the early 1900s as a space for the articulation of various concepts of learning difficulty. Somewhere between normal and defective, often under the early term "backward," a group of struggling students was represented by educational thought.

Carrier's sweeping treatment of learning disabilities in America emphasizes the political development of the disorder within the social activities of researchers and parent advocacy groups. For Carrier, it is impossible to distinguish between the science of learning disability and the words and actions of political activists pushing for special legislation in the 1960s and 1970s. The learning disability, from this stance, is a tainted product of a flawed and politicized science.

PHILOSOPHIE(S) OF SCIENCE(S)

This book explores the vast expanse of intellectual development across much of the twentieth century *behind* what American educators now casually know as a learning disability. This scientific activity includes an abundance of theories of learning and learning failure framed through numerous philosophical orientations to the practice of doing science employed by researchers in Europe and the United States.

A brief pause is necessary here to define some basic terms. The two primary epistemological traditions in the human sciences are objectivism and subjectivism. *Objectivism* involves the appropriation of the philosophy and methods of the natural sciences to the study of human activities.[70] It begins with "the belief that a mind-independent fixed reality forms the essential absolute or foundation for all knowing."[71] An objectivist social science attempts to accurately represent, often but not only through systems of measurement, realities of human living assumed to exist independent of scientific observers. Objectivist social scientists tend to seek nomothetic knowledge, rule-like generalizations that apply with accuracy across a wide range of cases or instances. *Subjectivism*, typically viewed as an orientation to social science standing starkly opposite to objectivism, emphasizes the socially and historically situated ideation of the scientists involved in acts of observing and interpreting social realities. Social science, in this light, involves multiple interpretations from human standpoints or perspectives that offer both compelling insights and distinct limitations. Frequently, subjectivist social scientists pursue ideographic forms of knowledge that recognize the unique qualities and features of individual cases while also recognizing commonalities across cases.[72]

The two main orientations in the social sciences to the scope of analysis are atomism and holism. *Atomism* "demands that all phenomena be understood as analytically decomposable into discrete, isolated, and fixed elements that operated jointly in a strictly additive fashion."[73] The task of science is to identify the distinct subelements of the entire entity, comprehend each in isolation, and then aggregate the small units of knowledge into a total picture of the whole. Atomistic approaches to social science often involve the measurement of parts of the whole collected within mechanized schemes of causal interaction between the parts. *Holism*, by contrast, begins with the assumption that the structural arrangement and character of the total observed entity tend to organize the functions and meanings of individual parts. Holistic approaches to human science often consist of organic interpretations of the structure and relationships between operating parts within the overall functionality of the total entity.

The learning disability construct erupted in the 1960s from a complex intellectual mélange fed by multiple traditions of research involving various understandings of the human being and the environment, and manifold approaches to the scientific treatment of the mind that fails to learn. From Germany came a turn-of-the-century neurology detailing the workings of the brain and the central nervous system as well as a pre-World War II Gestalt psychology. These German traditions offered a series of deep and often contradictory scientific attitudes: an atomistic view of mental functions and bodily reflexes, a holistic orientation toward understanding and valuing human life, an experimentalism emphasizing precision in measurement and observations, and a rich phenomenology of observation and clinical appraisal.

On American soil, these concepts of humanity and human science were admixed and layered with the eclecticism and practicality of pre-World War II functionalist psychology. Theories and practices were construed as tools to be valued primarily for their utility in effecting improvements in children's learning. Central to that functionalism was a growing field of educational measurement, a psychometric approach to dissecting the internal mental operations and observable behaviors of the struggling learner. Mingled with this quantitative, nomothetic orientation to science was a deep brand of practice-based qualitative analysis, a medical and psychological tradition of clinical research focusing on documenting the particularities of a single case. Objective and subjective forms of psychological appraisal operated in close tandem.

By the late 1960s, among leaders in the new American research field of learning disabilities—names such as Samuel Kirk, Newell Kephart, Marianne Frostig, Raymond Barsch, William Cruickshank, and Helmer Myklebust—the science they shared was an epistemological and methodological mongrel. To a philosopher of science seeking some kind of epistemological clarity and perhaps even a dose of purity, their multiform science would seem to be a patchwork muddle of antagonistic opposites. Objectivism shared the bed with subjectivism. Atomism broke bread with holism. Quantitative correlational analyses of experimental groups mixed with clinical observations of individual behavior as well as the expertise-based insights of practicing physicians and psychologists. Psychological measurements that chopped the child's intellectual life into tiny pieces and measured samples of those isolated segments walked hand-in-hand with Gestalt-inspired frameworks of whole organisms consisting of integrated nervous systems and musculatures.

To the leading researchers in the field of learning disabilities, a science that appeared to be philosophical chaos was, rightly viewed, a rich and varied field of inquiry with an intensive, creative focus on the practical art of educational treatment. As an outgrowth or continuation of the functionalist American psychology of the early decades of the twentieth century, the 1960s learning disabilities research field was an example of professionalized pragmatism, a philosophically thin version of the kind of American pragmatism touted by William James and John Dewey. To borrow Richard Shusterman's words, that pragmatism

> was primarily motivated not by the wish for neutral, accurate reflection of what is or logically must be the case, but by the desire to effect a worthy change or improvement. [The] goal was not so much to get things descriptively right but to make things better.[74]

Or, to turn the matter slightly sideways, getting things right descriptively was understood to be merely a means to a larger scientific end, a tool to be utilized in the pursuit of real improvements in the learning and lives of children. The validity of the researchers' scientific descriptions, theories, and analyses was judged by the fruitfulness of their treatment activities with children. Consequences of treatment activities dominated their evaluation of the utility and value of scientific concepts.

By not taking an epistemological hard-line in favor of either objective measurements or subjective clinical observations, but through the pragmatic and often muddy mixing of the two, the field viewed itself as intellectually open to all possible insights and understandings that might lead to new forms of treatment and instruction. The scientific activities, as well as the researchers themselves, were intimately tied to the clinical treatment of children with behavioral and learning difficulties. Often the experiences of these leading researchers in their direct diagnostic and treatment work with children and families served as the primary crucible for the development of scientific concepts and clinical treatments. It was not a system of a science informing educational practice, although that certainly happened, but of a science that included practice at its core, tightly uniting professional thought and action in an imminently practical orientation.

Scientific openness was not without boundaries. What the group of prominent learning disabilities researchers understood as a practical orientation to science, built mostly on the historical foundation of American psychological functionalism, assumed that the source of childhood learning problems resided in the individual. In the early decades of the twentieth century, a distinctly American psychology, drawing from the evolutionary naturalism of William James and John Dewey, was framed around the general goal of studying how the human organism adapted to the requirements of the environment. Harvey Carr, the leader of the well-known Chicago School of functionalism, guided his prominent department in studying how the activities of the mind contributed to "the adjustment of the organism to its environment."[75] Quite intentionally, in studying the organism within the environment, functionalism supported intensive investigations of the inner workings of the organism, leading to the development of multiple theories of psychological activity, while avoiding formal theories of human social and political life.

Lars Udehn has described "methodological individualism" as an orientation to the scientific analysis of human behavior through which the "actions of individuals are seen as resulting from (a) her/his psychology, (b) the physical surrounding, and (c) the actions of other individuals."[76] The particular form of methodological individualism employed by the learning disabilities researchers of the 1960s tried to disregard the latter two categories. Childhood learning difficulties were routinely explained as expressions of faulty internal psychology and/or neurology. Udehn explains that this version of methodological individualism was originally espoused by John Stuart Mill in the mid-nineteenth century.

> [Mill] argued that all social sciences are based on laws of mind, or on human nature. It is possible to find empirical laws, or generalizations, describing large-scale social phenomena, but a causal explanation of these empirical laws requires psychological laws.[77]

The American researchers in the field of learning disabilities believed that when children did not learn under the typical schooling arrangements and practices, the problem existed within the psychological or biophysical constitution of that individual. The child was placed under the proverbial microscope. Questions involving the practices, beliefs, and dynamics of larger social groups in which the child lived—the school, neighborhood, community, and society itself—were beyond the formal scope of scientific investigation. Bluntly stated, social theory or political exploration was not allowed.

This is not to say that social theory did not occur or did not play an important, although often quite awkward, role in the intellectual work of the researchers in the history of learning disabilities. Perhaps due to the fact that social theories concerning factors such as poverty, immigrant status, race, and gender in the lives and learning of children were generally understood to be beyond the acceptable boundaries of science, such notions slipped into the field only through the back door. They entered the scientific discourse as tacit understandings, what the researchers believed were established facts about social life in the United States—conventional truths not requiring support from data or rigorous analytic procedures. Such social and political beliefs could only be smuggled in under the cover of obviousness.

While social theories varied across eras and individual researchers, by the late 1960s, the greater part involved beliefs about the relationship between social class and childhood learning problems. Eugenic racism that blamed myriad social ills such as crime, unemployment, prostitution, and alcohol abuse on the inherited defectiveness of individuals had been a staple of mental retardation research prior to World War II. As the field of learning disabilities emerged out of the older science of mental retardation, lingering elements of eugenic thought continued, albeit in muffled and restrained forms. The Iowa Station environmentalism offered the possibility of intellectual growth through the intentional mental stimulation of educational programs. But the darker side of environmentalist thought was the contrasting notion that non-stimulating, or frankly "bad," home environments produce deficient child minds. Skeels and the Iowa Station researchers often assumed that lower-income families tended to raise children with correspondingly low intellectual levels. By the 1960s, the echoes of eugenic thought formed an undercurrent in the field of learning disabilities in theories that construed economically disadvantaged families as the frequent purveyors of insufficient environments that harmed or limited child intellectual development.[78]

TWO RESEARCH STRANDS

By the late 1960s, as the young field of learning disabilities produced the ideas that, carried forward by the political advocacy movement, became enfranchised in the learning disability construct, there were two main lines of clinical science. One focused on learning problems as psychological difficulties in the utilization of spoken and written language. Sam Kirk was the leading researcher in this psycholinguistic tradition. Drawing extensively from Marion Monroe's application of educational testing methods to diagnosis and treatment of reading disorders, Kirk began his career as a specialist in reading disorders. In the 1950s, he started to broaden his thinking about learning problems into a theory of psycholinguistic functioning. He built the Illinois Test of Psycholinguistic Abilities as the psychometric fulcrum of a clinical practice of language deficit remediation. He theorized learning disabilities primarily as psychological disorders involving deficits in the mind's management of linguistic information. This became the most prominent language-based approach to learning disabilities.[79]

The second line of learning disability theory emphasized the young child's development of sensory motor and perceptual skills based within the central nervous system. Wayne School researcher Alfred Strauss applied the aphasia research of German neurologist Kurt Goldstein to learning problems of children. The neurological system of the brain-injured child was, at the physiological level, misperceiving environmental stimuli and, therefore, operating ineffectively in the world. Well-known figures such as Raymond Barsch, Marianne Frostig, Newell C. Kephart, and Gerald N. Getman adopted Strauss' ideas as the foundation of clinical programs for the treatment of sensory motor disturbances. They prescribed a carefully designed regimen of movement activities and perceptual development tasks to prepare the child's neurological apparatus for academic instruction.

Although the two lines were conceptually quite distinct, they shared a model of clinical treatment that attempted to heal the neurological and psychological foundations viewed as underlying traditional academic learning. Both viewed the learning-disabled child as mentally incomplete, as lacking specific psychological or physiological capacities that supplied necessary substrates for the development of academic skills. In this sense, the two main lines of learning disability treatment targeted a physiological or psychological level assumed to be deeper and more essential than the more superficial activities of school learning. The goal was to (re)build the damaged or underdeveloped child as a neurological and psychological organism for the demands of the school curriculum.

For the limited purposes of this study, I have selected Sam Kirk and Newell Kephart as the exemplars of two primary lines of research leading to the learning disability construct. My strategy throughout is to trace the intellectual development of each man, tracking the influences and experiences that contributed to his theories and research. As Hayden White has advised, this critical undertaking requires analyses that go beyond simply recounting the scientific ideas and practices.

> In order to write the history of any given scholarly discipline or even of a science, one must be prepared to ask questions *about* it of a sort that do not have to be asked in the practice *of* it. One must try to get behind or beneath the presuppositions which sustain a given type of inquiry and ask the questions that can be begged in its practice in the interest of determining why this type of inquiry has been designed to solve the problems it characteristically tries to solve.[80]

At each step, the goal is to understand the historical development of the rich constellation of each researcher's ideas, where those concepts and practices came from, and how they coalesced within his overall approach to a science of learning failure. The challenge is to both venture into the science as understood and practiced by researchers as well as behind those practices and concepts to examine why the researchers framed human issues as they did.

Kirk and Kephart make for ideal subjects because they embodied the central conceptual features as well as the historical roots of the two strands of learning disability research. Their lengthy academic careers began in the 1930s and touched almost all of the intellectual traditions that ultimately fed the birth of the field of learning disabilities in the 1960s. Kirk's intellectual life was founded on the functionalism of the University of Chicago and the psychometrics of Marion Monroe. He continued his study of reading disorders with Thorleif Hegge at the Wayne School. After World War II, influenced by Alfred Binet's notion of the educability of intelligence and Harold Skeels' grand narrative of environmentalism, he carried out a large experimental study of the effects of preschool education on developing intelligence. Ingredients rendered from Chicago functionalism, Monroe's psychometrics, Hegge's unflinching clinical optimism, and the Binet-Skeels archetypal narrative were all crucial to his ultimate scientific contribution to learning disabilities, a psycholinguistic model of treatment based on the ITPA (Illinois Test of Psycholinguistic Ability).

Kephart's science of learning disorders began with his doctoral training at the Iowa Station. He then worked as a researcher under Strauss at the Wayne School. His psychological science blended an exuberant environmentalism with features of the aphasiology of Goldstein and Strauss. Kephart was also very interested in the relationship between learning and vision skills, including basic visual acuity but expanding into a broader concept of skills of visual perception. In the early 1950s, he began a close collaboration with an optometrist named Gerald N. Getman. The duo created a clinical process for understanding and treating childhood learning and behavioral problems through a program of perceptual and motor development activities. Often Kephart, Frostig, Barsch, and others described their work as movement education, a holistic clinical practice of healing minds by teaching the body.

In spotlighting the intellectual roots as well as the scientific orientations and practices of Kirk and Kephart, this book inevitably gives scant attention to a number of important scientists and clinicians. Perhaps most notable among the neglected are Helmer Myklebust, who developed an important variation of the language-based model, and William Cruickshank, whose efforts to build stimulus-free classroom settings exemplified a direct instructional application of Strauss' research. Also, I unfortunately attend little to the significant work of Marianne Frostig, Raymond Barsch, and vision specialist Gerald N. Getman. Each shows up briefly, given my strategic emphasis on Kirk and Kephart, but all are deserving of more historical study.

In closing this introductory chapter, I must state my overwhelming awareness of how limited this historical analysis is. This is a history of ideas, an exploration of the living and multiple trajectories of human thought over time. It is more of a history of the ideas themselves than a study of personal biographies of the contributing scientists. It is also more of an examination of a distinct series of scientific concepts and practices than an investigation of the cultural milieus and frameworks that fostered those sciences. It is no more than an initial stroll through the intellectual traditions, including the scientific ideas and practices, that produced the symbolic complex that we now know as the learning disability.

CHAPTER TWO

A Biological Holism OF Brain Injury: The Science OF Kurt Goldstein

PERCEIVING WITH SCHNEIDER

In 1915, a 23-year old German soldier named Schneider suffered a severe head injury causing damage to the occipital lobes at the back of the brain. He received medical care at the Institute for Research into the Consequences of Brain Injury, a specialized facility for military personnel in Frankfurt that was founded and directed by Kurt Goldstein. A clinical neurologist and psychiatrist by training, Goldstein worked closely on treatment and research with Adhemar Gelb, a Gestalt-oriented psychologist. The Institute offered a comprehensive research and rehabilitation program that included a laboratory for physiological and psychological examination, a school for the training of patients' residual capacities, and occupational workshops where the soldiers were prepared for return to the workforce. According to a 1919 hospital report, the program was highly effective: 73% of all patients were able to return to their old jobs or similar positions, 17% successfully found jobs in different fields, and only 10% did not gain employment.[1]

After Schneider's head injury had physically healed, Goldstein and Gelb administered the usual battery of psychological tests. The standard format for such tests involved making plus or minus notations regarding the patient's success or failure on a sequence of tasks of increasing difficulty, a procedure that the two clinicians viewed as helpful yet insufficient for diagnostic purposes. The results

confirmed the medically obvious, that the patient suffered from a series of perceptual deficits. Goldstein and Gelb's analysis, in contrast to customary medical
practice, supplemented the patient's quantified level of achievement on the tests
with a variety of qualitative data. Working in a step-by-step, experimental fashion,
they placed the patient into a succession of conditions designed to illuminate different aspects of his overall functioning. They closely observed every detail about
the manner in which the patient approached and attempted tasks, taking careful
note of the entirety of his behavior in relation to the environmental conditions.[2]

The resulting analysis concluded that Schneider suffered from a unique form
of word-blindness, a disturbance of perceptual ability in relation to letters and
words, that the two researchers termed "psychical blindness."[3] The patient was able
to read, but only under certain modified conditions. When words were presented
by a tachistoscope, a device used to flash images for brief time intervals, he was
unable to read words at one- or two-second exposures. If exposures were length-
ened to ten seconds, he could successfully read any word presented.

The clinicians were struck not only by the conditions under which the patient
could read but also by his peculiar, bodily way of reading. As Schneider read words
aloud, he simultaneously engaged in

> a series of minute head- and hand-movements—what his eyes saw he "wrote" with his
> hand. He did not move the entire hand as if across the page, but "wrote" the letters
> one over the other, meanwhile "tracing" them by head-movements.[4]

If the patient was asked to "trace" the letters in a different direction, or if he was
not allowed to trace at all, he was completely unable to read the same words.
Additionally, the patient had no awareness that he was physically "tracing" the
letters as he read them aloud. He thought that he was reading just as anyone else
would.

When the researchers put strike marks across a word, Schneider's tracing
behavior was disrupted and he could no longer read effectively. His tracing behavior and his corresponding attempt to read were completely derailed. His vision
tracked the wrong lines on the page, veering along the irrelevant strike marks
rather than sticking to the outlines of the letters themselves. The patient's perceptual capability was specifically limited to traveling along the lines on the page,
thereby gaining an awareness of a row of letters by physically traversing the length
of each stroke. Gelb and Goldstein concluded that "the word as a whole was not
present in his perception."[5]

The researchers decided to further investigate this perceptual oddity by presenting the patient with visual shapes formed out of arrangements of dots. In each
trial, Schneider was unable to "see" the shapes contained within the patterns of

dots. For example, given an equidistant arrangement of four dots that appeared as the corners of the square, Schneider did not apprehend any order or grouping of the dots. He could perceive all the dots as individual marks but noted no systematic relationship among them. It was not a square.

In additional tests of his visual perception, the patient was able to perceive still objects but he failed to identify the same objects in motion. If an arm moved back and forth between a straightened and a bent position, he could "see the arm in [only] one position and then in the other, but between these two he saw nothing."[6] If the arm motion was slowed down, he could see the arm at various places in the space along the moving path, like catching individual movie frames in still isolation, but he could not see the entirety of the arm in swinging motion. His perception was limited to incomplete units, to the most immediate, concrete, and partitioned details—the line strokes of letters, individual dot marks on a page, motionless frames of a moving object—while missing the complete configuration of letters, words, objects, and shapes.

Goldstein and Gelb arrived at a diagnostic interpretation that was highly unusual in the context of early twentieth-century German neuroscience. The atomistic reflexology of the day generally theorized direct connections between symptoms of sensory distortion and related areas of tissue damage on the brain. Functional losses were evidence of disease or injury to specific localities of the brain.[7] Goldstein and Gelb rejected the atomistic neurological tradition for a more holistic understanding of the operation of brain and body. They theorized a decentralized disorder of perceptual experience. Schneider's brain injury had left him with a general nervous system failure to experience visual phenomena in their complete wholeness.

> It seems likely that our patient had lost the ability to experience compactly organized visual impressions. A normal person hears melodies and sees spatial forms, both of which are composed objectively of successive or spatially separate parts. Were one, however, to describe a melody or a rectangle as consisting of such parts, one would be stating their *objective*, not however their psychological character. As experienced these phenomena are normally not "sums" but unitary, self-contained wholes.[8]

Schneider's head wound had resulted in a profound disorganization of sensory experience such that he was unable to perceive specific visual features in their contextual relationship to other features or the entire wholeness of the scene. This disturbance involved a variety of traditional brain functions, including visual perception and language production, in a comprehensive, neurosensory disorder of human experience.

Goldstein and Gelb concluded that "though the patient's behavior is certainly determined by the brain defect, it can only be understood as a phenomenon going on in the totality of his modified personality in relation to the world."[9] The standard neurological practice in the field at the time was to match symptoms with the location of the brain injury in order to create a clinical explanation based on the cerebral localization of functioning. Finding themselves unable to adequately explain the variety of presenting symptoms, Goldstein and Gelb broke ranks with the classical reflexology of the times that viewed thought and language as complex reflexes "involving information flow from the sensory to the motor centre."[10] They diagnosed not a functional pathology based on the location of tissue damage but a distributed neurological disturbance of the patient's entire experience of and relationship with the world. They were unaware at the time that a similar organic theory had been developed by the American neurologist Hughlings Jackson. From the whole cloth of their own clinical experiences, the German researchers built their own biological holism.[11]

Many decades later, during an audiotaped discussion at a rehabilitation psychology conference held at Clark University, Goldstein explained the clinical origins of his organismic approach.

> May I say how I came to the whole thing! Absolutely from the aspect of practice. There was no theory about the organism or anything at that time.[12]

In the 1959 conversation with his colleagues Heinz Werner, Martin Scheerer, and others, he described his own focus on the facts of clinical investigation colluding with the Gestalt theoretical orientation of the psychologist Gelb within the context of treating particular patients. Practice supplied the unavoidable facts from which and within which the two men built their holistic theory.

GERMAN ROOTS OF AMERICAN SCIENCE

The clinical neurology of Goldstein provided the intellectual underpinnings of the research of Alfred Strauss on brain-injured children at the Wayne School in the 1930s and 1940s as well as the prominent tradition of movement education treatment programs developed in the 1950s and 1960s by Newell Kephart and others. In this chapter, I outline Goldstein's science of brain injury, paying particular attention to aspects relevant to the further development of the science of learning disabilities in the United States. My focus here and throughout this work is not only on what researchers found—that is, their neurological or psychological knowledge of particular forms of human failure—but also on how they conceptualized and carried out the scientific work they were accomplishing. The building of specific slices of scientific knowledge occurred within the entirety of a researcher's orientation, epistemological and methodological, toward the practice of psychological or neurological science. The goal is to illuminate both the intellectual dimensions of scientific practice and the knowledge thereby produced within a historical narrative.

If, to borrow an oft-quoted truism, modern philosophy is little more than "a series of footnotes to Plato,"[13] it may be only minor hyperbole to claim that the American field of learning disabilities consists of a series of footnotes to Goldstein. Goldstein's ideas about brain injury and his philosophical approach to a clinical science of language, memory, behavior, and learning difficulties initiated lasting ideas and also deep conceptual tensions that continued in multiple forms through the developing field of learning disability research for many years. Exploring those ideas and tensions in terms of philosophy of science, methodology, and theory, and how they arose in the work of Goldstein is important preparation for comprehending the various intellectual and practical turns taken by those who later appropriated and continued his work.

An investigation of Goldstein's science of brain injury necessarily begins with an initial survey of the intellectual traditions that informed and contextualized his work. Three important influences deeply impacted the substance and philosophical orientation of his science: Carl Wernicke, Johann Wolfgang von Goethe, and the original Berlin School Gestalt psychologists, most notably Max Wertheimer. Wernicke, the renowned aphasiologist who literally drew the map of nineteenth-century brain science, was Goldstein's mentor during his medical education at Breslau. His research on aphasia, and perhaps more importantly his entire approach to medical science, was symbolic of the atomistic philosophical culture of late nineteenth-century Germany. Goethe, the Romantic Era writer and holistic natural scientist, might be viewed as Goldstein's spiritual advisor, a guiding wisdom in the development of his own philosophy and practice of science. If Goethe served as the historical herald of a holistic intellectual tradition, then the Gestalt psychologists were the current embodiment of holism in Goldstein's lifetime. Though he built his own unique brand of holistic science, Goldstein found social support and intellectual accord in the company of the growing Gestalt psychology community of the early 1900s.

EARLY TWENTIETH-CENTURY GERMAN CULTURE

Goldstein's integration and employment of these three profound intellectual influences took place within an early twentieth-century German cultural and scientific climate of widespread despair and revolt. The late and abrupt inception of the industrial revolution in the 1870s led to a harsh onslaught of mechanized production and thought. The loss of World War I was viewed as a shameful national failure and as a further indication of the decline of traditional order and spiritual moorings. Severe postwar economic woes further fueled the sense of German cultural crisis. The rise of machine symbols, concepts, and themes was felt at the cultural level as a loss of human and spiritual values. The objectivism and materialism of the machine metaphor devoured the subjectivism of life, community, and social order.[14] Mechanism—what Anne Harrington has called "a ruthlessly objectifying spirit that made people into things"[15]—had stolen the soul of German society and left the people in chaos.

Among university faculty who had traditionally served as cultural and literary standard bearers, this was widely understood as a violent encroachment of Western (e.g., European, primarily French) forms of spiritually empty intellectualism into the deep soul of German *Kultur*. The agonized belief among intellectuals was that the German society was losing nothing less than its very identity. "By the early 1920s," writes historian Fritz Ringer, "they were deeply convinced that they were living through a profound crisis, a 'crisis of culture.'"[16]

The rebellious and distressed response across multiple levels of German society, especially among the unified fraternity of university intellectuals, was the growth and embrace of holistic thought. The fragmentation and objectification of humanity and community experienced under the rise of positivistic science and modern technology were countered by a longing search for wholeness and unity. What had been stripped of meaning, ravaged and desiccated by hyper-rational technicism, could be restored only through ideas of integral union. Multiple sciences—including biology, mathematics, physics, medicine, and psychology—turned toward theories of systematic structure, of synthesis and comprehensive organization. In the human sciences, emotion was welded with reason, body unified with mind, thought connected to movement. In the natural sciences, pastoralism reunited man with nature, returning humanity to its proper ecological place in the spiritual fold of life.[17]

Goldstein's biology, as well as the Gestalt psychologies of the Berlin and the Leipzig Schools, developed within the explosion of holistic thought during the cultural crisis years of the early twentieth century. It grew within an effort to eclipse the kind of atomism and objectivism that Goldstein's mentor Carl Wernicke had made famous.

WERNICKE: A MECHANIZED BRAIN SCIENCE

Goldstein earned his medical degree at Braslau in 1903 under the tutelage of the renowned neurologist Carl Wernicke, an iconic figure in the history of medicine described by Harrington as "that guardian of classical mechanistic brain science."[18] For many years, the mentor and the student maintained a warm and thoughtful correspondence. Despite the obvious differences between Goldstein's holistic approach to organismic functioning and Wernicke's atomistic science of functional localization, Goldstein repeatedly described Wernicke as playing a vital role in the development of his thought.[19]

An understanding of Wernicke's approach to a science of aphasia not only provides us with significant insight into the medical education that Goldstein received and greatly rebelled against but also serves as a prominent example of the atomistic intellectual culture of German medical research in the early twentieth century. Goldstein worked as a physician in Germany for almost three decades, until the Nazi regime forced him to flee in 1933. He went to Amsterdam for one year, a highly productive time when he wrote *The Organism*,[20] his classic volume on brain injury, and then he immigrated to the United States where he lived for the rest of his life. His medical thought during his decades in Germany may be viewed as evolving in a crucible fired both by the immediate exigency of understanding and treating brain-damaged soldiers and by the cultural struggle between holism and objectivism. Wernicke's brain research was emblematic of the powerful objectivist intellectual orientation to medicine and science that served as conceptual background to Goldstein's holistic innovations.

Wernicke's status as the foremost figure of German neurological research in the late nineteenth and early twentieth century began in 1874, when he wrote his famous study that established "Wernicke's Area" as a functional hub of speech comprehension activity. In that study, Wernicke discovered that patients with lesions in the left superior temporal region of the brain produced speech that was fluent but also confused, involving frequent transpositions of sounds, words, and phrases. Some of these patients used "neologisms," constellations of sounds that sounded like but were not actual words. Building on an earlier finding on the left frontal lobe by Paul Broca of a speech production center, this work provided additional support for the localization thesis that theorized the existence of a series of brain centers that housed and coordinated different psycholinguistic functions.

In multiple ways, Wernicke's research on aphasia set the scientific standard for neurological research for an entire era of German neurologists and psychiatrists. His brain model incorporated the concepts of the reflexology of his day into a connectionist scheme that aligned a psychology of faculties with networks of energy transport and exchange. His theory, especially as displayed in the form of his oft-imitated diagrams of the brain that mapped out areas of functioning and various neural crossroads, became the standard of the dominant neurology of brain localization. His work became the scientific template for an entire era of brain researchers in a grand effort "to correlate nervous or mental processes with discrete regions of the brain."[21]

Closely related to this functional localization was an associationist psychology that theorized a fragmented nervous system of numerous, isolated operations related through chains of interaction and sensation. Associationism, a popular strand of psychology traced historically to Scottish philosopher David Hume and English physician David Hartley, theorized mental activity—consciousness—on a physiological basis. Nervous sensation was taken to be the basic unit of physiological activity. According to laws of association—resemblance, temporal and spatial contiguity, or contrast—sensations, and the images they carried, formed relationships and connections within the brain. The occurrence of one sensation, the delivery of one mental image, stirred related image memories into activation. In this atomistic manner, psychic phenomena were built up from the accumulated patterns and relationships of neurological sensations. Like gathering particles of sand into bricks, and then accruing bricks into buildings, complex brain activities such as thought, memory, and language were built of the gradual aggregation of connections among solitary incidents of neural sensation.[22]

Wernicke's theory correlated brain anatomy consisting of a network of cortical centers and neural fiber systems as supported in pathological examination with a psychology of the action and interaction of different mental faculties. He theorized a complex hub and spoke system of reflex transmissions and memory communications built on two primary constructs: (1) a center of cortical functioning and (2) a fiber tract system connecting both cortical centers to one another (association fiber system) and connecting centers to peripheral senses and musculature (projection fiber system).[23]

A "center," as understood within this articulation, was a region of the brain anatomy that accomplished a psycholinguistic function through the accommodation of a linguistic representation. Wernicke's Area, for example, was a section of brain tissue that achieved the psycholinguistic function of understanding spoken language and the linguistic representation function of storing the sound patterns of words (auditory imagery). The systems of fiber tracts provide the neural highways of sensation and association, spanning from the sensory organs to the cortical centers of memory storage to the muscular extremities of motor action. Fiber tracts allow for the transportation of all manner of nervous stimulation—from raw reflexes, mere enervations based on stimuli, to complex multibundles of sensory and motor memory appurtenances—across a vast transportation system linking different sensory inputs, numerous internal image stores, and resulting motor outputs.[24]

Reflexology of the late nineteenth century relied on the fundamental idea that all bodily movement was based on the same neurological activity as involuntary reflexes. The primitive neurological action of an involuntary reflex consisted of what was known as a reflex arc, a simple nervous circuit between a sensory nerve, brain motor center, and peripheral musculature. A peripheral sensory nerve is stimulated; that stimulation travels along a loop that carries the enervated energy—theorized by Wernicke as electrical in nature[25]—to the motor center of the frontal region, thereby stimulating a motor response. For example, a tap on the patella quickly results in a knee-jerk response in which the lower leg shifts forward.

Consciousness and voluntary action, according to Wernicke, involved a more complex version, a "schema of reflex action"[26] incorporating communication between the two brain centers—a sensory image area and a motor image area. An involuntary reflex consists of a simple pattern of stimulation that travels with no memory images. The individual person asserts no volition within the automatic system. A voluntary action, on the other hand, involves accessing an additional component in the reflex arc, what Wernicke called "sensory residuals of memory images"[27] stored within the motor and sensory image centers. The reflex stimulation flows from the peripheral sensory organ to the appropriate (e.g., auditory, visual) brain center where prior sensory image activities are stored. The nervous stimulation reanimates "memory images of earlier experiences,"[28] stirring up and adding the physiological remnants of prior nerve activity to the stimulation bundle that is then passed along to the anterior brain motor center. The motor center not only responds by impelling physical action. It also contains motor memory images stored from past neurological activity. Sensory image memories and motor image memories provide the neurological reflex components of conscious decision making.

Central to Wernicke's theory of voluntary behavior was a reflexology of human memory, specifically motor image memory and sensory image memory. Sensory image memories could be multiple in nature; for instance, the act of reading aloud implicated visual and auditory memory images in conjunction with the stored motor imagery required for speech production. He viewed memory itself as "permanent modifications of nerve tissue as the result of stimulation,"[29] a gradual tuning of the nervous fiber pathways based on the repetition of arousal patterns. Resistance within the pathways is reduced through repetition, creating what Wernicke called "well-worn connections…favoring ready translation of imagery into action."[30] Like walking trails worn through a grassy glade by the pounding of many footsteps, a neural connection gains receptive readiness to specific nervous transmissions. The brain fibers are physically modified by use, imprinted with the residue of past activity—the record of sensory images previously received. To Wernicke, this physiological alteration of the brain tissue through repetition was memory.

Wernicke also theorized about the combination of individual units of memory imagery into more complex combinations of associations. His theory drew directly from the associationist psychology of his era, emphasizing the relation-ship between psychic events (and, therefore, neural sensations) that occur in close physical or temporal proximity.

> The association of many memory images occurs simply by chance, because they are produced by a common external stimulus. In the same way, various images of motor patterns at the terminal of the reflex arc become associated with each other because they occur in the same time or in close succession. In this way different motor memory images may be called up into consciousness simultaneously.[31]

Auditory images, such as spoken sounds, and visual images, such as letters on a page, may become associated over time through repeated juxtaposition. The resistance is worn away, and correlations between different memory images may become actively supported by the brain's connecting pathways.

> Memory images of sensations as well as forms of motor response patterns function as elements provided by the outside world. Together they constitute the content of conscious thought.[32]

Maintaining the standard reflex concept of his era, Wernicke was able to theorize conscious action in a complex neural network involving the association and com-bination of prior sensory and motor images.

Armed with his "scheme of reflex action,"[33] an enhanced version of con-temporary reflexology, Wernicke then theorized three different types of aphasia depending on the location of brain lesions. Wernicke's cerebral network consisted primarily of a frontal motor center and a posterior sensory center. A brain lesion in the motor center would result in Broca's Area aphasia, a disorder of speech pro-duction often accompanied by no difficulties in understanding speech. Damage in the posterior sensory region resulted in Wernicke's Area aphasia, a disorder manifested in a variety of symptoms involving the disorganization of sounds and syllables. Speech production was typically confused due to issues of poor storage of auditory input, a failure of sensory image memory.

Wernicke called his third type "conduction aphasia... [a] disruption of the fiber tracts connecting the frontal lobe with the temporo-occipital area."[34] Conduction aphasia, Wernicke theorized, was unlike the two center-based aphasias of the frontal motor area and the posterior sensory area. It did not involve tissue damage at the site of a specific functional activity. Instead, it consisted of a blockage or disruption of the connective fibers that allowed the motor and sensory centers to communicate and cooperate.

What Wernicke introduced as an advance to Broca's earlier research was an expansion of the role of neural connections between functional centers in understanding brain activity and disease. Wernicke's research paved the way for the development of a full-blown connectionism (reaching greater complexity in Ludwig Lichtheim's expansion of Wernicke's model[35]), creating a cerebral road-map of neuroanatomic features explaining psychological operations. By the late nineteenth century, Wernicke-inspired connectionist diagrams tracking localized brain functions and conduit networks of neural communication became the standard framework of German medical training and practice, allowing physicians to quickly relate patient symptoms to a handy cerebral geography.[36]

Certainly, there was much of his mentor's research—and indeed the entire intellectual disposition of the German medical establishment, of which Wernicke was the standard-bearer—that Goldstein could not support. Wernicke's connectionist model of the brain became the archetype of a dominant neuroscience of cerebral localization that Goldstein found deeply flawed.[37] Moreover, the philosophical physicalism of Wernicke's brain model reduced psychic activity to matter in motion, tightly appending psychological activity to neuroanatomy in a manner that became the established neurological science of the early twentieth century. Wernicke described his scientific goal in terms of building upward from the physical to the psychological.

> There is a significant difference between the invention of various theoretic centers—with complete neglect of their anatomic substrates, because the unknown functions of the brain up to the present have not completely warranted anatomically-based conclusions—and an attempt, based on an exhaustive study of brain anatomy and the commonly-recognized laws of experimental psychology, to translate such anatomic features into psychological data, seeking in this way to formulate a theory by use of the same material.[38]

To Wernicke, the human mind and consciousness were contained in the nervous system: "Central nerve endings are invested with the role of psychic elements."[39] While Goldstein held that it was vital to base psychological explanations on the biology of the human organism, his organic science veered sharply from the atomistic practice of mapping specific psychological processes or behaviors to corresponding features of the material brain.

Gertrude Eggert has pointed out that despite the physicalism that was common in nineteenth-century German medical research, Wernicke's 1874 work was subtitled "A Psychological Study on an Anatomical Basis," an indication that the researcher intended to use a natural science approach to enlarge the account of the human body to include related aspects of human consciousness.[40] This same aspect of Wernicke's research was repeatedly praised by Goldstein in his various autobiographic writings.

> With Wernicke I became aware of the interrelation of matter and function, which led to a psychological interpretation of the symptoms of nervous diseases. His

recognition of the significance of psychology for psychiatry was far beyond that of other psychiatrists of his time.[41]

What Goldstein found laudable in Wernicke's work was his attempt to study the organism in a comprehensive way, unifying psychic and physical activity, mind and body, consciousness and sensation.

Further, Goldstein and Wernicke shared an approach to scientific research that was thoroughly clinical, holding fully to the empirical validity of the experiences of physicians in their examination of patients both live and deceased. Their epistemology was housed in the practical actions and cognitive activity of a physician, in his intellectual and professional capacity as a trained observer, a careful experimenter, and a cautious theorizer. David Caplan has observed that neurological research remained a primarily clinical affair until after World War II. In many cases, a scientific finding of profound consequence in the field was drawn from the analysis of a very small number of cases. The body was understood to operate in a systematic way, on the basis of natural laws that could be gradually unveiled through the close and painstaking analyses of individual cases. The observant and rational mind of the clinician was a primary instrument of scientific research.[42]

GOETHE: RELATING TO WHOLE NATURE

Despite his affection for his mentor, and a common utilization of clinical observation as the central practice of medical science, Goldstein shared only a small territory of agreement with Wernicke's fragmented worldview. Goldstein looked to Goethe, the cultural sage of German Romantic thought, for a scientific vision that maintained the wholeness of the world and human experience. In the context of cultural and scientific rebellion against atomism, the Gestalt psychologists and Goldstein turned to Goethe for a philosophical orientation that retained a unity of science, spirituality, and the depths of human experience. Goethe offered Goldstein a rich, distinctly German scientific heritage that blended holistic understanding of natural phenomena with a phenomenology of aesthetic appreciation. For all those who found Wernicke's reductionism and materialism devoid of human soul, Goethe was a fountain of spiritual energy flowing through an intensive scientific practice.

Goethe's entire approach to natural science—a very intentional, thoughtfully considered orientation to issues of philosophy and practice—diverged sharply from the Newtonian mechanistic orientation that was commonplace in the nineteenth century. In 1812, Goethe wrote to a colleague: "We have no need to concern ourselves with atomistic, materialistic, mechanistic approaches, for those ways of thought will never lack for supporters and friends."[43] Certainly, Goethe knew that his ideas were in the minority and, therefore, subject to frequent criticism and misunderstanding. By midcentury, German physiologist Emil du Bois-Reymond concluded: "There is no knowledge other than mechanical knowledge, no form of scientific thinking but mathematical-physical."[44]

The Goethean critique of Newtonian hypothetico-deductive science was multifaceted, raising a series of philosophical concerns more allied to the post-Kuhnian twentieth century than to the peremptory scientific discourse of Goethe's era. Most obviously, he criticized the overuse of quantification, the routine conflation of measurement with science itself. In his view, mathematics had become the too-powerful sine qua non of scientific discourse instead of a useful tool to be handled with strategic discretion. He believed that all forms of measurement leave a remainder, an aspect of a natural phenomenon that lies beyond the mathematical representation and, therefore, unnoticed by quantification. The result of quantification is a highly convincing veneer of exactitude that, by ignoring aspects of the phenomenon, falls far short of the necessary scientific precision. Furthermore, measurement captures only isolated bits lacking reference to the whole. For Goethe, procedures that fragment a natural phenomenon into partitive components without analyzing the relationships between them and their interactions with the structural totality amounted to a dull and thin scientism.[45]

Goethe was also concerned that scientists often replaced a deep and solitary focus on the natural phenomenon itself with abstract hypotheses and theories, resulting in a distorted and partial experience of the object of study. Rather than developing a discourse of direct appreciation and description, operating in a mode of open and genuine engagement with the phenomenon, the mechanistic science of his time frequently leaped past the object into a theoretical rhetoric once-removed, displacing the phenomenon with an effusive abstraction.

> Man takes more pleasure in the idea than in the thing, or rather, man takes pleasure in a thing only insofar as he has an idea of it.... This is the tendency to hypotheses, theories, terminologies, and systems.[46]

In his critique of Isaac Newton's theory of color, Goethe found that Newton had rendered the phenomenon of color as a series of mechanical properties, thereby creating a complex theoretical explanation that eclipsed a deep appreciation of the phenomenon itself. Again, Goethe was worried that scientists were using discourses and practices that actually lost the very phenomena that they were supposed to be scrutinizing.[47]

In Goethe's view, this proclivity to engage in surrendering the phenomenon to an external discourse of hypotheses and abstractions was closely related to the misguided Newtonian goal of seeking cause and effect relationships. It was not that Goethe opposed the use of theory in scientific research. He certainly understood the need for the development of theory; indeed, he believed that all observation and experience is theory-laden. Writing in words that anticipated the later hermeneutics of Hans-Georg Gadamer,[48] Goethe noted that "it is evident that we theorize every time we look carefully at the world."[49] An investigator "never sees the pure phenomenon with his own eyes"[50] but only with eyes dependent on his own multidimensional and contingent subjectivity. Eyes focused by a theoretical formulation, by an appreciation funded by prior concepts and experiences, whether acknowledged or unacknowledged, allow an observer to differentiate, value, and attach meaning. In this sense, theory is not only unavoidable but also necessary.

Given the robust complexity and continuous motion of nature—for Goethe always conceived of nature as immense, enigmatic, restless, and ever-changing—theory provided a useful heuristic for freezing the moving and scattered scene, for speaking of what surges and bounds just beyond human grasp in a language that facilitates access, observation, and reflection. Human words and ideas inevitably fall short of representing nature, but theory could provide at least a cognitive means of engagement, an incomplete but necessary conceptual connection between humans and the natural world.[51]

What Goethe found troubling in the nineteenth-century mechanistic science was both the prematurity and the excursivity of cause-effect theoretical assertions. The race of science seemed to be based not on thorough and intensive observation and description but impatient and triumphant lunges for the prize of discovery. The hasty propagation of cause-effect relationships ironically occurred concurrent with an inadequate appreciation of the natural phenomenon. This was a matter of reaching around and behind the object of study to assemble mechanical schemes of weights and pulleys, turning wheels and interlocking cogs, artificial concatenations rendered as logicomathematical sequences. Nature itself was avoided and misunderstood as the desires for mathematical purity and mechanical elegance were satisfied.[52]

The proper goal of science, according to Goethe, was "not to unveil but to hold 'in contemplation,'"[53] not to hypothesize external relations of cause and effect but to appreciate nature as experienced, to distill nature in a language that enhances human activity and cultural life. Science is the intentional development of a beneficial, nurturing relationship between humanity and nature, a process that allows humans to enjoy and submit to the complexity and fullness of nature. Science in a Goethean posture facilitates a gradual refinement of human thinking and social organization leading to an ethical and aesthetic enlargement of culture.

Science is rightfully a higher form of comprehension developed in thoughtful and cautious interaction with nature. Dennis Sepper has described Goethe's
orientation to science as

> a seeing embedded in the fullness of phenomena. The proximate goal of Goethe's
> method is to achieve what he called a *naturgemässe darstellung*, a presentation in
> accordance with nature, which implies that the presentation has to correspond to the
> fundamental elements of the phenomenon in question, such as continuities, associa-
> tions, contrasts, and wholes that give it structure.[54]

Science is a mode of apprehension that achieves a presentation in harmony with the
phenomenon by finding recurrent patterns and consistencies, the structures and
relationships that are intrinsic and indispensable to the phenomenon. Additionally,
it necessitates a placement of the object of study in a broader context, tracing
the associations and relationships between that object and the larger contextual
whole.[55]

Here is where Goethe's holism is most apparent. His science was "directed
toward the organic, striving to see the whole through the part and the part through
the whole."[56] Part and whole, due to their systemic continuity and functional interdependence, were each viewed as offering dynamic insight into the structure and
activity of the other. His scientific contemporaries often subdivided organisms or
the natural world into parts and then analyzed those parts under the assumption
that an additive knowledge of an accumulation of constituents would comprise an
understanding of the whole.

Goethe viewed natural phenomena as dynamic and changing wholes that
broke down into functional parts only within the contrived heuristics of scientific
observers.

> The things we call parts in every living being are so inseparable from the whole that
> they may be understood only in and with the whole.[57]

Parts themselves are distinct from the whole and from one another only on the
basis of the specific theoretical framework asserted by the researcher. This stance
allowed Goethe to conduct research involving systematic analyses of parts (for
example, structural features of the human skeleton) even as he held that any fully
scientific comprehension must construe parts within the broader operations of
the whole. For this reason, Goethe typically proposed that scientific observation
proceed from the whole to the parts and then back again to the whole.[58]

The required scientific orientation for an organic appreciation and comprehension was not reductionistic but aesthetic. Careful scientific observation and
theoretical work required not an objectivity devised of fragmented cognition,

not a partial intellectual modality exercising without the taint of subjectivity, but a gradual refinement of what Goethe called "our innate gift of observation."[59] Goethe believed that scientific research is a human art requiring the intense and purposeful direction of the full imagination of the investigator toward the object of inquiry. That refined and cultivated mode of seeing, of appreciating in fidelity with the natural phenomenon, is objectivity. This scientific practice of seeing the world in fullness and complexity, as R. H. Stephenson explains, shares much with the aesthetic orientation of a poet or artist.

> Just as an artist coordinates forms abstracted from the world with a chosen medium, in order to produce a new form, the work of art, so too the observer of nature (*Naturschauer*) intent on seeing into the life of things, matches whatever heuristic intellectual forms are available with the welter of concrete particularly which sensibility provides.[60]

By combining the concepts available, the findings and theories offered by past and current research, with his own aesthetic perception, a scientist disciplines and enriches himself as an instrument of observation and analysis. The most insightful and reliable scientific apparatus is the very humanity of the investigator, the creative and attentive focus of a human being in deep engagement with a phenomenon of study.[61]

What demands such a phenomenal aesthetic is Nature itself. Goethe believed that Nature is a creative and productive force to be treated with awe and reverence. It is immense, complex, alluring, and confounding.

> Nature! We are surrounded and embraced by her—powerless to leave her and powerless to enter her more deeply. Unasked and without warning she sweeps us away in the round of her dance and dances on until we fall exhausted from her arms.[62]

Scientific comprehension, at best, attempts to apprehend enduring patterns within the depths of the complexity, as displayed in transient moments and intermittent flashes. What humans can aspire to, and very intensively work towards, is a refined intellectual sensitivity, a heightened mode of perception—a "qualitative scientific cognition"[63]—that attends to what is most significant, enduring, and life-enhancing in the glorious and mysterious maelstrom of natural activity.[64]

It may appear that such a holistic, aesthetic phenomenology devised in sharp contrast to a quantitative, mechanized science would lead to a research method more akin to a poetic meditation than a rigorous scientific procedure. To the contrary, what is perhaps most enlightening about Goethe's approach to science was his systematic inductive method of experimentation. Goethe's method involved careful observation under a series of experimental conditions designed to display the phenomenon in all relevant variations. Often each successive experiment involved slight adjustments of the conditions present in the prior trial, a purposeful modification intended to open a different path of perceptive access to the phenomenon. The overall effect was a tightly coupled sequence of observations under a systematic array of conditions moving from simplicity to greater complexity. The bundle of adjacent experiments served as a single, large experiment offering a nearly comprehensive range of condition variation.[65]

With patience and discipline, Goethe used this inductive process not to validate theory but to illuminate the phenomenon in as many aspects as possible. Sepper observes,

> Each step, each discovery suggests new possibilities that are in turn tested circumstantially. The method depends above all on the utter familiarity with the phenomenon and on the exhaustive enumeration of all contributing conditions and their variations. The experiments continue until a limit is reached, the point beyond which the phenomenon itself…disappears.[66]

Goethe criticized the common nineteenth-century scientific practice of devising only a few exemplary experiments said to demonstrate the prime features of the causal mechanism underlying a natural phenomenon. Experimental procedures must be exhaustive, covering all conditions in which the phenomenon might be displayed with some modification.[67]

Most importantly, Goethe stressed that all elements of an experiment must be repeatable. He took great care in replicating his own experiments in order to check results and also in documenting the specific conditions of his experiments so that other investigators could conduct their own repetitions.

> The main value of an experiment lies in the fact that, simple or compound, it can be reproduced at any time given the requisite preparations, apparatus, and skill.[68]

Goethe emphasized the gradual accumulation of evidence, a form of Baconian induction, in order to systematically produce a description of the phenomenon that "excludes the accidental, sets aside the impure, untangles the complicated, and even discovers the unknown."[69] The final result was a careful documentation "not…of causes, but of conditions under which phenomena appear."[70]

GESTALT

Gestalt theory developed in early twentieth-century German universities, offering a provocative intellectual mixture of traditional experimental research methods popularized by Wilhelm Wundt and the so-called brass instrument psychologists with a thoroughly holistic approach to human consciousness and thought. It began in 1910 when Max Wertheimer met Kurt Koffka and Wolfgang Kohler in Frankfurt. The trio became friends and collaborators, working together to build Gestalt psychology as a radical critique of atomism and a holistic natural science of the human experience of the world.

With one foot in the natural sciences and one in philosophy, the Gestalt theorists ambitiously strove toward the creation of an empirical synthesis that would resolve longstanding philosophical problems through experimental methods. German psychology researchers of the era were empirical philosophers, researchers who tackled questions concerning the nature of human consciousness in the scientific laboratory. Wertheimer, Koffka, and Kohler served as university faculty members within philosophy departments, an institutional arrangement that facilitated the impressive intellectual and historical breadth of their work. Mitchell Ash notes, "In Germany, at least, psychologists' self-assigned task remained the development of an empirically based philosophical worldview."[71] American psychologists of the early twentieth century, working in an institutional and cultural context that frequently split the natural sciences, social sciences, and the humanities into fairly isolated enterprises, sought legitimacy through professionalization and procedures of quantification. By contrast, German psychology was already established as a socially sanctioned enterprise in a university disciplinary structure that greatly integrated the sciences and philosophy. The work of the Gestalt theorists in Germany addressed a broad intellectual audience that included biologists, physicists, psychologists, and philosophers.[72] In that context, they effectively articulated a new vision of how the human mind understands the world.[73]

An 1890 paper entitled "On Gestalt Qualities" written by Austrian philosopher Christian von Ehrenfels is often regarded as the conceptual birth of Gestalt theory.[74] Von Ehrenfels posed a particularly confounding problem to the standard bottom-up atomistic psychology of the day, the question of how the mind builds up a meaningful, orderly experiential world from a physiological basis of isolated sensational elements. As one American commentator later described the dilemma:

> How can these elements get reunited into a psychic continuum, that meaningful world of experience, which is after all what the psychologist is trying to explain? By what kind of mental chemistry can these psychic "atoms" be compounded into the more complex "molecular" mental states? What is the principle of psychic synthesis?[75]

The strategy ultimately employed by von Ehrenfels was to drop the entire notion of building a mental synthesis from disparate sensory fragments in favor of theorizing a consciousness that actively framed perception in organized forms, structures of ordered meaning. Rather than moving from parts to pieced together wholes, his theory came from structural wholes down to constituent parts. In doing so, he shifted the location of functional emphasis from the periphery of sensory reception to the central operations of the mind.

The specific question von Ehrenfels posed concerned the conscious perception of a musical melody. By the conventional atomistic account, each individual note served as an independent auditory stimulus to which the nervous system responded with a single unit of sensation. The entire melody, as perceived by the nervous system, amounted to a succession of isolated sensations, an additive phenomenon built of singular sensory bits. After a melody has been played, human memory consisted of a sequence of single memory images corresponding to each sensation, a sequential string of memory units traced back to each individual auditory tone. The entire experience or the complete memory of the melody consisted of a summative aggregation of the many constituent sensation elements.

To this atomistic psychology, von Ehrenfels challenged, how do we explain the fact that a familiar melody, if played in a different key, is recognizable as the same song despite the fact that not one of the individual notes is the same? The entire sequence of stimuli is different, yet a listener easily knows the two melodies as the same song.

> Thus we have on the one hand two complexes of tone presentations, made up of wholly different components, which nevertheless yield a similar (or, as one normally says, *the same*) melody, and on the other hand two complexes made up of exactly the same elements which yield entirely different melodies. From this it necessarily follows that the melody or tonal Gestalt is something other than the sum of the individual tones on the basis of which it is constituted.[76]

The philosopher proposed that the perception of a melody consists of both the parts—the individual notes and corresponding nervous sensations or memory images—and a superstructural feature involving the relational arrangement of the parts into a coherent whole. He coined the term *gestalt-qualitat* ("form quality") to mean the positive content of consciousness comprising the organization of the otherwise isolated elements.

He further theorized that Gestalt qualities "comprise the greater part of the concepts with which we operate."[77] Effectively, this was the assertion of a new epistemology of human consciousness. By this account, human apprehension of physical and social reality was not accrued as an additive function of isolated sensory snippets. Conscious perception and understanding were primarily founded on central mental activity involving perceptual *Gestalten*, structural forms bringing organized unity, coherence, and order to everyday experience.

Science of Structured Experience

While von Ehrenfels was theorizing conscious form in musical melodies, Max Wertheimer, who years earlier had taken courses under Professor von Ehrenfels in Prague, came to similar conclusions in a series of experiments on concepts of number among "primitive" peoples. In his research on the numeracy utilized by primitives, Wertheimer discovered an approach to many daily living tasks that relied not on abstract concepts of number but on situation-based orientations to form and structure. For example, when a primitive man builds a hut that utilizes a series of posts, he does not count the number of posts needed. He proceeds with an orientation toward the structure of the hut, the specific framework of walls and corners, and builds posts to fulfill that schematic arrangement of objects and space.

Wertheimer likened this to a large family sitting down for dinner. Someone notices that a person is missing. This act of noticing could be accomplished by a calculation, by subtracting the number of family members seated at the dinner table from the total number of persons in the family. But this is not how one would typically realize that a family member is missing. What is noticed is the absence of a particular family member. One integral aspect of the familial whole—a specific member—is missing.

In this analysis, Wertheimer explained the difference between numbers and structures. Numbers are abstract, context-free, universal, and uniform in application. The primitives' approach to number concepts relies on structures, natural groupings of objects or people in relationships within specific lived contexts. While numbers are central to the abstract mindset cherished by Western civilization, structures dominated the primitives thought processes in regard to daily tasks involving multiple elements.

Even at this early stage of his career, Wertheimer's first concepts already surpassed von Ehrenfel's construction of gestalt quality as an overarching additive to the piecemeal sensory data. Von Ehrenfel's version tended to position *gestalten* as augmentative supplements cooperating with and supporting notions of sensory atomism and association. Wertheimer took a significant step beyond atomism by positing the experienced existence of

> wholes, the behavior of which is not determined by that of their individual elements, but where the part-processes are themselves determined by the intrinsic nature of the whole.[78]

He found that the primitives' apprehension of their world relied not on schemes of dissection and calculation but on cognitive frameworks involving structured arrangements of vital elements. A square is not a square because it has four corners or four sides but because the sides operate in a specific structural relationship to one another. Or, better put, the whole of the figure occurs as a specified form consisting of lines arranged in parallels and perpendiculars. The structural form of the whole defines the constitution of the parts. As Wertheimer later wrote:

> I stand at a window and see a house, trees, sky. Theoretically, I might say there were 327 brightnesses and nuances of color. Do I have "327"? No. I have sky, house, and trees.[79]

In direct perception, one does not experience segments but forms, "the arrangement and division which is given there"[80] in the scene at hand.

Orientation to Science

This research conducted early in Wertheimer's career demonstrated what would become the Gestalt orientation to experimental science. Influenced by phenomenologist Edmund Husserl's *Logical Investigations*, Wertheimer maintained the typical practices of empirical experimentation while importing a phenomenological epistemology that focused research questions squarely on the content of the primitives' mathematical thought.[81] His goal was to ascertain, as interpretive anthropologist Clifford Geertz would write some seven decades later, "what the devil they think they are up to."[82]

> It is not enough to ask which numbers and operations of our mathematics are used by the peoples of some other (especially a so-called primitive) culture. Instead the question must be: *What* thought processes do they employ in this domain? *What* are their problems? *How* do they attack them? What are the results?[83]

Wertheimer attempted to comprehend the number concepts employed by primitive peoples on their own terms, as a socially meaningful and legitimate form of cultural practice, not as a lesser intellectual achievement in contrast to a more advanced numeracy of Western civilizations.

The coupling of a phenomenological orientation to epistemology with the traditional psychological experimentation methods became the hallmark of Gestalt empiricism. It was a flexible methodology that employed both quantitative and qualitative data, often leaning toward the latter due to a general skepticism about statistical comparisons across groups such as the personality and intelligence testing pursued by American psychologists. They opposed the attempt to use statistics to identify laws or generalizations based on probabilities. The Gestalt psychologists's goal was "to convey the inherent orderliness of nature in immediate phenomenal form,"[84] to grasp the essence of nature as experienced by humans.[85] This was a scientific goal accomplished best through direct observation of human experiences under a variety of experimental conditions.

"Let us, therefore, turn to the experience itself,"[86] declared Koffka at the onset of one research project. Science itself, in this approach, begins with a full confrontation of the facts of the phenomenal situation. This requires not the artificial baggage of abstractions and concepts born of earlier research projects but immediate contact with the fullness of experience. The central research focus of Gestalt psychology was a rigorous analysis of the content and process of phenomenal experience. Inquiry begins with a shining of the empirical spotlight on what humans undergo and go through as sensory, perceiving, and thinking organisms.

Phi Phenomenon

Perhaps the most famous experiment of Gestalt psychology was Wertheimer's discovery of the Phi phenomenon. This was an investigation of what was known as the stroboscopic effect, the appearance of motion given flashing lights or objects occurring at specific time intervals. A version of this that is familiar to many readers today would be the large outdoor signs that create an impression of motion by lighting a series of bulbs or lamps in rapid succession.[87]

Using a tachistoscope set at varying speeds, Wertheimer had his subjects observe a sequence of two flashed objects (lines or angles). At some speeds, the subjects saw both objects A and B, as well as a motion from A to B. At other speeds, the subjects reported that they no longer saw A and B at all, only a visual trace of movement. They perceived only the motion itself shifting across the visual field. One subject described this Phi phenomenon as "only a passage across, a strong motion in itself."[88] Another subject reported: "I have seen a strong motion (showing correct direction) but I know nothing of the objects."[89] Absent from their perception were the constituent elements presented before and after the perceived motion. These objects as the sensory results of visual stimuli had been crucial to the prior psychological explanation of the stroboscopic effect. In the tradition of atomistic psychology, perception was understood as built of separate sensory elements traceable back to external stimuli—in this case, to the two individual objects that seemed logically to be the starting and ending point of the motion. The perceived motion between the two objects was typically explained as an illusion, an additive dimension supplied by subjective mental activity.

In the case of the Phi phenomenon, however, Wertheimer discovered a perceptual experience lacking dependence on isolated sensory elements. He concluded:

> The impression of motion is materially not constructed from the subjective supplementation of the intermediate positions of the object. In certain experiments,

though there was nothing seen or even thought of the objects.... the impression of the motion over the field was itself compellingly present.... The phi phenomenon exists separately from the appearances of the two stimulus objects.[90]

In Gestalt terms, a "unitary continuous whole process"[91]—a perceptual whole— was grasped without the need for isolated parts.[92]

Basic Principles

In 1913, prior to most of the extensive experimental work on human and animal perception and thought, Wertheimer gave a lecture that contained what would become the basic conceptual outline of Gestalt theory. Ash has reconstructed three primary principles based on the notes taken by a woman attending that lecture.[93] Below, following each statement of principle, I have provided a demonstrative quotation from Wertheimer's 1922 overview of Gestalt theory.

1. The contents of human consciousness are not a summation or aggregation of individual psychic or physiological units, mental images or nervous sensations. The contents—what is actually experienced—are organized on the basis of structures called *gestalten* (forms).

    What is given is "formed," in and of itself and to varying degrees: what is given are more or less structured, more or less definite wholes and whole-processes, for the most part with high concrete whole properties, with internal regularities, characteristic whole-tendencies, with whole-determinacies for their parts.[94]

2. Sensations and impressions are perceived and comprehended within structural impressions, whole images or concepts that are often grasped prior to any awareness of the existence of constituent parts. The meaning of fragments or part contents is derivative of the structural whole.

    Thus, the pieces are not to be initially posited as the "prius"...Rather, their status is largely one of parts subject to material determinacies that emanate from the whole.[95]

3. Human epistemology is a process of knowing that typically involves reaching a centered impression, a structural understanding that allows for an orderly range of impressions and sensations.

    What joins itself with what is given in the psyche—in a complementary manner—is not in principle determined by external, content-foreign factors...but by material, whole-factors, by concrete laws of form, of Gestalt.[96]

Figure-Ground Perception

The concept of visual perception occurring in a relationship of figure to ground, of object to contrasting backdrop, is likely the most well-known development of Gestalt theory. Kohler borrowed the notion from Edgar Rubin, a Danish psychologist who is known for the widely distributed double image of a light goblet consisting of two dark face silhouettes on each side.[97] Kohler theorized the act of perceiving a gestalt in terms of seeing a differentiation between a well-defined prominence and less-defined or homogeneous surrounding material.

> A visual object is a total form bounded by definite contours enclosing a surface and this whole is experiences as set off against the surroundings in which it occurs. The less this condition of "being set off against" becomes, the less we are likely to consider the object a "thing."[98]

The contrast between figure and ground supplied a format for a variety of investigations of visual perception, most notably the work of Adhemar Gelb and Ragnar Granit on thresholds of the visual perception of color.[99]

Perhaps more importantly, the figure-ground concept became an icon of holistic perception that echoed beyond the boundaries of Gestalt psychology. Goldstein often used the figure-ground metaphor as a framework for epistemology and ontology, as a systematic format for his own analytic thought in his research and as an assumed organizational structure for the experienced world. Later, Alfred A. Strauss and Heinz Werner would lead two generations of brain-injury and learning disabilities researchers in the United States with a general conflation of visual figure-ground discrimination with perception itself. Failures to accurately distinguish between figure and grounds in visual stimuli became synonymous with central nervous system failure.

A HOLISTIC BIOLOGY

> The knowledge we need, can be comprehended only by a special mental procedure which I have characterized as a creative activity, based on empirical data, by which the "nature" comes, as a Gestalt, increasingly within the reach of our experience.[100]

Goldstein's philosophy and practice of biological science arose from his experiences of frustration as a young clinician. In 1907, he accepted a position at a psychiatric clinic in Konigsberg. There he found that the standard medical practice consisted of a classificatory diagnosis according to a symptom-based nosology devised by noted psychiatrist Emil Kraepelin. This was followed not by treatment but by custodial care. Like many such clinics in Germany at that time, the treatment culture at Konigsberg was hampered by what Anne Harrington has called "therapeutic nihilism," a detached and arrogant science paired with an empty repertoire of rehabilitative protocols. There was a widespread belief in German neurology that explaining phenomena was enough. Many physicians remained indifferent to the needs of patients and the challenges of healing and treatment.[101]

Goldstein concluded that the entire clinical science was inadequate to the medical and human challenge of helping suffering patients.

> While concentrating on investigation of organic neurological and psychiatric cases, I became aware that the usual procedure, following the method of natural science, studying carefully the outstanding symptoms and trying to base therapy on these results, revealed many interesting phenomena but was very unsatisfactory for the purposes of therapy. When I began to examine also the other manifestations of pathological behavior of the same patients, which were usually considered simply concomitants and were more or less neglected in the interpretation, the results seemed more promising.... I felt that we are confronted with a basic problem in our scientific approach to understanding the behavior not only of patients but of living beings in general.[102]

This early experience of dissatisfaction with an insufficient medical science was formative for the young clinician, the promising first step on what would become a lifelong path pioneering a holistic approach to understanding psychopathology and, indeed, human nature itself. In his time at Konigsberg, and later in his fruitful collaboration with Gelb at Frankfurt, Goldstein worked to replace a flawed medical science with a "holistic approach, which assumes that every phenomenon—normal as well as pathological—is an activity of the whole organism, in a particular organization of the organism."[103]

The holistic approach to a clinical, biological science of the human organism was informed by a twofold critique of an atomistic, mechanistic science as a form of medical knowledge. First, he found that natural science created distorted understandings through the fragmentation of the whole organism into artificial parts. For example, in discussing the tradition of reflexology and localization in neurology, he explained that breaking human activity into analytic pieces tends to result in obscure analytic units that are primarily discursive products.

> Even in the analysis of behavior, the attempt to reduce the more "complex" performances to the "simpler" ones has met with the greatest difficulties. Very often, the "simpler" performances have been found to be abstractions, and the events which the latter aim to explain turn out to be "simple" only in the presence of a specific, habitual, technical attitude of abstraction.[104]

This mode of simplification, of division into functional components, creates an artificial picture based on a theory of partition. The picture renders separate elements in accord with that theory of partition, not in agreement with the wholeness of the organism itself.

The natural science attempt to comprehend the human organism through a reductionistic analysis—"divide the organism…into parts, and then to reconstruct it"[105]—had failed due to a basic philosophical error: the assumption that "the organism is such a sum of parts."[106] If the organism is divided into sections for the purpose of studying each in isolation, the actual functioning of the sections is "modified by their isolation,"[107] altered by the analytic detachment from the dynamic of the whole. When the analyses of the separate sections are brought back together, the flawed accounts of the multiple sections add up to an incorrect, ostensibly total portrait.

Although this sharp critique, consisting of arguments in the Goethean tradition, was compelling, Goldstein's main concern was the effective practice of medicine.

> The basic motive, however, was not primarily a dissatisfaction with the theoretical results, but with their inadequacy in medical practice. Despite great strides in certain fields, patients as well as physicians began to lose faith in the practical value of a scientific theory.[108]

Here Goldstein not only enacted a clinician's devotion to the health and well-being of his patients but also asserted a form of clinical pragmatism valuing knowledge to be as humanly useful as, in this case, medically practicable.

> Knowledge in biology always has to stand the test of usefulness. We do not want merely to understand the nature of an organism and to use our understanding secondarily for practical purposes; we are primarily interested in guaranteeing the existence of the living being.[109]

His epistemological position held much in common with American pragmatists such as William James and John Dewey in their support for a systematic and open-minded brand of empiricism. Goldstein viewed scientific knowledge as provisional, as beliefs warranted by human observations gathered under a variety of salient conditions yet ultimately open to modification or replacement given sufficient evidence.[110]

What was this holistic science that Goldstein developed? Christopher Lawrence and George Weisz place Goldstein's work in the context of a broader movement of "medical holism"[111] that occurred between the two World Wars. Holistic medical practitioners who were dissatisfied with the reductionistic models of the body and the diagnosis of disease via brain localization attempted to fashion an alternative science. In a broad, cultural sense, they "represented a proposed solution—or at least a complex response—to the problems of modernity,"[112] to regain something very human and even spiritual that many felt was lost in the expansion of mechanistic ways of dissecting life and society. Despite its countercultural ethos, this movement did not involve a significant questioning of the centrality of laboratory science and experimentation in the furthering of medical knowledge.[113] Goldstein, in fact, working in a tradition greatly informed by Goethe, placed rigorous procedures of clinical experimentation at the heart of his science.

Medical holism, developing in a manner that echoed the possible types of holistic analysis articulated by Wertheimer,[114] took on two forms—internal and external. Internal medical holism involved a systemic theoretical stance concerning physicality, a particular view of the relationship between entire body and its constituent parts. This stance generally privileged the overall organismic state, thereby framing the health or illness of specific organs or subcomponents as derivative of that state of the whole. "The parts," Lawrence and Weisz note, "in turn are perceived to have many intense and multidirectional interconnections."[115] From this position, the essence of the organism is the interconnectedness and interdependence of the various structural and functional components, the inseparability of parts from the entire organism.

The external form of medical holism focused on the analyses of the interaction between the organism and the surrounding environment. One might view this interaction as taking place on multiple levels running along a continuum from micro-environmental to macro-environmental. The environment included physical features such as "swamps, marma...climate, air pollution," and social factors like "poverty, various forms of behavior deemed unhealthy, the political system, even Western civilization itself."[116] The medical holists of Goldstein's era tended to view the organism-environment relationship as a one-way interaction occurring generally at a micro-level, framing the immediate social and physical environment as causal and the human organism as the receiver of environmental effects.

Goldstein's science combined the internal and external forms of medical holism. His principal focus was the activity of the organism, what humans actually do, within the larger frame of the ongoing interaction between the organism and the environment. He examined the external space of organism-environmental interaction in order to understand the internal, biological organization and functioning. The external interface between organism and environment was the locus of his investigation, the site of clinical observations that informed him of the state of organismic processes.

In his analysis of the psychophysiological effects of the environmental demands on the organism, Goldstein utilized the Gestalt figure-ground framework as an archetypal model of bodily organization and activity. For example, in a discussion of visual response to light stimuli, Goldstein explained that the neurological excitation in and around the eye itself could be understood only in terms of corresponding relationships to neurological activities in other parts of the body. The stimulus does not only result in a "near effect" in the receiving organ. Investigation must appreciate the numerous neurological activities throughout the organism that are prompted by the stimulus and by the eye's excitation.

> We speak of this connection of the near effect as the *figure* process and of the excitation in the rest of the nervous system as the *ground* process…. Any excitation in the nervous system has the character of a figure-ground process.[117]

By employing this figure-ground scheme, Goldstein attempted to describe all responses to the environment as simultaneously consisting of localized forms of functioning as well as a complex of processes over the entire organism.

Methodologically, Goldstein's approach to scientific research involved three practical features: (1) inductive clinical experimentation, (2) qualitative data collection (what he called "phenomenological observations"[118]), and frequently, (3) an extended, single case study design. He and his partner Gelb developed a systematic procedure of observing patients under varied conditions—a grand multitask experiment in the Goethean tradition—in order to see not only what patients could or could not do but also how they operated in relation to a specific set of environmental conditions. With each step, each variation of the conditions, Goldstein and Gelb availed themselves of another opportunity for gaining insight into the patient's mode of adaptation to the environmental demands. The data collected was the densest, most thorough form of "thick description" long before anthropologist Clifford Geertz coined that term.[119] One of Goldstein's cardinal methodological postulates stated that investigators must "consider initially all the phenomena presented by the organism, giving no preference in the description to any special one."[120] Everything that could be observed was initially noted. Only later on would the data be analyzed for purposes of interpretation.

As mid-twentieth-century medical research shifted toward statistical analyses involving measurements of variables over large numbers of patients, Goldstein maintained the value of a comprehensive, iterative analysis of a single case over years. He and Gelb studied the German soldier named Schneider for almost a decade. This practice became a cornerstone of Goldstein's clinically based research regimen. The value of intensive study of a single case, Goldstein held, was in the comprehensive character of the knowledge gained. Studying (or measuring) many patients in partial and brief fashion left investigators unaware of the phenomena they were missing, the data not collected. They were, therefore, were unable to understand how that missing information might cause them to rethink their entire interpretation of the other facts at hand. Partial pictures are often distortions. Although one could never fully reach a complete account for all observations or a final description of a phenomenon, a prolonged and meticulous procedure of observation and description offered at least some assurance of avoiding at least gross errors.[121]

CONCRETE AND ABSTRACT BEHAVIOR

Elements of Goldstein's holistic science of brain injury played prominent roles in the future development of a brain-injury science and the subsequent learning disability science in the United States. Central among these was what he called the "abstract and concrete attitudes."[122] He defined attitudes as *capacity levels of the total personality in a specific plane of activity.*"[123] Each distinct attitude brackets an overall range of mental, physiological, and behavioral performance exhibited in relation to a given situation or experience. Although everyday living requires that a person utilize both abstract and concrete attitudes depending on the requirements of situations, Goldstein found that his patients frequently had lost much or all of their ability to engage in abstract behaviors.

This is demonstrated clearly in a case example that Goldstein explained in his 1937–38 William James Lectures at Harvard University. He described a series of clinical experiments conducted with a 30-year-old man with a frontal lobe lesion.

> We place before him a small wooden stick in a definite position, pointing, for example, diagonally from left to right. He is asked to note the position of the stick carefully. After a half minute's exposure the stick is removed; then it is handed to the patient, and he is asked to put it back in the position in which it was before. He grasps the stick and tries to replace it, but he fumbles; he is all confusion; he looks at the examiner, shakes his head, tries this way and that, plainly uncertain.[124]

The patient failed at what seemed to be a simple task. But then Goldstein presented the patient with a more complex assignment.

> Next we show the patient a little house made up of many sticks, a house with a roof, a door, a window, and a chimney. When he is asked to reproduce the model, he succeeds very well.[125]

Why would the patient fail at a simple task with only one stick and succeed at a complicated task involving intricate arrangements of numerous sticks? Goldstein immediately ruled out specific functional defects of perception, memory, and motor activity. Function-specific explanations for the patient's failure on the first task would be contradicted by the impressive demonstration of skills on the second task.

Goldstein proceeded with the investigation by devising a new pair of experimental tasks.

> We put before the patient two sticks placed together so as to form an angle with the opening pointing upward. The patient is unable to reproduce the model. Then we confront him with the same angle, the opening pointing down this time, and now he reproduces the figure very well at the first trial.[126]

When the patient was asked to explain the difference between his two performances, he stated plainly that the two tasks have nothing to do with one another.

> Pointing to the second one, he says, "That is a roof"; to the first, "That is nothing."[127]

From the patient's perspective, the first task involved representing an imaginary figure, an abstraction that does not exist in real life. The second task consisted of constructing a roof, a concrete object that the patient had experienced first hand.

Goldstein explained that his case example demonstrated the difficulties encountered by a patient who had lost his ability to engage the world through an abstract attitude. His interaction with the environment consisted only of concrete behaviors "confined to the immediate apprehension of the given thing or situation in its particular uniqueness."[128] He was unable to experience the specific situation in ways that connected with objects and concepts beyond his direct experience. His restricted range of behavior was "determined by a stimulus,"[129] compulsively tied to features comprising a portion of the immediate environment. He was seemingly bonded to particular elements of the environment such that imaginative or symbolic activity transcending the specificity of the scene was not possible.

In contrast, the abstract attitude is exemplified by symbolic activity and extra- or trans-experiential connectivity. Persons with an abstract attitude

> transcend the immediately given situation, the specific aspect or sense impression; we abstract common from particular properties; we orient in our action by a rather conceptual viewpoint, be it a category, a class, or a general meaning under which the particular object before us falls. We detach ourselves from the given impression, and the individual thing represents to us an accidental example or representation of a category.[130]

Although an individual engaging in concrete performances often seems passive, compulsive, reacting automatically as if the environmental situation were pulling his strings, the abstract attitude involves an element of distance, of thoughtfulness, of measured consideration.

With an abstract attitude, a person also has a perspectival dexterity that creates space for judgment and choice. He can "consider the situation from various aspects, pick out the aspect which is essential, and act in a way appropriate to the whole situation."[131] The abstract attitude facilitates behavior that is "conscious and volitional," allowing the person to adapt effectively to a variety of contexts under numerous environmental conditions.[132]

While the abstract attitude is marked by facility in multiple environmental situations and an ability to successfully navigate contextual shifts such as changes in conversation topics or the composition of a social milieu, in the concrete attitude, "action is set going directly by the stimuli,"[133] compelled by specific subsets of the context rather than a flexible appreciation of the total situation. A person behaving in the concrete attitude is unable to effectively perceive and adapt to the many environmental situations that arise in life.

What was notable about Goldstein's formulation in terms of his approach to a science of brain injury was the decoupling of localized tissue damage and mental symptoms that marked the aphasiology of his era. Rather than tying a small set of behavioral or linguistic symptoms to the location of the cerebral damage, Goldstein created an explanation of a wide range of human behavior based on the general orientation of patient to environmental demands. His patients' numerous symptoms included distractibility, difficulty making choices, cognitive and behavioral rigidity, lethargy, problems participating in conversations across changing topics, inappropriate emotions, and a lack of social relationships. Goldstein was able to explain all of these apparently disparate manifestations as a loss of abstract capacity resulting in the overutilization of concrete behaviors.

For example, Goldstein employed the Gestalt figure-ground concept to explain the difficulty that many patients had in understanding and participating in a social conversation that meandered across a variety of topics. The figure, in this instance, was the specific statement or parcel of information that a person was relating in the conversation. The ground was the background information necessary to understand the specific statement, including the narrative sequence of prior statements in the discussion and the general storehouse of information on the topic and allied topics necessary to comprehend the single statement. Brain-injured patients were able to grasp some of the concrete details—some figure elements—of the moving conversation, but they lacked the abstraction capacity necessary to relate those isolated elements to the ground, the background information providing a meaningful context. The result was that in the stream of everyday conversations, Goldstein's patients clung fast to the jutting rocks and floating logs while failing to comprehend the flow of the river itself.[134]

The figure-ground scheme became the centerpiece of Goldstein's entire psychopathology. The figure represented a concrete object of perception within human experience. The ground represented the vastness of historical, social, and physical context that, in relationship to the figure, granted the conditions for a concrete figure to gain human meaning. The characteristic feature of brain injury was a figure-ground disturbance, a psychophysiological failure of the organism to behave within an orientation to the world that perceives details in light of totality.[135]

CATASTROPHIC REACTION

Central to Goldstein's holism was an avoidance of theoretical formulations that rendered the body distinct and isolated from the mind. His orientation to the human organism as an organic whole was founded on what he called the "psychosomatic relationship,"[136] the inseparability of physiological processes and emotional activity in the general interaction of the organism with the environment.[137] His emphasis on the unity of mental and bodily aspects of human activity foreshadowed much of the movement education work of 1960s learning disabilities researchers such as Newell C. Kephart and Marianne Frostig. The most striking and illuminative example of Goldstein's psychosomatic thought was his concept of a "catastrophic reaction."[138]

Understanding the psychophysiological condition of catastrophe as a state of dire inadequacy, a human situation of failure and suffering that Goldstein expanded to existential dimensions in his later writings,[139] requires first a comprehension of Goldstein's theory of how an organism achieves "adequacy"[140] in relation to the environment. In *The Organism*, his classic treatise on holistic biological science, Goldstein used the process of learning to ride a bicycle as an analogy for the general process of achieving adequacy.

> We execute inappropriate movements of the body...until suddenly we are able to maintain our balance and to move on in the correct way...by continuous modification of the movements, the correct performance will be reached.... the correct movements appear suddenly *when a state of adequacy between the procedure of the organism and the environmental conditions* is attained.[141]

Gradually, through a process of self-modification that can best be described as learning, the organism achieves a physiological adaptation to the physical demands of the environment, thereby producing an effective alignment between person and environment. Goldstein framed human learning within this naturalistic concept of adaptation as "the realization of adequacy between the organism and its environment."[142]

Drawing from Darwin's concept of evolutionary adaptation as the alteration of species over generations to functionally fit their environmental conditions, Goldstein described human learning as the immediate or short-term, physiological process whereby the responses of the human organism are modified to fit external stimuli in ways that achieve greater practical compliance to the requirements issued by the environment. For Goldstein, this process was both physiological and psychological in that it involves the entire body-and-mind of the person, and it relies heavily on the complex activities of the central nervous system.

To Goldstein, effective learning was the "actualization of organisms,"[143] a process of achieving successful or normal organismic functioning that results in an orderly or stable relationship between the organism and the environment. Goldstein also described such a state of order or balance as "health…the condition of order by which the realization of the organism's nature, its 'existence', is guaranteed."[144] An organism that is functioning correctly is learning or adapting effectively, and this is demonstrated in the achievement of psychophysical coordination with the environment across the widest variety of situations and environmental conditions.

In contrast to a Darwinian understanding of adaptation, Goldstein held that, given the requirements of the environment, health involves more than the survival of the human organism. Goldstein maintained that health as a state of effective equilibrium between the biology of man and the demands of the environment was a matter of the "preservation of his being,"[145] the fulfillment of the most essential individualities of the person. The human drive is not only to survive but "to actualize itself according to its potentialities in the highest possible degree,"[146] to become the most developed version of itself within the scope of constant challenge of interacting effectively with the environment. Growth, development, and the fulfillment of the individual personality—the most essential aspects of the changing biology of the human being—are achieved in acts of effective adaptation to the environment. Goldstein's biological humanism, by the latter portion of his career, became the source of the notion of self-actualization that was espoused by American humanistic psychologists such as Abraham Maslow.[147]

Catastrophic reaction is a profound experience of sickness, a diminution of health, an organismic failure to reach adequacy. It is a situation of organismic disorder resulting from a performative incongruity between human behavior and the environment, a human failing to meet the demands of the environment concomitant with a temporary state of emotional deterioration and cognitive disorganization. Frequently, patients who experience a catastrophic condition are, in the short term, rendered unable to accomplish tasks that they typically have mastered. In many cases, they are unable to even explain why they feel so overwhelmed. The entire organism is functionally subdued.

In his 1937–1938 William James Lectures, Goldstein gave the example of a patient confronted with a multiplication problem that he could not perform. The totality of his state included this failure and an overwhelming experience of anxiety.

> He looks dazed, changes color, becomes agitated and anxious, starts to fumble. A moment before, he was amiable; now he is sullen and evasive or exhibits temper. He presents a picture of a very much distressed, frightened person, a person in a state of anxiety.[148]

Once again Goldstein's analysis demonstrated the holism of his clinical science. It has become common in the context of modern functionalist psychology to explain that a student who fails on an academic task might then experience feelings of sadness, anger, or nervousness in response to the failure. Goldstein believed that such atomism artificially teases apart the whole phenomenon into causally linked aspects. His concept of a catastrophic condition holds to the unity of the phenomenon. The patient's experience of intense feelings was not caused by his failure on the multiplication problem. Instead, the emotional state "belongs to the situation of failing."[149] The entirety of the disordered situation falling short of human health consists of an act of inadequacy in relation to the environment in combination with an intense and incapacitating sense of anxiety.

TO AMERICA

In 1927, a young physician educated at Heidelberg took a position as a research assistant under Goldstein's supervision in Frankfurt. That physician worked for Goldstein for only one year before moving on to a number of other German posts and ultimately emigrating to the United States. In 1937, that doctor began a new job as a researcher at the Wayne County Training School in Michigan. His name was Alfred A. Strauss. In the following 10 years, his research team, that included psychologist Heinz Werner and teacher Laura Lehtinen, migrated Goldstein's research on brain injury from wounded soldiers to institutionalized children with mental retardation, reframing learning and behavioral difficulties as a disorder of psychological perception and bodily adaptation to the environment. By the early 1960s, the Wayne School research spawned dozens of parent organizations devoted to what became known as the Strauss Syndrome. Treatments specialists such as Newell Kephart, Marianne Frostig, and Raymond Barsch applied Strauss's revision of Goldstein's work to entire regimens of movement education therapy for the rehabilitation of brain-injured children. Little did Goldstein ever imagine when he first hired that young physician to his staff in 1927 that Strauss would carry his holistic biology to America where it would become the foundation of a new disorder called learning disability.

CHAPTER THREE

Building THE Strauss Syndrome AT THE Wayne County Training School

At the May 1940 meeting of the American Psychiatric Association in Cincinnati, two researchers announced the discovery of the "mentally crippled child."[1] German neuropsychiatrist Alfred A. Strauss and Heinz Werner, a Viennese psychologist who received his experimental research training in Munich and Hamburg, had presented similar ideas a year earlier at a meeting of mental retardation researchers and institution directors—the primary audience of most of their research presentations. But this time their presentation gave a far more definitive and comprehensive declaration, a forthright pronouncement of the discovery of a previously unknown medical syndrome. Equally important was the scientific stature of the venue. This was the big time—the medical research community with the authority to grant scientific legitimacy to new mental diagnoses was present.

In their investigations with mentally deficient children living at the Wayne County Training School in Northville, Michigan, Strauss and Werner discovered a subset of the population with a distinct collection of learning and behavior difficulties due to what they theorized as peri-natal brain injuries. The specific constellation of symptoms—perseveration, distractibility, forced responsiveness to stimuli—was not only unlike the typical psychological profile of other mental deficients, it was also remarkably similar to what Kurt Goldstein had found among brain-injured soldiers.

In proclaiming a new diagnostic category of childhood mental pathology, Strauss and Werner coined the term *mentally crippled child* to draw a clear analogy between physical disability that was fully visible and a handicap hidden in the recesses of the brain. The metaphor linked the child who, due to a physical impairment, is unable to walk or run and the child who, due a physiological impairment within the veiled territory of the brain, is unable to learn or behave normally. The new syndrome would be taken seriously by psychiatric researchers and clinicians only if that audience believed that an unobservable impairment of the central nervous system was the scientific equivalent of a visually apparent bodily defect.[2]

Strauss and Werner struck out with the psychiatrists. The proposed "mentally crippled"[3] diagnostic category never caught on among medical researchers, or among anyone else, for that matter. But there would be success in the identification of a new childhood learning disorder. What the Wayne School researchers first described in 1940 as "a definite sensori-motor syndrome characterizing the brain-injured mentally defective child"[4] became the basis for what later gained widespread renown as the "Strauss Syndrome."[5] What Werner and Strauss did not realize at the time was that their research would gain national acclaim and practical application not among physicians but with educators and parents.

This chapter explores the intellectual history of the Strauss Syndrome through an analysis of the scientific research of Alfred Strauss, Heinz Werner, Laura Lehtinen, and others at the Wayne School. Over the course of nine highly productive years of research, beginning in the late 1930s, often in close collaboration with Werner, Strauss drew a concise, clinical portrait of the etiology and symptomatology of childhood brain injury that would form the conceptual core of the learning disability construct. During these years, Goldstein's research on brain-damaged soldiers found new life in its application to a childhood population that had little obvious history of brain trauma.

THE WAYNE SCHOOL RESEARCHERS

The scientific captain, the man at the organizational helm of the Wayne School research venture, was Alfred Strauss. Born in Germany, he completed his medical degree at the University of Heidelberg in 1922. He then received five years of advanced training in psychiatry and neurology at the University's Polyclinic for Internal Medicine and the Psychiatric Clinic. He then served one year as research assistant to Kurt Goldstein at the Neurological Institute in Frankfurt.[6] Strauss worked in a number of research and administrative posts, rising finally to become director of the Neuropsychiatric Polyclinic at Heidelberg in 1930. There he focused his research and clinical efforts on the neurology of mental deficiency.

In 1932, he published his earliest work on the diagnosis and treatment of mental defect.[7] He fled Nazi Germany in 1933 for Spain where he joined the University of Barcelona. When anarchists seized the Child Guidance Center that he had founded, he went briefly to Switzerland. He accepted the position as a research psychiatrist at the Wayne School in Michigan in 1937.

In his position as leader of institutional research efforts, Strauss was known less as a commander than as a collaborator, a team player who facilitated a fluid and vibrant dialogue among the Wayne School scientific staff. A young graduate research assistant named William Cruickshank, who later reached prominence for translating Strauss's ideas into a highly articulated pedagogy for brain-injured children, described the "second floor of the School's research building" as "an active place with ideas constantly being verbalized and integrated." In this intellectually lively environment, the "roles of theoretician, 'idea man,' conceptualist, implementor, and writer were shared, and these roles passed easily from one to another."[8]

Since opening in 1926, the Wayne County Training School had pursued a strong research mission combined with a fairly standard program of rehabilitation for high-grade mental defective children, yielding an impressive output of research in the fields of medicine, psychology, and special education. In the early 1940s, the Wayne School became the national epicenter for research on children with mental deficiency and brain injury. Led by Strauss and Werner, and supported by a grant from the McGregor Fund, the Wayne School research program gained a strong reputation in the psychological community. Several researchers who would later become central to the field of learning disabilities participated in research and training activities at the School: Newell Kephart, Samuel A. Kirk, William Cruickshank, Laura Lehtinen, and Ray Barsch. Other noted psychologists who were involved with research at the school included Sidney Bijou, Maurice Fauracre, Charlotte Philleo, Betty Martinson, Boyd McCandless, and Bluma Weiner.[9]

Despite the evident leadership of Strauss, one can make the case that much of the quality and tenor of the Wayne School research program was due to Heinz Werner, a brilliant psychologist whose extensive career of academic accomplishments in both Germany and the United States included six brief years of collaboration with Strauss. Elected to the prestigious American Academy of Arts and Sciences in 1956, he was a world-renowned psychological researcher who concluded his career as the chair of G. Stanley Hall's celebrated psychology program at Clark University. Two edited volumes of work in celebration of his research contributions have been published. The first, produced to mark his seventieth birthday in 1960, included chapters by such luminaries as Jerome Bruner and Abraham Maslow. At the time of his death in 1964, he was writing an invited autobiography for the esteemed *A History of Psychology in Biography* series. After Werner's death, two lengthy obituaries in leading American psychology journals extolled his many scientific accomplishments while offering only passing mention of his collaboration with Strauss. It would seem that, to the mainstream of American psychology, the Strauss years counted for little within the distinguished career of Werner.[10]

Conversely, Werner's presence meant a great deal to the science of Strauss. Much of the distinctive character of research at the Wayne School was drawn from Werner's strong knowledge of experimental and developmental science.[11] Raised in Vienna, Werner was a scholar with a broad intellectual background that included musicology, neo-Kantian and neo-Hegelian philosophy, and experimental psychology. Central to his early interests were thinking and perception, two themes that continued throughout his career. By 1914, when he had received a Ph.D. at the University of Vienna, he had already published an article expounding a "thesis that sensorimotor activity constituted the underpinning of higher reaches of conceptual thought," a notion that would become vital to the formulation of the Strauss Syndrome and the later treatment work of Newell Kephart and the movement educators.[12] When Werner arrived in Hamburg in September 1917 to serve as William Stern's research assistant, he was already capable of running an experimental laboratory. The young scholar had already assisted Sigmund Exner in the Physiological Laboratory in Vienna and worked under Oscar Kulpe and Karl Buhler at the University of Munich.

Between 1920 and 1933, Werner was a faculty member at the University of Hamburg. He wrote books on the psychology of metaphor and children's musical melodies. His most noteworthy work, first published in 1926, was his classic developmental psychology text *Einfuhrung in die Entwicklungspychologie*. Over the next three decades, it was issued in four German editions and translated into numerous foreign languages, including an English volume in 1940.[13] Werner fled from persecution at the rise of the National Socialist Party in 1933, immigrating first to Holland and then to the United States.

Through a complex series of experimental and clinical investigations, the Strauss-Werner partnership built the conceptual content of the Strauss Syndrome, a group of identifiable behaviors linked to an underlying brain injury etiology. They developed a manifold scientific procedure devoted to understanding the psychological functioning of an individual child in reference simultaneously to both the general population and his diagnostic group. Mixing a medical phenomenology of clinical judgment with quantitative analyses of group performances, they steered zigzag lines of inquiry through alternating phases of clinical subjectivity and experimental objectivity. This open-ended and ambitious approach to scientific inquiry enacted Werner's understanding of research as what his biographer Herman Witkin described as "an evolving affair.... an indefinite project."[14] Werner's approach to science was both exploratory and ambitious, pursuing not a finalized confirmation of hypotheses, but an unending and intensive examination that yielded, at best, moments of superior insight and understanding.

Wayne School thinking on instructional practice was influenced by educator Laura Lehtinen, especially as Strauss began to shift in the mid-1940s from the task of distinguishing and conceptualizing a distinct brain injury syndrome toward the challenges of educational treatment. She was the teacher in the experimental classroom at the Wayne School and Strauss's collaborator on the highly influential book *Psychopathology and the Education of the Brain-Injured Child.*[15] In 1947, at the time of the volume's publication, Lehtinen and Strauss left the Wayne School to found the Cove Schools—the first educational programs specifically designed for students with brain injuries—in Racine, Wisconsin and Evanston, Illinois. Lehtinen earned her Ph.D. in educational psychology at Northwestern University in 1960 and served as the Cove Schools clinical director until she retired in 1984.[16]

GERMAN SCIENTIFIC ROOTS

The science of Strauss and Werner was an extrapolation of early twentieth-century German scientific ideas and practices within an American context. Like many German scientists and academics of the era, these two researchers immigrated to the United States to escape the reign of Hitler.[17] But they shared far more than an experience of political persecution and immigration. Both received their scientific training in the intellectual fire of the German culture crisis of the early twentieth century. The foundational intellectual development of each took place within the rise of holistic psychology and medicine, at the crossroads of intellectual and moral conflict between Goethe's holism and Wernicke's mechanism, between a phenomenology of inherent structure and an atomistic science of schemes of causality.

Although thoroughly schooled in the more mechanistic traditions of neurology and psychology, Strauss and Werner each had particularly strong personal and theoretical ties to holistic psychology and medicine. Strauss's time working as a research assistant under Kurt Goldstein left a lasting impression on him. After her husband's death, Marie Strauss described Goldstein's work as a singularly profound and lasting influence on her late husband's research.[18] Strauss also studied neurology in Heidelberg in the early 1920s where groundbreaking holistic physician Viktor von Weizsacker held the prominent Chair of Neurology. Undoubtedly, he was fully educated on Weizsacker's "medical anthropology," an approach to medicine that expanded the holism of Wertheimer and Goldstein through admixture with the patient's subjective experience.

A central figure in the German holistic science community, Weizsacker added a strong experiential and perspectival dimension to the perceptual theory of his Gestalt colleagues. He believed that positivistic medicine suffered from the impossibility of the achievement of scientific objectivity. In a stance that succinctly exemplified the holistic response to mechanistic objectivism, he wrote, "To understand someone and to understand something are two incomparable cases."[19] The patient, as an experiencing and knowing subject, was not merely an object of study but a cognizant participant in a "transsubjective" social exchange with the physician.[20]

The physician's goal, in Weizsacker's theory, was to combine his physiological knowledge of the diseased body with the patient's autobiographic interpretation of his own illness experience in order to comprehend the narrative course of the condition. This goal relied not merely on traditional medical expertise but on a distinct phenomenology of relationship, a shared experience and communication between doctor and patient. Through an interpersonal "contact in experience," a reciprocal interaction whereby both the physician and the patient change one another, the most comprehensive and effective therapy takes place.[21]

> This *contact in experience* is thus the *via regia* to the real world, and through it and *only* through it do those sciences participate in the actual history of the patient, in the real human being. At the instant when the judging mind disengages itself from the moment of the experiencing contact, when he merely imagines the person in space as a spatial structure, in time as a process that is running down, only thinks of him as a soul, as an I or as a character—in that instant a false theory of man is generated.

Natural science approaches to medicine produce false theories through detachment and objectification, while a relational epistemology and human interaction deal in medical truth within lived social experience. Weizsacker created an innovative psychophysical holism that unified biological processes of matter with human activities of symbolic meaning. Medical knowledge, in this account, was a social and experiential phenomenon, produced and continuously refashioned by the experiences of physicians working with, listening to, and learning from patients. It amounted to a deeply personal accrual of the subjective wisdom of numerous clinical encounters.[22]

Heinz Werner's German intellectual roots similarly grew in holistic science circles, revolving most notably around his close identification with the so-called Leipzig School of Gestalt Theory, a somewhat less renowned rival to the famous Berlin School of Wertheimer, Kohler, and Koffka. In particular, his thinking owed much to the work of Leipzig School founder Felix Krueger.[23]

In 1917, Krueger accepted the same Leipzig professorship once held by his mentor William Wundt, the father of experimental psychology. Wundt had favored an experimental psychology that measured sensory experience as an objective phenomenon. Differing with his mentor, and also with Wertheimer and the Berlin Gestaltists, Krueger espoused a phenomenological psychology that examined human experience. He believed that the only access a scientist has to external reality occurs through the medium of consciousness. Therefore, the proper focus for science was not sensory activity but conscious processes such as perception and affect. Additionally, he infused his version of Gestalt theory with developmental emphasis, an attention to human change over time.

Perhaps where Krueger and the Berlin School most diverged was in Krueger's assertion that gestalt structures occur not within nature but only within the mental activity of the organism working to bring order and meaning to diffuse experience. In this sense, form was taken to be wholly psychological. The human organism has a biological impulse to make sense of his world by organizing conscious experience into meaningful structural units. Krueger's phenomenal experientialism did not avoid essentialism. He endowed this concept of psychological structure with existential depth. In his theory, all human experience involves, at the essential bottom of it, unconscious structures that become conscious gestalts only in acts of experiential meaning.[24]

HOLISM AND POLITICS

Strauss and Werner cut their intellectual teeth in the theoretical richness and social revolt of an early twentieth-century German scientific holism that sought to restore humanity—feeling, subjectivity, dignity, and community—to a cultural scene depleted by mechanistic thought. The theme of holism as a remedy for hyper-technicism and the attendant alienations of modern life would recur in the history of research on childhood brain injury and learning disabilities. Strauss's followers in the 1960s, movement educators Newell Kephart and Marianne Frostig employed holistic psychology within a liberatory framework that attempted to reclaim what is most human and subjective from what they viewed to be the cold machinery of industrial progress. Even later, in the 1980s, special educators Mary Poplin and Lous Heshusius led a sharp intellectual rebellion against the positivism and behaviorism of learning disabilities research. Their passionate support for holistic forms of qualitative educational research coupled with their ardent critique of the barren narrowness of quantitative research was a more recent reincarnation of the liberatory politics of holism.[25]

If we were to halt our examination of the early origins of Strauss and Werner's science at this juncture, it would fix upon the notion that the pair carried a deeply humanistic form of holistic psychology from the German context to American soil prior to World War II. Such a belief in the dignity of the human organism would meld neatly with the American humanistic thought of the environmental school of Harold Skeels and his colleagues at the Iowa Child Welfare Research Station. Yet the political content of holism, as Anne Harrington and Stephen Cotgrove acknowledge, is far more flexible than it might first appear. The historical record of the involvement of Viktor von Weizsacker and Felix Krueger in the National Socialist Party stands as an object lesson in how a holistic philosophy designed for one political orientation could be steered toward darker purposes.

In the latter years of his career, Krueger expanded his Gestalt psychology into a spiritually infused political holism that contributed public support to the cause of the National Socialist Party. He made numerous public speeches during the 1930s that praised Hitler as a "farsighted, courageous, and soulful Chancellor."[26] He clothed fascist ideology in a holistic worldview that quickly became a common feature of the National Socialist rhetoric.

Quite ironically, the same holism that had been built as a German response to the perceived evils of positivist science and mechanized culture became a central feature of the social theory of National Socialism. For example, a 1935 study designed in the mode of many Gestalt studies of perception compared the drawings of Jewish and Aryan schoolchildren. This study concluded that the Jewish children had psychological deficiencies in spatial orientation and holistic perception. Holistic perception—broadly speaking, the ability to bring together diverse perceived elements into a structured whole—was interpreted as evidence of racial superiority. The singular mental skill of synthetic unification became an individual ability that demonstrated levels of intellectual hierarchy among peoples of the world.[27]

Krueger's intellectual contributions to National Socialism consisted of two primary concepts. First, he exported the common Gestalt psychology relationship between parts and the whole to the sociopolitical domain in a manner that espoused the dominance of the social whole over the individual parts, of society over citizens. In a 1932 speech to the German Boy Scouts, he encouraged the boys to subordinate themselves to the will of the larger community. He expressed the view that individuals should, by choice or by force, adhere to the greater structural unity of the state.

Secondly, Krueger espoused a eugenics philosophy built on the notion that defective elements of the national structure must be removed in order to preserve the purity and consistency of the racial whole. In 1935, he declared that the unwhole, the failures of health and ability of disabled persons, should be sacrificed under the direction of the common order.[28] He supported national policies involving the "eradication of the Jewish parasitic growth" and the forced sterilization of "inferior hereditary stock."[29] His beliefs echoed the frequent National Socialist assertion that Jews had been greatly responsible for culture-damning rise of modern science and technology.

Krueger's years of rhetorical support were surpassed by Weizsacker's direct participation in the activities of the National Socialist Party. During World War II, Weizsacker was the director of the Institute for Neurological Research in Breslau. Hundreds of children with various disabilities were killed at a psychiatric hospital in Loben-Lubliniec and then shipped to Weizsacker's Institute where their brains were used for neuropathology studies. Weizsacker's involvement was documented in written instructions that he gave for the proper preparation and transport of brains and spinal cords. He justified his actions by reasoning that Hitler stood as the supreme symbol of the national solidarity of which he was only a part. His unquestioning service to Adolf Hitler was, in his reasoning, equivalent to service to the greater good of his community, the spiritually transcendent nation. Like Krueger, he expanded holism from a psychological to a social theory, from an understanding of functional relationships between parts of an individual body and mind to a sociopolitical rationale for the sacrifice of citizens to the larger society. Both Weizsacker and Krueger crafted a cultural holism in which the hierarchical whole rightly defined, dominated, and even destroyed the constituent parts.[30]

The political redeployment of virtually the same holistic concepts that Strauss and Werner imbibed in their own graduate research education demonstrates the ideological flexibility of holism. The Gestalt theorists and Kurt Goldstein crafted their holistic orientations to science as part of a broader cultural backlash against what was experienced as the cultural dehumanization wrought by scientific and technological development. Contrary to the emancipatory intent of its origination, holistic thought was conveniently pirated to the purposes of authoritarianism. The same principle of political flexibility of psychological theory would later play out among the followers of Strauss and Werner, the American learning disabilities researchers of the 1960s. Holistic theory and functionalistic psychology would conspire toward a reactionary politics that actively framed children and families living in poverty as mentally deficient.[31]

PROCESSES AND DEVELOPMENT

Prior to joining Alfred Strauss at the Wayne School, Heinz Werner spent 1936 as a visiting scholar at Harvard University. A landmark paper that he wrote during that year outlined a series of proposals that set the tone for the ensuing, rich collaboration with Strauss.[32] In his few years in the United States, Werner had found academic psychology to be over-convinced of the unitary nature of mental activity. This was greatly due to the conventional summation of intellect under a single IQ score. It also had to do with the American aversion to depth psychology in an era chiefly dominated by behaviorism. Werner critiqued the conflation of mental activity with intelligence measures and offered a theory of learning that emphasized "the underlying mental processes" that occur beneath and behind observable and measurable behavior.[33]

For example, Werner posed, if one wishes to understand a child's arithmetic learning, standardized tests that focus solely on whether that child produces a correct or incorrect answer to a problem fail to provide sufficient insight into the psychological processes—the kinds of thinking and reasoning—that actually yield the child's response.

> Group tests reveal the product of thinking, not the processes responsible for the product.... The true measure of development is not accuracy, but the manner in which the pupil thinks of numbers.[34]

Werner proposed that psychologists and educators conduct research to identify and understand how young minds operate, how learning occurs within the realm of mental processes and functions. His ideas countered the predominant behaviorism and mental measurement strands of early twentieth-century American psychology. The former promoted a tendency to avoid analyses of mental activities, and the latter often framed learning as a unitary function fully represented on a quantitative scale. Faced with what he viewed as a tendency toward superficiality in the American context, a theoretical thinning out of the complexity and depth of mental activity, Werner posited an understanding of learning that presaged the development of the field of cognitive science two decades later. To his thinking, a psychology of learning required investigations of how the mind behind the test score actually worked.

Between 1937 and 1943, the research program of Strauss and Werner at the Wayne County Training School applied Goldstein's work with brain-damaged adults to a population of children with a range of learning difficulties.[35] Werner's theory of mental activity at that time supplied two vital ingredients to that project. First, childhood learning was developmental in nature. It involved an often-overlooked temporal feature: qualitative psychological change over time. Growing children undergo a path of change according to what Werner called "laws of mental growth,"[36] a sequence of qualitatively different levels or stages of activity.

Contemporary developmental theory of the era was dominated by G. Stanley Hall's principle of recapitulation—often stated as "ontogeny recapitulates phylogeny." Simply stated, this evolutionary theory held that as individual humans grow, they pass through the same stages of mental development achieved in the evolutionary advancement of the species over the course of history. Part of this theory was the notion that primitive cultures had stalled at lower stages of intellectual development while industrial, Western cultures had reached the evolutionary forefront of human progress. From this perspective, adults within primitive cultures were understood to operate at mental levels identical to those of young children or adolescents in today's Western societies.

Werner's developmental theory had been strongly influenced by Felix Krueger and William Stern, under whom Werner worked from 1917 until 1920 in the experimental psychology laboratory at Hamburg. In an attempt to distance his thinking from evolutionary biology, he borrowed Stern's principle of parallelism to produce a softened version of Hall's recapitulation concept.[37] Werner asserted that Western children and primitive adults, or Western children and higher functioning animals, do not share identical mental patterns. Instead, they utilize mental operations that are only roughly similar.[38]

Werner believed that psychological development "must be thought of in the form of typical mental patterns, with the higher levels being understood as innovations emerging from the lower."[39] Each level of intellectual activity involves a dynamic interaction of multiple psychological functions, not a static and singular mental operation. The primary principles of mental development are "an increasing differentiation of parts and an increasing subordination, or hierarchization."[40] Lower forms of mental activity, as demonstrated by the examples of young children, primitive cultures, and persons with psychopathologies such as brain injury and schizophrenia, involved frequent unities of subject and object, thought and emotion, objects and situational contexts, idea and concrete action. As individuals (and cultures) progress into advanced patterns of mental organization, psychological operations become differentiated and flexible. The advanced mind experiences objects without affective distortion and recognizes and knows objects outside of the limitations of personal purposes and experiences. Hierarchization consists of the neurological mind's achievement of centralized and stable control over mental and bodily functions. "The activities at the motor, sensory, or emotional levels are subjected to the dominance of the higher functions of mentality."[41] Diverse psychological functions are ordered and integrated in a coherent manner that supports the ongoing thinking and actions of the organism in relation to the environment.

This developmental emphasis in Werner's theory was articulated through his second central concept, an understanding of mental activity as an integrated series of psychological functions and processes. Mental development as a succession of stages, when cast in relation to psychological processes, is "conceived as a transformation of one pattern of processes into another."[42] Growth in learning ability during the childhood years should not be understood simply as the singular or homogeneous accumulation of mental power, as "an increasing efficiency in accomplishment"[43] or a refinement of one or more fixed processes. Rather it is best viewed "as transformation of mental processes from lower to higher forms,"[44] a progressive replacement of primitive or concrete modes of perception and conceptualization with more advanced and abstract processes.

Werner's 1937 paper set the learning theory for the entire Wayne Country Training School research project. Learning consisted of a directly observable dimension, overt behavior that was merely the most available tip of the iceberg. Surface behavior—psychometrically measured, clinically observed, experimentally provoked and isolated—provided only a point of entry into the deeper and more important psychological operations. Werner and his colleague Strauss framed brain injury research as the investigation of the internal workings of the developing mind.

A SCIENCE TO COUNT ON

Strauss and Werner's investigation of the psychological functions residing behind specific achievement deficits began with a small series of inquiries concerning teenage boys with finger agnosia and counting difficulties.[45] At first glance, these studies on the relationship between deficits in basic arithmetic skills and an inability "to recognize, indicate on request, name, or choose with open eyes, individual fingers either of their own hands or the hands of others"[46] would seem irrelevant to this research team's later work on brain injury. To the contrary, the finger agnosia studies served as the launchpad for the conceptual development of a brain-based learning problem syndrome, the initiation of what would be known as the Strauss Syndrome. Moreover, it provided the two researchers with a preliminary practice field where they could craft and refine their particular approach to neuropsychology.

As written documents, the finger agnosia studies were unique in the fact that they often included the researchers' explicit and often prolonged explanations of their methodology, an unusual openness in the field of psychology, providing a rich orientation to the unique combination of clinical and experimental research conducted at the Wayne County Training School. According to Thorleif G. Hegge, the research director at the school, the scientific approach implemented by his research staff consisted of the "correlation of...case studies with increasingly refined experimental investigations." The research attempted to simultaneously seek a "knowledge of groups" and "knowledge of types of problems as they exist in individuals."[47] Clinical examinations of individuals were counterbalanced by comparative analyses of groups.

The research at the Wayne County Training School drew its subjects from the institution's child and adolescent population. The Wayne School boys had significantly sub-average IQ's and were, therefore, understood as examples of a specific clinical-type, mental deficiency. The finger agnosia studies initiated a persistent theme in Strauss's research, the attempt to scientifically parse out a distinct sub-population from the larger group of children with mental retardation. If a clinical subgroup of those children conventionally understood as having mental retardation, in fact, had a different disorder altogether, such a differential diagnosis could lead to improved methods of educational treatment for the newly identified group.[48]

Strauss and Werner theorized the psychological character of finger agnosia as a particular example of a disturbance of body schema, "a sort of diagram of our physical selves existing in our minds,"[49] a mental model built of "kinesthetic, tactile, and optical factors."[50] Due to a brain lesion in the parietal-occipital area of the left hemisphere, the patient lacked a consciousness of the spatial configuration of his own hand, including the number and arrangement of his fingers. This spatial defect was construed within the Gestalt concept of figure and ground. The boys in the study failed to distinguish the fingers (figure) from the hand (ground).[51]

What intrigued these researchers was the fact that these boys were also unable to perform basic arithmetic operations such as counting. Strauss and Werner theorized a possible connection between "deficiency in finger schema and arithmetic achievement."[52] They conducted a series of experiments that compared small groups of boys with and without arithmetic disabilities.[53] In a design that would become characteristic of their approach to clinical assessment, they created a 13-item battery of finger schema tasks. The items were selected as a comprehensive battery on the basis of clinical experience. One task involved the examiner touching a finger on a subject's hand and then asking how many fingers had been touched. Another task consisted of touching a subject's finger and then asking the boy to locate the corresponding finger on a hand drawn on a blackboard.

The boys in the high arithmetic ability group fared well on the finger schema battery, making only 16 errors in 130 total trials. The boys in the arithmetic disability group fared dramatically worse, averaging 36 finger schema errors each.[54] The researchers concluded that the relationship between finger agnosia and mathematical counting difficulties was the result of a developmental failure to translate concrete, motoric operations into abstract, mental number concepts.

Finger agnosia as a disturbance of the body schema means the loss of an articulated instrument for mental operations, *e.g.*, as used in building up number concepts. We may assume that *the primary number concept exists concretely as a configuration of the fingers of the hand.* If such an articulated schema cannot be formed, a basic element for a nature development of the number concept is absent.[55]

An understanding of numbers as an abstract mental operation begins with a bodily phenomenon, a spatial awareness of articulated fingers arranged on the hand. The development of number concept proceeds from that concrete physiology to an abstract psychology. What starts, quite literally, with finger counting becomes, in a more advanced developmental distillation, an abstract operation involving mental representations.

Strauss and Werner wondered if this relationship between finger agnosia and arithmetic difficulties might indicate the presence of "a functional impairment of a more general nature."[56] Perhaps the two correlated defects were part of a clinical syndrome that was distinct from common mental deficiency. Exploring such a possibility would require a theory of child development that unified concrete, bodily experience and abstract, mental functioning. Werner's developmental theory provided the necessary link for further investigation, constructing a fluid developmental path from a concrete, motoric experience to abstract number concept through a central process level of visual perception. Perception, as a mental experience of the spatial configuration of objects, was to become the middle ground between concrete and abstract, between body and thought.[57]

This particular investigation serves as a suitable example of the complex scientific methodology employed by Werner and Strauss—an approach they termed "functional analysis"—that wove together subjective clinical interpretations of individual cases with experimental studies involving group comparisons of functioning.[58] The typical Werner and Strauss study was unusual in American psychology of the time because it did not involve a tightly defined, preplanned scheme of data collection and analysis. Readers of their research were treated to a peripatetic narration of multiple, small inquiries into a larger totality, long strings of inquiry structured by broad questions and jeweled with multiple clinical or experimental examinations. A concatenation of scientific moments sutured together a serpentine path of reason.

Werner described "the function of the scientist as discoverer and explorer of unknown lands rather than a deductive methodologist."[59] In the footsteps of an explorer on virgin soil, logic resides within each curious step, each decision to turn this way or that, emerging as the moment of investigation demands. Reason involves not a highly structured method but an openness of mind within a distinct sense of purpose. In the science of Werner and Strauss, experimentation alternated back and forth between an individual case and group comparisons, each step yielding "a momentary solution.... a hypothesis for further inquiry."[60]

It was only in the full journey of many steps, a narrative of multiple questions posed and examined, that the scientific nature of the discovery process was rendered.

This deeply inquisitive but methodologically flexible format for scientific inquiry was counter to the process rigidity that Werner believed hampered much of American psychology. When he first began working with psychology doctoral students in the United States, he found to his dismay that many believed the researcher's task was to "set up a rigid hypothesis, or set of hypotheses" in order "to prove or disprove the hypothesis."[61] The primary ideation occurred prior to the study, in the preparation of the hypothesis and design. The purpose of the scientific procedure was reduced to merely deciding thumbs up or thumbs down. Werner was deeply dissatisfied with what he viewed as the American narrowing of experimental psychology toward the goal of "proving" hypotheses. He viewed the scientific process as the space not only for the possible confirmation of a hypothesis but, more crucially, also for the thoughtful generation of new proposals. He also found the dominant American behaviorism of the era to be unsatisfying. It artificially froze the dynamic nature of human behavior into a static equation, continuing an outdated, nineteen-century physics in order to produce the ostensibly scientific elegance of precision and quantification. Yet, to Werner, the American hyper-focus on clarity and closure had obscured the "vague.... metaphorical.... not-quantifiable"[62] aspects of human activity. Werner believed in a more humble, open, and provisional science. He espoused a psychology oriented less "toward proving" and more toward "probing," replacing the common emphasis on "prognosis of behavior" with a conceptually deeper "gnosis of behavior."[63] In practice, working with Strauss, this approach to science helped to integrate the treatment specialist's clinical methods of phenomenal inquiry with the research psychologist's techniques of statistical comparisons of groups functioning in the same investigative strand.

A graphic depiction of the step-by-step reasoning employed in the finger agnosia studies offers an opportunity to better understand the Strauss and Werner path of experimentation. Table 1 represents the sequence of tasks, outcomes, and theoretical explanations conducted by Strauss and Werner in their research on finger agnosia and arithmetic disability. The *mode of analysis* column captures the general research method employed at each stage, typically a single clinical case analysis or a group experimental analysis. The *test or task* column details the 13 different tasks over 17 trials attempted by the individual subject and the 13-task test utilized for comparison of the two groups. The *outcome* column indicates the result of the test or task trial. The *theoretical explanation* includes both the initial hypotheses that drove specific phases of the inquiry and explanations that the researchers believed were empirically confirmed at specific points in the study.

Table 1   Investigation Process of Finger Agnosia Research[64]

Step	Mode of Analysis	Test or Task	Outcome	Theoretical Explanation
1	Clinical case—JB, 15-year-old male, with arithmetic disability	With eyes closed, point to own finger that was touched.	Frequent errors	Does JB have both an arithmetic disability and a finger schema deficiency?
2		With eyes closed, point to sequence of two fingers that had been touched.	Increase in errors	
3		With eyes closed, after finger is touched, select touched finger on examiner's hand.	Failed frequently	
4		Count with fingers on one hand	Satisfactory	
5		Count with fingers on two hands	Multiple errors	Confirmation of JB's finger schema deficiency
6	Group experimental comparison—two groups of 14 males from Wayne County Training School	High-achievement arithmetic group vs. low-achievement arithmetic on 13-item finger schema test.	High-achievement arithmetic—few errors Low-achievement arithmetic—mean 36 errors each	Is a finger schema deficiency related to arithmetic disability? Yes.
7	Clinical case—JB, 15-year-old male			Is the relationship between finger agnosia and arithmetic disability an indication of more general deficiency?
8		Copy simple designs	Satisfactory	Does this possible general deficiency have a

Continued

Table 1   Continued

Step	Mode of Analysis	Test or Task	Outcome	Theoretical Explanation
				visual perception or spatial component?
9		Copy complicated designs	Many errors	
10		Draw picture of a folded paper	Satisfactory	
11		Draw picture of hypothetical square paper cut on diagonal	Error	
12		Repeat, with opportunity to first view paper pieces together and then apart	Error	
13		Repeat, with paper pieces farther apart	Error	
14		Repeat, with paper pieces even farther apart	Error	
15		Draw picture of hypothetical square paper with corner cut off	Error	
16		Repeat	Error	
17		Repeat	Satisfactory	
18		Draw picture of hypothetical square paper with hole in upper left and paper turned upside down	Error	Confirmed severe spatial construction impairment

The eighteen steps occurred in three distinct phases. First, a clinical investigation with one boy (JB) with very low arithmetic achievement explored the possibility of a coexisting finger schema defect. The researchers confronted the male subject with numerous "critical situations to discover if there is an impairment of functions."[65] After confirming that JB had both deficiencies, the experimental phase examined the question of whether, among mentally deficient boys in general, there existed a concurrence of the two defects. The comparison on the 13-item finger schema test demonstrated a dramatic difference in performance between the high- and low-achieving arithmetic groups. This evidence supported the concept of a general relationship between the two deficiencies. Working in the Gestalt tradition, Strauss and Werner theorized that the neuropsychological relationship between functional deficiencies might consist of an "impairment in the ability to perceive spatial directions and relate forms spatially to one another."[66] In the third phase, the researchers returned to a clinical analysis of this theory by confronting JB with a series of experimental conditions.

In the final clinical phase, the researchers subjected JB to tests of visual perception. He was able to copy a series of basic shapes. But he performed poorly on more complicated figures that combined lines and figures. The researchers then cut off various sections of a piece of paper and asked the boy to draw the remaining portions. JB struggled on repeated trials. Werner and Strauss described these "tests of mental operations in visual space" as routinely "performed by our children of seven years of mental age." Given JB's measured mental age of 10, his achievement on these tests demonstrated the fact that he was "severely impaired in the ability of spatial construction."[67] It appeared that a deficit in perceptual functioning, an impairment of the psychological ability to construct an effective orientation to physical space, explained the relationship between difficulties involving finger schema and counting.

Drawing heavily from Gestalt psychology research on visual form perception, Werner's developmental theory informed the finding of three distinct stages of number orientation within the growing physiology and psychology of the child.

> First we may find a primary form of the number concept linked up with body activity, motor rhythm, counting by fingers, etc. An important step is understood when numbers are understood as perceptually organized units (especially in the optical field), the so-called concrete number forms. In order to teach a still higher level, another metamorphosis of the process-pattern must occur. The number forms are then stripped of their picture-like properties, and one reaches the level of abstract number concepts.[68]

Bodily motoric activity develops into visual form perception, which then grows into a mental symbolic appreciation.

The finger agnosia research prepared Werner and Strauss for further studies between 1939 and 1942 that fully developed, confirmed, and fleshed out the Strauss Syndrome. They had created a workable scientific practice, a unique way of combining Strauss's skills of neurological interpretation of individual clinical cases with Werner's rich background in Wundtian experimentation, melding what they viewed as medically enlightened subjectivity with a pre-statistical form of quantitative objectivity.

Further, they had discovered strong initial evidence supporting the possibility of a clinical sub-type of the mentally deficient population. This evidence rested on an underlying belief in the existence of natural types within the human population, discernable groups or classifications of neurological and psychological variation within the species. Material differences in the structure and functioning of neurological systems allowed for the differentiation of distinct types of human defectives.[69] Research must achieve a fully elaborated discernment, a clear description of the many ways in which the newly discovered type differed from the larger mental deficient classification and the normal population. The practical import of this differentiation of types was educational, the development of "methods of training"[70] with specific application to the psychology of the type. Fueled by the finger agnosia studies, this belief in a neuropsychology illuminating the boundaries of discoverable natural types was carried aggressively forward into the series of Strauss Syndrome studies.

It should be noted that a general assumption throughout the Wayne School research was that the children housed in the institution were undeniably examples of the mental deficient type. The social factors and processes that lead to the diagnosis and residential placement of children at the institution were beyond question. All of their analyses began with this typological assumption about the inherent nature of the defective child. Then they built forward toward a further refinement of the sub-typology through the development of what they called "exogenous" mental defectives, children with low IQs due to brain injury.[71] With one notable exception, a paper coauthored in 1939 with Newell C. Kephart, Werner and Strauss did not venture into questioning the possibility of social or political processes behind decisions to institutionalize children.

Kephart, while certainly not a sociologist by any account, brought a somewhat larger sense of social and environmental awareness to the research team. He was a recent graduate of the Iowa Child Welfare Research Station, the hub of environmentalist thought and the front line of psychology's struggle over the impact of environment and heredity on intelligence. He had studied with such environmental luminaries as George D. Stoddard and Harold Skeels. His participation in a small number of collaborations with Strauss in the late 1930s resulted in the only Wayne School studies involving any demonstrable—though very limited—concern with the social world around the child. Kephart steered the Wayne School into a brief dalliance with a science of human activity that might examine more than the workings of the mind.

Strauss and Kephart observed that the child population of the Wayne School was predominantly male. They gathered data indicating that over 62% of the child residents at the time were boys. Briefly, Strauss and Kephart theorized the social causation for the gender disproportionality.

> In the selection of individuals for institutional commitment social maladjustment is the dominant criterion. Sincere their social inadequacy is more easily recognized, therefore, boys are more likely to be selected for commitment.[72]

While this analysis admitted to the role of preadmission social interactions and cultural conditions in the creation of the population assumed to represent a natural type, it captured those processes only under the idea of accurate recognition, of finding or failing to find what was actually there. Boys of the defective type were more easily recognized in community life, and the result was that mentally deficient girls were underrepresented at the Wayne School.

This example of a rare and very limited examination of social factors behind the diagnosis of mental defect by the Wayne School researchers only serves to emphasize the methodological individualism that guided their thinking. Strauss and Werner were convinced that the true focal point for their scientific work was the further delineation of clinical types within the feebleminded population, the identification of what they would call endogenous and exogenous types of mental defectives. Building from Goldstein's work and the Gestalt psychology tradition of perceptual research, they believed that what differentiated one type of disordered child from another was the psychological perception of figures in relation to backgrounds. As it would turn out, in the mind of the new type of defective child that they discovered, figures and grounds were all confused.

CLINICAL SCIENCE AND THE EXOGENOUS TYPE

In three papers presented at the 1939 meeting of the American Association on Mental Deficiency, Wayne School researchers Strauss, Werner, and Kephart began the task of detailing the multiple psychological contours of the exogenous type.[73] These three papers initiated a series of scientific and practical examinations that would remain prominent throughout the work of the Wayne School researchers and, to a great extent, into the next generation of learning disabilities science. Strauss provided an overview of a new clinical type of mentally deficient child, a step that opened the door for the full delineation of a new neuroperceptual disorder. Strauss and Werner presented a study examining the perceptual and motor functioning of children of the new clinical type. Combining Strauss's clinical phenomenology with the procedures of experimental psychology, they explored the figure-ground perceptual functioning of brain-injured children. The third paper, coauthored by Strauss and Kephart, launched two additional areas of research interest, (1) the influence of the environment surrounding the child on intellectual functioning and (2) the practical development of forms of pedagogy specifically suited to the brain-injured child. The areas of research interest articulated at the 1939 conference papers comprised the most significant research strands at the Wayne School and foreshadowed the central concerns faced by the following generation of American learning disabilities researchers.

In his solo conference paper, Strauss offered a description of two distinct types of mental deficients, exogenous and endogenous, based on his own clinical observations of patient behavior. The endogenous type served only as a character of psychological contrast for the real agenda, the full delineation of the exogenous or brain-injured clinical type. This paper also displayed Strauss's reliance on an epistemology of clinical judgment as a vital feature of the Wayne School approach to neuropsychological science.

Strauss described the endogenous type as a child having the conventional form of mental retardation: "any mental defective in whose immediate family (grandparents, parents, or siblings) there occur one or more cases of mental defect, and in whose case history there is no evidence of brain disease or injury."[74] He used the term "familial" to capture two possible causes of the disorder that trace back to family or parental origins, an inherited mental defect or "a form of social deprivation, a restriction of the sphere of social-cultural influence."[75]

In contrast to the standard endogenous retardation, the term "exogenous" referred to a "more specific type of mental handicap in an individual with otherwise normal potentialities and normal environment."[76] The exogenous mental defective had no familial background of feeblemindedness, due to either heredity or a limiting or deprived environment. The child's case history indicated

> a pre-natal, natal, or post-natal disease or injury which appears to have damaged the brain. There should be a strong probability that this brain defect is the cause of his mental retardation.

A likely peri-natal insult to the neurological system—the "probability of brain damage by trauma or inflammatory process"—resulted in a mental defective that physicians and psychologists had erroneously viewed as indistinguishable from his endogenous peers. A clinical examination of the exogenous case was utilized to determine the "presence of neurological signs" as post hoc evidence of the peri-natal brain injury.[77]

The timing of Strauss's clinical description of the exogenous case was a clue to his orientation to science. He presented this very full account of the new type in 1939, in the early stages of the program of Wayne School research. The primary

experimental research through which Strauss and Werner investigated and ultimately defined the neuropsychological nature of the exogenous condition was
far from complete. It certainly had not been presented in public research forums
or published in scientific journals. At this national meeting of mental deficiency
researchers, Strauss felt comfortable providing a description of psychological and
behavior features of the exogenous type based almost solely on his own clinical
observations. His scientific strategy opened with a phenomenology of clinical
observation and then followed later with a series of experimental studies that
would provide greater clarity, dimension, and legitimacy to his initial observations. This exemplifies Strauss's position that a tradition of clinical examination,
a medical practice of the interpretation of neurological functioning as exhibited in
observable patient behavior, stood at least as an epistemic co-equal to the experimental methods favored by American psychology. This understanding of a clinician's interpretations as a form of refined and elevated subjectivity constituted
a central (and later, a much-questioned) aspect of Strauss's neuropsychological
science.

The clinical practice of appraising the presence of a brain lesion on the basis
of neurological soft signs, subtle abnormalities of physical response, would ultimately become the most vulnerable aspect of the science of Strauss and Werner.[78]
Perhaps the earliest public critique took place at the 1940 meeting of the American
Psychiatric Association, during a discussion among session participants of Strauss
and Werner's paper announcing the discovery of the mentally crippled child. In
attendance was Leo Kanner, a Johns Hopkins University child psychiatrist who
would soon become known for his own dramatic pronouncement. His 1943 paper
on "autistic disturbances" identified a new psychiatric and educational disorder
on the scientific basis of 11 clinical case descriptions.[79] After opening his remarks
with multiple statements of praise for both the paper and the esteemed researchers,
Kanner asked "what the authors consider as 'evidence of brain lesions' in 20–25
percent of the children examined."[80] His question directly requested what Strauss
and Werner habitually did not provide for, a detailed account of the process of neurological examination that had resulted in the conclusion that a brain lesion was
present. Their understated, standard explanation on the matter used pat phrases
such as "evidence of early acquired brain lesion,"[81] a "neuropathological pattern
demonstrated by clinical signs,"[82] or "indication of an early brain lesion."[83] Kanner
quite casually asked how such evidence, signs, and indications were ascertained
and interpreted.

The record of the 1940 American Psychiatric Association meeting reports
five questions asked by the audience and only four answers provided by Alfred
Strauss. The single unanswered question was Kanner's inquiry about the "evidence
of brain lesions."[84] It is very possible that Strauss's reply to Kanner's question came

only days later at the annual meeting of the American Association on Mental Deficiency in Atlantic City. In a presentation made without Werner, Strauss paused before presenting his study in order "to clarify our viewpoint on the evaluation of neurological signs."[85] His goal—in this rather lengthy tangent, evidently set in response to Kanner's critical query—was to both define and defend his practice of neurological interpretation. Strauss framed his defense through an analogy.

> When an adult patient is admitted to the hospital after an apoplexy which results for example in a hemiplegia, you find paralysis, spasticity, pyramidal reflexes, and so on, on the side afflicted. After weeks and months the gross disturbance decreases, the pyramidal signs disappear and as so-called "residual" signs you may find only a hyperactivity of the tendon reflexes on the afflicted side. Now let us imagine that some time afterwards this patient is again admitted to a hospital. You find him unconscious with no one to give you a history. You find in the neurological examination only the hyperactivity of reflexes on one side. What would your diagnosis be?[86]

The problem, as Strauss understood, was the case of a patient who had suffered a severe head injury in the past, then recovered such that major signs of neurological damage were no longer apparent, but had no communicative ability to inform the physician of the original injury. Strauss lamented that a young child was unable to provide an accurate history, and parents gave historical information that was "nil or incomplete."[87] The physician's only clue in Strauss's narrative was the relatively subtle "hyperactivity of the tendon reflexes." What should the neurologist to make of this sign?

Strauss's narrative example revealed his framing of the diagnostic situation. He was the physician seeking undisclosed past brain damage on the basis of mute traces of reflexological evidence. He gathered an elusive set of physiological whispers, mere hints of possible neurological anomalies, and heard them speaking of a hidden traumatic incident at some point in the past. Armed only with "the imperfections of objective criteria in child neurology," he worked to piece together a puzzle comprising unexplained neurological signs resulting from the original brain injury.

The science of the interpretation of neurological signs blended together prior research on three factors: the developmental stages when specific signs typically appear or disappear, the localization of lesions on the brain, and the coincidence of multiple signs. For example, Strauss explained that the Babinski sign, "the extension of the big toe on stroking the sole of the foot with a pencil or pin,"[88] typically was present in infants and disappeared before the age of two years. Yet research had demonstrated the presence of this sign among mentally deficient children, those considered to pass through developmental stages at a slower pace, up until ten years of age. Since the Babinski sign had been localized to the extrapyramidal system of the brain, the presence of that sign among adults would demonstrate a pyramidal lesion. Further, the coincidence of this sign with other signs yielded an even more complex but insightful matrix of clues to brain damage.[89]

The remaining portion of Strauss's defense consisted of a detailed description of the "short scheme for neurological examination" developed over the course of "several thousand examinations with normal children and mental defective children of all grades."[90] It was not the discovery of "gross neurological disturbances"[91] but the illumination of one or more neurological "signs as indication of a lesion in the central nervous system"[92] that was the goal of the examination procedure. He expressed disappointment in the fact that his institutional responsibilities with such large numbers of children limited his neurological examinations to abbreviated versions of standard medical practices. Yet he maintained the scientific validity of his procedure. Strauss described the scientific basis for his examination regimen as a series of "longitudinal studies in our clinical investigations,"[93] an accumulation of professional experience and wisdom over decades of neurological practice. Using the best available neurological knowledge, paying close attention to his many patients, he had refined what he considered to be a viable process for the interpretation of minor neurological signs.

Strauss concluded his argument with a claim that might be viewed as compensatory hyperbole. Certainly, any critique of the interpretation of subtle neurological signs, even the mild and polite inquiry posed by Kanner, suggested the possibility that minor behavioral quirks might exist without the presence of underlying brain damage. To some extent, human bodies and their functions vary. Irregularities of the minor variety are part of physiological variance often caused not by neurological illness or damage. Strauss's defense must be viewed as answering primarily this charge. Yet his conclusion reversed the tables on the relationship between brain injury and neurological signs.

> We must bear in mind the fact that in children with brain damage we may have no neurological findings. Thus, the absence of neurological signs is not a conclusive proof that no lesion in the central nervous system exists.[94]

Faced with the question of whether a few reflex irregularities might occur without an etiology of brain lesions, a hypothesis linked to the possible over-diagnosis of brain injuries, Strauss countered with the inverse claim. What was more likely was that some brain-injured children lacked observable neurological signs. What was more probable, to Strauss's thinking, was that he and his colleagues at the Wayne School were actually under-diagnosing the number of cases of brain injury.

The most prominent critique of Strauss's clinical science of neurological interpretation came a decade later, in 1949, in Yale psychologist Seymour Sarason's widely read *Psychological Problems in Mental Deficiency*. Sarason compared Strauss's analysis of brain injury among children with Goldstein's work with soldiers. The soldiers had clearly suffered combat injuries to brain tissue. Goldstein's conclusions about the relationship between the soldier's various behaviors and their brain injuries met scientific standards of evidence. Strauss's conclusions, on the other hand, fell short.

> In those exogenous cases where there are only minor neurological symptoms one might also ask (1) with what frequency these minor signs would appear in a group of clearly normal people, and (2) how reliable is the neurological examination in the sense a group of neurologists examining the same patient will come to similar conclusions.[95]

Sarason offered an extensive review of neuropathology research in which knowledge of specific relationships between localized brain injuries and behavioral manifestations had been developed. The misuse of this research, Sarason contended, involved assuming that the exhibition of certain behaviors inevitably pointed back to abnormalities of brain functioning. In the vernacular, while fire produces smoke, a sighting of smoke in the air is not a confirmation of fire.

The critique of the validity of neurological examination in Strauss and Werner's research struck a blow against a clinical science based in phenomenology. Drawing from Goethe, Goldstein had utilized a science of careful observation and situational experimentation that relied on the refined subjectivity of the medical investigator. His science required insight, intuition, and the accumulation of lessons drawn from personal experiences working with patients over time. Strauss carried a very similar clinical phenomenology into his medical procedures. Unlike Goldstein, though, Strauss's patients did not have confirmed brain injuries. The Achilles heel of Strauss's continuation of a Goldstein-inspired phenomenology was the ambitious and far-reaching nature of his attempts to directly connect what can be observed, human behavior, to what cannot be directly observed, the biological matter of the human brain.

While the critique of the clinical aspect of Strauss and Werner's approach to science was substantial, it probably did little to deflate the influence of the Wayne School research among special education researchers. The writings of William Cruickshank, Newell Kephart, Ray Barsch, and Marianne Frostig reanimated and propelled the Wayne School account of the brain-injured child from the 1950s through the 1970s. The blended science of Strauss and Werner, the combination of subjective phenomenology of clinical observation and a quantitative method of experimental group comparisons, was respected and, with some modifications, utilized by Kephart's movement educators as well as Sam Kirk's psycholinguistic process trainers. Like Strauss, they would experience a sharp critique that questioned the validity of their clinical interpretations. Unlike the critique of

Strauss, the 1970s assault on the clinical treatment and research programs of Kirk, Kephart, and Frostig would have a more profound and unsettling impact on the standing of their research within the scientific community.[96]

ENVIRONMENT AND EDUCATION

The Kephart and Strauss 1939 conference paper explored two areas of thought that remained significant among brain injury and learning disability researchers for decades: (1) the relationship between the child's family environment and the child's disorder and (2) the challenge of developing a pedagogy specifically for brain-injured students. Environment, a vague term used most evidently to question how the social and physical world around the child influenced his psychological functioning and learning, was a theoretical topic that Strauss and Werner generally avoided. Their work concerned how the neurological and psychological activity of the child understood and responded to the environment, a line of inquiry that tended to under-theorize the very meaning of environment by rendering it static and unproblematic. From their standpoint, this stance was quite reasonable. The source of the brain-injured child's difficulties resided in the damaged biological matter of the central nervous system. Serious attention to the environment amounted to tangential activity, given the neuropsychological nature of the problem. Nevertheless, it would prove difficult in the decades to follow for Strauss's intellectual ancestors—most notably, the movement educators Newell Kephart and Marianne Frostig—to study the child in clear isolation from complex and troubling environmental questions. The movement educators would interpret the environment in a variety of ways, including the nurturing behavior and intelligence of the parents, the social class and race of the family and community, and the physical characteristics of the school classroom as a field of immediate sensory inputs.

One must wonder to what extent even Strauss could maintain the scientific clarity of the hermetically isolated individual as the neurological being that he and Werner pursued. The fact is that, in a few rare instances over the course of his career, Strauss wandered quite awkwardly into theorizing on environmental questions. Collaborations with Kephart[97] and Boyd McCandless,[98] psychologists with strong interest in the impact of the social environment on the behavior and learning of the child, produced unusual departures from the standard individualized science of the Wayne School. What stands out most notably in these quick splashes of environmental theory was the atypical willingness of self-conscious empiricists, researchers whose scientific conclusions were routinely based on a thoughtful mixture of careful clinical observations and experimental data, to theorize the quality of family and home environments without any evidence. Strauss and Werner's overarching neglect of questions about the social environment surrounding the child was matched only by what might be called the scientific strangeness of Strauss's rare ventures into that arena of psychological concern.

For example, in their 1939 conference paper, Strauss and Kephart analyzed IQ data from hundreds of children admitted to the Wayne School to examine the influence of the (assumed to be positive) institutional environment on general intelligence. They found that exogenous mental defectives tended to experience a loss of intellectual ability in the institution environment while the children with endogenous retardation tended to increase in intelligence. It appeared that the intelligence of the endogenous type was subject to greater improvement in the standard institutional milieu. Therefore, the brain damage of the exogenous group would require a different training approach altogether.[99] Kephart and Strauss followed this in 1940 with a very similar study that reconfirmed the thesis that "a change in environment for these exogenous cases would not be expected to produce a change in the course of mental growth."[100]

These two intelligence studies created a thesis regarding the home environments where children of the exogenous and endogenous types were raised. A central defining difference between the two populations was the source of the retarded intellectual performance. The endogenous child was theorized as a physiologically intact organism that had suffered retardation due to a "generalized impoverishment of the environment."[101] Stated otherwise, healthy minds had been damaged by bad home environments.

> The environment in these cases would appear to be so circumscribed that it is impossible for the child to absorb from it the skills, knowledges, and attitudes necessary to the development of intelligence.[102]

These researchers freely theorized the quality of the child's home environment without any supporting data. The same researchers whose empiricism would not allow them to make strong assertions about a child's behavior or psychological functioning without a thorough process of scientific inquiry quite casually defined the unobserved and unmeasured environs of the child's home and family life, concluding that the endogenous organism was physiologically endowed with the capacity to absorb concepts and skills but had been environmentally underfed by deficient families.

The importance of the various descriptions and details concerning the endogenous type for understanding the role of the home environment among children of the exogenous type amounts to a point of sharp debate. The exogenous cases had a "relatively circumscribed physical defect of the nervous system" that "blot out certain circumscribed sensory and motor responses and thus leave the organism incapable of responding to certain groups of items."[103] If the endogenous child's brain was a fully operational sponge that failed to thrive in a dry desert environment, then the exogenous child's brain was materially impaired such that the rich waters of an intellectually enhancing family experience failed to achieve a full developmental result. By definition, then, the family environments of exogenous mentally deficient children were assumed—again without data—to be "adequate"[104] and not the source of the disorder.

This 1940 study endorsed the need for a distinct pedagogical approach to the exogenous child. It should not attempt to elevate the general level of intelligence the way a training program for endogenous cases required. Instead, it should provide "some compensatory mechanism," devising an instructional route around the defective aspects of neurological functioning and "through some other portion of the nervous system which has not been impaired by the defect."[105]

Strauss's approach to the educational treatment of childhood brain injury developed—during the Wayne School research and in his subsequent years as director of the Cove Schools—a program specifically for children with brain injuries. His pedagogy would typically consist of two simultaneous processes, one curative and one adaptive or compensatory. Curative treatments were designed to improve neuropsychological functioning in problematic areas, for example, "training in visual perception of form and size" in order to enhance the ability to discern structural wholes from constituent elements.[106] The adaptive pedagogy emphasized the situational development of instructional procedures to "circumvent the limitations"[107] imposed by the disorder. This pedagogy of circumvention featured a modification of the conditions of a given task, "accentuating the essential parts of an activity and eliminating those less elements that may interfere."[108]

BIRTH OF A SYNDROME

The 1939 Werner and Strauss conference paper, building on the finger agnosia studies, initiated an extensive investigation of modes of visual and sensory perception that ultimately framed the Strauss Syndrome as a neurosensory "disturbance of the foreground-background relation."[109] This line of inquiry began with studies of visual perception among exogenous defectives and comparison groups and later extended into other sensory modalities such as tactile and auditory processing.

The 1939 study involved a comparison of the performance of two groups—endogenous and exogenous matched on mental age measures—on the kind of Gestalt perceptual task that became the centerpiece of Werner and Strauss's research. The children watched an examiner create a design with marbles on a mosaic board consisting of 10 rows of 10 possible holes. Then they were asked to reproduce the figure, first by using marbles on a second mosaic board, and then in a pencil and paper drawing. These copying tasks involved visual perception of a structural whole consisting of component parts in conjunction with the motor skills required for hand drawing—multiple aspects of the neurological system undergirding spatial orientation and environmental manipulation. The endogenous group clearly outperformed the exogenous group on both tasks. Moreover, Werner and Strauss noticed a distinct difference in the kind of strategy employed by the children in the two groups. The endogenous defectives generally utilized a "global procedure,"[110] an approach to drawing the figure in one, coherent movement "by going around the outline in an unbroken sequence."[111] The exogenous defectives lacked this holistic rationality, as evidenced in their tendency to "perform in an arbitrary and incoherent manner."[112] Werner and Strauss concluded that the global approach was a demonstration of a strategy typical of an earlier level of development, indicating that the endogenous type was a more general form of genetic retardation, a developmental delay. The disorganized strategy of the exogenous type was evidence of physiological defect due to brain injury. They concluded, "Incoherent visuo-motor activity points to a defective organism and can be interpreted only in terms of pathology."[113]

The exogenous type children seemed to have a functional defect in the area of visual perception. Citing Edgar Rubin, the Danish phenomenological psychologist who designed the famous black and white figure-ground vase image, and Kurt Koffka, whose 1935 *Principles of Gestalt Psychology* brought the basic concepts of Gestalt psychology to psychologists in the United States, Werner and Strauss next attempted an experimental group comparison of the figure-ground disturbances. They devised a series of Gestalt perception tests for this purpose.

Three groups of children—30 normal, 25 endogenous, and 25 exogenous or brain-injured—undertook a series of visual perception tasks that challenged them to distinguish a foreground object from a background. First, using a tachistoscope, the children were exposed for one-fifth of a second to nine images: black and white line drawings of common objects "embedded in clearly structured homogeneous backgrounds consisting of jagged and wary lines, squares, crosses, etc."[114] The children were asked to verbally describe what they saw. They found that the "normal child responds predominantly to the object,"[115] not to the background. Children with endogenous mental retardation performed similar to normal children of the same mental age. Over 75% of the responses of the brain-injured children were directed toward the background.

Next, the researchers compared a group of 27 brain-injured children with the same number of endogenous defective children on a visual perception task involving a "geometrical figure constructed of heavy circular dots embedded in a configuration of small dots."[116] The image was flashed for half a second using a tachistoscope. The subjects were then presented with three cards and asked to select the card that appeared most like the original figure. One card (B) depicted only the background design of the figure. A second card (DF) presented the same background with a different foreground figure. A third card (F) portrayed the original geometrical figure on a different background. As in the prior experiment, this scheme was designed to challenge the children's ability to perceive foreground objects without perceptual confusion with the background. Strauss and Werner found that the brain-injured group selected the B card during 52% of the trials. The non-brain-injured children chose the B card during only 27.5% of the trials. The researchers concluded that "the two tachistoscopic tests demonstrate the existence of a disturbance in the differentiation of the figure and ground in the brain-injured child."[117]

In the three visuo-motor studies involving the marble board and the tachistoscope, children with brain injuries had performed poorly on visual perception tasks.[118]

> The constructions as well as the drawing indicate that the performance errors of the brain-injured and the generally retarded child are different in nature. The reproduction of the generally retarded child may be crude, resembling only vaguely the original pattern, but it still retains characteristics of an integrated whole. The brain-injured child fails to discriminate clearly between figure and background. A performance which follows partially the lines of the figure and partially those of the background, must lack completeness and unity of form.[119]

The brain-injured child suffered from a syndrome that, at the very least, included a disorder of visual perception, an inability to differentiate between a foreground object and the background scene. He experienced a "disintegration of form" due to "background interference,"[120] a neurovisual misrepresentation of the object world surrounding the child.

But was this only a problem of visual perception? The holistic tradition of Goldstein typically favored explanations of human behavior that unified different forms of sensory processing and mental functioning. Strauss and Werner wondered if this might be a more general issue involving central nervous system distortions of multiple forms of sensory input. They proceeded to address this question by designing a new pair of figure-background tests, this time focusing on a second sensory area: tactual-motor operations.

The researchers asked the same two comparison groups of brain-injured and endogenous children to, without looking, use their fingers to examine two small boards affixed with tacks. One board was covered with a background of flat thumbtacks and a figure made of hemispherical rubber tacks raised 5 mm above the background. The second board had the same flat background with a figure made of "raised wooden solid"—an intentionally easier task, given the complete and unbroken form of the foreground design. After examining each board with their fingers, the children were asked to "draw what is there."[121] Irrespective of the correctness of the resulting drawings, they fell into three categories: (a) drawings of foreground, (b) drawings of background, and (c) combined drawings of foreground and background. The endogenous group drew just the foreground in 93% of the trials and the brain-injured in 26% of the trials. The latter primarily represented either the background alone or the background and the figure without differentiation.

"None of the children in either group had difficulty"[122] on the second board. The confusion of figure and ground occurred only when the foreground design was built of intermittent objects. When it lacked a self-evident wholeness, the brain-injured children were unable to provide the unifying structure based on a sensory experience of the isolated elements. In their experience, parts of a coherent whole were more likely to deteriorate into the background than rise into an integrated and cohesive gestalt.

Werner and Strauss had found that children with brain injuries had neuropsychological deficiency "in three fields: in visual perception, in visuo-motor performance, and in tactual-motor activity." The "disturbance of the foreground-background relation is not caused by an impairment of a circumscribed function."[123] The three flaws were, to holistic theorists, undoubtedly related. Due to the multisensory nature of the disorder, they posed two possible ("not necessarily mutually exclusive"[124]) theoretical explanations. First, drawing heavily from Goldstein, they proposed that the brain-injured children had

> a disturbance of…schemata (body schemata, spatial schemata) in pathology. The figure-background schema may be considered one of the reference frames by which the human organism is able to organize a given field in an adequate manner. The brain-injured child shows evidence of an impairment of this capacity.[125]

This was a general neurosensory disorder concerning the child's orientation to the spatial-object world.

A second hypothesis raised the question of the attractive powers of the various elements of the object world over the central nervous system. On the tasks involving the figures constructed of tacks, the examiners noted that the brain-injured children seemed to spend an inordinate amount of time fingering the individual tacks, a behavior that appeared related to their poor apprehension of the total figures consisting of multiple tacks. It may have been that "the attraction exerted by some object in the environment may interfere again and again in the completion of the task."[126] This hypothesis proposed a theory of distractibility founded on the notion that the organism's disproportionate and impractical attraction to random stimuli acted as an interference, a form of sensory confusion, a misappraisal of the value of various concurrent or adjacent stimuli. The children with brain injuries, in this hypothesis, were "at the mercy of outside forces,"[127] unable to neurologically make a distinction between what mattered and what did not.

"A MORE GENERAL FACTOR"

The syndrome, whether labeled as exogenous, brain-injured, or mentally crippled, was now ripe for dramatic expansion. To Werner and Strauss, the neurological system served as the bedrock structure for all mental and bodily activity; indeed, it was the physiological organizing principle of human life. If their research had halted after the initial studies with marble boards and tachistoscopes, the syndrome would have been limited to the field of visuo-motor operations. Their Goldstein-inspired holism suggested that the neurological underpinnings of visuo-motor activities did not occur in physical or psychological isolation from other mental and bodily functions. Once this hunch was confirmed through the tests of tactile-motor functions, the door was opened wide to an expansive search across multiple neurological domains. Subsequent research would scour the far corners of the exogenous child's body, mind, and actions, seeking and finding evidence of a multiplicity of related functional disturbances.

The first area of scrutiny, following the pattern of analysis employed with the visuo-motor and tactile-motor studies, was auditory-motor organization. Drawing from his strong background in the psychology of music, Werner conducted an experimental study that compared 22 endogenous children with 26 exogenous on tests involving the vocal reproduction of melodic patterns played on a piano. The two subject groups were similar on IQ. Only children with average singing skills were allowed to participate. The performances of these two groups were also compared to the responses of a group of 30 normal children who had been tested on the same 17 melodic patterns in a prior study.

The difference between the endogenous and exogenous groups relative to errors made was slight: 72% of the endogenous group trials were incorrect, and 83% of the exogenous group attempts were in error. The difference, though, was in the kinds of errors made. Werner analyzed the performances in terms of 16 different types of errors of melodic reproduction. The errors of normal children tended to fall into a cluster of types involving functional regressions to lower levels of development. Like the normal children, the endogenous group tended to make errors demonstrating regressions to the strategies of lower developmental levels. The errors of the exogenous group, however, were inconsistent with this genetic pattern, an indication that the auditory-motor functioning of the exogenous children was disturbed in a manner that could not be explained by a concept of delayed development.[128]

In the multiple comparisons of endogenous and exogenous groups, Werner and Strauss had clearly demonstrated that

> the difference in performance is not due to a deficiency in a specific sensori-motor field, auditory or visual. It seems to be based on a more general factor, inter-sensorial in nature. We may speak of a sensori-motor syndrome characterizing the exogenous type.[129]

The syndrome had been expanded to include a deficit of auditory-motor functioning.

The general sensori-motor syndrome involved an underlying neurological defect manifested not only in visual, tactile, and auditory perception but also in a wide range of linguistic and behavioral disturbances. Clinical observation found a host of language oddities, rational absurdities clothed in an eloquent and impressive verbosity. Brain-injured children often engaged in a "peculiar use of unusual words and an affected style" of speech, resulting in phrasings that were "sometimes queer, irrelevant, and dyslogical."[130] Similarly, the behavior of exogenous children was frequently "erratic, uncoordinated, uncontrolled, disinhibited, and socially unaccepted."[131] Educationally, these children suffered from problems of attention, learning, and social adjustment.[132] The exogenous child was "erratic" and "lacking in control and discipline."[133] The sum total of all of these areas of defect amounted to the discovery of "a personality that is fundamentally different from the personality of the endogenous type."[134] Top to bottom, it appeared that the brain-injured child was a uniquely impaired character.

The next phase of the experimental expansion of the syndrome investigated processes of cognition. This scientific move made good sense in light of Werner's view of childhood mental development as progressing from motor activity to perception to conception, from concrete simplicity to symbolic abstraction.[135] Further, it can be understood as pushing the Wayne School science of brain injury into what was perhaps the most coveted and under-examined area of human psychological activity. Between approximately 1930 and the early 1950s, American psychology chiefly employed various forms of behavioral theory. Depth psychologists such as Strauss and Werner found conventional stimulus-response theories too cumbersome to support analyses of psychological processes occurring *behind* human behavior. Despite their affinity for psychological depth, they also rejected a Freudian description of the hidden recesses of mental life. Undoubtedly, Werner and Strauss were driven by the same intense desire to get at the inner essence of human thought—to surrender what Werner called "a deeper insight into the genesis of abstraction"[136]—that consequently led to the multidisciplinary cognitive revolution in the United States beginning in the 1950s.[137] Defining the brain injury syndrome in a comprehensive science that would inform pedagogy required an exploration of mysteries of human thought.[138]

DISORDERED THINKING

A thorough reading of the scientific development of the brain injury syndrome by the Wayne School researchers raises the question of the expansionist tendency of a science of individual mental defect. Like miners who strike gold in one hillside and then quickly decide to explore the surrounding hills, it is perhaps not surprising to observe the scientists rushing to check for deficiencies across many areas of psychological functioning. Perhaps this is less surprising among holistic theorists who assume underlying order and structure unifying distal elements. In the line of research by Strauss and Werner, an original concept of visuo-motor deficiency was, through gradual steps of experimentation and clinical case observation, extended into successive functional areas of tactile-motor and auditory-motor activity. At this point, the scientific aggregation of partial functional defects allowed for a structural reframing of the syndrome as "inter-sensorial in nature,"[139] involving the entirety of the neuro-sensory apparatus. If the total central nervous system had been compromised due to perinatal brain injury, thinking itself would be implicated.

The investigation of cognition consisted of a series of experimental comparisons of exogenous and endogenous groups on thinking tasks (by Strauss and Werner) and a cluster of clinical case studies (by Strauss alone). The first two experimental studies compared 10 exogenous and 10 endogenous children on object grouping tasks. In the first experiment, given 56 common objects, the children were directed to "place those things together which go together, which fit together." The examiners then asked the children, "Why did you put these things together?"[140] The exogenous group chose a far greater number of objects and used them "to form more groups than the non-injured children." The brain-injured children also created far more "infrequent" or unusual combinations of objects. Any combination that occurred only once was considered infrequent or uncommon by the researchers. The exogenous group created 30 uncommon combinations while the endogenous group produced only 11. The second object-grouping task involved far fewer objects and produced similar results. Again the brain-injured children, in comparison to the endogenous group, produced many more combinations and uncommon groupings.

The researchers were "struck by the marked peculiarity of the point of view upon which the brain-injured children relate the objects."[141] For example, one

brain-injured child grouped a picture of a bell with that of a whistle. His rationale was that "both sound loud." Another unusual combination was the coupling
of a razor blade and a stamp showing a king with a beard. The child reasoned
that the "man should have a shave." Werner and Strauss interpreted these infrequent groupings produced by the brain-injured children as "psychopathological."[142]
Common or socially conforming forms of cognitive categorization were viewed as
indications of mental stability and health.

In order to present "experimental conditions which permit greater freedom
of mental activity and which are closer to the exigencies of reality,"[143] Strauss and
Werner devised the Picture-Object test. The examiners presented the subjects
with two black and white, *Life* magazine photographs: a boy drowning in ocean
waves (photo D) and a large building on fire with firemen attempting a rescue
(photo F). The children were also given 86 common toys such as cars, human
and animal figures, and furniture. The task was to place "those objects which go
with the picture."[144] The children could place each object with photo D, photo F,
or neither.

Similar to the prior experiments, the brain-injured children "placed twice as
many objects before the pictures" and "chose the common objects less frequently
than the endogenous children."[145] Werner and Strauss identified four additional
pathological features in the performance of the exogenous group. First, they often
engaged in a "deviation from the standard meaning of objects," demonstrating a
"pliability of the meaning of objects with respect to the situations."[146] An example
of this behavior is a child who

> places a wire before the fire picture saying, "That's a hose." The wire can represent a
> hose to this child because essential qualities of the object have been neglected while
> less significant characteristics have been considered.[147]

This example demonstrates the researcher's interpretation of an unusual coupling
of objects as a perceptual error. The child's appropriation of the wire as a hose
occurred because his sensory perception—primarily visual—attended disproportionately to the irrelevant features of the wire.

Throughout this line of research, cognition was merely a beefed up version of
neuro-perception. The meaning of the objects and the situation portrayed by the
photo was reduced to the accurate perceptual reception of the physicality of the
objects. As late as 1955, in the second volume of *Psychopathology and the Education
of the Brain-Injured,* co-authored by Strauss and Kephart, thinking was theorized
not in terms of internal processes of symbolic activity or information exchange
but as mental operations organizing multiple sensory stimulations into coherent
patterns. Chained to a theoretical vocabulary of mental activity as perception, the

Wayne School researchers theorized cognition as the coordination and integration of perceptual inputs.[148]

The second form of deviant thought involved the "organization of the objects in circumscribed small units."[149] Although the examiner's instructions directed the children to simply place the objects in front of the appropriate photograph, the brain-injured children went a step further by arranging the objects into groups based on relationships between the objects. For example, the subjects often formed groups based on physical commonalities such as openings or holes. They also interpreted thematic relationships between objects, such as placing a stop sign next to a fire engine so that the vehicle would stop.

Strauss and Werner described the third form of deviant thought process of the brain-injured children as "conspicuous formalistic behavior," a preoccupation with "orderliness, a pedantic systematization" in the selection, arrangement, and discard of objects. The physical motions of the brain-injured children in handling the objects involved multiple hesitations, and repeatedly shifting and replacing objects. For example, after the task was completed, when the brain-injured children were clearing the table and putting the objects away, they often grouped objects together prior to removal. The researchers viewed this behavior as unnecessary pickiness and unreasonable "pedantry."[150]

The fourth form of cognitive pathology replicated Goldstein's findings of a "concrete attitude"[151] among brain-damaged soldiers. Strauss and Werner described the brain-injured children as failing to appreciate objects as abstract members of a general class. They were unable to see the task as "a sober logical problem." Both the endogenous group and a group of 10 normal children viewed the situation as a "static, logical, rather than general relationship."[152] For example, one endogenous child placed a rope in front of the drowning boy photo, saying, "You can save him." The cognitive attitude of the endogenous and normal groups was direct, realistic, and without supplementary tangents or creative enhancements.

On the other hand, the brain-injured children tended not to view the objects as general elements of a formulaic scheme but "as concrete elements of a situation."[153] Moreover, they understood the specific situation "as a temporal series of events,"[154] a narrative "extended into the past and the future."[155] Often they added "fanciful elements which go far beyond the content of the pictured situation."[156] For example, one subject talked about taking the drowning boy in the photograph to the hospital where Santa Claus would visit him. A subject who paired the picture of the drowning boy with a ball said, "Before going into the water, the boy had it in his pocket."[157] A child who placed a table, chair, fork, and spoon in front of the drowning boy photograph explained, "After the boy has been saved he has got to eat."[158] The researchers interpreted these narratives consisting of past, present, and future with creative embellishments as examples of concrete thinking due to the child's intensive focus on situational details.

In Strauss and Werner's final conclusions to the Picture-Object study, it was evident that their formulation lacked a serviceable theory of cognition. Although their investigation had explored dimensions of thinking behavior, and they found a series of pathological cognitive processes specific to the brain injury syndrome, their final theoretical formulation reverted directly to Goldstein's original list of brain injury symptoms. Mental activities of meaning attribution and delineation were framed as elements of defective neurological responses to the environment.

Uncommon object groupings were a demonstration of "forced responsiveness to stimuli." The children had selected odd combinations due to an inability to screen out "extraneous stimuli," resulting in difficulties in focusing on the relevant features of objects.

> Since the child cannot help turning his attention to such stimuli, any background noise, brilliant object, moving object, or other such extraneous element may be a source of interference.

When irrelevant or unimportant aspects of the sensory environment intrude upon the child's perception, the child then interprets the meanings of objects or their relations in unconventional ways.[159]

"Deviation from the standard meaning of objects"—what later cognitive psychologists might have called cognitive distortions and what laypersons might describe as just creativity—amounted to a perceptual hyper-focus on the environmental elements lacking the correct meanings for the situation. Here the scientists' utilization of a metaphor of perception of physical details as short-hand for thinking activities ran thin. The various modes of thought that Strauss and Werner found particular to the brain-injured group were reduced to questions of focus and attention. Thought patterns that the researchers described as pathological were theorized as the neurological result of imbalances and interferences in sensory attention.[160]

The problem of "conspicuous formalistic behavior" was explained under the umbrella of Goldstein's "pathological fixation," of perseveration, a behavior of "exaggerated attentiveness" to a stimulus.[161] The case of a child repeatedly moving, re-moving, and re-shifting objects about was an example of being captured by the "inertia of the organism, the inability to shift from one nervous activity to another."[162] Rather than moving on to the next object task, the child remained neurologically entrapped in the cul-de-sac of the current stimulus environment, unable to achieve completion. This behavior was also evidence of "disinhibition," the children's inability to "restrain themselves from manipulating handles of doors, turning knobs, rolling round objects, etc."[163]

Finally, the intellectual confusion of the brain-injured children was encapsulated under the broad notion of "disassociation," a "lack of integration of elements into a more comprehensive configuration."[164] Not only had the children focused disproportionately on misleading aspects of the physical environment, they also suffered from a "lack of organization,"[165] an inability to correctly integrate the variety of sensory stimulations into a coherent overall understanding of the situation.

Noticing the temporal and narrative aspects of the brain-injured children's thinking, Strauss and Werner's final experiment featured a new test: a story task. The children were presented with three story prompts: (1) "What happens when children are getting up in the morning?" (2) "What happens on the street when children are on their way to school?" and (3) "What happens when the children are in the school room?"[166] The children were asked to represent each story with a set of three pictures. As in prior experiments, the "brain-injured children tended to remove the boundaries of the presented event, expanding it into the past and future."[167] This "trend of temporal expansion" was viewed by the researchers as further evidence of "an organism whose intellectual processes appear impaired."[168]

In 1944, Strauss summarized the brain injury syndrome as

> a thinking disturbance characterized by a lack of ability to discriminate essential from non-essential details, evasion from reality, escaping in grotesque phantasies, incoherence, and flight of ideas.[169]

The Strauss Syndrome had expanded, albeit somewhat awkwardly due to a theory of cognition crafted out of Gestalt notions of perception and Goldstein's organismic attitude, to become "a thinking disturbance."[170]

EXPANDING BEYOND MENTAL DEFICIENCY

Consistently, Strauss and Werner described the exogenous child as having mental retardation but differing from the endogenous type in terms of etiology and psychological characteristics. The brain injury syndrome was a specific subtype of mental retardation. In 1944, for the first time, Strauss and Wayne School teacher Laura Lehtinen hinted that the syndrome might not be synonymous with mental deficiency. They theorized that the multiple functional difficulties associated with the brain injury could mask the child's actual intellectual potential.

> With a brain-crippled child...the actual mental capacity may not be evident because of the general disturbances which befog or overshadow the underlying mental elements. We are prevented, therefore, from its measurement through tests by the

barrier of general disturbances (which of itself lowers the test score) and because of failures in achieving skill and accurate experiences due to the handicap of general disturbances in learning situations. If the general disturbances can be removed or remedied or improved, then the real ability and the true developmental period become apparent.[171]

Strauss had long been a strong supporter of the validity of intelligence measures for the purpose of assessing general intellectual capacity.[172] In three brief sentences, he and his coauthor opened up the possibility that the global inadequacy that an observer or an intelligence test might discover could be a smokescreen. What appears as general intellectual deficiency might actually be the far-reaching neurological defect resulting from brain injury. If one could arrange to see past that façade, it might be concluded that the true intellectual potential beneath is substantial. This was the first time that the Wayne School researchers had theorized that some children with brain injuries might have normal, or even superior, intelligence.

By the 1947 publication of *Psychopathology and the Education of the Brain-Injured Child*, Strauss and Lehtinen's classic summation of the Wayne School research, the authors had completely isolated the brain injury syndrome from mental retardation. Reasoning that "clinical and psychological examination yielded similar results with all types of brain-injured children irrespective of their placement on the Binet scale of intelligence,"[173] they defined the syndrome without reference to intelligence level. This reconceptualization of the Strauss Syndrome was important due to the popularity of the 1947 book. Many researchers and educators in the ensuing years understood the Strauss Syndrome not in terms of the many prior Strauss and Werner research articles that categorized the Syndrome under the umbrella of mental retardation but based on the Strauss and Lehtinen text that distinguished the new disorder from mental defect.

This new idea of the brain-injured child of normal intelligence became the basis of a successful entrepreneurial project for Strauss and Lehtinen. In 1947, they left the institution setting to found the Cove School, a private residential school in Racine, Wisconsin, for students with brain injuries. They were able to secure strong financial backing from a number of local companies as well as private citizens to pay the tuition for some children from families who could not afford the new school.[174] In June 1948, Strauss happily wrote to the Members of the Cove Schools Corporation (a group of supportive experts that included Sam Kirk, Newell Kephart, and Heinz Werner, as well as William Cruickshank of Syracuse and Leo Kanner of Johns Hopkins): "we started the second year with the number of pupils up to the limit of our capacity and with a demand by parents wishing to place children in our school which exceeds our physical plant."[175] By the end of 1948, Strauss announced that the Cove School had signed an agreement with the State Teachers College in Milwaukee to prepare teachers specifically for the School's brain-injured students.[176] Lehtinen and Strauss's new residential program was off to a roaring start.

As the two took on a variety of new administrative and clinical duties, their formal research activities waned; at least, their production of research publications decreased. The Wayne School team had never drawn a sharp distinction between intensive clinical work—observation, documentation, and analysis of child behavior—and the traditional processes of psychological research. It is probable that they considered themselves to be just as fully engaged in research at the Cove School as they had been at the Northville institution. In 1952, Strauss wrote that he and his colleagues had found the syndrome characteristics among many types of children—"not only mentally retarded children, but also children with normal intelligence quotients"—and the brain-injured population included children of all intelligence levels. Strauss described this idea as found "in the course of our research,"[177] a phrase offered without reference or elaboration. It is likely, at this point, that he was referring to unpublished, clinical observations made at the Cove School.

The second volume of *Psychopathology and the Education of the Brain-Injured Child* included a lengthy appendix written by Laura Lehtinen describing a number of "case histories of some of the children who have been or are now enrolled in The Cove Schools and whose intelligence quotients on standardized tests are within the normal range."[178] The expansion of the brain injury type to include children of all levels of intelligence drew strong support from parents of children who could not be classified as mentally retarded but had significant learning difficulties. In 1950, Lehtinen and Strauss opened a second Cove School, a day program in Evanston, Illinois.

A MOVING TREATMENT

Published in 1955, the second volume of Strauss's influential *Psychopathology* was coauthored by ex-Wayne School researcher Newell C. Kephart. After serving in the military during World War II, Kephart joined the psychology faculty at Purdue University. In 1950, he teamed with functional optometrist Gerald N. Getman in developing a clinical approach to the treatment of children with perceptual and sensory motor deficits. By the early 1960s, Kephart, and other educators such as Marianne Frostig and Ray Barsch, employed the popular Strauss Syndrome construct as the conceptual foundation of their programs of movement education. Through bodily activities and visual perception exercises, the movement educators treated childhood learning and behavioral deficits. The movement educators pursued the novel notion that learning disorders—even reading problems—could often be resolved by a curriculum of physical activities.

"A New Perception OF Things": Movement Education AND Newell C. Kephart

MOVEMENT AS EDUCATIONAL TREATMENT

In a 1960 book providing parents with guidance on how to develop their child's perceptual abilities in preparation for school success, Purdue University researcher Newell C. Kephart related the case of a boy named Jim. A child of normal intelligence, personality, and visual acuity, Jim failed to learn to read through his first three years of schooling. He was frustrated by overwhelming academic challenges, and his behavior and attitude deteriorated badly. A psychologist found that Jim performed very poorly on the draw-a-maze subsection of an IQ test and referred him to a therapist who specialized in the treatment of perceptual disorders.

The specialist administered a series of perceptual performance tests. When given basic figures to copy, such as a square and a triangle, Jim drew scribbled distortions. When asked to draw two squares side-by-side, although he typically wrote with his right hand, he drew the left square with his left hand, switched the pencil to his right hand, and then drew the right square with that hand. The psychologist asked Jim to draw a line on the chalkboard, using his right hand, beginning from a point at his right side and angling across to a point to the left of his body. As his right hand crossed his middle torso, the boy stopped, shifted the chalk to his left hand, and then completed the line. In tasks involving letter identification, Jim confused the letters b and d, p and q. When asked to read a series of words, he also experienced reversals: he read *saw* as *was*, *dog* as *gob*, and *or* as *ro*.

"The midline of his body," Kephart observed, "served, then, as a barrier to his movements."[1] The underlying problem was "that Jim never really learned to distinguish between the two sides of his body," a skill called "laterality."[2] He had failed to develop an accurate

> image of his own body, a visual and kinesthetic awareness of how he fills the space within his own skin.... [This is] an awareness...basic to motor control...funda- mental to our perception of the world outside our skins, the left and right or up and down of things.[3]

The specialist concluded that what young Jim needed was an educational program that would teach him

> a new perception of things as they are, a new sense of identity with other children, a new feeling of self-confidence—and, of course, a new level of school achievement.[4]

Children who did not learn to accurately perceive the world struggled not only to learn to read. Often the perceptual handicap resulted in higher-level cognitive difficulties, including the development of concepts that are "weak, restricted, or bizarre."[5]

In order to learn to read, to think properly, and become a successful student, Jim would require a program of activities designed to develop the abilities neces- sary for realistic perception. For in "the normal human visual mechanism, things are *viewed* accurately—but they are only *understood* as the result of learning."[6] In the 1940s and the 1950s, scientists had developed "simple, clinically proven techniques"[7] for teaching the necessary skills. Jim would benefit from these spe- cialized techniques.

During the 1960s and the 1970s, educators and psychologists across America discovered many Jims, young children who required formal training or remedia- tion of a specific set of perceptual abilities as a prerequisite to standard kinds of school learning. Preschools, kindergartens, elementary schools, and special schools for struggling learners nationwide initiated perceptual development screening and training programs. A group of prominent educational therapists, most notably Kephart, Marianne Frostig, Gerald N. Getman, and Ray Barsch generated the theoretical accounts and programmatic tools for this national popularization of perceptual-motor training for young children.[8]

At the Longfellow School in Madison, Wisconsin, young children engaged in a program of physical activities that included hopping, jumping rope, walk- ing on rails, rhythmic walking (to a metronome), bouncing on a trampoline, and copying shapes on a chalkboard.[9] Children with severe reading problems attending the Reading Research Unit in Lexington, Massachusetts, spent "an hour a day on rhythmic-motor exercises to learn to control their bodies in a coordinated way. They [were] taught to skip rope, walk a rail and to bounce a ball to music."[10] Elementary schools in Chicago Ridge, Illinois, offered first- and second-graders a sensorimotor development curriculum involving, for instance, walking a wooden balance beam. The program was designed to enhance language development.[11]

"You must first develop the skills that underlie reading," explained Frances McGlannon, a private school director in Miami, Florida. The perceptual development activities at the McGlannan School included having blindfolded students identify shapes by feeling objects with their hands. At both the McGlannan School and the Dewitt Reading Clinic in San Rafael, California, motor skills activities involved walking on a balance beam as well as other coordination and balance exercises.[12]

Public schools in Muncie (Indiana), Trumbull (Connecticut), Ramapo (New York), Salisbury (North Carolina), Newton (Massachusetts), and Richardson (Texas) put kindergarten students through an intensive series of tests designed to catch early learning problems. Educators guided the young children through a range of important screening and development activities: walking on stilts, drawing lines between two points on a chalk board, "walking on balance beams, drawing circles, listening to recorded tones, repeating numbers and words, and drawing pictures of people."[13] Movement education, as a developmental preparation for academic learning, was a national phenomenon.

In this chapter, I examine the development of perceptual and sensory motor development programs designed to either alleviate or forestall the educational problems of brain injury and learning disabilities. I conglomerate a range of similar instructional programs intended to foster programs and efforts for the development of young children's motor and perceptual skills under the broad heading of *movement education*. Foundational to the movement education approach was a threefold theoretical assumption:

(1)   Motor activity and sensory perception are inseparable aspects of the physiological development of children;

(2)   Adequate motor development, in the early years, leads to the acquisition of adequate neuropsychological skills of sensory (primarily visual) perception; and

(3)   Adequate perceptual skills (primarily visual) are a physiological and developmental prerequisite to learning standard academic skills such as reading.

Building on the neurological research of Kurt Goldstein and Alfred Strauss's Wayne School team, the movement educators created and popularized programs of physical activities and perceptual development for young children.

Although dozens of educators and psychologists across the country developed and implemented movement education programs during the 1960s and 1970s, the leading national figures were undoubtedly Kephart, Frostig, Getman, and Barsch. In their own research and practice with struggling learners, and frequently in mutual collaborations that cross-pollinated their concepts, they built a complex theoretical understanding of how children failed to learn and how to treat educational retardation. James M. Kauffman and Daniel P. Hallahan noted in 1976 that, for all practical purposes, with some minor variations in emphasis, the perceptual development programs developed by these leaders were virtually interchangeable in both theory and practice.[14]

This chapter will explore the work of a single researcher, that of Newell C. Kephart, as a suitable representative of the broader science and practice of movement education. Kephart embodied the movement educators' eclectic, practical blending of neurological holism and functionalist psychology within a clinical orientation toward the learning difficulties confronted by individual children. The movement educators' focus on struggling young learners located them in a disciplinary intersection, at the crossroads of the fields of education, psychology, neurology, and optometry. They were able to draw quite freely, and in some eyes too liberally, from a variety of disciplines because of their clinical orientation that placed pragmatic concerns of treating an individual child at the forefront.

PRACTICAL CLINICAL EXPERIENCE

Kephart is an excellent example of the movement educators' practices of diversified theoretical borrowing in service to a clinical focus on the individual as a unique case. In a volume published after his death, Kephart's wife Martha wrote:

> He was concerned with the whole child and any problems the child might have with learning. His was a very eclectic approach and he believed that anything that worked was right. He resented being accused of having a theory—he said he had no theory, only methods and techniques.[15]

It is an overstatement to say that Kephart had no theory. He was clearly a very comprehensive and sometimes daring theoretical thinker who often united seemingly disparate conceptual elements in complex and new ways. Yet it is also quite true that he did not settle on or cling to a single theory. He was singular only in his devotion to doing what yielded positive results in each case. This clinical focus was supported by a habit of wide-ranging theoretical scavenging, the constant, utilitarian appropriation of ideas from multiple places and sources, brought together to face the practical challenge of treating the individual child who failed to learn.

This was the bold yet practical style of Kephart and of the movement educators. One might say that both the strength and the weakness of movement education as an area of professional work were derived from its fierce attitude of innovation and independence. The principal allegiance was not to a specific tradition of psychological research or to an identified theory of human behavior or learning, but to a child's well-being. Yet, even this bare statement of child-oriented purpose is far too simple, for the child's learning and educational needs were construed within a clinical practice that relied heavily on the experiential judgment of an educational therapist. Direct experience with many children over time and face-to-face interaction with a given individual child were prized by the movement educators as the most promising epistemology—a pragmatic and results-driven way of understanding a child's development, difficulties, and progress. It was believed that the struggling learner, if provided with the properly designed regimen of developmental exercises, could make great strides toward adequate functioning and that proper regimen was best devised by thoughtful clinicians who crafted a refined mode of understanding and judgment from experiences obtained working with children and fortified by the best knowledge from a number of disciplines.

For the young Kephart, this independent and assertive orientation toward clinical knowledge was greatly cultivated in his collaboration with optometrist Gerald N. Getman in the early 1950s. But long before he and Getman teamed up in the creation of perceptual-motor development exercises for children, Kephart had been schooled in the promise of early educational intervention. The intellectual growth potential of young children was matched only by the influential power of educational professionals and their programs. Kephart's doctoral studies at the Iowa Child Welfare Research Station took place at the most progressive edge of the prewar nature-nurture controversy, a vibrant and optimistic intellectual climate where child psychology shook off its moribund conservatism to become the progressive voice of an unlimited human potential.

THE IOWA CHILD WELFARE RESEARCH STATION

As a doctoral student at the University of Iowa in the mid-1930s, Kephart worked as a researcher at the well-known Iowa Child Welfare Research Station. At that time, the Iowa Station was fast becoming the empirical catalyst in the development of the concepts of the plasticity of early childhood intelligence and the influence of environmental stimulation. During the decades prior to World War II, the fields of psychology and medicine generally maintained that the human mind was relatively unchanging in its intellectual capacity. Child development research, although a relatively young science, chiefly concurred with this deterministic thesis. Whatever innate capacities one was born with were understood to frame a circumscribed range of lifelong mental abilities. The development of normal children was understood as a rational, orderly process in which physiological and psychological maturation proceeded in a linear progression.[16]

A seminal example of this deterministic concept of maturation and intelligence development was the popular 1931 volume *Experimental Child Study* by Florence L. Goodenough and John E. Anderson, codirectors of the Institute of Child Welfare at the University of Minnesota. Goodenough had completed her doctoral study under the mentorship of Lewis Terman, the famous Stanford psychologist who created the English translation of Binet's original intelligence scale. He was the most visible researcher articulating the concept of intelligence as an innate and unchanging mental characteristic.

Child development, wrote Goodenough and Anderson, consisted of a series of growth achievements occurring in an invariable sequence. The most important single concept in this field of research was that child development conformed to "the law of the constancy of developmental order."[17]

> Although children vary greatly in rate of development, the order of development as marked by the successive appearance of various developmental events varies but little from one child to another. This sequential order is apparent at all ages and in all functions.[18]

The primary and trusted measurement of growth or advancement within developmental steps, not surprisingly, was intelligence testing. The mental age of a child, as measured by an intelligence test, was an accurate assessment of that child's location on the fixed "serial order" of developmental stages.[19] Intelligence was relatively constant, a stable feature inherent to the biological constitution of the individual child. The social order, as exemplified in various levels of employment involving a hierarchy of skill and, quite typically, corresponding grades of financial compensation, could be readily explained by the innate intelligence of the individual. The deep conservatism of the deterministic thesis construed social and political structure as outward expression of the natural facts of differential endowment.[20]

The Iowa Child Welfare Research Station, under the leadership of outspoken and politically connected director George D. Stoddard, provided the leading advocacy for a more progressive, Dewey-inspired notion of child development. During Kephart's years of doctoral study in the mid-1930s, Station researchers conducted empirical studies that challenged the staid notion that the individual intelligence was primarily static, stable, and relatively immune to environmental influence. Stoddard, prolific child development researcher Beth L. Wellman, and the soon-to-be-famous Harold Skeels defied the status quo of child development research by positing that intelligence was highly variable during the first five years of life, and that environmental stimulation played a central role in either fostering or squelching intellectual development.[21]

The Iowa Station researchers occupied center stage of a heated national debate over the constancy and elasticity of intelligence. A November 1938 *Time* magazine article entitled "IQ Control" placed the Station and director George Stoddard in the public spotlight as the discoverers of the environmental keys to unlocking hidden intellectual potential. *Time* celebrated the revision of the traditional concept of IQ constancy with the updated, progressive vision pronounced by the Iowa researchers.[22]

At the February 1940 Yearbook convention of the National Society for the Study of Education in St. Louis, the progressivism of the Iowa Station squared off against the determinism of Terman and Goodenough. Since the aging Terman did not attend the meeting, the real scuffles occurred in planning sessions leading up to the conference. At the May 1939 planning session, Terman supporter Quinn McNemar presented a harshly worded review of the Iowa Station environmental research.[23] When McNemar and Beth Wellman spoke at a September 1939 meeting, Wellman chastised her opponent, "You should realize that Lewis Terman has poisoned your mind."[24]

Terman, perhaps realizing that he would not attend the upcoming Yearbook conference in St. Louis, organized a small panel of the National Education Association in July 1939, at Stanford, to discuss the upcoming "nature versus nurture" yearbook. But rather than allowing equal time for the presentation of the two opposing positions, Terman was scheduled for a one-hour address and Stoddard was granted only 10 minutes. Stoddard later described the whole meeting as "rigged" against him.[25]

At the St. Louis conference in February, Terman relied on surrogate John E. Angerson to argue for his side. In his paper published for the conference, Terman openly accused the Iowa Station researchers of inaccurately reporting their own data.[26] But Anderson was a milder figure, and the heated conflict foreshadowed in preliminary scraps did not erupt. Ernest R. Hilgard, the moderator of the debate, recalled later that "the audience was with" Stoddard and the environmental argument.[27] Terman's heyday had passed. Psychology had already shifted away from a purely deterministic understanding of human intelligence toward a model that mixed the factors of nature and nurture.

The prominent national role of the Iowa Station in the pitched IQ battle had not come about without some degree of happenstance. Perhaps the initial spark was supplied not by a profound new theory or piece of scientific research but by a dramatic personal series of events involving Stoddard's predecessor, Station director Bird T. Baldwin, and Station researcher Beth L. Wellman. When Baldwin's daughter enrolled in the Station preschool, her IQ was measured at 84, a level considered at that time to be feebleminded. Against all conventional sense at the time, Baldwin refused to send his daughter to the state institution for feeble-minded children. Instead, she attended the Station preschool program, where she prospered. Testing conducted 18 months later measured her IQ at 143, an incred-ible increase of almost 60 points. Baldwin's wife died in 1925. He soon thereaf-ter became engaged to Beth Wellman. When Baldwin died in 1928, Wellman adopted Baldwin's daughter.

Subsequently, Wellman initiated a series of studies of the effects that nursery school attendance had on young children's intelligence levels. At first, she began mining the piles of IQ score data that had been gathered on 600 children who attended the Station preschool between 1921 and 1932. She found that the IQs of students increased substantially between fall and spring and then dropped slightly during the summer months when the children were not attending preschool. Moreover, she found that the more years of preschool that children attended, the greater the IQ benefit. Children who attended for three years gained 26.3 per-centiles. Children who attended for two years increased by 19.9 percentiles, and children who attended only one year rose by 15.6 percentiles. Similarly, children who attended for full days gained more IQ points than children who attended only half-day sessions.

Wellman concluded, "Gains in intelligence test scores are associated with pre-school attendance.... Intelligence is modifiable by environmental conditions."[28] The Station preschool data indicated that the "greatest gains were made by the children in the lower levels of IQ."[29] The maximum potential for the environmen-tal enhancement of intelligence resided among the youngsters with the lowest IQs. It was clear to Wellman and her Station colleagues that preschool environments made a substantial difference in the development of intelligence. Wellman's sub-sequent empirical work through the remaining years of the 1930s investigated the question of environment itself, seeking to understand more specifically how envi-ronments modify intelligence.[30] Her conclusions have become the basic philosophy underlying most early childhood educational programs, including Head Start. Not only is intelligence highly malleable, especially in the early years, it also responds most vigorously to a pedagogy of experiential fullness and diversity.

> The best type of mental growth is not accomplished by putting the child through paces like a race horse, or by practicing something over and over like the scales on a piano. It is accomplished in part by providing the child with the opportunity for a life rich in experiences.[31]

Wellman believed that children progress best in environments that support their natural curiosity and independent thinking.

Similar but far more famous conclusions were reached by Wellman's colleague Harold Skeels. When Skeels, a Station doctoral graduate who had studied under Stoddard and Wellman, accepted a job administering IQ tests to children placed in a Davenport (Iowa) orphanage, he had no idea that his rather pedestrian testing responsibilities would throw him into the national limelight. By State of Iowa law, all children in the orphanage were given an IQ test, and those who were deemed too feebleminded for foster placement or adoption were sent to live at the state institution in Glenwood. Skeels started his mental testing position in January 1934. Part of his responsibilities included checking on the general well-being of the children that he ordered transferred to the state institution. On one of those routine visits, he discovered that two infants, a 13-month-old with an IQ of 46 and a 16-month-old with an IQ of 35, had been placed on an adult female ward. The institution was chronically understaffed, so the staff had entrusted the care of the babies to a group of women institution residents.

When Skeels returned for another routine visit six months later, he saw a dramatic improvement in the two infants' behavior. They were far more playful and interactive than would be expected of children of their intellectual level. Skeels was afraid that he had made an error in his original testing and classification of the youngsters. He decided to retest them on the Binet. This time the two children scored 77 and 81, an increase of 31 and 46 IQ points respectively in half a year. 21 months later, he again retested the two children. They scored 95 and 93, well within the average range. He ordered them to be transferred back to the orphanage where they were permanently adopted by families. Skeels and environmental stimulation had saved the toddlers.[32]

Behind the highly provocative notion "that social intervention could make a beneficial difference"[33] in young children, the Iowa scientists employed relatively uninventive research methods. The primary investigative designs involved simple experiments, statistical comparisons of mean scores between treatment and control groups. In some instances, this practice took on a longitudinal trajectory as groups of preschool students were tracked into later school years. The general assumption was that such comparisons of group means provided insight into both normal and abnormal development.

What marked the Station's research was not methodological innovation but the novel thesis that human capacities unfold in an unscripted manner. A child's intelligence, narrowly speaking, and physical and psychological abilities in general are not predetermined by inheritance or social position. What a person is ultimately able to do depends greatly on how that individual is nurtured and taught, especially during the formative preschool years. This almost open-ended optimism about the future possibilities for all children chimed a theme of American egalitarianism. The centrality of early schooling in this scheme placed educators at the heart of democratic civilization.

MODIFIED BY THE IOWA STATION ENVIRONMENT

For doctoral student Kephart, the Iowa Station was a dynamic context of remarkable social consequence, a heady research environment where science suddenly and quite triumphantly leaped to profound heights of social and political importance. Seemingly overnight, in a small intellectual enclave in the Midwestern moderation of Iowa City, the research and actions of psychologists mattered far more than the profession had previously imagined. Human nature itself was up for grabs, both in its very definition and, perhaps more importantly for Kephart's intellectual development, in the pronounced import of educational programs designed to promote improvements at the deepest of psychological dimensions.

Doctoral student Kephart certainly experienced both the bright light of prewar psychological science—the embattled heat of intellectual controversy—and the sanguine expectations of psychology and education becoming the pacesetters of social engineering. In his own research at the Iowa Station, Kephart participated in a lesser priority of the institute: mental health and juvenile delinquency. He worked closely with fellow doctoral student H. Max Houtchens on the development of a psychometric measurement of neuroses among juvenile delinquents.[34] This line of research brought him under the supervision of Harold M. Williams, a psychologist who collaborated with Skeels on one of the influential studies of intelligence in a local orphanage.[35]

Kephart's dissertation was supervised by Williams, and his committee included both Stoddard and Skeels. In the Acknowledgments page, Kephart warmly thanked both men for their "valuable suggestions and criticisms,"[36] an indication that Kephart's decision to conduct research in the seemingly less exciting area of juvenile delinquency did not remove him from the social envelope of the progressive child welfare ethos of the Station.

Beyond that one note, a casual reader of Kephart's dissertation research would be more easily convinced that he had studied with Max Wertheimer and the Berlin Gestalt theorists than with Stoddard and the Iowa progressives. Citing Wertheimer, Wolfgang Kohler, Kurt Koffka, and Kurt Lewin, Kephart theorized that the many aspects and elements of normal personality constitute "an organized whole" that brings about a meaningful synthesis and integration of mental and sensory data.[37] A normal personality unifies the otherwise disparate elements of human experience into a coherent and meaningful structure. Juvenile delinquents, Kephart hypothesized, "display personality defects which may be described as disorganization of mental data.... a disconnectedness between the elements of psychic material."[38] Quite literally, he investigated the notion that juvenile delinquents simply cannot get their "stuff" (mental, sensory, and experiential) together.

Methodologically, Kephart's study melded procedural commonplace with a hearty exploratory reach. He set up five separate experiments involving comparisons of group means between randomly selected samples of delinquent youth at the Iowa Training School for Boys and males from the local public schools. The five areas of experimentation involved widely varied areas of psychological functioning, each presented by Kephart with little theoretical explanation. Yet taken individually and as a carefully selected composite, the areas demonstrate the expansive holism of the young researcher's thinking. It is evident that, despite the thin vagueness of his articulation of the various areas of functioning and their relationships to one another, the doctoral researcher understood vast areas of mental activity, language, and motor behavior to be implicitly and deeply connected.

The first experiment investigated the relationship between motor behavior and verbal association or language-based thought. The second examined what Kephart called the "smoothness of the flow of mental processes at the verbal level,"[39] a construct aiming generally at the rate and regularity of linguistic output. The third experiment looked at a Gestalt theory staple, the development of visual form perception in tasks utilizing traditional black and white silhouette figures. In all three experiments, the delinquents performed at a significantly lower level of psychic organization than the control group.

The fourth was perhaps the most creative and theoretically unbounded experiment, an examination of the psychological utilization of past experiences to provide structure and coherence to the present. Kephart had the subjects in both groups memorize the Gettysburg Address. Then he gave each subject six minutes to memorize a sequence of nonsense syllables that sounded like the Gettysburg Address, assuming that the most capable individuals would employ the Address as a device for memorizing the new material. His concern was not only whether they used the Address as a mnemonic aid but also whether the subjects were aware of doing so, if they had insight into their own memory strategy. Delinquents demonstrated less insight in this experiment, leading Kephart to conclude that "in delinquents past experiences are less dynamically connected to present problems than in nondelinquents."

The fifth experiment of Kephart's dissertation was the only one that attempted to examine the boys' social relations and friendships with peers. This experiment held true to Kephart's focus on the delinquent's individual personality as the location of problems that ultimately played out in the social world. He analyzed the boys' preferences within their peer group, asking each to name 10 boys that

he liked best, under the theory that a normal personality develops social preferences and attachments within the local peer group. Abnormality, in this regard,
was indicated by a large percentage of preference selections from outside of one's
group of daily peers. Kephart found that few of the delinquent boys in the Training
School named their fellow inmates as preferred peers, while many of the boys in
the local public middle school selected classmates as their favorites. This difference
was evidence, in Kephart's reasoning, that "delinquents show less synthesis in their
social relations than do nondelinquents."[40]

Writing in concepts that foreshadowed his later understanding of learning disability, Kephart found that the problem of delinquency could be reduced to a specific personality defect. Delinquents lacked a capacity of "mental organization,"[41]
a functional ability to bring the pieces of sensory, perceptual, and mental data
together into a synthesis that supported conforming behavior. Why such an internal synthesis of psychic and even physiological dimensions would lead to behavior
that conforms to conventional expectations of childhood and youth behavior was a
stretch for Kephart. His explanations on this issue were confusing. His main reasoning employed a general analogy between social harmony and psychic balance.
Discord in the community, in families and schools and neighborhoods, must be
mirrored in the internal psychological disorganization of the problematic individuals. Drawing heavily from the Gestalt concept of perception as a task of integrating fragmented elements into a coherent structure, he posited the delinquent
boy as unable to unify his experiences into mental cohesion, thereby rendering
him unable to notice and accept the social norms of the community. Simply put,
internal disorganization within the problematic individual was the source of social
incongruence and deviance in the community.

Kephart's dissertation exhibited his early attraction to the far-reaching and
often ambitious holism of the Gestaltist theorists. He proudly defied the typical
mind-body split of contemporary American psychology by examining linkages
between motor behavior and mental activity. The wholeness of human physiology, he believed, could not be arbitrarily divided into bodily and psychological
functions. Instead, he theorized a dynamic synthesis of all physiology, a structural
unity at the core of all of human activity.

His holism, however, stopped at the skin's edge. His notions of wholeness and
order were fully ensconced within the individualized psychology employed by both
Terman's deterministic old-schoolers and the more progressive Station researchers
who supervised his research. Juvenile delinquency, a phenomenon consisting at
face value of repeated conflicts between identified teenagers and their authority
figure parents and teachers, was distilled by Kephart's analysis into a failure of the
teens' internal Gestalt mechanisms. Social conflict in the community is merely an
outward expression of the jumbled mess within the delinquent's character. Even

with Skeels and Stoddard on his dissertation committee, Kephart's conclusion reiterated the longstanding determinist belief that problems in society are to be blamed on flawed individuals. Quite logically, from this standpoint, healing social ills of America required the educational and psychological alteration of defective individuals.

Failure of internal mental organization was a psychological explanation that Kephart carried forward into his later work with children with brain injuries or learning disabilities. In 1967, he described learning disabilities in terms reminiscent of his 1936 dissertation: "One of the major aspects of the learning problem is the organization and integration of perceptual and conceptual information." As a child with a learning disability moves through the school grades, he "achieves well until he reaches the third or fourth grade; and then suddenly begins to fail for no known reason." At this level of schooling, "more emphasis was placed on organization of material" and "the pressures for organization became too great" for the child to succeed.[42] Kephart's early notion of mental disarray among juvenile delinquents remained a central feature of his later thinking about learning disability.

WAYNE COUNTY TRAINING SCHOOL

After finishing his degree at Iowa in 1936, Kephart took a position as a mental hygienist at the Wayne County Training School in Northville, Michigan. He moved from one intellectual hotbed to another. The Wayne School was an unusual institution. Superintendent Robert Haskell, noting the scientific work of Henry Goddard and Edgar Doll at the Vineland Training School in New Jersey, established a research department with the goal of national prominence. During the late 1930s and the 1940s, it became a recognized leader in the neurological study of mental retardation and brain injury.

For five years, until he was called into military service in 1941, Kephart worked as a researcher at the Wayne School. His first research projects revived the themes of the Iowa Station, particularly the heated IQ war between the two sides representing explanations for individual differences in intelligence: hereditarian and environmental.[43] In a series of small studies, he investigated the question of environmental influence on institutionalized boys described as "high grade morons and borderline defectives."[44] Working within the Skeels environmental thesis, Kephart theorized that some of the Wayne County adolescents had intellectual deficits caused by a lack of proper stimulation in their families and homes, and these cases could be effectively remediated through designed programs of stimulation.

In 1939, Strauss and Kephart explored the relationship between environment, intelligence, and etiologies of mental defect. They sorted the population of the Wayne County Training School into different clinical types based on the apparent etiology of each child's mental deficiency. They then compared IQ changes during time of residence at the institution across the various etiological types, working under the assumption that the institution presented a generally favorable and stimulating environment for intellectual growth. They found that the endogenous types, that is, children who "have an essentially intact nervous system,"[45] generally experienced a gain in IQ in the institution environment. These children were understood to have a retardation that was "due, in part at least, to an environment so circumscribed that the child is unable to absorb from it the skills, attitudes, and knowledges necessary to the development of intelligence."[46] By contrast, exogenous types, children with apparent damage to or disease of the brain or central nervous system, generally experience a decrease in IQ.[47]

Kephart also tracked the measured IQ of 50 Wayne County children prior to admission, during the time when they lived at home with their families, and after admission to the institution. He found that, in general, IQs gradually decreased during the preadmission period and increased during residence as the institution. He explained these trends as supporting the thesis that poor intellectual stimulation at home caused intellectual deficiency and the more stimulating institutional environment produced mental gains.[48]

These studies led Kephart to believe that "the provision of an environment, within the institution, which is specifically planned to offer additional stimulation to these children, should result in a further rise in IQ."[49] With the hope of more dramatic results, Kephart further tested the environmental thesis by exposing a group of 16 institutionalized boys to a specially designed program of educational stimulation. He theorized that such a program would produce even greater intellectual gains than those fostered by the typical institutional environment.

The actual content of the 18-month stimulation program was somewhat vague. The theoretical basis for the program and the scientific definition of what constituted "stimulation" were murky notions. The children engaged in construction activities using materials such as wood and metal. Children were supported in designing and carrying out their own products. In addition, "abstract problems were presented for solution"[50] to the boys. It seemed that these problems were presented on an informal or impromptu basis. Kephart described these problem-solving activities as fostering logical forms of thought. Furthermore, in social situations, rather than telling the children what to do, the staff engaged them in problem-solving discussions involving explorations of possible actions and consequences. Again, this aspect of the intervention appeared to occur in an unplanned or spontaneous way.

While the treatment activities were loosely conceived and organized, the intent of the stimulation program was clear.

> The interest of the experimental program is primarily in the child's own original development, of means toward the end. Free choice, both of the end and the means, stimulates ingenuity, spontaneous evaluation of methods and similar qualities.[51]

Kephart wanted to increase the amount of "internal productivity,"[52] meaningful thinking and reasoning activity, in order to provoke growth in the cognitive apparatus.

All evidence pointed to the success of the experiment. Prior to the stimulation treatment, the mean IQ score of the group was 66.3. After the treatment, the mean IQ gain for the group was 10.1 points. Kephart concluded that "the rate of mental growth can be significantly increased in a favorable institutional setting by specific programs of stimulation."[53]

Kephart's research at the Wayne County Training School consisted primarily of the transportation of the central themes of the Iowa Station from the preschool to the institution context. His methods and findings greatly mirrored the work of his mentors at the Station. The environment and educational intervention again won the day.

Two components of the environmental hypothesis were central to his thought at the time and remained at the heart of his subsequent work in the area of brain injury. First, he believed that a young child's early experiences in the family and home had a profound, formative effect on mental development. The central nervous system of children was, to some extent, a malleable system developed in interaction with early environments. Second, he believed that carefully designed programs of training based on psychological knowledge could effectively ameliorate cases of lagging neuropsychological development. What had been molded in five early years could be greatly remolded, retrained, through professional intervention. Each of these beliefs carried on the social engineering tradition of the Iowa Child Welfare Research Station.

Perhaps more profound in the long run for Kephart's thinking about children was the initiation of his professional collaboration with Alfred Strauss. The publications completed by the pair during Kephart's time at the Wayne County Training School were certainly more Kephart than Strauss, more the environmentalism of Iowa Station than the holistic neuropsychology of German extraction. This is not to say that Kephart did not work closely on Strauss's neurological examination of brain injury. Kephart's professional style was to learn from each professional relationship that he experienced. He drew in the conceptual elements and features that he believed could supply improvement to his own theoretical approach. Perhaps more pointedly, he refined his own clinical skills and knowledge by appropriating new concepts and tactics from his intimate collaborators. The partnership that Kephart and Strauss initiated in the late 1930s was maintained for decades, long after Kephart had moved on to Purdue. The most significant product of this affiliation for both parties was not Kephart's early environmental thesis studies but the coauthored 1955 publication of Strauss's second volume of *Psychopathology and the Brain-Injured Child*.[54]

VISION AND WORK

Kephart's work on environmental stimulation at the Training School was interrupted by World War II naval service, and he never directly returned to the question of the programmatic enhancement of IQ. After the war, he accepted a faculty position at Purdue University where he joined the highly productive Occupational Research Center that gathered statistics on industrial labor. Although his research at Purdue then turned to empirical investigations of the relationships between visual skills and adult behavior in the workplace, his prior experiences designing environmental treatments for mental deficiency remained influential.

After World War II, Kephart applied the environmental thesis to the occupational investigations of the visual skills of industrial workers, a series of studies that led him to conclude that visual skills, like mental skills, could be improved through training.[55] In the late 1940s, he focused on the analysis of visual phoria, a problem concerning ocular movement and the coordination of the two eyes to achieve binocular vision. Working with his occupational research colleagues at Purdue, Kephart measured phorias among workers in textile factories and corporate offices. His research with industrial workers repeatedly documented the relationship between levels of visual skill and gradations of worker effectiveness. In numerous studies, he demonstrated "the relationship between measurements of visual phorias and increased industrial production."[56] Good vision and good work, it would appear, were closely related.

For example, in a study of 97 electric accounting card key punch machine operators, Kephart found that 20 workers simply did not have the basic visual acuity or depth perception skills necessary for their jobs. Of the 77 remaining workers, 19 failed a battery of phoria tests; 13 of the 19 had been rated as less satisfactory workers by their employers. A battery of phoria tests served as a fair predictor of worker effectiveness.[57] In a similar study among workers in the lens inspection department of an optical goods manufacturer, Kephart found that measures of visuals skills correlated closely with tenure on the job. Workers with vertical or lateral phoria difficulties tended to leave the job after a brief time while those with no phoria problems tended to remain in their positions.[58]

SIGHT AND VISION

In 1950, Kephart began a close partnership with Gerald N. Getman, an optometrist who later became a leading figure in the field of learning disabilities in his own right, on the development of a clinical approach to the treatment of childhood brain injury.[59] The two collaborated on the development of perceptual-motor training for children, first at Getman's optometric practice in Minnesota and later at Kephart's educational clinic at Purdue. By the early 1970s, the names Kephart and Getman would be inextricably linked by many in the field of learning disabilities and synonymous with perceptual-motor education.

If Kephart can be called the optometrist's psychologist for his exploration of mental activities of perception in relation to visual skills, then Getman was the psychologist's optometrist. An unusually adventurous thinker, Getman mined the intersection of optometry and educational research that most researchers viewed as obviously unrelated. In the 1940s, Getman spent over four years studying with the famous Yale developmental theorist Arnold Gesell, a highly unusual training for an optometrist.[60] Often teamed with Kephart or Raymond Barsch, Getman spent many decades treating children who, although they scored within the normal range on all the standard optometric measures, struggled to utilize their visual skills in reading and other academic work. As a functional optometrist, his concern was not merely how well the children saw within the examination room but how and why they utilized that vision in the many contexts and activities of daily life.[61]

The keystone of Getman's theory was what he understood as the oft-confused difference between sight and vision. Sight is merely the sensory organ response to light, a physiological reaction involving the retina. But vision is a larger organismic process of interpreting the environment, a neurosensory dynamic that only begins with sight.[62]

> Vision is a very complex process which includes more than the eyes. Certainly the visual process originates when light reflection from objects, or brightness contrasts like print, strikes the retina and is then transmitted as neurological beeps to the entire central nervous system. However, the completion of a visual act involves the entire organism and all of the relevancies and interrelationships which exist between all information systems.[63]

Vision, in this broad and holistic view, involved all of the complex neurological exchanges and interactions that result in making sense of the environment. Light input must be integrated with other sensory and motor information in order to result in a meaningful and useful interpretation that derives meaning and facilitates action. Getman's expanded concept of vision harkened back to Goldstein's holistic view of the organism as a complex physiological architecture-in-motion, a structural dynamic geared toward understanding and operating within the environmental context. What Getman added to Goldstein was a heightened emphasis on the centrality of vision in a physiological system of learning.

While sight constituted a mere sensory reaction, visual skills had to be learned through practice and experience. Getman contended in his work with children and families that the development of vision was a frequently neglected area of early learning that often resulted in otherwise unexplained learning difficulties. Many struggling young learners with 20/20 sight had failed to acquire the necessary visual skills, especially those required in learning to read, to succeed in school. In his clinical practice, Getman gradually developed a regimen of exercises designed to help children develop their visual-perceptual skills. This perspective jibed neatly with Kephart's developing understanding of the relationship between visual skills and academic success among children.

Equally noteworthy was Getman's orientation to a science of learning and learning difficulties, his intense phenomenological focus on the needs and satisfactions of the individual. He was a devoted experimental clinician, again greatly in the Goldstein tradition, who addressed each individual case as a site of scientific and practical exploration. He traced his own practices of what might be called a pragmatic clinical empiricism to his father's experiences as a turn-of-the-century druggist and optometrist. In the 1890s, prior to the modern standardization and mass production of pharmaceuticals, a druggist worked closely with patients and their physicians to formulate chemical recipes specific to the medical needs of individuals. The elder Getman's 1894 apothecary notebooks included numerous formulae for ointments and liniments contrived for and often named after specific patients. The practice of the druggist was to make continuous adjustments in the formula of the medication based on the response of the patient, an experimental and gradual process that was completed only when the patient had shown satisfactory improvement.[64] This orientation to science placed great faith in the validity of the information communicated by individual patients, in their words and behavior, and the responsive judgment of an astute clinician.

Getman viewed his individualized clinical science as chiefly opposed to the common psychological analyses of groups involving statistical means and standard deviations, the very methodological apparatus that was the mainstay of Kephart's doctoral training. Working as a devout clinician within an educational and psychological field that often prized statistical analyses, he described himself as feeling pushed "away from the statistics of the multitudes and toward the clinical results on one patient at a time."[65] Individual abilities and needs often lost in the statistical sciences were retained only in a clinical approach founded on the direct communication between patient and practitioner.

At first glance, it would seem that Getman's ardent form of clinical episte-mology was an ill fit for Kephart. Of all the movement educators, Kephart had the firmest foothold in a more traditional functional psychology that frequently relied on quantitative research methods. His training at the Iowa Station had involved a basic method consisting of comparisons of means between experimental and treatment groups, a general practice that he continued in his quantitative work. Yet, over the course of Kephart's career, his path of inquiry gradually moved from an early interest in statistical, experimental research to a later emphasis on clinical, experiential learning. After Getman's Minnesota-based educational therapy clinic was moved to Kephart's Purdue campus in 1956, Kephart's quantitative research days were over. With one exception, his research activities in the prime years of the development of the learning disability concept consisted solely of clinical experi-ences with children and families.[66]

PERCEPTION AND SCHOOL SUCCESS

Buoyed by his work with Getman, Kephart shifted his line of empirical work in the early 1950s from the vision of adult workers to that of children in the public schools. If the job performance and longevity of adult workers were related to visual skills, then, perhaps, it would follow that young children who achieved poorly in schools could be failing due to vision problems. Kephart leaped from factories to schools in order to test that hypothesis. To his thinking, this shift of location and population was quite reasonable. He viewed himself as approaching

> the problem of the school situation in much the same manner in which we approach it in the industrial situation.... The school child can be thought of as being engaged in a task which is not dissimilar in many respects to the task in which the industrial worker is engaged.[67]

The similarity of intellectual and visual requirements of adult employment and childhood academic work warranted a migration of his visual skill research pro-gram into the realm of education.

Kephart began testing his theory that success in academic learning was directly related to a child's level of visual skills. In a study undertaken with 52 boys at the Colorado State Industrial School, a clinical eye examination was conducted on all subjects. The boys were sorted into an experimental group and a control group that were matched on IQ and a standardized academic achievement test. Based on the clinical examination results, the boys in the experimental group were given corrective lenses as needed. Visual acuity problems among the boys in the control group were left uncorrected. After a four-month period in which both groups received the same academic instruction, the two groups were again given standardized academic achievement test. The experimental group had advanced 1.21 grade levels, and the control group had progressed by only .62 grade level on academic achievement. Kephart found that "at least a certain proportion of low school achievement may be due to the existence of visual problems which can be alleviated by professional eye care."[68] He further concluded that "the correction of visual difficulties leads to more rapid progress in school achievement."[69]

This first investigation into the relationship between vision and academic success had merely echoed common sense. Of course, we might say, children who need glasses but do not receive them will have difficulty in learning. If children are unable to see the chalkboard or their textbooks, we would only expect them to achieve poorly. Give them glasses and they will do better.

Kephart's next step drew more heavily from Getman's expanded concept of vision and, therefore, had far greater implications. It depended on a concept of visual skills, the learned habits of the eyes moving and working together to perceive the dimensions of physical space and supply accurate sensory images to the brain. In Getman's terms, Kephart had moved—at least partially—from examining issues of sight to vision, from a rather mundane question of visual acuity toward the broader, ultimately more conceptually rich area of neurosensory perception.

Three studies of the visual skills of schoolchildren convinced Kephart that visual perception was a key prerequisite to academic success. And conversely, weakness in visual skills explained a significant portion of all school failure. First, he compared the measured level of visual skills of 2200 children in grades 3 to 12 with the visual skill scores of 7655 industrial workers. The visual skill battery utilized included quantitative measures of vertical and lateral aphoria, acuity, depth perception, and color discrimination at distances both near and far. This expanded construct called visual skills, as enacted within a battery of measures, went far beyond visual acuity as routinely assessed on a Snellen letter chart in an optometrist's office. Although his more comprehensive attempts to theorize sensory perception as neurological activity would come later in his career, even at this relatively early point Kephart was already concerned with an enlarged, multi-faceted concept of visual perception, an amalgam of the multiple ocular capacities by which we visually capture useful images of a variety of objects under a range of conditions.

In this large-scale comparison of industrial workers and public school students, Kephart found that "the distribution of [visual skill] scores of school children was strikingly similar to that of scores of industrial workers."[70] The differences between the two groups on the complete battery of tests and on a number of key subtests were very slight. In prior studies of industrial workers, Kephart and his occupational research colleagues had found that "between 40 and 50 percent of the industrial population is visually handicapped on their jobs."[71] His goal was then to figure out what percentage of all schoolchildren did not have the necessary visual skills to accomplish typical academic tasks. Theorizing that the pencil, paper, and book activities of schoolchildren were essentially similar to the work tasks of adult office workers, he then applied the minimum standards for clerical and administrative employees to the visual skill scores of the schoolchildren. On that basis, he concluded that half of all children in the public schools likely lacked the required level of visual skills to succeed in academic work.

While this large-scale comparison of public school students and adult workers made only scant progress toward a satisfactory understanding of the relationship between visual perception abilities and school achievement, it provided Kephart with evidence that a comparison between the vision of young children and that of adult workers in relation to their daily work tasks was a legitimate question for psychological science. This was the empirical support that Kephart needed in order to move forward with further research.

The next two studies looked directly at the connection between visual skills and academic achievement. In a study with high school students, Kephart investigated the utility of the adult clerical workers' visual skill standard in predicting levels of reading achievement. A total of 250 high school students took the visual skill battery. Comparing their scores to the standard previously set for clerical and administrative workers, he then ranked the students as either meeting or not meeting the required visual standard for success. The students were also administered a standardized reading achievement test.

> Among those students who met the visual standard, 46 percent were above their grade level in reading achievement. Among those students who did not meet the visual standards, only 28 percent were above their grade average in reading achievement.[72]

Correlation coefficients indicated that this difference was statistically significant. Using rather simple procedures of grouping scores of continuous variables, Kephart had found a relationship between visual perception and reading ability.

A similar procedure was carried out with a group of 468 seventh-grade students. All were given the full visual skill battery. Again the visual standard of adult clerical workers was applied. The students were also ranked by their classroom teachers on their level of general academic achievement. Kephart found that 56% of the students who met the visual skill standard were rated in the upper half of their class on achievement. Only 47% of the students who did not meet the visual skill standard were rated by their teachers as achieving in the upper half of this class.[73]

Kephart concluded that a "relationship can be demonstrated between the visual skill status of school children and their academic achievement."[74] Many school children, by his analysis, did not have the level of visual skills necessary for academic success. If these children were provided with professional services designed to improve visual perception, he reasoned, that would lead to "rapid progress in school achievement."[75]

At this point, Kephart was convinced of the relationship between visual perception and school achievement. In the years to come, he directed a number of graduate thesis studies on the topic, but his own line of statistical research had concluded.[76] By the mid-1950s, Kephart was a mature scholar who believed that he held a crucial insight into the education of young children. Based on his own clinical experiences, and his quantitative studies of visual skills among adults and children, he had developed a central commitment that served as the purpose and blueprint of his research for the remainder of his career. His work in the ensuing years, until his death in 1973, involved theoretical and practical refinements of his central notion that the programmatic enhancement of the development of perceptual abilities prepared young children for standard academic challenges, such as reading, in the early grades. His theoretical writings increasingly paired his early notion of visual perception with concerns with motor skills and development. Perception was an activity of a physical organism within a bodily effort to achieve coordination with the surrounding environment. He came to believe that vision was a primary feature of the physical body's attempts to operate effectively within the contours and dimensions of physical space.[77]

One seemingly odd tangent was a final quantitative study, conducted with colleagues in physical education in the early 1960s. Essential to the movement education theory and practice of Kephart and his colleagues Frostig, Getman, and Barsch was the idea that perceptual functioning and motor activity could not be separated. Framed within a neurophysiological holism, the idea was that visual interpretation developed and occurred in concurrence with bodily movement. Only as the body moves, senses, and experiments in the physical environment do the capacities of visual perception develop. In this unusual study completed with two physical educators, Kephart assessed whether motor activity, isolated from perception, could stand alone as a predictor of school learning. The group attempted to identify a distinct set of motor performance factors that correlated with and, therefore, predicted academic achievement. Kephart and colleagues correlated measurements for 37 separate motor performances—for example, hopping on one foot, shooting basketballs through a goal, or sprinting a 40-yard dash—with the standardized academic achievement scores of 120 fifth- and sixth-graders. The goal was to ultimately select a battery of motor items that would predict academic achievement. The results, not surprising in afterthought, were weak. The team was unable to identify a consistent set of motor activities that were related to school learning success. This failed effort was Kephart's only deviation from the common movement education belief in the unity of perceptual and motor development.[78]

PERCEPTUAL-MOTOR DEVELOPMENT THEORY IN FINAL FORM

The second half of Kephart's research career involved a shift from quantitative, experimental science to a clinical science combining direct service to children and families with a phenomenology of professional learning by experience. At Purdue, he established the Achievement Center for Children, a remediation program for children with learning difficulties, in 1960. It was largely an expansion and institutionalization of the program that he and Getman had initiated in 1956. Kephart served as director until he left Purdue in 1968. Then he returned to his native Colorado, to found and run the Glen Haven Achievement Center, an expansion of his long-running summer camp program, on a full-time basis. Working in cooperation with the University of Northern Colorado, he directed that instructional program specifically for children with learning disabilities, until his death in 1973.[79]

It is difficult to put forth a single delineation of Newell Kephart's theory of perceptual-motor development because his thinking on the subject grew and changed over time. What can be submitted is the final form of his understanding, a description of how he seemed to understand childhood development and learning in the period preceding his death. This final form represents the central currents of his contribution to learning disability theory in the late 1960s, at a time when University of Illinois special education professor Samuel Kirk and others were working on legislation that coalesced and enshrined the learning disability concept in federal law.

By Kephart's appraisal, the central problem faced by the public schools was that children with learning disorders—a group comprising "at least 15 to 20 percent of our school population"[80]—showed up for the first grade lacking a range of developmentally acquired skills, psychological capacities of interpreting and interacting with the environment, that were necessary for school-based learning. These children were "unqualified by lack of adequate basic training to cope with the demands of the curriculum."[81] A series of preliminary, foundational skills were understood as growing in the malleable yet enduring materiality of the central nervous system, the brain and the network of sensory organs. The acquisition of these skills both required learning and preceded further learning. In the early childhood phase of development prior to the formal academic lessons of school, a healthy neurological apparatus gained dexterity and acuity as machinery for perceiving, comprehending, and responding to the world.

An athletic analogy may provide some assistance at this point. It is common today for athletes who participate in collegiate sports such as football to attend the first session of organized, team practice only after completing an extensive program of fitness preparation. A football player often undergoes many weeks of grueling physical training involving weight lifting and aerobic workouts in order to prepare his body for the demands and rigors of the game. The assumption is that the athlete's body, at a material-physical level, should achieve an advanced state of preparedness consisting of the development of generic abilities and skills (strength, agility, speed, flexibility) that provide a foundational basis for the further development of the specific skills required for achieving success in the game of football. The athlete's responsibility during the off season is to reach that level of physical preparedness such that the more specific football skills (throwing, catching, blocking, tackling) might be built on a solid and capable physical fitness foundation.

Similarly, Kephart maintained that "readiness is necessary before academic skills can be taught successfully."[82] Readiness, in the educational context, was understood as a neurologically based, multiple skill preparedness for the tasks and tests of academic learning. Success in school required the childhood development of what Getman and Kane termed "physiological readiness,"[83] which Barsch defined as "a level of total (neurosensory) organization which would enable them to profit from the existing curriculum."[84] The activities and experiences of early childhood serve as a period of preliminary perceptual, sensorimotor, and mental training. In non-disordered cases, the child's "neurological structure...a large, elaborative, highly active system"[85] advances developmentally into a state of psychophysiological effectiveness and balance that allows the young child to respond successfully to classroom instruction.

This state of neuroeducational fitness consists of patterns of advanced cooperation and coordination throughout the central nervous system, a mechanized notion of a learner operating in dynamic efficiency. Sensory activities in the bodily extremities and organizational processes of the centralized brain hum along in a polished state of functional harmony. Communication and organization across the sensory-perceptive system is refined, efficient, and accurate.

As a functional achievement, the state of readiness described by the movement educators involved the development of a neurological armature of sufficient consistency and refinement to support the capture of accurate pictures of the child's world. The human task of the brain and nervous system was understood as providing an unclouded mirror of objective reality, of downloading, organizing, and utilizing correct representations of the environment. Kephart explained that the brain builds up "a little model of the universe"[86] that neatly encapsulates "the laws of the universe,"[87] a neurologically based orientation to the spatial and temporal patterns of reality. If the child achieves an accurate model, then "his responses will come out right."[88] He achieves an adequacy of interaction with the environment. If the neurological system is working effectively, that facilitates the child's success in school and, more broadly, in life. If not, there is a disruption of perception—a learning disorder.

Failures of physiologic readiness occur when youngsters do not develop efficiencies of sensory input and concomitant accuracies of neuroperception. Speaking clearly for the entire group of perceptual-motor theorists, Barsch captured the main problem with these children:

> At age six they have not yet become efficient listeners, although their auditory system is intact. They have not become efficient visualizers although their visual systems are healthy and their sight is adequate. They have not learned to appreciate texture for learning even though their hands and bodies have no impairments. They move but do not transport their bodies easily and gracefully.... Despite the presence of basically adequate physiology, the perceptual processes have not been refined to the complex sharpness required for academic efficiency.[89]

The sensory organs themselves are functional as receivers of environmental stimulation. The problem resides in the brain's failure to adequately organize, integrate, and interpret the various, simultaneous streams of sensory data. Just as Kephart and Getman had found that sufficient sensory capabilities for sight required experiences of the development of vision, of learning how to see, a child had to learn how to utilize the inputs from all physiologically intact sensory organs. Neurological learning was required in order for the child to develop the ability to perceive the world and the symbols on the schoolbook page. What occurs in the case of disordered learning is a failure of neurological development. As Kephart stated succinctly, there is "a disruption in the processing of information within the central nervous system."[90] Put briefly, the young brain of a child with a learning disorder is not fit for school learning.

MOTOR TO PERCEPTUAL TO COGNITIVE DEVELOPMENT

Child development was understood by Kephart as gradual demonstration of the underlying concept that "motor activity of some kind underlies all behavior, including higher thought processes."[91] He once quoted a passage from British neuroscientist Charles Sherrington that captured the progression of human development: "muscle is there before nerve and nerve is there before mind."[92] Human growth begins with a basic motor foundation of bodily movement, proceeds to a visually dominated activity of neuroperception, and culminates in perception turned abstract and generalized, the achievement of higher-level cognitive conceptualization.

The early motor achievement necessary to the proper development of perception and higher conceptualization was posture—a balanced and coordinated orientation of the body in relation to the immediate physical environment at a given moment. The centrality of posture arises from the body's adaptation to gravity in space. Kephart theorized that the spatial environment consists of no constants. Every object is understood only in directional relation to other objects. The only reliable feature offering consistent orientation to human perception is gravity, a force that pulls in one direction at all times. Posture is the body's way of developing a trustworthy bodily relationship with gravity, a physiological accomplishment that allows the human body to orient itself in a constant fashion to the environment. All motor activity begins with and relies on solid bodily posture.[93] Barsch similarly placed what he called "postural-transport orientations"[94] at the heart of his theory, a series of physical skills such as balance and strength that facilitated purposeful and efficient bodily movement in the spatial environment.

Posture involves verticality, a bodily alignment in space with the force of gravity. The midline of the body, a column running vertically down the center of the torso, was theorized as the physiological fulcrum of proper posture. Successful motor development consists chiefly of two underlying components of physical coordination: laterality and directionality. Laterality is the "inner sense of one's own symmetry,"[95] a kinesthetic and perceptual understanding of the physical constellation of the body in systematic arrangement. The child who develops a strong capacity for laterality has a reliable "map of internal space"[96] that allows for successful perception of the environment on the left and right of the midline and seamless motor cooperation of left and right extremities.

In Kephart's developmental theory, children progressed through six sequential (but often overlapping) stages. Children who failed to successfully complete the developmental objectives of a given stage before moving onto the next phase were defined as children with learning disorders.

1. Motor

"The first 'space world' develops within arm's reach."[97] With hands, feet, and mouth awkwardly probing into immediate space, the infant gradually builds what might be called motor knowledge, a kinesthetic understanding of body and environment acquired through motor activity. The child learns "how to initiate a contact with the environment and how to control this contact."[98] Through that contact, the child gradually accrues sensory information concerning her body and its interaction with the environment. The objective of this stage is the development of "control over the organismic end of the interaction,"[99] a working awareness of the moving body in the context of the immediate environment. The child's "major problem is how to produce a movement among parts or combination of parts,"[100] a coherent coordination of torso, limbs, and extremities. The child learns to coordinate many discrete motor behaviors into structured sequences of activity, organized and intentional motor patterns. At the completion of this stage, "the child's interaction with the environment is no longer random, it is purposeful."[101]

2. Motor—perceptual

Concurrent with the prior motor stage begins the "long process of matching perceptual data to motor data."[102] The young child begins to coordinate perception—primarily visual, but more broadly involving the integrated interpretation of all sensory stimulation—with motor information and bodily movements.

> Perceptual information is matched to the previously developed motor information. At this stage, however, the motor information is the controlling factor...Perceptual information is manipulated against motor data until consistency between the two sources of information is achieved.[103]

For example, in the development of eye-hand coordination, the child's ability to move and control his hand is primary and develops first. The perceptual factor of visual stimulation provides an additive, lesser source of neurological information. The child attempts to understand and control his hand movements by coordinating motor data with information gained by visually tracking the hand in motion.

3. Perceptual—motor

After motor data are aligned with perceptual input, the functional balance begins to shift; "the primary information is perceptual. Motor information is used only to confirm or augment."[104] Rather than knowing the environment and his relationship to the environment through the inefficient and strenuous labors of bodily movement, the child begins to rely more on visual information. Central to the achievement of adequate visual perception is the ability to distinguish figure from ground, to devote selective attention to individual elements of the environment. Kephart explained:

> There is a contrast between the figure elements and the ground elements so that the figure seems to stand out from the ground. Attention can then be directed to the figure and diverted from the ground.[105]

Through learning and growth, a functional psychological advance that is based in the refinement of the neurological system, visual perception becomes the central faculty for the development of school readiness skills and the early acquisition of reading skills. The ability to accurately discern visual figure-ground relationships is the physiological basis for attending to and comprehending letters, groups of letters, and words printed on a page.[106]

4. Perceptual

Perception, although frequently described by Kephart and Marianne Frostig to be primarily visual,[107] is a multiple modality consisting of continuous streams of input from the various sensory organs. The child begins to tackle the task of organizing and integrating the multiple perceptions into stable and useable maps of environmental reality.

> Here he deals with perceptions in groups. He identifies characteristics of objects through perception and manipulates those characteristics to elaborate an extensive systematized body of information. On the basis of such perceptual manipulations he can predict what will happen in the event of a given response.[108]

Perception management, so to speak, involves an ability to build abstract generalizations from multiple pieces of perceptual data. Language begins to have an important symbolic function in the efficient manipulation of perceptions.

This stage culminates in the achievement of what Kephart called a "perceptualmotor match,"[109] an active congruence between the two different physiological apprehensions of the environment. Kephart provided an example:

> A child systematically explores a square form with his hand. At the same time, he watches his hand and pays attention to these visual data. Since his hand keeps telling him "this is a square," he can manipulate the visual information until this also tells him "this is a square." The visual data have been matched to the motor data.[110]

This match of different forms of neurological information is a necessary step in the development of a perceptual apparatus that accurately and efficiently captures external reality such that the child's actions in relation to the environment may be realistic and effective.

Laterality, "a right-left gradient by which he can identify any response in terms of its relation to the midline of the body,"[111] gradually develops from the second stage forward. The earliest forms of laterality simply involve an experienced awareness of two sides of the body and the spatial relationship between the two: right hand and arm opposite left, right leg and foot opposite left. By this fourth stage of the scheme, Kephart viewed laterality as an active projection that the child learns to make from his bisected body out into the physical environment. This projection allows the child to create stable representations involving directionality and secure spatial coordinates in the surrounding world. Essentially, there is a left and a right side of the body in the environment, and the bodily midline serves as the vertical equator of physical space. This consistent orientation toward space helps the child to advance "from subjective spatial estimates to objective spatial relationships."[112]

5. Perceptual —conceptual

This stage completes the abstraction task of the prior stage as the child transitions from combining and organizing mere sensory data into the advanced utilization of fully abstracted concepts. "Perception gives rise to conception,"[113] a neurological advancement that facilitates greater efficiency, dexterity, and accuracy in inter-action with the environment. Conceptualization allows for the most useful and stable features gathered from many perceptions to be aggregated into an idea or image that is useful across many environmental contexts.

> Thus, the child has experience with the perceptual object, chair. This initial expe-rience is elaborated by a large number of experiences with similar articles. He had perceptual experiences with hard chairs, soft chairs, wooden chairs, metal chairs, overstuffed chairs, etc. Out of this myriad of perceptions he identifies common ele-ments. These common elements are brought together into a new whole.[114]

The new whole is an abstract generalization built of many perceived specifici-ties, a generic notion of a chair suitable for a variety of purposes. The child uti-lizes the generic concept, a "disembodied form without further reference to the concrete situation,"[115] as a format for operating effectively in multiple "chair" circumstances.

It should be noted that this new whole, in Kephart's thinking, involves a material change within the cellular operations of the brain. His thinking about the mental utilization of concepts was an elaboration based on his notion of the individual perceptual unit (or "percept"[116]), a momentary apprehension of some aspect of the environmental field. Each percept, as a neurological activity, leaves a trace record in the form of a modification within the neurons of the brain. The progress to more consistent frameworks for apprehending the environment consists of modifications at the material level.

These frameworks provide psychic and sensory organization that facilitates perception and action. In this sense, not only are concepts derived from perception, the concepts in turn feed back into perception to provide temporal, spatial, and informational context to an individual's experience in a given moment.[117]

6. Conceptual

At this advanced stage, mental activity is symbolic and linguistic, involving the most complex and efficient use of abstractions. As in the prior stage that involved complex tasks of relating perceptions to one another for purposes of aggregation, organization, and abstraction, in this stage too the child manipulates multiple concepts. Memory plays an increasingly important function as "information both past and present is integrated and systematized."[118] Concepts amassed and coordinated from multiple experiences, past and present, interact to support the organism's fluid and efficient interaction with the environment.

Language serves a vital function, allowing for complex concepts to be captured quickly and neatly so as to be organized toward specific purposes. Clarity of thought, language use, and action are demonstrated by the efficient coordination of ideation and linguistic signs. Just as motor and perceptual data must match in earlier development, so too concepts and language must align in advanced development.

At this high level, the child's interactions with the environment rely more on internal mental guidance than external sensory input. The stability of the external world, of an orderly physical and social environment, has been effectively internalized.

> It is no longer necessary for the child to be dependent upon outside stimulation for all information necessary for the solution of problems.... Now a small model of the universe has developed within the child's head. This small universe is an operating model and the child can manipulate his universe within himself with only occasional reference to the concrete environment for the purpose of checking.[119]

The social and physical world surrounding the child, in this view, is relatively static and constant. Like an automobile driver who travels the same road every day and learns to do so without paying much attention, the developmentally advanced individual has an internal operational map that provides consistent guidance.

LEARNING DISABILITIES AND ETIOLOGY

In the simplest terms, Kephart understood learning disabilities as the result of a "gap,"[120] an absence of physiological and psychological growth, occurring at any stage of this developmental sequence. This developmental failure is a neurological fact, occurring within the cellular activities of the brain, demonstrated in corresponding psychological processes or capacities. Within the brain, a "neuron is anatomically missing or it is non-functional,"[121] thereby creating a disruption within the processing of sensory, motor, perceptual, and conceptual information. The necessary neurological networks required for adequate organismic functioning, for effective interpretation of the environment, are only halfway constructed. The child is, in Kephart's words, an "incomplete organism."[122]

Kephart theorized three specific etiologies for a learning disability: brain injury, emotional disturbance, and "experiential deprivation."[123] The first of the three coincides with the definition of learning disability as a defect of neurologically based, psychological processes that became part of the federal special education mandate of 1975. The latter two etiologies were specifically ruled out of that law as types of learning problems. Emotional disturbance became its own category of disability, separate from learning disability. The federal law specifically denied that a child's prior experiences, whether understood in terms of cultural factors, familial background, or the quality of prior educational instruction, could be the cause of a learning disability.

Brain injury involved the kinds of cases that Kephart and Alfred Strauss had described in their work together. Originally, these children were understood to have experienced some kind of brain damage, a "direct destruction of nervous tissue, as in a lesion or concussion."[124] Over time, Kephart acknowledged, clinicians had migrated to a "broad classification" that involved "other forms of disturbance" that "affect nervous tissue either directly of indirectly."[125] Generally, there were a variety of illnesses and genetic conditions that obstructed central nervous system development and yielded the same symptoms found in children with verifiable brain damage. He seemed to concede a difference between the prior notion of *brain damage* and the common usage of the term *brain injury* by researchers and clinicians while also tending toward a conflation of the two. He described brain injury as "an extension of the original classification" (e.g., brain damaged) while noting that "not all cases will respond to the same educational program."[126] His primary concern, even in a discussion of etiology, was not causation but treatment.

Emotional disturbance, in Kephart's thinking, occurred in two ways. A child suffered either from a "traumatic disturbance…limited in time but extremely intense" or from a more "prolonged" disturbance that was "less highly charged emotionally but…extended over time."[127] He believed that brief but highly volatile experiences of emotional trauma often produced deviant behavior but not learning difficulties. In contrast, a child experiencing an extended period of lower-level emotional distress would often develop disorders of both behavior and learning. In the case of the prolonged, less charged emotional trauma,

> among the results appears to be an interference with functional relationships within the central nervous system. This prolonged emotional disturbance produces effects very similar to brain injury.[128]

A disturbance of a child's emotions, in one of the two forms, could result in a neurological disruption equivalent to a brain injury. This idea basically agreed with the definition of learning disability offered by Samuel Kirk—in January 1963, to an audience of neurological researchers—that included the possible causation "from...emotional or behavioral disturbance."[129]

A holistic understanding of a common neurological basis of both emotion and thought, the inseparability of the two realms of mental activity, and the relationship of the entirety of human neurology to an individual's experiences was generally shared by the movement educators. Neither Kephart nor Frostig felt comfortable with the conventional tendency among psychologists of their era to separate cognition and affect.[130]

The third cause of learning disabilities was experiential. Failures to achieve the performance goals of the lower stages of development, according to Kephart, often occurred due to a lack of necessary life experiences. He believed that such children were "experientially incomplete."[131]

> Certain readiness skills are dependent upon each other in the same way that certain academic skills are dependent upon each other.... If the necessary learning experiences in the readiness stage are not presented, the hierarchy of readiness skills may be upset with resulting confusion at higher levels. For these reasons certain deprivations of experience may lead to learning disabilities.[132]

Dysfunctional voids within the child's neuropsychology are absences of experience, markers of privations of family and community life. Internal gaps in neurological development and the corresponding failures of psychoperceptual abilities are remnant consequences of inadequacies that were present in the social environment of the child.

Kephart agreed with many of the cultural deficit theorists of the late 1960s that young children living in poverty frequently had learning disabilities due to a lack of the necessary life experiences.[133] His thinking relied on the common, loosely formulated notion that certain families offered their children an environment lacking the stimulation or experiences required for complete neuropsychological development.

LINGUISTIC POTENTIAL

A similar belief was held by Samuel Kirk. In the early 1950s, Kirk carried out a large experiment testing the effect of preschool education on the intellectual development of young children. His results supported the environmental thesis that IQ could be promoted by early educational programs. But the project also solidified Kirk's belief that that low-income families often provided dramatically limited home environments that failed to nurture the development of young minds.[134]

Like Kephart's concept, Kirk's social class–based understanding of insufficient family environments was a political outgrowth of his psychological study of the plasticity of intellectual maturation. Similar to Kephart's doctoral education at the Iowa Child Welfare Research Station, Kirk's early experiences as a researcher involved a powerful apprenticeship in psychological environmentalism. From 1931 until the fall of 1935, Kirk worked under Thorleif Hegge, research director at the Wayne Country Training School in Michigan. A strong believer in the environmentalism of Stoddard, Wellman, and Skeels, Hegge applied concentrated doses of educational stimulation—specifically, intensive reading instruction—to the minds of mentally defective children. Later, in 1939, while teaching at Milwaukee State Teachers College, Kirk met Harold Skeels and heard first-hand from him the miraculous narrative about the two infants saved from the confines of an Iowa institution by the intellectual stimulation provided by two maternal surrogates. The enhancement of child intellectual potential through educational training, greatly due to Kirk's leadership, became a central maxim of post-World War II special education. By the late 1950s, Kirk was the preeminent voice in the rise of the profession of special education in the United States and primary articulator of a psycholinguistic theory of learning disability. While Kephart and the movement educators were developing sensory motor treatment programs throughout the 1950s and 1960s, Sam Kirk was building a parallel therapeutic agenda for childhood language difficulties.

CHAPTER FIVE

Diagnosing AND Treating Psycholinguistic Deficiencies: The Practical Science OF Samuel A. Kirk

In 1951, Samuel A. Kirk spoke at the twenty-fifth anniversary celebration of the Wayne County Training School in Northville, Michigan. The special education professor had worked at the Wayne School as a teacher and researcher in the early 1930s, immediately after receiving his bachelor's and master's degree in psychology at the University of Chicago. During his four years teaching children with mental retardation in the institutional setting, Kirk was also a doctoral student at the University of Michigan. In his anniversary address, he joked about the personal impact of the educational experiences he had at the two Michigan establishments.

> At a conference at which I was a speaker several years ago, the chairman of the meeting asked where I had worked and studied. I informed him that I had worked at the Wayne County Training School and that I had obtained my doctorate from the University of Michigan. The chairman inadvertently introduced me as one who had worked at the University of Michigan and had obtained his doctoral degree from the Wayne Country Training School. I did not contradict the chairman because there was probably more truth in that statement than one would suppose.[1]

At the University of Michigan, Kirk focused on studies of physiology and neurology, culminating in a dissertation on brain dominance and handedness in rats.[2] He later described his Ph.D. research as an informative "digression" that taught him to avoid impractical concern "with such terms as 'brain dysfunction' or 'brain damage'" in favor of more matter-of-fact statements such as "the child has not learned to read."[3] He often had little patience for complex technical terminology that elevated professionals while offering little guidance for how to treat or teach children. Much of his career was devoted to replacing medical explanations of learning difficulties with educational concepts that he believed were more useful. At another important conference, in 1963, when Kirk responded to the urging of a parent advocacy group to supply a term and definition for a new learning disorder, he would hold to that same principle of describing in the barest practical terms.[4]

This man who would, greatly as a result of that 1963 definition, often be called the father of learning disabilities did not begin his life's work in the hallowed halls of Ann Arbor but in the pale tile and dim shadow corridors of residential institutions for children with mental retardation. From the beginning, Kirk's interest in the depths and functions of the mind was steered by his desire to figure out how to teach children who could not read.

At an experimental school for delinquent youth in Oak Forest, Illinois, as a University of Chicago graduate student in 1929, he met a 10-year-old boy who had not learned to read. With those first lessons in the practical science of remedial reading under the doorway of the boy's bathroom, Kirk began his professional quest to teach reading to struggling learners.[5] After completing his doctoral studies, Kirk continued this pursuit by taking a position at the Wayne County Training School. Under the supervision of research director Thorleif G. Hegge, he created an entire systematic approach to teaching reading to children with severe reading difficulties.

At the Northville (Michigan) institution for mentally defective youth, the strongest early influences on Kirk's thinking about reading and disabilities came together with coherence and purpose. Working under Hegge, one of the few researchers searching for the key to effective reading instruction for mentally deficient youth in the 1920s and 1930s, Kirk united with a fellow follower of Marion Monroe's approach to understanding reading disabilities. Together, Hegge and Kirk adapted Monroe's phonics-based reading remediation program to the Wayne School population "using the principles of learning from the Chicago school of functional psychology."[6] Monroe herself had earned her MA (1924) and Ph.D. (1929) at Chicago, completing both of her graduate research projects under the supportive supervision of department chair Harvey Carr.[7] She authored the earliest research diagnosing specific reading disabilities through the use of a mathematical calculation of discrepancy between reading achievement and general ability. She developed a diagnostic instrument for the measurement of specific areas of reading error, and she personally passed on her approach to Kirk during his graduate studies, introducing him to the idea that learning difficulties might be profitably analyzed through the utilization of psychometric instruments.[8]

Marion Monroe was a reading disability researcher who worked for a brief time with the noted Samuel T. Orton at the University of Iowa but who should be viewed as a substantial scholar in her own right. She was one of the first psychologists to apply early mental testing procedures to the diagnosis of reading difficulties. In the early 1930s, she taught Samuel Kirk how to administer her Monroe Diagnostic Reading Test to identify specific reading errors.[9] Her science of reading analysis and remediation was the conceptual and practical forerunner to Kirk's later development of his own diagnostic language instrument, the Illinois Test of Psycholinguistic Ability. What Monroe created for the diagnosis of reading problems, Kirk later built for the identification of specific psycholinguistic weaknesses.[10] Later in her career, she coauthored a number of the wildly popular *Dick and Jane* children's series.[11] In recognition of the longstanding impact of her research, she was elected to the Reading Hall of Fame in 1973 as a member of the first class of inductees.[12]

Unlike Marion Monroe's work, Thorleif G. Hegge's research on reading disorders achieved little national recognition. Toiling for decades in the underappreciated shadows, Hegge's science took a back seat to his prominent work as research administrator. Prior to becoming the research director at the Wayne School, he worked for one year in the research department of the Vineland Training School in New Jersey, a unit made famous by renowned mental deficiency researchers Edgar Doll and Henry H. Goddard. Superintendent Robert Haskell hired Hegge with the specific goal of building the Wayne School into a national center for mental retardation research.[13] While achieving this feat, Hegge simultaneously carried on his own line of research on the educational treatment of specific reading disabilities. During the early 1930s, Hegge and his associates were a rarity, a team of researchers carrying on a continuous scientific program focusing on reading difficulties among children with mental retardation.

As his anniversary address joke implied, Kirk's focus was imminently practical. He employed and tolerated theory only to the extent that such formulations would drive remedial instruction forward. This ethos of useful knowledge in action, of an applied, no-nonsense science of psychology, was the progeny of the functionalist school of psychology developed by James Rowland Angell and Harvey Carr at the University of Chicago in the early twentieth century. Kirk and his wife Winifred studied at Chicago while Carr was the department chair and took to heart the functionalist creed of an eclectic science serving practical ends.[14] Carr was an integral figure in the development of functionalism as the fundamental approach to American psychology, directly continuing the work of his esteemed predecessor James Rowland Angell. He was revered and beloved by generations of Chicago graduate students for his broad understanding of a psychological science with inclusive space for multiple perspectives and research methodologies, for his belief in science as more of an attitude of inquiry than a specific theory of human activity.[15]

In his autobiography, Kirk cited the Chicago functionalist school and specifically Harvey Carr for supplying his general orientation to the science of psychology.[16] Kirk was far from alone in this regard. The Chicago functionalist tradition that developed under the leadership of Angell and Carr provided American psychologists of the pre-World War II era with a powerful and broad organizing notion, an evolutionary science of organismic adaptation that offered direction and identity for the growing profession. It would be difficult to understand not only Kirk's work but much of American psychology in the twentieth century without exploring the foundational role of Chicago functionalism.[17]

In the first part of this chapter, I will explore the scientific roots of Samuel Kirk's thinking about a psychology of language development, reading, and disability. Three early intellectual influences had a profound and lasting impact on the character and content of his work through his career: the Chicago functionalist school under the leadership of Harvey Carr, reading diagnostician Marion Monroe, and Wayne School researcher Thorleif G. Hegge. From this basic foundation, I will then examine Kirk's research that led him to develop the Illinois Test of Psycholinguistic Ability (ITPA) as a clinical tool for the diagnosis and remediation of language deficits. The ITPA was the centerpiece of Kirk's approach to clinical treatment, his understanding of learning disabilities, and his most significant scientific contribution to the young field.

THE CHICAGO SCHOOL

Harvey Carr's four-decade involvement in the development of functional psychology at the University of Chicago spanned roles ranging from novice to expert, from a new doctoral student attempting to gain an initial conceptual grasp to department chair and articulate national spokesperson. He entered the doctoral program in 1902 and completed his degree in 1905. Three years later, after a brief stint as high school teacher, James Rowland Angell hired him back as an assistant professor. He remained on the Chicago faculty, spending the final twelve years as department chair, until retirement in 1938. He entered the university when functionalism was in its unsteady infancy as a wide-ranging, new approach to psychology and left when functionalism was all but synonymous with American psychological science itself.[18]

What the young doctoral student Carr encountered in 1902 at the University of Chicago was an impressive faculty of philosophy and psychology that was busy shaking off European intellectual roots to forge a new, distinctly American scientific identity. William James's *Principles of Psychology*[19] in 1890 and John Dewey's "The Reflex Arc Concept in Psychology"[20] in 1896 spearheaded the break from Wundtian experimentalism toward a psychological naturalism that examined consciousness in relationship to the observable achievements of action. James rendered human mental activity along a Darwinian theme, embedding consciousness within the physiology of the organism while asserting the role of thought in acts of adaptation to novel circumstances. Mind, in James' analysis, was a system of biopsychic functions that help an organism adapt and survive. Similarly, Dewey's landmark paper recast an old reflex arc concept within an evolutionary naturalism. He fused the standard reflex scheme of sequential elements—stimulus, sensory activation, mental association, and motor response—into a single, psychophysical coordination within an environmental context.[21]

The tenor of the nascent American science of psychology brimmed with a forthright pragmatism fashioned chiefly by Charles Sanders Pierce, Dewey, and James. Pierce's 1878 essay "How to Make Our Ideas Clear" initiated an American disenchantment with traditional philosophies based on epistemological allegiance in favor of understandings pinned to the experienced consequences of belief. Put briefly, Pierce and the pragmatists set aside customary concern with the epistemological moorings of ideas in order to embrace meanings in their applied utility.

> Consider what effects, that might conceivably have practical bearings, we conceive the object of our conception to have. Then, our conception of these effects is the whole of our conception of the object.[22]

The truth value of ideas could best be attained through examination of the practical difference those ideas make within lived experience. What James, Dewey, and Pierce sought was a scientific approach that understood ideas in light of their practical consequences, an unvarnished and useful empiricism that required no transcendental support. As neopragmatist Richard Rorty would later say, "We should not look for skyhooks but only for toeholds,"[23] ways to better understand and act within the present historical and cultural context. It was a stripped-down empiricism that traveled the grounded messiness of experience, working solely within the verifiable and useful realities of human activity.

The new American pragmatism embraced a Darwinian naturalism, an understanding of the human organism as operating in adaptation to the social and physical environment. Biology and psychology were understood to be continuous disciplines, linked sciences dedicated to the empirical examination of animals and humans as organisms of psychophysical unity adapting to environmental requirements. This evolutionary framework was coupled with the pragmatic epistemology of empirical consequence, an understanding of knowledge within the scope of experiential utilization. As capable philosophers and first-generation American psychologists, Dewey and James forged a bridge from the epistemologically based (or metaphysical) European thought of the nineteenth century to the bare problem-solving impetus of twentieth-century America.[24]

The forward abutment of that bridge, so to speak, was anchored firmly in the psychology faculty at the University of Chicago. Harvey Carr's early development as an experimental psychologist was nurtured by the faculty that built "a new system of philosophy," an American psychology that James triumphantly christened in 1904 as "The Chicago School"[25] At that time, the department included a long list of important figures in psychology and philosophy: Dewey, George Herbert Mead, James H. Tufts, John B. Watson, and Angell.

If Dewey and James provided the theoretical turn that initiated what Edward B. Titchener called "functional psychology,"[26] it was Angell and Carr who presided over the implementation of that new approach. Historian of psychology and longtime Chicago faculty member Forrest A. Kingsbury divided the development of the Chicago School into two distinct periods: the early years under the leadership of Angell, and the later years when Carr was the central organizing force. Angell was department chair from 1902 until he left Chicago in 1920 to run the Carnegie Foundation and then become the president at Yale University. Carr provided leadership in the later years, until his 1938 retirement,[27] including the time when Marion Monroe, Samuel Kirk, and Winifred Kirk attended.

FROM STRUCTURALISM TO FUNCTIONALISM

The science that Carr encountered at Chicago in 1902 was in the midst of a dramatic transition. The primary approach to psychological research in the United States was the introspective experimentalism (often called structuralism) of Edward Bradford Titchener. A graduate of Oxford University, Titchener had studied at Leipzig under Wilhelm Wundt, the German scientist who created the first experimental psychology laboratory. Arriving at Cornell University in 1892, Titchener applied Wundt's experimental approach to the contents of human consciousness. His main investigative technique was called introspection.

Introspection was a process of subjective self-observation employed with a goal of identifying the individual elements of consciousness and their arrangement or relationship to one another. Research subjects were trained in the method of self-observation, an inward-looking activity of noticing and reporting conscious impressions. For example, an examiner would give a research subject a card with a word written on it. The subject would then look within and carefully report the mental activity stimulated by the word, producing an accurate record of a conscious event. Through repeated laboratory experiments with many trained subjects, psychologists held that a record of the relatively static structures of the mind could be carefully documented. Titchener's goal was the development of a pure science of description unmarred by concern for causation or application to the world.[28]

By the late 1890s, Titchener was entangled in a heated controversy with James Mark Baldwin, the founder of the experimental laboratory at the University of Toronto, over a question of sensorimotor reactions. Titchener supported what was known as the Lange thesis, a position maintaining that reaction time varied depending on whether a person focused on the stimulus or the muscular response. Baldwin's 1885 study with four subjects contradicted this thesis. Based on his data, Baldwin proposed a typology of humans with differing reaction speeds: for example, motor types with faster muscular responses and sensory types with quicker sensory responses.[29] The ensuing published debate between Titchener and Baldwin was further fueled by an 1896 study by Angell and Addison W. Moore that greatly supported Baldwin's findings while adding a functionalist element, a focus on the function of attention in relation to habit.[30]

Titchener gave his response to the Angell-Moore study in two papers in which he contrasted his structuralism with the theory held by his scientific opponents, what he, for the first time, called functionalism. In defending his own scientific program, Titchener claimed that the purpose of experimental psychology was "to discover, first of all, what is there and in what quantity, not what it is there for."[31] Analogous to the biological subfield of morphology, experimental research should document the structure and contents of the human mind. In contrast, the new "functional psychology" was "chiefly occupied with problems of function,"[32] which to his thinking was a misguided attempt to understand how the mind is "employed for the procurement of results"[33] in everyday life. Among a host of other harsh criticisms, many related to the inferiority of a science that is applied rather than pure, Titchener characterized the functionalist program as teleological, beginning with an assumption about the ends that human organisms seek.

> Introspection, from the structural standpoint, is observation of an Is; introspection from the functional standpoint, is observation of an Is-for.[34]

A science devoted to the compilation of natural facts, by Titchener's account, should constrain its attention to matters as they actually are, offering no opinion on what the mind is attempting or accomplishing in relation to human action and social living. Titchener was the first to articulate the approach of the functionalist interlopers, the new psychology of the Chicago School that would fully replace his own tradition of structuralism over the next three decades.

In his president's address at the meeting of the 1906 American Psychological Association in New York, James Rowland Angell presented the most comprehensive and forthright articulation of the functionalist position to date. Extending themes from his 1904 text *Psychology*,[35] in which he traced the initial outlines of functional psychology, Angell captured the breadth and complexity of the new psychology in a concise and clear statement. As a conceptual critique aimed at Titchener's defense of structuralism, it was a mild rhetorical move that aimed to supplement rather than replace introspection as the central experimental research method. As a political event in the rising narrative of the young field of American psychology, the president's address was a coming out party for the Chicago School, a full rebellion against the weaknesses inherent in the old structuralist program coupled with the instantiation of a new human science.

Angell issued a full account of the functionalist project as a science endeavoring to understand the moving and practical workings of the mind rather than a set of static mental elements. Minds, in this formulation with heavy nods to the pragmatism of William James and John Dewey, are active organs in accomplishing real ends in human activity. Functionalism was a psychological

> effort to discern and portray the typical operations of consciousness under actual life conditions as over against the attempt to analyze and describe its elementary and complex contents.[36]

Psychology, Angell held, should be concerned not with the atomistic and impractical artifice of an "isolated 'moment of consciousness.'"[37] Instead, it "should report upon conscious processes as they are really found amid the heat and battle of the actual mind-body life."[38] Angell's response to Titchener's charge that functionalism offered an applied and, therefore, impure science was to embrace the goal of pushing psychological research into the muddy contingencies and exigencies of real living. A philosophically lofty purity was replaced with a nuts and bolts brand of authenticity.

Angell forwarded three basic objectives that became the standard principles of American functional psychology. First, it involved the "identification and description of mental operations,"[39] setting forth the working mind in action rather than the invariable contents of consciousness. Second, it "constantly recognizes and insists upon the essential significance of the mind-body relationship for any just and comprehensive appreciation of mental life itself."[40] Within a naturalistic account, conscious activity cannot be understood in isolation from the material body in which it occurs. Third, mental operations must be understood within the context of an organism adapting to the environment. Drawing from the writings of Charles Darwin and Edward Spencer, Angell framed psychology as a strand of evolutionary biology, thereby understanding human activity within the natural goal of organismic adaptation to the requirements of the environment.[41] Psychology should work to "discover the exact accommodatory service represented by the various great phases of conscious expression,"[42] how the mind operates to facilitate acts of adaptation.

A MODERATE SCIENCE: HARVEY CARR

Harvey Carr is easily viewed as Angell's scientific descendant, the man who carried the functionalist torch for the second leg of the Chicago journey. Carr's orientation to the science of psychology greatly continued his predecessor's broad and moderate path. He maintained the key principles of Angell's functionalism. Carr believed that the central focus of psychology was "the study of mental activity,"[43] of the operations of mind that are "in reality psychophysical."[44] Given the "essential unitary character of the human organism," Carr held, "the distinction of mind and body is merely a distinction of two systems of organic function."[45] In his account, the organism engages in two types of inherently interrelated activities: adaptive and vital. The latter preserve the general organismic structure and processes required for bodily integrity and health. Adaptive processes, often with support of mental activities, seek "the adjustment of the organism to its environment."[46] Carr's clear goal as leader of the Chicago School was to maintain the intellectual commitments that Angell had so fully established.

Such preservation did not prove a simple matter. While the central challenge facing Angell's functionalism was the articulation of a new approach to psychology in contrast to structuralism, Carr faced a more complex situation. He found that the straightforward hope of shifting American psychology from a single nineteenth-century science to a single science for the new century was soon complicated by the development of multiple theoretical schools. In the wake of the waning structuralism, the professional climate of American psychology in the early decades of the twentieth century was quickly marked by division and conflict among groups espousing competing views.

The fragmentation of American psychology into what Carr bitterly called "warring camps"[47] was demonstrated clearly in books by Robert Woodworth and Carl Murchison that offered geographical surveys of the contested intellectual terrain. The dominant theme of each account was theoretical division and disagreement. Murchison's two volumes summarizing the field of American psychology in 1925 and 1930 featured separate chapters on six different schools—including behaviorism, Gestalt, and structuralism—by leading researchers in each area.[48]

Woodworth's 1931 *Contemporary Schools of Psychology* similarly offered his own summations of the various theoretical traditions.[49]

As the field of American psychology developed, the growth or importation of new theoretical perspectives such as behaviorism and Gestalt theory introduced disciplinary splintering that irked Carr. When Carl Murchison asked him to write a chapter on functionalism for the *Psychologies of 1925*,[50] Carr refused, saying "I don't like your damn book."[51] Carr later agreed to write the functionalism section for the 1930 edition when Murchison warned that if Carr did not write it Murchison would just get someone else to do it.[52] In that volume, Carr described functionalism as "a movement that embraced a large number of psychologists who had certain principles in common," a shared scientific project involving numerous strands of thought.[53] What Carr did not like about Murchison's book was the notion that there were multiple schools or opposing camps within the field of psychology. He preferred to think of psychology as eclectic yet systematic, unified in purpose and advancing forward due to empirical contributions from multiple viewpoints. A diversity of research methods or theoretical dispositions should not fragment the young field into isolated schools but should instead exemplify the "catholic attitude [that] is supposed to be one of the essential characteristics of the scientific spirit."[54]

Methodologically, that spirit required but did not solely rely on experimental research methods.[55] Carr's concept of experimentation was both broad and conservative, consisting of "the usual laboratory practice of eliciting certain modes of activity under specified conditions."[56] He supported the use of both subjective and objective—quantitative and qualitative—forms of observation as equally necessary. His understanding of science placed psychology at the practical nexus of multiple disciplines, taking "facts from sociology, education, neurology, physiology, biology, and anthropology."[57] He frequently advised psychology graduate students at Chicago to take courses in neurology, education, and philosophy.[58]

W. B. Pillsbury described Carr as exercising tremendous "care in experimentation and caution in interpretation."[59] Given his sprawling eclecticism in relation to research methods, epistemology, and other disciplines, Carr's science was primarily guided by his sober and temperate approach to interpreting human activity. His science was forged not on the mightiest method or the truest theoretical formulation—the cornerstone of some of the psychological schools that Carr saw popping up around him—but on a circumspect attitude of deep care and analytic focus.

Fred McKinney, a doctoral student in psychology at Chicago from 1929 to 1931, later recalled that the development of numerous theoretical schools within American psychology was often downplayed or even ignored in Carr's department. Carr tried to maintain a broad, diverse, and inclusive psychological science in the face of evident fragmentation, an effort that seemed to lead, quite ironically, to some degree of intellectual isolation. Theoretical rifts and scientific schisms were often ignored. For example, "behaviorism was rarely mentioned"[60] by the Chicago faculty.

John B. Watson's famous essay "Psychology from the Standpoint of a Behaviorist" was published in 1913, launching the growth of behavioral theory as a resounding rejection of consciousness as the proper object of psychological examination. "The time seems to have come," Watson declared, "when psychology must discard all reference to consciousness."[61] Watson maintained that a truly objective natural science would engage in the experimental study of behavior. Watson had been the first doctoral graduate of the Chicago psychology program, and he had served on the faculty briefly before moving to Johns Hopkins in 1908. His work launched a new field of behavioral psychology that included leading researchers such as Edward C. Tolman at the University of California, Berkeley, and Clark L. Hull at the University of Wisconsin. To Carr, the behaviorists' attempt to create a supreme theory or one best approach to psychology was counterproductive, turning a unified science into a field of intellectual argumentation. Not surprisingly, doctoral students at Chicago in 1930 primarily learned about behaviorism not from faculty members but through discussions with other students.[62]

Similarly, McKinney reported that Gestalt psychology was viewed by Carr with some level of doubt and annoyance. By 1920, Gestalt theory had been fully established within German psychology by Wertheimer, Koffka, and Kohler. In the mid-1920s, English translations of works by Koffka and Kohler were widely read by American psychologists. A series of over 30 lectures in the United States by Koffka, including an invited session at the 1925 conference of the American Psychological Association, quickly gained Gestalt psychology a new following within the United States.[63] Carr thought Gestalt theory was just one more unnecessary division within a scientific field that should remain whole.

Carr was not alone in his concern over the possible decomposition of the field of psychology. One reviewer of Murchison's *Psychologies of 1925* noted:

> In no other branch of modern science can one imagine a book with a similar title. Such titles as "Physics of 1925" or "Physiologies of 1925" would, indeed, sound strange.[64]

Another reviewer expressed concern at the harsh tone of rivalry and acrimony between the various theoretical camps. He concluded quite ironically that "it took courage to publish a book which would reveal to the general public how little psychologists agree and how little they think of each other."[65] A third reviewer described the field of psychology as "confusion" and asked "whether psychology is to split up into mutual intolerant schools teaching different subject matters."[66]

The question of the scientific character of a divided discipline was also raised by a reviewer of Murchison's *Psychologies of 1930*. What central and advancing notion of science inheres amidst the numerous, greatly isolated theoretical camps? Is there a science of psychology if the field chiefly consists of a series of separate schools vying for epistemic superiority?

> Schools and theories are isolated from one another to a degree that suggests no real substratum of scientific connection.... If the different schools were only so many facets of a common science, each would show concern to absorb into its own body results arrived at by the others.[67]

Perhaps the field was going through what Woodworth called "adolescence,"[68] a painful growth stage hopefully leading to a later maturity. Or, as one scholar theorized, it might be moving through a preliminary "exploratory"[69] phase that would ultimately weed out the less scientific schools in favor of a single evolutionary victor. Psychology might become one science, many sciences, or a degraded proliferation of dogmatic positions constituting no science at all.

Carr's response to this complex situation was demonstrated in a brief review that he wrote of Woodworth's *Contemporary Schools*. In his own conclusion to the book, Woodworth attempted to carve out a middle way, a path of pluralism and moderation to ride out the storm of conflicting views. He strongly advised readers to do likewise. He claimed that there was a

> giant middle body of psychologists who do not admit allegiance to any of the schools.... They refuse to swallow the medicine offered by any one of the schools... Such refusal need not in the least debar us, if we belong in the middle group, from recognizing good work where we find it.[70]

Carr placed himself squarely within this reasonable middling group, denying fealty to any theory or school, in order to appreciate whatever good work arose in any area of psychology.[71]

Positioning himself and functionalism as a moderate middle way between extreme positions was a common strategy for Carr. In 1917, he described the functionalist tenet of psychophysical unity as "a mediating point of contact for the two extremes of subjectivism and behaviorism." On the subjective end of the epistemological spectrum were data collected from introspection and clinical observations. Behavioral data constituted the objectivist pole. At the center, to Carr's mind, was a "modest program" drawing equally from both ends, respecting both epistemologies and avoiding the dogmatic downfalls of either extreme.[72]

Neither Carr nor Woodworth, the advocates of the middle way, directly addressed the question of what constitutes "good work" within such a moderate science of psychology. Certainly what divided Titchener from Watson from Koffka was the very definition of what each considered good psychological research to be, in regard to both theory and method. Research that earned accolades within one theoretical camp received intense criticism from other schools. Perhaps Carr and Woodworth were simply naïve in their desire for a pluralistic psychology characterized by cross-theoretical unity.

Additionally, though, one can see Carr's tendency toward a broad and inclusive unity as an example of his flexible and lean brand of pragmatism. He viewed the various theories not as opposing sets of scientific principles or competing philosophical doctrines, each self-righteous and leveraged against the rest. He understood theories as simply useful intellectual tools available to psychological researchers who might need them. Theory, in this sense, was a necessary intellectual fuel for research, but it did not hold the steering wheel that guided the journey. The practical focus of examining a given psychological problem, the human issue of actual living, took precedence over theoretical formulations. Rather than employing psychological theories as the armaments for competitive debate, he preferred to appropriate them as functional implements in the service of psychological inquiry.[73]

FUNCTIONALISM AND EDUCATIONAL TESTING

An influential movement within psychology in the early twentieth century that was easily and fully supported by Carr and the Chicago functionalists was mental measurement. Prior to World War I, Henry H. Goddard, of the Vineland Training School, and Lewis M. Terman, of Stanford University, had each produced revised versions of Alfred Binet's intelligence test. Measures of mental level initially garnered little professional or public respect. Then the development of measuring intelligence and ability exploded during World War I, when the U.S. Army commissioned 40 leading psychologists—led by Robert M. Yerkes of Harvard, and including Goddard and Terman—to develop tests to match large numbers of soldiers to ranks and jobs. Although the testing program was the source of some conflict within military ranks, the work quickly boosted the popularity and legitimacy of intelligence testing. After the war, public schools avidly sought uses for mental testing, and businesses began work on developing personnel exams. In under a decade, psychometrics became a staple of professional psychology and education.[74]

In his 1925 introductory book entitled *Psychology*, Carr included one full chapter on intellectual testing. He covered basic concepts of ability testing, distinguishing between tests of general ability (such as IQ) and those designed to measure a specific ability (such as academic subject tests). His rationale for supporting the use of mental measures was purely pragmatic. A helpful test has the partial capacity to predict a human performance in a specific area of activity. The social utility of testing relies on the "economy of test measurements," the fact that one can use a reliable test to quickly predict the behavior of large groups of persons with some accuracy. While some psychologists (such as Yerkes) viewed mental tests as an opportunity for psychology to become more objective and, therefore, more scientific,[75] Carr never imagined tests doing anything more than saving some time and effort. He viewed psychological measurement as just one contributing player in a large ensemble cast.[76]

Similarly, the psychology department at Chicago embraced mental measurement as useful without making psychometrics a central feature of the graduate program. The first psychometrician was hired to the faculty in 1924 when L. L. Thurstone, a graduate of the program, returned to Chicago from the Carnegie Institute of Technology. Graduate students typically took only one course on mental measurement and statistics.[77] When Samuel Kirk studied for his master's degree at Chicago, in order to access a complete series of statistics classes, he had to attend courses offered at the Institute for Juvenile Research.[78]

As one might expect, Carr's position on intelligence testing avoided extremes. But finding the temperate middle ground was not always easy. Despite Carr's avid attempt to hold together a divided field within one large scientific vision through a pragmatic understanding of science, or perhaps because of it, he sometimes espoused contradictory views. In his 1925 text *Psychology,* Carr incongruently coupled the standard principles of Angell's functionalism with a thoroughly deterministic and mechanistic science. Two specific quotations will suffice to demonstrate the conflict between a functionalist eclecticism and an objectivist mechanism in his text. In an early passage, Carr supported a broad and plural science.

> Psychology, like other sciences, utilizes any fact that is significant for its purposes irrespective of how or by whom it was obtained. No single avenue of approach can give a complete knowledge of a mental act. The various sources of knowledge supplement each other and psychology is concerned with the task of systematizing and harmonizing the various data in order to form an adequate conception of all that is involved in the operations of the mind.[79]

The mysteries of the mind require a flexible science open to facts gathered via many research methods and from multiple disciplines.

In a later passage, Carr espoused the "doctrine of determinism" affirming that "every aspect of mental life can be accounted for in terms of cause and effect." The "character of any human personality" is wholly determined by a combination of "the nature of his inheritance" and "the various extraneous influences to which he is subjected throughout life."[80] His articulation of psychological science, in this statement, sounded more like the rigid objectivism of Watson than the dexterous functionalism of Angell.

> The deterministic conception of mental life is a necessary postulate of any psychology that pretends to be a science. The practical concern of every science is the prediction and control of the phenomena with which it deals, but this prediction and control of any phenomenon is possible only in virtue of our knowledge of causal relationships. Science is thus primarily engaged in a search for causal relations.... Psychology as a science must necessarily proceed upon the assumption that all phases of mental life can be reduced to mechanistic terms, while any psychologist ceases to be a scientist in so far as he admits that any of his data are not amenable to a causal treatment.[81]

Carr painted a picture of human mental activity as a mechanized system involving lockstep cause-effect relationships, and psychological science as the precise means to chart those causal links.

Quite understandably, after rendering the mind as a virtual automaton, Carr then struggled with the notion of free will as he attempted to hang on to an image of humans thinking and making real choices. He wondered how a mind directed by levers and pulleys, triggered through causal schemes, could involve some element of intentionality and agency. He backpedaled from the lockstep determinism of his mind-as-machine image to conclude that (somehow) "purposes and intentions do influence conduct."[82] He was unable to explain how an individual's creation or selection of such purposes takes place in light of the air-tight doctrine of determinism. Somehow freedom of thought and choice occurs within the machine.

Carr's simultaneous embrace of features of extreme objectivism—mechanism, linear schemes of cause and effect, and determinism—within his pragmatic, eclectic orientation to science provides a brief glimpse into the difficulty he faced in attempting to maintain functionalism as the conceptual umbrella for all of American psychology. If psychology were narrowed down in terms of epistemology, methods, and theory, as occurred in the case of behaviorism, the result would be a high degree of internal coherence and agreement. Consensus and clarity could reign among researchers sharing a single grammar. If, on the other hand, psychology included a wide expanse of researchers with only marginal agreement on methods, theories, or epistemology—essentially, little to unite them beyond the shared use of the term "psychology"—then contradiction and disjuncture would be common. Carr believed "that functional psychology *is* American psychology,"[83] and he earnestly tried to create a broad and embracing discipline supporting a wide range of epistemological stances and methodological practices.[84] At some moments, he was able to find a middle road of moderation. Other times, his approach sounded a medley of discordant tones.

DIAGNOSING READING DISABILITIES: MARION MONROE

After Samuel Kirk had spent seven months in 1929 teaching a 10-year-old boy how to read at the Oak Forest (Illinois) institution, he sent the child to the Institute for Juvenile Research in Chicago for evaluation. There Kirk met Marion Monroe, a research psychologist who was developing a new, psychometric procedure for the diagnosis of reading disabilities based on analyses of error patterns. Kirk fondly recalled later that she "was kind enough to tutor me in diagnosis and remediation of severe cases of reading disabilities."[85]

Marion Monroe had completed her master's and Ph.D. research under the warm and thoughtful direction of Harvey Carr. In an era when graduate schools and fields of advanced science were dominated by men, Carr was a strong sponsor of women doctoral students.[86] Like Samuel Kirk, though, Monroe took a fair portion of her research education on the side. While she was faithfully completing two investigations of questions relating to the perception of color with Professor Carr, she launched her career as a reading remediation researcher, working first at the Iowa State Psychopathic Hospital in Iowa City and then at the Institute for Juvenile Research. Her work in Iowa City was supervised by Samuel T. Orton, a physician at the University of Iowa who theorized childhood reading difficulties as a matter of mixed hemispheric dominance, a problem of the brain working against itself, resulting in symbolic inversions and mirror images in the brain. He later developed what became known as the Orton-Gillingham approach to reading remediation, a system of instruction that combined phonetic training with Grace Fernald's multisensory methods.[87]

Monroe quickly set aside Orton's brain-based theoretical orientation to apply her strong knowledge of psychometrics to the diagnosis of reading disabilities. Her research in both Iowa City and Chicago derived less conceptual benefit from Orton's work than from the research of University of Chicago education faculty member William S. Gray. Orton's *Foreword* to Monroe's 1928 study was an awkward testimony to his less than ardent support of her research. He used the few introductory pages primarily to present his own theory of reading disorders, an approach that Monroe's volume offered only passing, noncommittal mention. His stiffly worded preface to Monroe's book supplied not a single supportive comment about her formulation of reading disabilities.[88]

In the foreword to her 1932 book, Monroe politely thanked Orton for calling "my attention to the unusual facility which poor readers sometimes have in mirror-reading and mirror-writing."[89] She described her research as moving beyond Orton to offer "extensions, modifications, and new points of attack."[90] In the same foreword, she thanked "Dr. W. S. Gray, of the University of Chicago, for reading the manuscript and making helpful suggestions."[91] The Monroe-Gray professional collaboration that began during her graduate school studies lasted for decades. The two worked closely together from the 1940s through much of the 1960s on the popular *Dick and Jane* children's book series.

A pivotal figure in the early application of the practices of mental measurement to the evaluation of reading, William S. Gray led the movement to bring quantitative precision to the analysis of reading and reading-related problems.[92] He studied under Edward L. Thorndike, the so-called father of educational measurement, at Teachers College from 1913 to 1914 when Thorndike was creating his first tests of reading. He also learned from Teachers College progressives John Dewey and William H. Kirkpatrick. Gray began the development of his own reading measure as part of his master's thesis with Thorndike, and he continued this test development work in his doctorate at Chicago under Charles Judd. Gray's *Oral Reading Paragraphs Test*, published initially in 1915, was one of the first standardized tests of oral reading proficiency.[93]

The widespread influence of concepts of efficiency and scientific management entered public education just after 1900, quickly leading to a shift toward quantification and technical precision among reading researchers.[94] The World War I boom in the development and use of mental measures by educators included dramatic growth in the creation of standardized reading tests. By 1926, at least 30 different standardized tests of reading achievement had been developed, including measures of silent reading, oral reading, and vocabulary.[95] Statistically similar to their intelligence test predecessors, the new reading tests mapped the performance of individual students onto a bell curve format, thereby comparing individual scores to the achievement of other students in the same grade. Often reading tests of the period created a total reading index score based on the combination of two subtests, one measuring speed and the other reproduction. Speed involved the rate of oral or silent reading. Reproduction was a narrow construct that predated what would later be called comprehension. It consisted of written or sometimes oral recall of sentences read, often supplemented with responses to highly focused factual recall questions, emphasizing raw recollection of words and facts rather than a deep understanding of content.

A strong advocate for the systematic use of standardized reading tests, Gray called on school districts to identify and assist the many students whose reading difficulties were otherwise going unnoticed.[96] "There are thousands of boys and girls in school each year," he argued in a rare moment of overt passion, "who make little or no progress because of inaccuracies and personal handicaps which could be eliminated."[97] With proper testing, children with reading difficulties could be identified, and then teachers could provide remedial instruction in areas of weakness. Students who scored "lower than the desirable standards," for example, in the area of oral reading rate, should be "given help in oral reading in proportion to their needs."[98] Although he admitted that researchers had not yet figured out the best ways to remediate reading disabilities, "diagnostic and remedial studies which have been made of such cases demonstrate that a very large percentage can be materially helped."[99]

Gray was a vocal and prominent proponent for the widespread employment of the new standardized reading tests in the 1920s, and today he is often remembered as an influential purveyor of an objective science of reading research and instruction. But his approach to the diagnosis and remediation of reading defects did not rely primarily on tests. As Allan Lukes has noted, "Gray's was not a wholly mechanistic reading psychology by any means."[100] He incorporated objective measures as useful elements within a larger framework of subjective analysis and clinical judgment. His approach to the diagnosis of reading disabilities started with the use of standardized measures, providing a "preliminary diagnosis"[101] outlining "the symptoms of strength or weakness in specific phases of reading"[102] relative to other students of the same grade or age. After the prefatory identification of a child with reading achievement below the norm and a general appraisal of subskills of reading and reproduction, psychometric instruments served no further clinical purpose. The remaining process of diagnostic appraisal relied on the subjective insight and expertise of a professional educator gathering facts about the individual child, an activity that went beyond the limited capacity of tests.[103]

Why was the utility of Gray's beloved tests so restricted in his own approach to diagnostic work? To Gray, a thorough diagnosis included both an identification of the specific reading performance difficulties encountered by the child and the underlying causes. Tests fell short on both accounts. "The standardized measures which are now available do not measure accomplishment in all phases reading,"[104] he contended, requiring clinicians to seek multiple forms of additional information.

> Before the specific nature of the child's difficulties was actually determined it frequently became necessary to observe his classroom work, to secure information from his teachers concerning his reading errors and difficulties, to compare him with a good reader for the purpose of determining differences, and to make use of the child's own introspections and comments.[105]

Moreover, Gray asserted, "the most helpful records are those which are secured when a pupil is working under normal conditions" of everyday classroom reading instruction, not under the somewhat artificial testing conditions. "A continuous series of records, such as can be secured only through the informal tests given day after day, is essential to a clear understanding of a case."[106] More could be learned from observing a child's everyday reading activities in the classroom than from the administration of standardized tests.

Certainly, one reason Gray's diagnostic science cast a wide net of data collection was his belief in the complexity of causation. He described the possible sources of reading disabilities as almost innumerable; these include poverty, intellectual defect, word blindness, vision and eye movement problems, inadequate phonetic training, health issues, home environment, and inadequate prior instruction.[107] The broader field of reading research, as researchers' interest in reading disability increased dramatically between 1935 and 1950, would generally embrace Gray's theory of multiple causes.[108] To Gray's thinking, the investigation of causation involving a variety of possible factors in a specific case required far more than what any test or group of tests might provide.

Further, Gray's thoughts on the limited role of tests in diagnosis provide some insight into his understanding of an educational science of reading disabilities. During the 1920s, when both Gray and Monroe were keenly focused on the diagnosis and remediation of reading disabilities, the Chicago professor's scientific orientation placed central epistemic authority in the thoughtful, organizing role of the clinician or remedial teacher. Only a person of balanced judgment could gather and analyze numerous forms of data—family history, school history, health information, and reports of academic progress in multiple subject areas—into a thorough, detailed study of the case. Objective measures were understood as helpful but insufficient tools to be used by an educated, insightful professional in the complex practice of clinical diagnosis. Gray generally downplayed the importance of standardized testing in the diagnostic process.

> Experience with more than one hundred remedial cases has shown clearly that the specific nature of a pupil's difficulties can be determined in a large majority of cases through the use of no more technical devices than informal tests of reading accomplishment.[109]

Contrary to his public role as banner bearer in the expanding march of an objective, quantitative science of reading, Gray limited standardized tests to the status of useful but not fully necessary instruments in service to the clinical task of diagnostic analysis.

As an advanced student of Gray's nuanced blend of mathematical objectivity and clinical subjectivity in the diagnosis of reading disabilities, Marion Monroe clearly gravitated toward her professor's psychometric side. While he cultivated a constrained role for educational measurement within reading disability appraisal, Monroe saw great potential for the epistemic elevation of quantitative instruments within the procedures of diagnosis. Her primary goal was to bring mathematical precision into the interpretations and decisions of the diagnostic process. To her thinking, and contrary to Gray's, the diagnosis of reading disabilities required less clinical judgment and more technical precision.

MATHEMATICAL ACCURACY IN DIAGNOSTIC PROCEDURE

Starting with Gray's diagnostic approach as a foundation, Marion Monroe worked to reduce what she called "the subjective element"[110] through the development of forms of statistical procedure within the appraisal process. In two large studies comparing the performance of children with deficient reading achievement with normal readers, Monroe introduced psychometric elements into what she viewed as weaknesses in the Gray diagnostic approach. The first study, conducted in 1926 at the Iowa Psychopathic Hospital, compared the reading performance of 120 normal and 175 retarded readers seven through twelve years of age.[111] The second large study involved a similar comparison, this time with over 500 children at the Institute for Juvenile Research in Chicago, resulting in the 1932 publication of Monroe's classic book *Children Who Cannot Read*.[112] Kirk once described this influential study as "my bible,"[113] his first guide to profiling abilities and disabilities in reading. The two main goals of these large-scale studies were to create a psychometric approach to determine whether an individual child's "reading is normal or not,"[114] and to characterize an individual's reading defect within a standardized algorithm of oral reading mistakes, what Monroe called a "profile of errors."[115] Such a profile would then serve as the basis for corrective training.

Differentiating between normal and retarded reading, to Monroe's thinking, was a matter of collating the level of reading expected of an individual with that child's actual reading performance, a comparison facilitated by advances in educational measurement. Through the comparative contrast of "intelligence and achievement tests,"[116] a child's reading performance could be viewed as distinct from his general intellectual capacity. This discrepancy notion was not at all new. In James Hinshelwood's medical research, he had concluded that "the general intelligence, powers of observation, and reasoning" were "unaffected in true cases of word-blindness."[117] What made word-blindness so fascinating and troubling was the existence of a distinct reading disability in a mind that was otherwise without disease. Monroe marshaled the technical apparatus of early educational measurement to this discrepancy concept, thereby discovering those children "having a special defect" in reading, "the atypical children who do not learn to read so well as would be expected from their other intellectual abilities."[118] Her diagnostic regimen could "differentiate them from the general defectives in who the entire pattern of intellectual traits is more or less uniformly retarded."[119] In its initial formulation, Monroe defined a "specifically retarded reader" as "reading below his school-grade level" and "reading below his obtained mental-age level."[120] From this preliminary notion of deficient reading achievement falling below grade-norms and IQ-norms, Monroe developed a discrepancy formula that became the foundation for the current standard practice of diagnosing learning disabilities.

In the final form, Monroe's formula for discrepancy yielded "a single measure of reading defect" called a "reading index."[121] She calculated an average of mental age, chronological age, and a measure of arithmetic achievement as a single score of Expected Reading performance. Chronological and mental age were used as factors indicating a general level of mental development in comparison to peers. Arithmetic level was added to provide a measure of the child's typical competence in academic subject learning. The Actual Reading level was a mathematical composite of four well-known standardized reading tests. Where Gray had found reading tests wanting in their uneven treatment of the many areas of reading activity, Monroe strategically stitched together multiple measures for maximum coverage, reasoning that what one test failed to do could be addressed by another. The Reading Index was calculated by dividing Actual Reading level by the Expected Reading level. In her Chicago study, Monroe found that the mean of the normal group's Reading Index was 1.02, while the reading defect group had a mean score of .49.[122]

Monroe admitted that, contrary to the goal of increased precision, selecting a specific Reading Index score where normal reading ends and defect begins was, however, an arbitrary decision.

> In the general population there is no hard-and-fast line of demarcation between reading-defect cases and normal readers. There are all degrees of gradation from very severe discrepancies between reading and other accomplishments to very mild disparities.[123]

Despite an admission that declaring such a line was "subjective,"[124] Monroe set the diagnostic standard for reading disorder at 2.75 standard deviations below the mean Reading Index. Seemingly ignoring her own recognition of the random nature of setting a boundary of normal performance, she nevertheless concluded: "The reading index discriminates very well between the reading-defect cases and the controls."[125] Monroe was satisfied that she had met the efficiency goal of building a statistical procedure for distinguishing between normal and deficient readers.

Central to this research was the idea that some children without a condition of general mental retardation had a specific defect in the area of reading. This added a new explanation to the age-old educational maxim that children who failed to learn to read must "be either lazy or stupid."[126] By teasing apart reading defect and intelligence level, Monroe created the possibility of a child of average or even high IQ having a reading disability. Or, to put it simply, mental deficiency was not the only plausible explanation for a case of reading defect. Monroe had formulated a third account: a specific learning disorder among otherwise normal children.

Simultaneously, Monroe also maintained that a child with mental retardation could also have a specific reading defect.

> The generally subnormal child is below his age level in other of his mental capacities and achievements as well as in reading and could not be regarded as a case of special disability so long as his achievements are harmoniously low. The defective child could, however, have a reading defect in addition to his general subnormality if his reading achievements were still more retarded than his other accomplishments.[127]

Monroe's procedure for diagnosing a specific reading disorder based on discrepancy also allowed for the possibility of a child with a subnormal IQ having a reading achievement level that was substantially lower—an indication of a specific reading disorder. She concluded that her "data emphasize that reading disability may occur at any intellectual level."[128]

ERROR PROFILES AS DIAGNOSIS

The Reading Index created an aura of mathematical clarity in identifying cases of specific reading disabilities, effectively shifting the determination from the realm of subjective clinical judgment to a standardized calculation. But it did not point to underlying causes or effective strategies for remediation. In order to provide a child with remedial training, Monroe believed that she must accurately document the "nature of his difficulties. His errors in reading give us an indication of his particular difficulties."[129] Monroe's research provided detailed overviews of the research on reading disability causation, maintaining Gray's concept of multiple etiological factors with scientific competence if not evident enthusiasm. She put discussions of causality aside from her ultimate goal—the development of programs of remediation. Her focus on developing strategies for corrective training was directed wholly toward remediation based on an "analysis of errors,"[130] a documentation of patterns of incorrect oral reading behavior regardless of etiology. She constructed her measurement diagnostics in response to the challenge of further refining Gray's ideas on patterns of oral reading errors. Although she made no reference to a behavioral theory of psychology, her concept of early reading as the correct spoken production of a sequence of sounds in response to printed symbols traded Carr for Watson, deemphasizing attention to consciousness in favor of regular patterns of behavior. Improving reading behavior amounted to carefully documenting the incorrect behaviors and then providing training sessions to improve those specific areas of error.

Gray's work on remediation had utilized a number of schemes of oral reading error classification that generally included word or syllable mispronunciation, substitution, repetition, omission, and substitution. In at least one version, his scheme also analyzed errors in reading groups of words or phrases.[131] He lamented the fact that "no standard technique has been worked out for diagnosing individual cases."[132] Yet his expansive view of the variety of causes and practical difficulties facing poor readers offered little to the standardization of a single model of error analysis as the linchpin of diagnostic analysis. Monroe's concise, behavioral view of reading did. She devoted herself to the development of a comprehensive formula of error analysis that focused only on the smallest units of behavior: spoken syllables or words.

In her Chicago study, Monroe built a model consisting of 10 types of frequent oral reading errors: (1) mispronounced vowels, (2) mispronounced consonants, (3) reversals of sounds or words, (4) addition of sounds, (5) omission of sounds, (6) substitution of words, (7) repetition of words, (8) addition of words, (9) omission of words, and (10) refusals or words aided (i.e., words not read aloud). The standardization of the 10 types involved a fairly sophisticated statistical treatment that employed far more educational measurement than any prior research on reading disability diagnosis. First, examiners counted each type of error committed by each child on three different oral reading tests. From this data, a "proportionate error score"[133] was calculated for each error category based on the average number of errors per 500 words. Three to six months later, the reliability of each of the 10 categories of proportionate error scores was checked through retests of 50 (of the over 500 total) children. Correlations between first and second tests for the sample yielded coefficients ranging from lows of .55 (addition of words) and .60 (omission of words) to highs above .90 for five (vowels, consonants, reversals, additions of sounds, and refusals/words aided) of the ten types. This confirmed that "a child is inclined to maintain the same profile of errors"[134] over time and over multiple readings.

Monroe calculated means and standard deviations (Z scores) for each error type at each grade (1–5) level. This created a standard curve stretching from three standard deviations below the mean to five above for each error type at each grade. She then broke each grade level down into deciles, yielding extensive tables of error scores per each tenth of grade level. Similar calculations were conducted for Total Errors—a comprehensive score combining all ten error types.

Comparisons between the performance of normal readers and that of those with reading defect demonstrated numerous differences in error rates.

> The reading-defect cases as a group greatly exceeded the controls in their errors in the following types: total errors, vowels, reversals, omission of sounds, repetition, consonants, and addition of sounds. They exceeded the controls slightly but not significantly in the following types: substitution, omission of words, refusals and words aided, and addition of words.[135]

While the Total Errors Z score for the normal readers was essentially at the group mean, the Total Errors Z score for the reading defect cases was 1.127, indicating that these children generally had more errors than the normal group.[136]

The greatest practical utility of the profile of errors was its ability to point out specific areas of oral reading difficulty requiring educational attention. Monroe's approach to instructional methods borrowed widely from the variety of common practices of the day, including phonetic training and Grace Fernald's sounding-tracing method. Like Gray, Fernald, and others, her research reported positive gains made by children receiving corrective instruction. But her contribution to the psychology of reading disability was not specifically in the area of instructional methods. What she built was a systematic diagnostic approach utilizing the statistical techniques of the era that directed reading teachers to specific areas of reading behavior requiring focused instructional correction. Based on Monroe's approach, a child needing extra attention could be identified, and then a program of remediation could be neatly crafted to specifically target the areas of substandard reading functioning.

While Monroe's research on reading disabilities certainly continued and further strengthened many emphases initiated by Gray, Monroe's psychology of reading embraced a more objectivist orientation. Gray had viewed reading as a complex individual and social matter, and reading disability diagnosis as an activity requiring a range of data sources weighted by a temperate stance of professional discernment. Monroe theorized reading as a pattern of behavior occurring in response to printed symbols. Diagnosis was a highly technical task designed to minimize professional judgment through reliance on standard, objective measurements, thereby allowing reading clinicians and teachers very few degrees of professional freedom in interpretation and decision making. While Gray believed that practicality demanded flexibility of clinical judgment, Monroe maintained that practicality was best served by accurate measurement. Each approach fit within the expansive umbrella of Carr's functionalist psychology. Gray occupied a middle way between objectivism and subjectivism. Monroe employed a more atomistic and mechanistic orientation exemplified by behaviorism and educational measurement.

"A MORE OPTIMISTIC ATTITUDE": THORLEIF G. HEGGE

The 1920s was a decade when many leading researchers—including Gray, Monroe, Orton, and Arthur I. Gates[137] and Laura Zirbes of Teachers College[138]—turned their attention to the remediation of reading difficulties. Spurred greatly by the increased use of standardized measures of reading, researchers focused considerable effort on what Zirbes called the "removal of deficiency"[139] through special methods of diagnosis and instruction. Although remedial work quickly became a legitimate subarea of reading research, the skills and needs of mentally deficient children were commonly ignored.

For example, the National Committee on Reading was formed in December 1922 to review prior research in the area and to provide thoughtful direction to further inquiry. William S. Gray chaired the group of eight national leaders through two years of collaboration, resulting in 1925 in the first national report on the state of reading research and instruction. The report contained 11 chapters on a wide variety of topics, including one by Zirbes on diagnosis and remediation, plus a substantial list of recommendations for further research. The volume lacked any address of issues concerning the teaching of reading to children with mental defects.[140] Reading and reading instruction were generally understood within an assumed framework of intellectual normality.

Ted Hegge, the director of research at the Wayne County Training School, observed that the "problem of reading disability has hardly been touched upon in connection with the mentally retarded."[141] The general assumption among psychologists and educators was "that special reading disability in cases of lower IQ is an aspect of mental deficiency and that the case therefore is untrainable."[142] Hegge's experience at the Wayne School taught him, to the contrary, "to adopt a more optimistic attitude"[143] toward the treatment of reading problems among mentally deficient children, at least those with IQs above 60.[144]

In 1927, Hegge launched what would become a very unusual educational project. He started providing treatment for the reading disability of one mental defective child. Drawing from success in that experience, utilizing psychology graduate students from the University of Michigan as reading instructors, he expanded his research and treatment program. Between 1929 and 1937, Hegge and his team delivered reading disability training to 80 children at the Wayne School, carefully documenting the entire process of diagnosis, treatment, and the outcomes.[145]

Hegge's concern was twofold. First, he worried about the common assumption among researchers that mentally deficient children could not learn to read due to their general condition of intellectual subnormality. Hegge was a strong believer that, given proper instruction, at least some of these children, most notably those with higher levels of intelligence, could learn to read. He believed that many mentally deficient children failed to learn to read because they were provided with instruction too early in their delayed development, when their chronological age was similar to nonretarded peers but their mental age lagged due to intellectual immaturity. This instructional practice frequently resulted in a paralyzing sense of frustration for the mentally deficient child. It also reinforced the mistaken premise that few such children could learn to read. He advocated delaying academic instruction for "high-grade mentally deficient children until a mental age of eight has been reached."[146]

Closely connected to this position was Hegge's stance that remedial reading researchers were failing to acknowledge the occurrence of specific reading disabilities among the mental defective population. Beginning with case reports by James Hinshelwood[147] in 1895 and W. Pringle Morgan[148] in 1896, an important line of research on the problem of word blindness had supported the notion that "extreme special difficulties" in reading "may be present in children whose intellectual abilities are normal in other respects."[149] This idea had much support from medical researchers who theorized the possible variability of performance across different brain-based functions, yet it held little sway with American educational psychologists who tended to conceptualize intellectual capacity in a more unitary manner.

Hegge, Sam Kirk, and Kirk's wife Winifred worked closely for four years on the development of a system of reading diagnosis and instruction for children with both a mental deficiency and a reading disability. They were quite satisfied to borrow Monroe's approach to diagnosis with little modification in order to focus on their primary goal—the creation and testing of "a definite method of attack on the difficulties which present themselves in the correction of a reading-defect."[150] They utilized her Reading Index with one modification to the formula—dropping out the measure of chronological age from the calculation of Expected Reading performance for the institutionalized child population. They called their new index the "reading trainability quotient,"[151] a measure indicating not only reading retardation but also, more importantly from their perspective, the "trainability"[152] of an individual child. Hegge's research team were very concerned with the question of distinguishing between a child who could not read due to mental deficiency and a "true reading case" or "specifically retarded reader,"[153] a child with mental deficiency who also has a treatable reading disorder.

The goal of effectively discerning which children had reading difficulties that were caused by a specific defect was set partially due to practical worries about efficiency. Hegge believed that "almost all cases are trainable,"[154] but he did not want to waste time treating children who would not respond favorably. The larger significance of accurately diagnosing specific reading defects grew out of Hegge's belief that the future life possibilities of high-grade mentally deficient children could greatly be interpreted in the tea leaves of reading diagnosis. His thinking roughly continued an attitude within institutions for the feebleminded that harkened back to the distinction between "salvageable and unsalvageable" populations prevalently made in eighteenth- and nineteenth-century almshouses.[155] Some people could be redeemed to hold a proper place in society, and some were beyond the powers of intervention.

In the institutions for mental defectives, this distinction typically hinged on a concept that Phil Ferguson has called "chronicity," a general social status "of being judged somehow 'unfixable.'"[156] Hegge's practice of reading defect diagnosis determined which children were chronic cases to be maintained in custodial care and which could be taught enough reading skills to buoy their psychological and vocational rehabilitation upward toward eventual community living status. The mental capacity to read was singularly indicative of the character and personal preparedness for life outside the institution walls. The mentally deficient child who could learn to read was educable, treatable, and could effectively move beyond custodial care to a life in the community.[157]

Through trial and error in working with many children at the Wayne School, the research group determined that true reading cases had an IQ of 60 or higher, scored below a third-grade level on standard reading measures, and had a reading trainability index of less than .70. These criteria targeted the population that could, given a typical program of about 75 half-hour, one-to-one instructional sessions, advance about two grade levels in reading.[158]

The Wayne School orientation to a science of diagnosing reading disabilities mixed Gray's clinical format with Monroe's mathematical precision. Like Monroe, Hegge's team had only limited interest in the etiology of the disorder, for understanding causation played little role in instructional treatment.[159] Like Gray, they retained a strong element of clinical judgment in the diagnostic process. Only through close clinical observation of a child's reading and his/her response to reading instruction could a final determination be made as to the trainability of the child.[160] The scientific approach of the Wayne School researchers, while relying heavily on Monroe's scheme of reading evaluation and intelligence measures, incorporated quantitative instruments within a process that still maintained the final necessity and validity of a professional's clinical judgment. This orientation to a science of diagnosis combined an overarching subjectivity of clinical orientation with the mathematical objectivity of psychometric measures. It would become the hallmark of Sam Kirk's psychology for decades to follow.

The reading defect treatment program employed at the Wayne School was primarily devised by Kirk. He analyzed the many phonics-based instructional programs available in the early 1930s and found that because they were "designed primarily for classroom instruction" with an entire class or large groups, "such methods proved inadequate."[161] "The drill materials are too brief, and the exercises introduce too many problems at one time."[162] What was needed, Kirk believed, was an extensive set of phonetic drills designed specifically for children with reading defects that built up response habits gradually from small linguistic units to larger elements.

Research on reading instruction involving explicit teaching of phonics was certainly in its infancy. The few studies that had been conducted emphasized whole-group instruction in general education classrooms in the primary grades, with little attention to children with reading difficulties, and the results created a murky efficacy picture. Two experiments in the Rochester, New Hampshire schools, one involving first- and second-grade students and the second looking at fourth- and fifth-grade children, indicated that children taught with a phonetic method "read generally with less speed, less interest, greater fatigue, and with confusion of ideas."[163] In comparison, the "classes having no phonics were found to enjoy reading for the sake of study."[164] The children taught without phonics, while often "careless in pronunciation," "read with greater interest, increased speed, and more expression"[165] than the phonics-taught students. A large study in eight Newark, New Jersey schools comparing the progress of first-grade classes taught with traditional whole-word methods with those taught with traditional methods plus supplementary phonics found that "the instructor mattered more than phonics or no phonics."[166] Similarly, researchers from Peabody College who compared the results of phonics and nonphonics instruction across the first three grades found a weak positive effect for phonetic drills.[167]

Kirk's premise that a program of intensive phonetic drills would yield encouraging results for children with reading defects had inconclusive support from prior research. The New Hampshire researchers observed that students who struggled to learn to read, specifically "foreign children, those having impediments of speech, and those who had previously formed bad habits of pronunciation,"[168] profited greatly from phonetic drills. To the contrary, the Peabody College study concluded that "bright children seem to be helped more by training in phonetics than are the dull."[169]

The Kirk-Hegge approach involved an intensive regimen of synthetic phonetic drills, graduating upward from memorization of the most common single sound-letter combinations into blends, whole words, and finally sentences. The system relied greatly on the memorization of what would later be called word families, monosyllabic units that vary only in the initial or final consonant sound.[170] Drawing from his Master's thesis at Chicago, Kirk also employed a small element of Fernald's kinesthetic instruction, often involving manual tracing of letters in addition to phonetic training.[171] Hegge described the program as an attempt to build up the "necessary associative connections and desired perceptual and response habits,"[172] creating patterns of relationship between mental images within the child's brain through sheer repetition.

Kirk's years working with Thorlief Hegge and the children of the Wayne School bathed him deeply in the waters of practicality. Hegge placed a high priority on the development of a program of reading intervention for children with reading defects and the demonstration, through the aggregation of a large set of clinical cases of success, of the program's effectiveness. Hegge had little interest in pioneering new psychological or educational theory, and Kirk was thoroughly engrossed in the first serious challenge of his career—creating a way to teach reading to kids that most professionals had written off as uneducable.

EARLY MENTAL TRAINING

When Sam Kirk left the Wayne County Training School to direct the special education faculty at the Milwaukee State Teachers College, he threw himself headlong into meeting the administrative and pedagogical challenges of running a teacher education program.[173] He also undertook the writing of *Teaching Reading to Slow Learning Children*. The book proved to be significant not as an advance in his thinking on reading instruction, for it was primarily a summation of his Wayne School work, but because it was a rare volume written for public school teachers about the instruction of reading to children with mental retardation. Kirk broadened the IQ boundaries of reading potential that Hegge had pronounced, stating that most children with IQ levels above 50 could learn to read if provided proper instruction. The book gave great attention to the details of teaching practice, offering pages upon pages of useful exercises, lessons, and advice drawn from the Wayne School years. In line with his new role as teacher educator, Kirk wanted to communicate not with researchers but with teachers in order to not only convince them of the capacities of mentally deficient children but to also guide them toward effective classroom practices.[174]

Behind the practice focus of *Teaching Reading to Slow Learning Children* were the initial outlines of Kirk's next project—a psychological theory of language activity based in areas of mental functioning. Psychology could undertake the dramatic challenge of educating human intelligence through identifying and training the main functional activities of the mind. The basic intellectual concerns and contours that would come together ultimately in his development of the Illinois Test of Psycholinguistic Abilities in 1961 were present in his thinking by 1940.[175]

In 1938, University of Chicago psychometrist L. L. Thurstone published his factor analysis of 240 subjects taking 60 different intellectual tests, resulting in the identification of seven primary mental abilities constituted within the broad construct of intelligence.[176] Two years later, Kirk developed a special class curriculum for six to seven-year-olds with mental retardation in the Milwaukee Public Schools. The program specifically used games and exercises to train the children in Thurstone's seven areas of mental ability.[177] Kirk considered Thurstone's formulation to be only "a partial answer"[178] to the question of identifying the specific mental operations that constituted intelligence. But Thurstone offered compelling support for Kirk's understanding of the mind as a multifunctional entity. His experiences working with children had grounded him in the practical arts of devising many ways of improving levels of skill in areas such as language use, memory, visual memory, auditory memory, and oral pronunciation.

Once again, Kirk was to be strongly influenced by the work of Marion Monroe. In his days as a graduate student and a researcher at the Wayne School, Kirk had been a close follower of her work on the diagnosis of reading disorders through the use of educational tests. That approach primarily involved the measurement of surface behaviors, errors in oral reading, not the deep "study of mental activity"[179] that Professor Carr recommended for functionalist psychology. But Kirk had been attracted to the practical utility of her work in guiding reading remediation.

By the late 1930s, Monroe's latest instrument, her *Reading Aptitude Tests*,[180] had become the cornerstone of Kirk's thinking on the diagnosis of reading problems among mentally retarded children.[181] The *Tests* provided a "profile of abilities"[182] required for effective reading, a set of basic mental functions needed for reading that was analogous to Thurstone's primary mental abilities. In Monroe's measure of five areas of reading-related ability, Kirk saw an organizing scheme for the prophylactic treatment of reading defects and other learning difficulties. He envisioned a program of exercises designed to prepare the young mind to learn.

> Since no one has attempted to train the primary mental abilities, it is not known whether such training is possible. Furthermore training of specific functions may not transfer to other mental activities. Whether or not mental maturity can be accelerated.... must await experimentation in this field. However recent evidence on the educability of intelligence is a hopeful sign; if future experimentation shows the way, mental maturity can be accelerated.[183]

Kirk's initial outline of possible mental training involved exercises in the following five areas: language development, language and memory, visual discrimination and memory, auditory discrimination and memory, and oral pronunciation. These closely matched the five subtests of Monroe's *Reading Aptitude Tests*.

Kirk's vision of a program of early mental training based on Monroe's measure of reading aptitude seemed expansive and ambitious, given the highly circumscribed focus of Monroe's Tests. Kirk culled a powerful theory of intellectual operations from a virtually atheoretical psychometric instrument designed to predict only reading achievement at the end of first grade. Monroe's aptitude measure evaluated a small aggregation of behavioral performances closely connected to early reading success. More specifically, it was constructed "to indicate special weakness or peculiarities,"[184] to briefly tap into factors that correlated with future reading problems. The five subtests, each consisting of two or three brief exercises, were selected not because each addressed a necessary element of mental functioning necessary to reading performance. To Monroe's thinking, the value of each subtest as well as the composite score resided solely in their predictive capacity, the ability of the test to mathematically forecast which students would be strong or weak readers by the end of first grade. The correlation value of the composite score and two well-known tests of oral reading at the end of first grade was .75.

Monroe provided no additional rationale for the selection of areas of appraisal other than to note that they were drawn from her prior study at the Institute for Juvenile Research in Chicago and from unpublished research in the Pittsburgh Public Schools. Her strategy was not to formulate a theory of reading consisting of five elements and then devise measures of each. Rather, it would seem that she had endeavored to build a way to test for the tell-tale indicators of reading failure derived from years of her own experiences in the field.

Why did Kirk see a grand theory of intellectual functions and an initial framework for the "training of intelligence"[185] in what appeared to be a piecemeal bundle of factors that fairly reliably predicted the reading achievement of seven-year-olds? A partial answer begins with a dinner with Harold Skeels in Milwaukee in 1939. Skeels was a researcher at the Iowa Child Welfare Research Station who was in town to deliver a lecture on his latest research. He told a story at dinner that profoundly affected Kirk's thinking.[186] In a 1981 conference presentation, Kirk recalled Skeels' account:

> When visiting an Iowa orphanage, Skeels had been informed by the superintendent of that institution that two one-and-a-half-year-old babies who seemed unable to respond to their environment had been brought to the orphanage…The officials believed that the babies were "feebleminded" and should be in an institution for mental defectives. Skeels obtained a mental rating on these children on the Kuhlman test of mental development and found that the observations were correct; the IQ's were very low.… Skeels persuaded the superintendent of that institution to admit these two babies under special conditions. They were to be placed with adult mentally defective women, each child in a different ward. Later Skeels visited the state institution. In one of the adult wards he found the bright-looking little girl, talking, laughing and playing. He asked where she had come from and was informed that this was the girl that he had brought there some months before. He again administered the Kuhlmann Test to her and found that her IQ was near normal. The experience was repeated with the other child in the ward, who also was found to be of average intelligence. Apparently, these two little girls had tremendous attention from the adult women, who played with them and talked to them continually during the day. These two children had received an extraordinary amount of early stimulation.

This narrative, as well as the series of studies completed by Skeels and his colleagues at the Iowa Station supporting the plasticity of early intelligence, convinced Kirk "that there is a large range with which the environment can raise or lower IQ."[187]

Skeels' influence on Kirk was due to more than the Iowa Station research. Kirk's graduate work at Chicago had included a thorough study of the relatively new field of mental measurement, including the translated writings of French psychologist Alfred Binet, the inventor of the first scale of individual intelligence. At that dinner, Skeels shared with Kirk an unpublished English translation of a 1911 paper by Binet called "The Educability of Intelligence."[188] Kirk had never seen this Binet manuscript before. It contradicted Kirk's prior belief that Binet viewed intelligence as a constant trait, immune to environmental influence. The paper "presented a curriculum to develop memory, attention, reasoning, language, and other vectors of intelligence."[189] What Skeels taught Kirk was that Binet had developed his intelligence test with the specific purpose of turning immediately to training intelligence. He believed in the assessment of mental activity only as the first half of a complete process of education. But Binet died only six years after he created his IQ test, leaving his work incomplete. Subsequently, American psychologists proceeded under the mistaken impression that the measurement of intelligence stood alone as a valid psychological procedure. The lesson that Kirk drew from Binet's 1911 paper was that educational diagnosis requires the next logical step: practical utilization in instructional practices. Diagnosis and instruction must be unified.

The Binet thesis of the educability of intelligence—bolstered by Skeels' research, and further sanctified by Skeels' role as the traveling messenger bearing the unknown Binet manuscript—had a profound impact on Kirk. As he became an active public speaker in the 1950s and the 1960s, spreading the science and practice of special education across the United States and abroad, the powerful story of Binet's lost lesson became a central feature of Kirk's stump speech. Cloaked in all the dramatic mystery of a posthumous message delivered from the famous French psychologist, yet also supported by the scientific research of the Iowa Station, Binet's death-halted mission of educating intelligence was embraced by Kirk as his own professional calling. With Kirk as the primary voice of the developing field of special education, the Binet-Skeels ethos would become the proper objective of the new profession.[190]

Kirk's ambitious appropriation of Monroe's aptitude tests demonstrated his growing belief in the power of psychology and education to dramatically improve young minds. Certainly this was a strong theme in Hegge's research shop, the belief that even mentally deficient children had far more learning potential than most professionals assumed. Kirk believed that although inherited intellectual characteristics provided a general range of mental potential, environmental influences accounted for a significant portion of the final level of intellectual ability. For example, he explained that a child born with a specific inherited mental disposition might, due to environmental variation, achieve an IQ as low as 70 or as high as 110.[191] Given the wide breadth of possibility, the future of educational programming was in the deliberate and profound modification of the capacities of the human mind.

SPECIAL EDUCATION AT ILLINOIS

In 1947, after serving in the military for five years during World War II, Kirk accepted a faculty position at the University of Illinois. He almost immediately began forming the Institute for Research on Exceptional Children, the organizational home for his research and training activities for the next two decades. University president George D. Stoddard, formerly the director of the Iowa Child Welfare Research Station, served as a strong supporter of Kirk's early efforts to set up and seek external funds for the Institute.[192]

In 1949, Kirk embarked on an ambitious study of preschool education that he viewed as his continuation of the environmental work of Harold Skeels, his own embodiment of the legacy of Alfred Binet.[193] The large-scale experimental project would ultimately provide further confirmation of his belief in the educational training of the intelligence of young children.

Kirk and his Illinois research team compared four groups of young children (ages three to six) with low IQs (between 45 and 80) over three to five years of development: (1) 28 children living at home who took part in preschool programs, (2) 26 children living at home who did not attend preschool programs, (3) 15 children living in institutions who attended preschool programs, and (4) 12 children living in institutions who did not attend preschool programs. The purpose of the study was to investigate the extent to which early preschool programs could promote intellectual development for both mentally retarded children living in institutions and those living with their families, regardless of whether the low intellectual functioning had an organic or environmental cause. The children were tested at the beginning of the experiment, during the preschool period, prior to leaving the preschool, and then at regular intervals for up to five years.

Kirk calculated statistical comparisons of IQ scores between the experimental (preschool) and control (no preschool) groups. Since he believed that "this kind of statistical approach alone is limiting and narrow,"[194] case studies were also compiled for each of the experimental children. The case studies involved "clinical judgments of the dynamics of growth and the synthesis of nonquantitative information from observations."[195] Cases generally included information on the child's family, early developmental history, medical and psychological status of the child, educational progress within the preschool program, summaries of psychometric testing at various intervals, and follow-up data. Intelligence test measures were interpreted within an overall psychological profile of a developing, growing child.

Changes in intelligence measures provided strong support for the environmental thesis. The Institution Experiment Group began with a mean IQ of 61 and gained an average of 12 points by the completion of the preschool program. The Institution Contrast Group that did not attend preschool started with a mean IQ of 57.1 and dropped an average of 7.2 points during the project period. Neither group's IQ changed significantly in follow-up examinations. The Community Experimental Group had a mean IQ of 72.5 at the initiation of the project and gained an average of 11.2 IQ points by the end of their preschool education. The Community Contrast Group that did not attend the preschool program began at 75.8 mean IQ and decreased by less than one point during the preschool period. At one year follow-up, even after a year of attending the local public school, the Community Experimental Group's mean IQ was almost unchanged. The Contrast Group, however, gained an additional 7.5 points, "presumably...the result of school experience."[196]

Kirk later reported that "six of the 15 children" in the Institutional Experimental Group "were salvaged from institution life and paroled to family life: whereas none of the contrast group—not one child—was paroled from the institution."[197] One of that group of six later graduated from college and became a junior high school teacher. Accounts of this research project became a staple of Kirk's oft-told stories of Binet and Skeels, and a mainstay in his belief in the educability of intelligence, for years to come. It became the essential founding narrative of the new American profession of special education. Children who had hidden potential that could be effectively discovered and cultivated through professional intervention were saved from lives of isolation and degradation. The untold portion of the story was that those children who lacked such potential or who did not respond to professional treatment were, by default, left behind. Sitting on the shoulders of Hegge and Monroe, Kirk dramatically built optimism on a plan of individual correction and greatly expanded the bounds of that educational hope, but those bounds only extended so far.[198]

POOR MINDS

The Binet-Skeels narrative of hope and reclamation not only had a limited reach but also led to a profound assertion concerning the quality of home environment provided by lower-income families. The experimental study of preschools for mentally deficient young children convinced Kirk of the presence of child-rearing deficiency in low-income families. The environmental thesis of Binet and Skeels, of the Iowa Child Welfare Research Station and the Research Department of the Wayne County Training School, held that young minds could be greatly improved through educational provision and environmental enhancements. On the underside of that seemingly optimistic ethos was a much harsher proposal. If certain kinds of environments, such as preschool programs, supplied growing minds with the right kinds of stimulation, it only made sense to assume that certain other types of less stimulating environments actually constrained or even damaged young minds.

Perhaps there were home environments and families that offered young children environments of such insufficient stimulation and experience that they literally caused mental retardation. Kirk pursued this thesis and arrived at some troubling conclusions. One portion of his case study analysis involved the collection of information about the experimental children's families and home conditions. Three social workers employed by Kirk rated each home as adequate, semi-adequate, or inadequate in light of a list of six family or home conditions that "might retard the child's development."[199] Past research, such as the work of Harold Skeels, summed up the quality of the home environment chiefly through measures of parents' educational attainment and rankings of the father's occupational status.[200] This tended to perpetuate an assumption that families with low income provided deficient home environments for the intellectual development of young children. Kirk's approach expanded the usual measures of home quality to a list of six factors viewed as indicators of environmental inadequacy.

1. Low educational level of the parents, as indicated by leaving school prior to the completion of the elementary grades.
2. Below-average intelligence of the parents as revealed by available test records, or by impressions of the social worker and the preschool teachers.
3. Dependency of the parents on private or public social agencies, or on relatives, for financial support or social services.
4. Parent attitudes of overprotection or rejection, based on reports by the social worker and the preschool teachers.
5. Low moral standards in the home, as indicated by the police records or neighborhood complaints.
6. Inadequate housing conditions, such as gross overcrowding, or lack of minimal facilities for heating, lighting, and plumbing.[201]

The expanded framework generally maintained the prior assumption that social class correlated closely with quality of parental care and intellectual stimulation.

Kirk described families who failed to provide adequate environments as "psycho-socially deprived."[202] His explanation of the term illuminates the social class dimension in his thinking. "The term 'psycho-social' has been used here to emphasize the psychological climate of the home as well as the socioeconomic level."[203] This conflation of the family's psychological health with its social class status is evident in the fact that three of the six criteria (numbers 1, 3, and 6) used in the evaluation of family adequacy revolved around the family income factor. Low levels of educational attainment, acceptance of social welfare benefits, and substandard housing were all common features of lower class life in the early 1950s.

On the basis of the evaluation of the children's homes, done in conjunction with the trajectory of intelligence measures of individual children over time, Kirk concluded:

> Children living in psycho-socially deprived homes who do not attend preschool tend either to remain at the same rate of development or to drop to a lower level. On the other hand, a majority of the children from the same homes who attended preschool received compensation for their inadequate home environment sufficient to accelerate the rate of development.[204]

Environmentally deprived families harmed the intellectual growth of young children. Preschool programs could partially offset this damage, although "there is a point beyond which the effect of family conditions cannot be rectified by the school environment."[205]

The insult perpetuated by inadequate families on the minds of young children was sufficient for Kirk to raise an alarm to social welfare agencies.

> A study of these families and their influence on the development should be of some concern to those interested in cultural etiologies of mental retardation. It should make us reconsider the belief that "a poor home or a poor mother is better than no home or no mother."[206]

Kirk repeatedly stated that children from "inadequate" homes should be removed from their family homes and placed in foster care in order to improve reduced intellectual functioning caused by psychosocial deprivation.

> Attempts to change the attitudes of parents, their child-rearing practices, and other factors in the home through sporadic interviews will not be sufficient to change the course of development of the children. It is necessary for society to consider more intensive changes of environment for children from psycho-socially deprived homes.[207]

These aggressive recommendations to remove children from families to foster care were based on the belief that raising a child in a limiting intellectual environment was a form of parental neglect or abuse.

A year after the publication of the experimental study, Kirk summed up his stance on poverty and intellectual capacity: "Slow-learning children tend to come from low socioeconomic backgrounds."[208] Years later, looking back on the study, Kirk and his wife Winifred commented,

> It is interesting to note that among the culturally different or economically disadvantaged we find some deficits which are probably due to disuse and lack of training rather than neurological origins.[209]

As a result of this experimental study, Kirk espoused a political stance that closely paralleled other writings by cultural deprivation theorists in the field of learning disabilities in the late 1960s.[210] Kirk came to the conclusion that the insufficient environment in lower-class homes was a primary factor that constrained the intellectual development of young children. Poor families provided young children with a limited range of life experiences that contributed to and, indeed, frequently caused mild to moderate mental retardation. His class-based social analysis served to, in James Carrier's words, "locate the source of poverty in poverty itself, particularly the home and child-rearing practices of the poor."[211] Insufficient intelligence and lack of money went hand in hand in certain families. The solution was to educationally raise the level of children's intelligence through their removal from the deficient family.

HOW TO TRAIN THE MIND

In the early stages of the massive five-year study, Kirk and his team set up the preschool programs for the experimental groups. Traditional notions of mental retardation would suggest that all children with substandard IQs were essentially alike in their educational needs. The research team wanted "to organize an educational program for these children according to their needs."[212] Kirk was aware of the inability of existing psychological and educational tests to actually provide a detailed understanding of each child's abilities, to describe what each child "could and could not do."[213] Kirk was not thinking merely about what each child could do in terms of the curriculum or the range of typical classroom activities. What he wanted was a profile of mental functions much like what he had originally envisioned growing out of Marion Monroe's aptitude tests: "We concluded that what we needed for the educational assessment of these children was an intraindividual test; a test that would tell us in what areas a child was successful or unsuccessful."[214]

Between 1951 and 1961, Kirk developed the first edition of the Illinois Test of Psycholinguistic Abilities (ITPA). It became the paragon of psycholinguistic assessment instruments, often viewed as being synonymous with learning disabilities diagnosis, achieving widespread utilization in the United States. Its tremendous status as a means of diagnosing intraindividual mental and linguistic abilities supported the growing popularity of a psycholinguistic process approach to treating learning disabilities that remained popular through the early 1980s.[215]

The initial conceptual framework for the ITPA was a modification of Monroe's five areas of behavior related to reading success. Kirk dropped Monroe's tests of pure motor activity, activities such as tracing a line with a pencil and tapping dots in the center of circles as fast as possible. He was interested only in those motor activities that were directly related to language use. But he retained all of her areas that emphasized language, memory, and visual perception skills. The one area of deep psychological ability that was missing in Monroe's behavioral approach to pre-reading skills was mental association, the "mediating process of seeing relationships and integrating concepts."[216] Although Kirk's interests were no less practical than Monroe's, his goal was more far-reaching than the prediction of reading behavior. He wanted to appraise the psychological operations that serve as the functional foundations of childhood learning in order to design programs of intellectual training. That required some attempt to examine cognition, at least in relation to how the mind handles language-based forms of ideation.

NEURONS THAT LEARN

The ITPA, initiated in 1951, first published in 1961 and revised later in 1968, was the centerpiece of the psycholinguistic processes approach to learning disabilities treatment. Kirk and his colleagues developed the ITPA in an effort to build a clinical, psychoeducational framework that allowed remedial teachers to pinpoint specific areas of communication deficit and apply instructional treatments to improve functioning in those areas.[217]

Despite his frequent critique of the medical model of brain injury, and contrary to James Carrier's claim that the ITPA constituted an "abandoning of neuropathology,"[218] Kirk did not fully detach his theoretical work from the neurological concept of learning. His theory overlaid the neurological foundation with a fresh coat of early cognitive psychology. Kirk's psycholinguistic process theory of language functioning affixed a conduit model of communication transfer onto the prior concept of learning as biophysical activity in the central nervous system. He built the ITPA on the foundation of a neurological functioning model developed by cognitive psychologist Charles E. Osgood, augmented by aspects of a brain theory created by University of Chicago researcher Joseph Wepman.

The contributions of these theorists allowed Kirk to move forward into a clinical, educational practice dedicated to the remediation of basic psychological processes without neglecting a neurological explanation of learning difficulties made prominent in the Wayne School's brain injury science.[219]

Osgood was a psychologist who befriended Kirk at the University of Illinois. At Kirk's urging, Osgood developed a model suitable to Kirk's diagnostic-remediation needs. Osgood then served as a consultant in the development of the ITPA. When Kirk wrote to his colleague in March 1959 about the difficulties in developing tasks that fully measured all aspects of his friend's model,[220] Osgood wrote back, "I would like to see the new battery be as closely related to the theoretical model as possible—but I'm sure it's the obscurity of the theory as well as the limitations of our own ingenuity that has made this difficult."[221]

Osgood's obscure theory was crucial to Kirk's research, for it included the innovative and eminently useful idea that neurons learn. The Osgood model provided an explanation of linguistic processing that theorized neurons as biophysical components that are effectively modified by sensory experience. It imported then-popular concepts of behavioral conditioning into the gray matter of the brain, thereby explaining the brain's development of symbolic semantic operations, of attaching meaning to symbols, as a result of activities of neural conditioning based on human experiences with linguistic symbols. Simply put, through a process of cellular conditioning, the brain learns how to associate meaning with oral and written linguistic symbols.

Osgood theorized this neuro-learning through an application of the Hullian stimulus-response conditioning psychology of the 1950s to the relations between neurons in the brain and external stimuli received as sensory signals. In this theory, neurons in close proximity relate to one another through patterns of conditioning. The repeated, associated firing of two proximal neurons builds a tendency for each to then operate with some degree of dependency on the other. Just as an organism may be conditioned to exhibit a second behavior through repeated patterns of association with a first behavior, thereby creating a linkage between the two behaviors such that the stimulus promoting the first behavior will tend to also promote the second, so too occurs the activation of associated neurons in the brain related to one another.

When this co-stimulation of adjacent neurons occurs frequently, the stimulus for the firing of one neuron can become sufficient to provoke the firing of the associated second.

> I suggest that *with high frequency of stimulus or response pairing the central correlates of one will become a sufficient condition for the excitation of the other.* I shall call this *evocative relation.*[222]

The conditioned pairing of associated neurons is the linking mechanism that results in complex chains and intricate webs of stimulus-linked neurons. Given a complex arrangement of associated neurons, "it means that the initiation of some elements of a response pattern will set the whole pattern going."[223] Through the development of networks of conditioned neuron associations, the brain builds response patterns that operate as parallels to the complex sensory signals of linguistic input. The linguistic patterns of sounds and symbols experienced as sensory input by the human organism becomes, through gradual processes of neural conditioning, isomorphic with the mirrored internal patterns of neuron activity. In this way, the brain actually learns (or becomes conditioned) to respond internally with a complexity that matches the complexity of the linguistic signals received by the sensory nervous system.

In Osgood's theory, evocative relations explained on a neural basis how the brain develops the capacity to respond in an orderly, patterned way to the most basic units of symbolic formulation: phonemes and syllables. Additionally, he theorized that a less powerful version of such conditioned relations allows the brain to adapt to the broader regularity of linguistic input, the grammatical structure that limits linguistic input to formulae of repeated behavioral patterns. These less powerful neural relations occur when stimulus-response pairings occur at low levels of frequency.

> With a lower frequency of stimulus or response pairing, the central correlates of one will become merely a condition for "tuning up" the correlates of the other. I shall call this a predictive relation.[224]

Predictive relations as a form of neural conditioning are less certain than evocative relations, so they rely on the "probabilistic character with the grammatical restrictions in the language as a whole."[225] Due to the relatively low power of these associations between neurons, the stimulus-response pairings are patterned based only on probabilities of associated firing. But probabilities suffice when responding to a highly regular, static stimulus system. Osgood viewed the grammatical structure of language as just such a highly regular system, providing a consistency of input to which the predictive relations could respond effectively if not perfectly.

Osgood's theory supplied Kirk with a way of theorizing learning as simultaneously biophysical and psychological, as an activity both in the brain—the material activities of neurons that can be conditioned and reconditioned through modifications in human sensory experience—and in psychological behavior. This idea was central to his contention that a remedial program could yield improved functioning at a psychological process level that existed as a fundamental substrate to academic learning. If neurons, as the physical components that grant meaning to linguistic symbols, could be altered by intentional patterning of sensory input—indeed, if neurons could *learn* through strategic arrangement of specific kinds of sensory experiences—then a program of psycholinguistic remediation having lasting effects would be feasible. This was Kirk's goal, the development of a program of educational remediation that trained the deep psycholinguistic processes of encoding, associating, and decoding symbols, thereby building up the underlying neural capacities that he viewed as the essential fundament of school-based academic learning. His focus in the ITPA and the remedial activities was the measurement and treatment of ineffective psycholinguistic processes. By housing this practical activity within Osgood's model of neural conditioning, his work united the Goldstein-Strauss emphasis on neurological activity with his own interest in psychological process treatment.

BLOCKED CONDUITS: DYSFUNCTIONAL COMMUNICATION PROCESSES

Linguist Michael J. Reddy's description of the conduit metaphor of communication neatly captures the theory of language use encapsulated in Kirk's model of language learning. According to the conduit metaphor,

> Language *transfers* human thoughts and feelings.... A person who speaks poorly does not know how to use language to send people his thoughts; and, conversely, a good speaker knows how to transfer his thoughts perfectly via language.[226]

This understanding of language relies on the metaphorical assumption that thoughts and feelings are like parcels that are physically passed from one person's brain to another's through spoken or written symbols. Language difficulties, when viewed as inhering in an individual's neurology and psychology, involve failures of mental transfer—dysfunctions in the activities of receiving, emitting, or internally managing parcels of symbolic meaning.

Kirk's language learning model consisted of a multifaceted conduit system involving (a) two primary channels of communication flow, (b) three psycholinguistic processes, and (c) two levels of overall organization.

The two communication channels were theorized as "the routes through which the content of communication flows,"[227] the main sensory and motor modalities through which linguistic symbols are received (input) and then expressed (output). Kirk called these two "the auditory-vocal channel" and "the visual-motor channel," terms indicating the functional priority of hearing and vision as communication reception modalities and of vocalization or other motor activity as outputs.[228] The auditory-motor channel is "the course by which sensory impressions are received through the ear and responses expressed verbally." The visual-motor channel is "the course by which sensory impressions are received through the eye and responses expressed through gesture and movement."[229]

The three psycholinguistic processes "constitute learned habits necessary for language usage." These are specific activities of message transfer within a pathway that begins with sensory input, ends with communicative expression, and theorizes the hidden semantic activity occurring in between. *Decoding* is receptive translation of sensory inputs into meaning. *Association* is the central process by which decoded inputs are organized, managed, and symbolized such that encoding can occur. *Encoding* is the act of expressing ideas through words or gestures. These three interdependent processes operate in a sequential order from decoding to association to encoding.[230]

Osgood's original theory included three levels of representation: projection, integration, and representation. He described the projection level as comprising "wired in" neural activities involving simple reflexes. Osgood deemed these responses as "unaffected by experience," and thus without the possibility of learning or conditioning.[231] Given Kirk's emphasis on promoting learning in the neural and psychological process activity, he dropped this level out and adopted (with slightly different terminology) Osgood's two more complex levels for the ITPA. The simpler of the two was the *automatic-sequential* level (synonymous with Osgood's integration). It primarily involves Osgood's predictive relations for the purpose of basic sound and symbol sequencing. Additionally, Wepman's idea of a memory bank was incorporated to retain and retrieve a residue of psycholinguistic activity.

> Activities requiring the retention of symbol sequences and "automatic" habit chains are mediated at this level. A child repeating "da da da" to his father's urgings without having any established meanings for his utterances is operating at this linguistic level.[232]

This level involves all aspects of language learning that do not involve attaching meaning to symbols. It is structural, imitative, and pre-semantic.

The higher cognitive functions of issuing meaning to auditory or vocal symbols occur in the *representational* level. Activities at this level rely heavily on Osgood's evocative relations. Kirk's descriptions of activity at the highly complex levels of symbolic processing were generally very brief, little more than two to three sentences, and came with a direction to the reader to consult Osgood. By contrast, Osgood's theoretical explications were extensive and complicated.

Osgood's theoretical formulation of how patterns of neuron conditioning add up to symbolic comprehension began with an example of a baby responding to the sight of a bottle. The baby has already experienced milk, and the milk stimulus elicits her consistent responses of salivation and excited behavior. But how does the baby engage in symbolic behavior? How does the baby learn to respond to the bottle as a sign of the presence of milk? Over time, the baby's responses to the milk become extended to the bottle. When she sees the bottle, she salivates and demonstrates excitement. Osgood called the milk a *significate*.

> I define significate as any pattern of stimulation which regularly and reliably elicits a predictable pattern of behavior.... Whenever a neutral stimulus (sign-to-be) is paired with a significate and this pairing occurs sufficiently close in time to a reinforcing state of affairs, the neutral stimulus will acquire an increment of association with some distinctive portion of the total behavior elicited by the significate.[233]

Since the significate is a stimulus with a relatively reliable relationship with specific responses, the pairing of that significate with a second stimulus results in a less consistent but important new stimulus-response relationship. The second stimulus—in the baby example, the bottle—is now a sign, a symbol that stands in for the first stimulus because it elicits some subset of the total response effects of that significate. What Osgood accomplished in this theory of symbolic mediation was a design for a mechanism using the fairly limited stimulus-response psychology of his day whereby the brain develops habits of signification and meaning.

Kirk's utilization of this theory of psycholinguistic symbolic behavior was important for three distinct reasons. First, given Osgood's housing of this behavioral conditioning within the neural activities of the brain, Kirk's science remained tethered to the scientific legitimacy of the Goldstein-Strauss neurological foundation of a learning disorder. Second, Kirk added a layer of contemporary cognitive psychology. In practical terms, this provided some distance from the medical orientation of the older neuroscience and opened the door to a psychoeducational, clinical practice of diagnosis and remediation. Finally, with Osgood's orientation to the brain as a learning mechanism that is conditioned into semantic linguistic activity through the accumulated experience of sensory input, Kirk asserted that learning occurs at the deepest, most profound levels of psychological and neurological activity. The most fundamental communicative and symbolic activities of the brain—in this case, the defective or dysfunctional brain—could be permanently modified by the provision of a program of sensory experiences. This assertion fueled a professional optimism about the prospect of improving intellectual functioning through intervention.

ON HUMAN DIFFERENCES

The result of Kirk's ITPA-based approach to instructional remediation was a shift in educational emphasis from what he called "interindividual differences" to "intraindividual differences."[234] From his work with Marion Monroe and Ted Hegge, Kirk had learned that if education diagnosis was to supply useful information for treatment, it must move beyond simply classifying children under disorder categories. It must offer some insightful interpretation of the internal workings—most importantly failings—of the individual mind in order to provide guidance to remediation. The traditional practice of classificatory diagnosis discerned interindividual differences, understandings of how an individual child compared to others, mapping an individual child on a nosological scheme involving normality and numerous disorders. What Kirk had developed with the ITPA was an approach to diagnosis that compared numerous levels of psychological functioning within one child. Marked discrepancies between performances among a child's different psychological abilities often exhibited as a learning problem. Treatment sought to improve specific areas of retardation.

Kirk touted his new approach to diagnosis of intraindividual differences because it supported targeted educational intervention. To his annoyance, however, he was not able to completely swear off use of traditional schemes of classification. Indeed, he asserted the existence of a distinct, new psychoeducational disorder characterized by an individual psychological profile of dramatically uneven levels of ability. The learning disability construct that he coined was a new disorder classification, a novel type of interindividual difference based on a problematic individual profile of intraindividual differences. Classificatory diagnosis must clearly distinguish the new learning-disabled child from the normal learner, as well as from the child with mental retardation and the child with emotional disturbance. Kirk's expertise in a psychological science of intraindividual differences was demonstrated in the development of the ITPA. But his struggles with systems of classification, with explaining how learning disability differed from other childhood disorders of learning and behavior, would prove to be his most frustrating and lasting challenge.

CHAPTER SIX

"One Definition Doesn't Include Everything": Samuel A. Kirk AND THE Learning Disability Concept

In November 1960, Samuel A. Kirk expressed his frustration with the seemingly unending task of defining disorder terms and concepts to his colleague Norris Haring of the University of Kansas.

> I think that we are still struggling with terminology as we have for the last fifty years in this field. One definition doesn't include everything, hence more definitions.[1]

Special education research was filled with concepts medical, psychological, and educational, producing not clarity and consensus but a continuous cycle of reconsideration and redefinition. Conceptual flaws and fissures in old constructs led to fresh patches and refashioned articulations that inevitably satisfied only some of the researchers. Soon enough dissatisfaction brought about new phrasings and rehashed combinations of definitional elements. Fresh formulations soon left some researchers wanting. And around and around it went.

Kirk viewed this kind of work as endless and annoying. His comment to Haring served as ironic foreshadowing of the role that Kirk would play over the next two decades in the new field of learning disabilities. He was quite dissatisfied with the usual diagnostic practices that classified children into disorder types. Procedures of classification were "administratively helpful but educationally unproductive,"[2] assisting bureaucracies with typological headcounts while offering little guidance to actual instruction. "I am more interested in discrepancies in development within an individual," Kirk wrote to a colleague in 1959, "than I am in comparing him with other individuals."[3] Yet he also worked feverishly through much of the next two decades to raise the learning disability classification into scientific, political, and popular legitimacy. He shouldered a substantial intellectual load in building (and rebuilding) the contents and parameters of the learning disability construct.

To some extent, the irksome task of setting the conceptual boundaries of learning disability classification was thrust upon Kirk. As the man widely considered by parents, professionals, and politicians to be the leading voice in American special education, Kirk's written and spoken words carried great weight. If only he could arrive at an unambiguous proclamation, the field of learning disabilities would perhaps move ahead with a degree of unity and consensus. Research would progress. Strong educational policies would be written at the state and federal levels. Effective treatment programs and instructional techniques would be developed and proliferated. Universities would prepare diagnostic-remedial teachers to work with learning-disabled students. With an eye on all of these practical ends, Kirk spent much of the 1960s and 1970s chasing after numerous versions of the learning disability concept, adding, cutting, modifying, redecorating, and then—as he well knew even before he began—doing it all again.

The purpose of this chapter is to provide an examination of the multiple, varied, and contradictory articulations of the concept of learning disability forwarded by Kirk between 1960 and 1984. In doing so, I am seeking two specific goals. First, I want to put in perspective Kirk's contributions to the science of learning disabilities by displaying the many theoretical quandaries and tensions that he confronted. My purpose in relation to Kirk's repeated efforts to recalibrate the learning disability concept is to illuminate both his intentions for the new construct, what he wanted the disorder concept to achieve in public education, and the unrelenting conceptual problems he wrestled with along the way.

Second, by casting a focused spotlight on the intellectual struggles that dogged the leading figure in the new, American scientific field of learning disabilities, I hope to shine a partial but bright light on the puzzles and uncertainties that faced the entire scientific field during the fever-pitched period of parent advocacy that led to public school programs for learning-disabled students in the 1970s. When Alfred Strauss and his Wayne School colleagues sculpted the dimensions of the brain injury syndrome, they worked in relative peace and solitude. There was no public dialogue of any volume or import around the education of brain-injured children in the 1940s. By the early 1960s, greatly in response to the research done by Strauss's team at the Wayne School, the heightened interest level among parents had already begun to place learning disabilities researchers into a fishbowl atmosphere. Their work and words suddenly gained significance far beyond what had historically been a small, low-profile coterie of scientists. Recontextualized within a political movement, a field of clinical knowledge and practice was captured in a pressurized container of parent advocacy and legislative activity. No researcher exemplifies the strains and struggles of this fevered recontextualization of the field of learning disabilities research more fully than Kirk. Working at the forefronts of both scientific development and political advocacy, he attempted to remain true to two masters, one scientific and one political, maintaining the integrity of the research basis of the disorder while taking pragmatic steps to pass legislation to support research, training, and public school services. Pulled in various directions by the differing requirements of science and policy, Kirk often found himself dealing with his own confusion.

CONFUSION FOUND

As early as 1967, at the conference of the Association for Children with Learning Disabilities in New York, Kirk asked, "Are we confused?"

> As I attend conferences of "learning disabilities" and look over programs of conferences and conventions, I am wondering whether or not the term "learning disabilities" has not now become so broad that it includes all problems of children.[4]

The new term had been adopted so quickly by such a wide range of parents and professionals that the meaning of learning disability had become nonspecific, wandering and stretching to each new case of learning difficulty or behavioral deviance. Kirk feared that learning disability would be applied to all children achieving below average, and the concept as he had hoped it would be understood would be essentially lost. He reiterated this complaint for many years. In 1970, he dubbed this the "bandwagon effect" and griped that some new experts in the field were giving bloated prevalence estimates as high as 30% of the child population.[5]

Kirk's complaint was not new in special education. Diagnostic classifications often moved like rudderless ships. In 1921, psychologist Wallace Wallin carped that mental deficiency had become the all-purpose whipping boy for many social critics. At that time, led by Henry H. Goddard's warning that the feebleminded were "a distinct menace to society,"[6] numerous researchers and commentators pinned virtually any problem of society on the coat sleeve of mental deficiency. Wallin railed against the "present day tendency to play fast and loose with such vague and undefined concepts as 'defective children,' 'mental deficiency,' 'mental defect,' 'defectiveness,' 'subnormality,' and 'feeblemindedness,' 'moronity,' and 'criminal imbecility.'" If one were to believe those who liberally applied such notions, "it would be possible to report almost any person as a case of 'mental defect' and thereby secure his lifelong incarceration in a custodial institution."[7]

Similarly worried about the careless application of the learning disability label to a growing laundry list of childhood learning and behavioral concerns, Kirk repeated his bandwagon lament for almost two decades.[8] In his 1977 ACLD (Association for Children with Learning Disabilities) presentation, he stated that

> a persistent problem has been the clarification of the definition and the concept of learning disabilities.... It may be that our parent and professional groups, as well as our journalists, have differing concepts of the learning disabilities and have consequently confused the public and our legislators. I must admit, too, that this had confused me.[9]

Kirk was far from alone in this view. Over the years, numerous committees and commissions were formed for the purpose of creating a single, best definition of learning disability. In 1975, the Division for Children with Learning Disabilities of the Council for Exceptional Children convened a special caucus to develop a consensus definition. Three working groups were established. One produced no result. The other two groups could not reach a common agreement.[10] Six years later, the National Joint Committee for Learning Disabilities brought together representatives from six professional groups—Association for Children and Adults with Learning Disabilities, American Speech-Language-Hearing Association, Council for Learning Disabilities, Division for Children with Communication Disorders, Council for Exceptional Children, International Reading Association, The Orton Dyslexia Society—to build a consensus across conflicting professions. Even the committee admitted that what they had achieved was only partially satisfactory to the participating groups.[11]

The practical result of the confusion over the learning disability concept, in Kirk's view, was that "learning disabilities programs in public schools are now including a great number of children who should not be classified as learning disabled."[12] Public school learning disability programs of the late 1970s were filled with a wide range of failing students, thereby limiting the ability of those programs to focus specifically on providing educational treatments for learning disabilities. In 1983, Kirk again reported that

> school districts have identified many children as learning disabled simply because they did not perform at grade level. Many of these children are slow learners, culturally or linguistically disadvantaged, or have had inappropriate instruction...If this practice continues, the learning disability programs are in danger of becoming dumping grounds for all educational problems.[13]

Kirk observed in 1984 that the public schools were still misusing learning disability as a broad category for virtually any child needing extra help: "Today...the term learning disability applies to nearly every kind of learning problem a child may encounter."[14]

TOO MUCH MEDICINE

Sam Kirk wrote two very different drafts of his 1967 ACLD speech about confusion in the field of learning disabilities. Both versions describe the problem as the outcome of too many disciplines conceptualizing and describing the disorder in too many ways.

> The various medical specialties have long been concerned with the physiological and structural correlates of specific learning disorders. Therefore we find pediatricians involved with those children, pediatric neurologists, psychologists, ophthalmologists, orthopedic physicians, and a host of other medical specialists, each concerned with their specific aspects of the physical condition of the child. Among the psychological profession, we have a variety of points of view about the child who does not learn, which of necessity add to the confusion by their extreme diversity. Among the language pathologists and speech correctionists we have a variety of opinions and procedures which add to the confusion among the professions in the field. Between general and special education, we find conflicting points of view as well as varying degrees of knowledge which compound the difficulties.[15]

The result was a "great confusion in terminology"[16] that hampered the effort to pass legislation recognizing learning disabilities. Legislators who turned to professionals for assistance in understanding the disorder confronted a chaotic cacophony of terms, phrases, and concepts.

Where the two drafts of the speech differed was in the remedy. In the initial version, Kirk proposed a solution. Very briefly, he urged the many professions involved in serving these children to clarify what constitutes a learning disability within their own disciplinary area. Kirk soon realized that asking each profession to reach greater clarity within its own theories and terms would not alleviate the problems of working across the disciplinary lines. He scrapped this ineffective idea.

To Kirk's thinking, the problem included but was also larger than miscommunication between multiple professions. The dominant discourse across all of the professions was medical, an orientation that placed an inordinate emphasis on complex and authoritative diagnostic classifications driven by theories of etiology. It was standard practice among pediatric physicians, speech pathologists, and neurologists alike to classify deviance according to highly technical and esoteric physiological explanations for learning and behavior problems. Beyond its lofty expertise and polysyllabic erudition, medicine offered little practical assistance for diagnosed children and their families. Parents traveling the obstacle course of knowledgeable childhood professionals were overwhelmed by one diagnosis after another, too often accompanied by advice that there was no treatment for this ailment.

Even in cases in which a specific neurological causation might be positively located, Kirk maintained that this scientific insight rarely guided the instructional remediation program.

> Knowing whether a reading disability stems from a lack of development of, or injury to, the angular gyrus, or some other area, does not, in most instances, alter the remedial procedure. The latter is generally dependent upon the behavioral symptoms rather than the neurological findings.[17]

Treatment must begin not with medical investigations but with a clear description of what a child could and could not do. Kirk abandoned his futile proposal after a few sentences. There was no use even trying to improve communications among professions haunted by an unworkable medical nosology.

In the revised draft of the speech, Kirk proposed no solution. He described the confusion via narratives of three sets of frustrated parents playing a modified Monopoly game, moving by chance across the game board in search of knowledge, solutions, and services from the many professions. With rolls of the dice, the families stumbled through a nearly random circuit of programs and treatments, professions and professional jargon. Their children's problems were defined, redefined, and treated in various ways depending on which professions they chanced upon. Kirk concluded that "it is no wonder that parents find it very difficult to play this game in an expedient and direct fashion."[18] The purpose of the revised speech was to illuminate the urgency and complexity of the confusion without even trying to offer a remedy.

The revised 1967 ACLD speech was unusual for Kirk. He was a man who tried and tried again to bring a remedy to the confusion. Moreover, he believed that he had a solution. He recommended education rather than medicine, teachers instead of doctors. Many disorders of learning and behavior could be successfully addressed by special educators. What was required was what he and his colleagues Strauss, Kephart, Frostig, and Barsch had been doing effectively for decades: adopting a clinical approach to educational treatment that began with a thorough diagnosis of areas of ability and disability followed by a one-to-one, intensive instructional regimen. Proper educational diagnosis had little concern for classifying children in comparison to one another and even less curiosity for the etiological source of the child's difficulties. Kirk's experience teaching reading at the Wayne School had taught him to gather the best available pedagogies into an intense educational program focused explicitly on jumpstarting child learning in areas of retardation. Skills and behaviors could be directly taught to the child. This was the roll-up-the-sleeves kind of pragmatism that Kirk espoused for the new field of special education. Standard discussions of etiological theory and physiological causation amounted to little more than swirls of pipesmoke rising slowly from soft leather chairs to the ceiling in hospital physicians' lounge.[19]

EXAMINING KIRK'S RECORD OF CONCEPTUAL CONTRIBUTIONS

If, by Kirk's appraisal, the learning disabilities construct had quickly become muddled in the early days of the learning disabilities movement, it would seem obvious that he might attempt to clarify the situation. Certainly, that was his explicit goal. Analyzing the content of Kirk's contributions to the learning disability concept, especially in light of the immense volume of his scholarly productivity, is no small order. I have gathered documented records of 20 occurrences—in professional speeches and published writings—when Kirk offered a description of the learning disability concept between 1960 and 1984.[20] Of these, 18 were attempts to deliver a complete distillation of all essential aspects of the disorder. Twice Kirk spoke or wrote in a partial way, focusing only on specific subelements of the diagnosis without providing a more total articulation.

Given the difficulty of wading through and interpreting Kirk's extensive record of spoken and written articulations of the learning disability concept, I have broken them down into their conceptual building blocks that I am calling *components*. I have identified 15 separate components that Kirk used and reused over the years. Each component was a meaningful element that, in and of itself, made a substantive contribution to the larger description of the disorder. Further, the presence or absence of an individual component made an essential difference to the meaning of the entire articulation. Typically Kirk combined between six and ten components to form the entire learning disability construct.

A brief example of what I mean by the term *component* should help to demonstrate this approach to the analysis of how Kirk conceptualized and reconceptualized the construct over the decades. In his first four descriptions, published or spoken between 1960 and 1963, Kirk included both a psychological process dysfunction and a neurological impairment as central features of the disorder. In a 1960 speech to the Illinois Psychological Association, his first articulation of the disorder on record, he described a learning disability as "a condition of the child, psychologically or biologically, which inhibits his ability to learn in school."[21] In a 1962 article coauthored with Barbara Bateman, he defined a learning disability as a problem "resulting from a psychological handicap caused by a possible cerebral dysfunction."[22] These early versions of the construct employed two distinct etiological components: a problem of psychological activity and a neurological or physiological defect. Beginning with an April 1963 speech to parent advocates in Chicago, Kirk dropped the neurological etiology component from his description. His subsequent articulations over the many years included the psychological process disorder component without the biophysical component present in his earliest work.

Table 2 details the components present in each of the 20 articulations that he made between 1960 and 1984. The 15 components utilized in describing the learning disability concept are labeled with the letters *A* through *O*. I will briefly define each of these.

Components *A* through *C* involved etiological theories that provided some causal explanation for the learning difficulty.

A. Intrinsic cause—deficit in psychological processes
B. Intrinsic cause—defect in neurological or biological processes
C. Intrinsic cause—emotional or behavioral disturbance

Components *D* through *I* were exclusionary factors, reasons for the learning difficulty that, if present, indicated that the problem was *not* a learning disability.

D. Environmental or cultural disadvantage (a lack of proper intellectual stimulation)
E. Poor quality of prior instruction in school
F. Lack of prior instruction in school (often due to poor attendance)
G. Sensory (hearing, vision) or motor impairments
H. Mental retardation
I. Emotional or behavioral disturbance

Components *J* through *N* described the co-morbidity or co-occurrence of learning disability with other childhood disorders. *J* was an intensified version of co-morbidity that pointed to a high level of correlation between learning disability and emotional or behavioral disturbance such that the two disorders were understood to be constitutionally linked. Components *K* through *M* indicated a co-morbidity of distinct disorders. Learning disability and each disorder could co-occur to create what Kirk called a "double handicap,"[23] but the two impairments were framed as essentially unrelated.

J. Constitutional correlation with emotional or behavioral disturbance
K. Co-morbidity with mental retardation

L. Co-morbidity with sensory (hearing, vision) or motor impairments
M. Co-morbidity with emotional or behavioral disturbance

Component *N* demonstrated Kirk's attempt to distinguish between levels of mental retardation in relationship to the learning disability diagnosis. Due to the general and total nature of the intellectual defect, severe mental retardation was understood to be a disorder quite unlike a learning disability. But mild mental retardation, he sometimes claimed, proved to be only a learning disability concealed behind a diagnostic disguise. Proper educational treatment would bring to light the concealed mental assets, the hidden potentials, in order to demonstrate when mild mental retardation was actually a learning disability.

N. Mild mental retardation as disguised or undiagnosed learning disability

Component *O* asserted that students with learning disabilities, unlike other students with academic learning difficulties who could learn adequately in the general classroom, required a special education program consisting primarily of one-to-one diagnostic-remedial tutoring.

O. Need for special education instruction

Table 2 Components of LD Construct in Kirk's Writings and Speeches, 1960–1984

	Date	A	B	C	D	E	F	G	H	I	J	K	L	M	N	O
1	Mar. 1960[24]	X	X	X	X	X	X									
2	1962[25]	X	X	X	X	X	X	X	X							
3	1962[26]	X	X	X	X	X	X	X	X							
4	Jan. 1963[27]	X	X	X	X	X	X	X	X		X					
5	April 1963[28]	X						X	X							
6	Dec. 1964[29]	X			X	X	X		X	X						
7	1966[30]	X		X				X	X			X	X		X	
8	1967[31]	X			X	X	X	X	X							X
9*	May 1967[32]											X			X	
10	1968[33]	X						X	X		X	X			X	
11	1971[34]	X			X		X	X	X	X	X		X		X	
12	1972[35]	X			X			X	X	X						
13	Nov. 1972[36]	X						X	X	X		X	X	X	X	
14	1976[37]	X			X			X	X	X	X	X		X	X	
15	1977[38]	X					X	X	X	X		X	X			X
16	1979[39]	X			X		X	X	X	X		X	X			X
17*	Mar. 1979[40]	X			X	X	X									X
18	1983[41]	X			X	X	X	X	X	X						X
19	1983[42]	X			X			X	X	X		X	X			X
20	1984[43]	X			X			X	X	X		X	X	X		X
	Total	19	4	5	15	8	13	16	17	10	4	10	6	3	6	7

* Paper or speech devoted not to entire concept but only to a specific one or two aspects.

Of the 18 total or complete articulations of the disorder, only two pairs (2, 3 and 16, 19) were wholly consistent with one another in terms of the components present. Thus, this record of complete conceptualizations actually consists of 16 distinct delineations of the disorder over 24 years.

In the midst of extensive conceptual variation, it should be noted that a handful of components were relatively consistent features in Kirk's pronouncements. Certainly, the notion of a dysfunction of psychological processes (A) was a mainstay within his thinking over the decades. Also, he employed a small series of exclusion factors with some regularity: Environmental or cultural disadvantage (D), Lack of prior instruction (F), Sensory (hearing, vision) or motor impairments (G), and Mental retardation (H).

The fact that components K (co-morbidity of learning disability and mental retardation) and N (notion of learning disability often disguised as mild mental retardation) were utilized only one time less than H (exclusion of mental retardation) points to a troubling theoretical cul-de-sac concerning the relationship between mental retardation and learning disabilities. What was the difference between the two disorders? This question deserves a closer examination.

CONFUSION MADE

Kirk undoubtedly fanned the fires of confusion as he tried to snuff them out. The single best example of how he often fueled the very conceptual tangle he lamented was his numerous attempts to clarify the relationship between learning disability and mental retardation. One of the central challenges to the development of learning disability as a unique concept was to explain how it related to the older, more established, and greatly trusted classification of children with mental retardation. Kirk's seemingly endless struggle to make clear this relationship is a frustrating tale of theoretical ambiguities and rhetorical miss-steps.

In early 1963, separated only by three months, Kirk delivered two remarkably different speeches. In January, he spoke to a small conference of brain injury researchers at the University of Illinois, a group that included Newell Kephart, Helmer Mykelbust, and Joseph Wepman. At that meeting of neurological scientists, he said that learning disability refers to

> a retardation, disorder, or delayed development in one or more of the processes of speech, language, reading, spelling, writing, or arithmetic resulting from a possible cerebral dysfunction and/or emotional or behavioral disturbance and not from

generalized mental retardation, sensory deprivation, or cultural or instructional factors.[44]

It was a disorder of the psychological processes with possible etiologies of neurological damage or emotional disturbance. He listed mental retardation among the excluded conditions. Or so it appeared. Later in the same presentation, he backtracked on this, then asserting that learning disability "does not refer to most mentally retarded children since the discrepancy between their ability and their achievement is not great."[45]

Kirk's use of the modifiers "generalized" and "most" introduced the possibility of exceptions to the mental retardation exclusion. Latour and Woolgar have described words like these as "grammatical modalities" that operate as "an expression of the *weight* of a statement," a register of factual status.[46] A modality can be used to either increase or dial down the degree of rhetorical facticity. Similarly, linguists use the term "hedge" to describe a word, phrase, or clause that effectively reduces the certainty, authority, or truth value of a statement. George Lakoff defines a hedge as language "whose job it is to make things fuzzier."[47] Kirk demoted the truth value of his statements, creating some room for doubt or alternative interpretation. Perhaps children whose mental retardation was not "generalized" could also have a learning disability.

Three years later, he would more clearly take just this position. If a child with mental retardation "has discrepancies among abilities, or if he has special abilities and marked disabilities, he could be classified as a child with a learning disability as well as overall mental retardation."[48] One could have a generally depressed profile of intellectual ability that still included significant gaps between high and low areas of functioning. He would articulate this same notion of possible co-morbidity of mental retardation (at least) 10 times between 1963 and 1984 (see Table 2).

But on that day in January 1963, the audience of neurological researchers focused on Kirk's exclusionary language and ignored the small trail of qualifiers. They interpreted Kirk as declaring that mentally deficient children could not also have a learning disability. Some expressed concern that this exclusion "was unnecessarily restrictive if not arbitrary."[49]

Three months later, in April 1963, speaking to a very different audience of parent advocates, Kirk presented a definition of learning disabilities that differed significantly from his statement to the scientific assembly.

> Recently, I have used the term "learning disabilities" to describe a group of children who have disorders in development in language, speech, reading, and associate communications skills needed for social interaction. In this group I do not include

children who have sensory handicaps such as blindness or deafness, because we have methods of managing and training the deaf and the blind. I also exclude children who have generalized mental retardation.[50]

The various etiologies of the disorder—including cerebral injury and emotional disturbance—were dropped completely. There was no theorized line of causation, only an existing developmental language problem. In this revision, the phrasing concerning mental retardation constituted an unequivocal exclusion. Contrary to what Kirk had suggested with the modifiers "most" and "generalized" a few months earlier, a child with mental retardation could not also have a learning disability.

It would appear that Kirk's presentation to the conference of parent advocates was, at least to some degree, an example of telling the audience what they wanted to hear. His presentation distanced learning disability from the highly stigmatized category of mental retardation. He avoided any talk of the causes of the learning problem. Whether one pointed to the standard etiologies of early brain injury, flawed genetic inheritance, or deficient environmental stimulation, it would be difficult to fully disentangle the parents in the audience from possible blame. Perhaps it was best not to mention causation at all.

This suggests that Kirk felt pressured by the parents to make certain statements in his speech. He later admitted to having mixed feelings about offering a definition of learning disability at the conference. He was wary about adding yet one more diagnostic label of questionable pedagogical value to the professional repertoire.[51] Immediately prior to providing a definition for learning disability, he professed to the audience his strong reluctance to do so.

> I have felt for some time that labels we give to children are satisfying to us but of little help to the child himself. We seem to be satisfied if we can give a technical name to a condition. This gives us the satisfaction of closure. We think we know the answer if we can a name or a label—brain injured, schizophrenic, autistic, mentally retarded, aphasic, etc. As indicated before, the term "brain injury" has little meaning to me from a management of training point of view. It does not tell me whether the child is smart or dull, hyperactive or under-active. It does not give me any clues to management or training…. I should like to caution you about being compulsively concerned about names and classification labels.[52]

In fact, Kirk invested more time and effort in the speech attempting to convince the listeners of the lack of educational utility of childhood disorder classifications than he spent on actually offering a definition of learning disability. Later, he recalled that "several [parents] approached me with the admonition that they needed help in the selection of a name for their proposed national organization."[53]

Under pressure, accompanied by words of caution and even mild protest, Kirk gave the parents the term and definition they wanted.

STEP FORWARD . . . AND BACK

Kirk often ensnared himself in a rhetorical trap by first making blanket statements that fully excluded children with mental retardation from the learning disability category, only to later backtrack with some attempt at clarification that allowed for a degree of overlap between the two conditions. The first half of this rhetorical two-step provided what seemed to be a much-needed pronouncement of how the learning disability was different from mental retardation. The second move, the back step, sought a more nuanced and delicate arrangement between the two disorders. The combination of the two steps created added confusion and cornered Kirk into the repetitive cycle of definition and redefinition that he disdained.

For example, in his 1966 book *The Diagnosis and Remediation of Psycholinguistic Disabilities*, Kirk described the child with a learning disability on the very first page. He boldly declared, "These children are not deaf or blind or mentally defective."[54] Later, on the same page, he explained in more depth that a mentally deficient child was quite different from the learning-disabled youngster he was writing about.

> A severely mentally defective child may show extreme retardation in language, speech, and all other communication processes. This child does not necessarily have a learning disability since a learning disability implies certain assets in addition to specific disabilities or wide discrepancies between abilities.

Once again, his brief use of two modifiers, "severely" and "necessarily," raised the question of whether a learning disability might be possible for a child whose mental deficiency was not severe. In the next sentence, though, rather than explaining how the conditions of mental retardation and learning disability might coincide, he alluded to problems of misdiagnosis. It was the case that "some children appear mentally retarded in the classroom and on intelligence tests but are actually children with learning disabilities."[55] This statement appeared to indicate that the two disorders were clearly distinct, but also that there was a problem with the misdiagnosis of learning-disabled children as mentally retarded. If one disorder could be misdiagnosed as the other, it would appear that the two classifications were quite distinct.

Or maybe not. On page two, Kirk again returned to the relationship between the two disorders.

> This point of view does not imply that a mentally retarded child, diagnosed as such by ordinary mental tests, cannot have a learning disability. If he has discrepancies among abilities, or if he has special abilities and marked disabilities, he could be classified as a child with a learning disability as well as overall mental retardation.[56]

In the first two pages of the text, Kirk asserted three theses. First, a child with a learning disability could not also have mental retardation. Second, at the point of ostensible overlap between the two disorders resided the problem of the misdiagnosis of some children with learning disabilities as having a mental deficiency. Third, a child with mental retardation could also have a learning disability. This kind of tangle was not uncommon for Kirk. Nine times, in speeches or publications between 1963 and 1984 (see Table 2), he described mental retardation both as an exclusionary factor *and* as a condition possibly co-occurring with a learning disability.

In the same 1966 text, Kirk provided psychological case studies of 10 children with psycholinguistic disabilities, demonstrating the use of the ITPA as the cornerstone of the process of diagnosis and remediation. Seven of the ten example cases were children with mental retardation. Kirk described one other case subject as having a borderline level of intelligence. What was communicated quite openly in these examples was that the child's classification according to level of intelligence or type of disorder was not germane to the practical task of designing and carrying out a program of remedial instruction. Classifying the child as mentally retarded or learning disabled amounted to a tangent from what Kirk viewed as the real challenge: diagnosing areas of psycholinguistic strength and weakness in order to provide remediation.

TALES OF POTENTIAL

Two months after the 1967 ACLD conference, Kirk gave an address entitled "Mental Retardation vs. Learning Disabilities" at the University of Minnesota in which he directly confronted the question of the relationship between the two disorders.[57]

Noting that learning disability and mental retardation were "two somewhat ambiguous concepts,"[58] he told numerous clinical stories of cases of children in his experimental preschool study who appeared to have mental retardation. For example, a four-year-old boy had been committed to an institution at age two-and-a-half with a diagnosis of mental retardation and a convulsive disorder by two physicians. The boy had no convulsions at the institution, but an electroencephalogram (EEG) was abnormal. His IQ was 60 and his "babblings were not intelligible."[59]

With six hours of preschool education this boy showed marked acceleration in speech and language development. His IQ rose from 60 and 70, to 80 and 90. At this point (5 ½), it was felt that he was ready for parole from the institution. He was placed in a foster home and in a community preschool. At age 6 ½ he tested 104 IQ on the Stanford-Binet and was placed in a regular first grade rather than a special class.[60]

In these accounts of educational stimulation and intellectual growth, Kirk appropriated the grand environmental narrative, the archetypal Binet and Skeels story of human transformation due to psychological intervention, of hidden potential unlocked by heroic educational provision. Early education turned defect into normality.

While Binet and Skeels stopped here at victory, Kirk's story went on to add a new twist. It was soon discovered in the regular first grade that this now-normal boy had great difficulty learning to read. Tests "of his abilities revealed some major deficiencies in the integration of sounds, and in the ability to learn words."[61] The child was then tutored in a systematic program of phonics, and his reading skills improved dramatically. This boy went on to experience tremendous educational success, graduating from high school and attending college. Kirk had "many such experiences with young children classified as mentally retarded, but whose abilities and disabilities were obviously discrepant."[62] These were actually children with learning disabilities whose condition had been misinterpreted as mental deficiency.

Ironically, Kirk's revision of the archetypal narrative of the Iowa Child Welfare Research Station, the tale of environmental influence and intellectual growth, positioned mental retardation as a condition lacking substantial learning potential. The childhood disorder that was packed with latent mental assets and possibilities for future success was the learning disability. Plucked from the dead end of misdiagnosed mental deficiency, the learning-disabled child could grow and achieve. Perhaps he might even excel. As psychology and education located true human potential in specific children, thus availing those youngsters of proper treatment and optimistic futures, it separated the wheat of learning disability from the chaff of mental retardation. The former was the fulfillment of the Iowa Station legacy. The latter was the human remnant left behind. Kirk made this point clear to the Minnesota audience.

The label of mental retardation tends to classify a child as belonging to a group who requires certain kinds of care, management, and education. The diagnosis of learning disabilities in educational circles implies that the child has certain assets and certain disabilities that may be amenable to remediation, or amelioration. My thesis this evening is a plea that mentally retarded children should be evaluated further so that we may institute remedial procedures for those mentally retarded children who show significant discrepancies in growth, cognition, perceptual, and communications skills. It is possible that a certain percentage, I do not know how large or small, can be better managed as learning disabilities, than as mentally retarded.[63]

For Binet and Skeels and Wellman, optimism and hope abounded because education could raise children up from mental defect to normal intelligence. In Kirk's revision of the archetypal narrative of environmentalism, hope thrived because education could save children with learning disabilities from the depths of mental retardation.

A REVIVAL

Kirk's revision of the Iowa Station narrative of the educational redemption of mentally defective children to the new cause of learning disabilities occurred in a uniquely frenetic historical context that involved parent organizations, the national media, and extensive public policy activities. To many parents more than willing to view their children as the asset-filled wheat rather than the dull chaff, such a tale was welcome news.

Throughout the 1950s and early 1960s, organizations of parents seeking answers to their children's puzzling learning and behavior problems were formed around the Strauss Syndrome idea. Local advocacy groups—such as the Alabama Foundation to Aid Aphasoid Children, the Milwaukee Society for Brain-Injured Children, and the New Jersey Association for Brain-Injured Children—started up across the country. When Kirk made his public proclamation of "learning disability" at a 1963 conference in Chicago, often described as the moment of birth of the learning disabilities idea, the meeting was sponsored by a coalition of 15 different local parent organizations.[64] The many parent associations then combined to form one national group around Kirk's idea, the ACLD, which served as the organizing force of the popular learning disabilities movement.

Attendance at the original 1963 ACLD meeting in Chicago was estimated at about 200 participants. Four years later, over 6000 parents and educators attended the 1967 ACLD conference in New York.[65] In just a few years, the ACLD exploded in size as parents of children with learning difficulties across the nation flocked to the new organization. Edward Frierson, director of the special education teacher education program at George Peabody College, Vanderbilt University, described the early ACLD conferences as overflowing with "evangelical fervor."[66] Filled with desperation and hope mixed in equal parts, parents clamored for solutions. "By the mid-1960's," Frierson observed, "the learning disabilities movement had taken on the characteristics of a religious revival period."[67]

The national print media both reflected and fueled the popular movement. Publications such as the *Saturday Evening Post*, *Newsweek*, *The New Yorker*, *Look*, and *Reader's Digest* spread the fervor in melodramatic stories with titles such as "Children of the Empty World" and "They Said Our Child Was Hopeless."[68] Magazine narratives often employed a standard recipe of desperate parents, a child (frequently with the pseudonym Bobby) trapped in a mysterious and heart-wrenching ailment, and heroic professionals holding the key to the child's liberation. Whatever talents or abilities the child might have were concealed beneath a cloak of odd behaviors, bizarre communications, and nonsensical interactions. The child was "more monster than boy,"[69] a "hopeless"[70] case who "shreds the hearts of his parents."[71]

> Bobby lives in a maddening world, and he was trying to fight his way free. Most of the time he could not understand anyone. He could talk, he could see and hear, some of the time he could even read and understand words, but, at the crucial moment the real meaning of words and sentences would dissolve and leave him panic-stricken. Words, sounds, shapes, and feelings turned into a jumbled mess. In a quiet moment, he once said, "The blind have seeing-eye dogs, but I have no one."

In 1966, *Look* magazine announced that an "estimated five million children in this country, one of every ten school-aged youngsters" had a similar case of "minimal brain dysfunction."[72]

For parents, the long road of agony turned hopeful only after finding the right psychologist and treatment program. But first they often went through an endless series of diagnostic sessions with numerous specialists who "diagnosed [the child] repeatedly as mentally deficient, emotionally disturbed, uneducable."[73] Each new diagnosis brought the same devastating news that no effective treatment was available. Finally, the parents reached a point of complete frustration and fatigue, "the end of the line."[74] As one mother described her experience:

> After eighteen costly, heartbreaking months, we felt that we had exhausted all of the local medical resources. We faced the appalling truth that Chicago had no help for Ethan.[75]

But then there was redemption.

> Then what we firmly believe to be divine chance led us one evening to a lecture by Dr. Newell C. Kephart, professor of psychology at Purdue University. His subject was inspiring: For the first time in our experience, here was someone who was discussing *treating* deviant children instead of merely diagnosing.

Rescue was embodied in figures such as Kephart, Dr. Helmer Myklebust of Northwestern University, Dr. Ray Barsch of the Dewitt Reading Clinic in

California, and the team of Dr. Robert Jay Doman, Glenn Doman, and Dr. Carl H. Delacato of the Institute for the Achievement of Human Potential in Philadelphia. These enigmatic but wise, quirky but caring men offered troubled children a "last chance for a normal life."[76] With tremendous patience and a prescient vision, they disregarded all prior diagnoses, looking past the shroud of defects to uncover "the child's hidden intelligence."[77] Given proper clinical treatment, the children in these publications were able to "advance toward a normal boyhood."[78] Miss Johnson, the educational therapist in the Myklebust clinic, described the dramatic changes she had seen in one boy who had been successfully treated: "When he came in here, he wasn't anything. Not anything at all.... Now he's a boy again."[79] Such was the extraordinary gravity of the problem and the dramatic promise of proper diagnosis and treatment by professionals who specialized in the new disorder.

PUBLIC POLICY

The fierce advocacy energy of the popular learning disabilities movement was gradually reflected in the development of federal special education policies. The Kennedy and Johnson administrations both viewed the education of children with disabilities as high priorities within the expansion of federal influence on public education. Public Law 88–164, passed in October 1963, provided funds for research and personnel preparation to educate children with a variety of disabilities. It made no formal provision for children with learning disabilities, but it funded personnel training in this area at four universities under the miscellany category of children with other health impairments.[80] Perhaps more importantly, it established the first federal office devoted specifically to the education of disabled children: the Bureau of Handicapped Children in the United States Office of Education. Kirk had been an influential supporter of disability-related legislation in Illinois and at the federal level since the early 1950s. He was generally viewed by politicians as the leading expert in American special education.[81] When President Kennedy signed 88–164 into law, his signing statement specifically appointed Kirk to direct the new federal office. Kirk who was then working at the University of Illinois took a pay cut to accept the post.[82]

Amendments to the Elementary and Secondary Education Act of 1966 (Public Law 89–750) again left learning disabilities off the list of handicapping conditions targeted for federal funds. Reportedly, supporters of traditional categories of disability fought against the inclusion of learning disability in the legislation fearing that the new disorder would siphon out funds from research and programs for the more established conditions.[83] That legislation did, however, create the National

Advisory Committee on Handicapped Children, a group charged with general oversight of the federal programs for children with disabilities, providing recommendations directly to the federal commissioner of education. Chaired by Kirk, the committee developed a definition of learning disabilities that was later modified for inclusion in the Education of Handicapped Children Act (P.L. 94–142) of 1975.[84]

The National Advisory Committee strongly pushed for the first federal recognition of the learning disability construct in the Learning Disabilities Education Act of 1969 (P.L. 91–230).[85] The act provided funding for teacher education and research, but it did not create a federal definition of learning disability. States were allowed to utilize their own definitions.[86] That national policy consensus was reached only in 1975 when Public Law 94–142 forged a federal mandate for states to provide a public education for all children with disabilities, including those with learning disabilities.

SCIENCE IN A NEW CONTEXT

The intense energy of the learning disabilities movement, an expectant climate in which parents envisioned educational programs to reclaim lost children and heal fractured families, dramatically altered the social context of the work of learning disability scientists. A scientific community that had traditionally consisted of a series of low-key conversations among clinical research teams working directly with children, supplemented by occasional publications or conference discussions linking similar programs, was abruptly thrust into a furious national dialogue involving parents, politicians, and public school personnel. What had occurred in relative isolation among small research groups at various points around the country—Frostig in Los Angeles, Kephart in Indiana and Colorado, Myklebust in Chicago, Cruickshank in Syracuse—suddenly moved to a very public stage. Ray Barsch described the scene in the mid-1960s:

> In a relatively brief time the concept of Learning Disabilities catapulted from pencil sketches on the cognitive drawing board to the production line of the educational market place to satisfy consumer urgency. Almost immediately it was identified as a category, recently discovered, a previously neglected population deserving a distinctive identity and national concern.[87]

It was no longer just a congenial alliance of somewhat parochial research units operating in the contemplative and calm quarters of various universities, institutions, and clinics. It was no longer what some science studies scholars have called an "invisible college," a small and loosely knit network of similar researchers whose informal communications greatly define a given field of intellectual practice.[88] The science of learning disabilities was raised up on the shoulders of the bustling and chanting crowd who hung on researchers' every word, seeking hope and healing for children and families. Ideas traced in "pencil sketches," working hypotheses, experimental procedures, and provisional clinical understandings would not longer do. New pressures and unprecedented urgency surrounded the researchers' work.

No learning disabilities researcher felt those pressures more acutely than Kirk. Other researchers retained some degree of detachment from the fervor— for "revivalist tactics are suspect"[89] to the scientist—continuing to operate their schools, camps, and clinics just as they had for years, applying their concepts and practices without undue impingement. But Kirk was the one man who most represented the science of learning disabilities to the nonscientific public. He was the high-profile polyglot attempting multiple acts of translation, carrying the ideas formulated within a diverse scientific community into multiple social spheres with different needs and interests: parent groups, disability advocacy organizations, state-level public education administrators, local school district professionals, and state and federal lawmakers.

Perhaps the biggest challenge facing Kirk in those acts of translation was the packaging of learning disability into a singular form, one definitive and comprehensible description of the disorder. James C. Chalfant, one of Kirk's doctoral program graduates, issued a report on legislative issues to the 1966 ACLD conference that highlighted this requirement.

> Perhaps the greatest stumbling block to legislation for learning disabilities is the agreement on a common definition. It is extremely difficult to legislate for something which is not clearly defined.

Kirk well knew that a field of learning disabilities and a movement toward mandated public services for students with learning disabilities required that many parties rally around a single, fairly consistent concept of the disorder. But the science of learning disabilities of the early 1960s that he represented and drew ideas from had not arrived at such a consensus. Moreover, prior to the popular learning disabilities movement, there had been little impetus among researchers to seek any such agreement on the construct.

In the early 1960s, the field of learning disabilities research closely resembled University of Chicago psychologist Harvey Carr's vision of functionalist science as an eclectic collection of perspectives unified more by a broadly defined purpose than theoretical agreement.[90] Whatever differences that might have existed in regard to theories of human behavior or methods of research took a back seat to the common mission of seeking immediate solutions for struggling children and their families. Data collection and analysis freely intermingled subjective observations of children in clinical and school settings and objective measures of various forms of mental and sensorimotor activity. What united the many forms of data was a certain attitude of inquiry, a disposition that combined curiosity, creativity, and precision within an intense search for answers. What united the learning disability—brain injury–perceptual handicap—minimal cerebral dysfunction researchers of 1960 was not a common term or construct but a shared devotion to a flexible, practical science of individual functioning as a way of understanding a fairly wide range of childhood learning and behavior issues.

Prior to the popular learning disabilities movement, there was little inclination among the many researchers or the multiple professional disciplines to seek agreement on a single disorder construct because such a consensus served no immediate purpose in their treatment activities. Assisting children and families, in this mindset, relied on independent and informed clinical judgment, operating within the broad parameters of psychological and neurological science, directed toward the specific needs of each individual case. Scientific work and effective treatment at the many research sites around the country, as viewed from this clinical approach, operated at full capacity without conformity to a single construct.

Most learning disabilities researchers of the era were active clinicians providing psychoeducational remediation and treatment to children and families in residential or out-patient settings. Each clinical program had idiosyncratic features, distinctly local ways of understanding children and treating educational retardation. Despite substantial variation in approach, Kirk and colleagues such as Kephart, Frostig, Strauss, and Myklebust were mutually supportive of one another's efforts. Although Kirk rejected Alfred Strauss's brain injury etiology, he was encouraging and complimentary in his communications with Strauss.[91] Despite the apparent nonalignment between his theory of psycholinguistic processing and the movement educator's emphasis on perceptual-motor functioning, Kirk was an avid public supporter of the clinical treatment programs of Frostig and Kephart.[92] In January 1965, Kirk served as a warm host to Marianne Frostig when she visited the University of Illinois for a series of lectures. She thanked Kirk for providing her with advice on how to increase the language emphasis in her program.[93]

The general perception among these researchers was that some degree of intellectual and practical diversity across the field was healthy, given the multifaceted and elusive nature of the problems they were addressing.[94] Kirk's words captured the shared sensibility among the scientists of the era.

> One of the easiest points to see is that the child with learning disabilities is a child with a complex problem for which there is no pat solution. The program of diagnosis

and remediation which may work for one child may be completely inappropriate for another.[95]

From this standpoint, many research programs were required, simultaneously approaching and attempting to solve the problems from multiple angles. Aside from having to respond to the pressures of the popular movement, the researchers of the 1960s generally favored a variegated science involving multiple theories of learning failure and a variety of treatment programs. To their thinking, the complexity and enormity of the challenge demanded multiple affiliated but not wholly similar clinical research programs.

The popular movement, however—hitched to new organizational bodies such as Association for Children with Learning Disabilities and the federal Bureau of Education for the Handicapped—demanded greater conceptual homogeneity. Parents had already experienced an inconsistent hodgepodge of professional services that varied greatly depending on geography and luck. Parent groups and policymakers pressed for a standardization of concepts and terms in order to legislate for and build a national system of educational provision for learning-disabled children. What the ACLD and Kirk strove for was a single, homogeneous system of diagnostic and remediation service located within all public schools, thereby guaranteeing all American parents access to learning disabilities services.

Kirk's work during this period was demonstrative of the transfiguration of an eclectic and flexible scientific field, a creative and open informality of a few members of varying treatment orientations, into an enormous, professionalized educational system consisting of regulated orthodoxies. Due to what James J. Gallagher called "the enormous popularity of his [Kirk's] newly minted category,"[96] the mom and pop corner stores tried to become a national chain of standardized franchises. Only one sign could hang above each store and decorate the logo on the movement letterhead, and the forces of organizational and professional regularization leaned on Kirk at every step.

Much of Kirk's career as a scientist can be understood as an effort to shift from theoretical frameworks that classified children in comparison to others to examinations of psychological patterns of strength and weakness within an individual. He typically described this as a transition from an emphasis on "interindividual differences" to an appreciation for "intraindividual differences." He viewed the latter as far more useful for educators designing instruction for individual students.

The pressures of the popular learning disability movement—the push to pass educational policies mandating the identification and special education of learning-disabled students as well as the parents' need for a single disorder construct—pushed Kirk to employ schemes of diagnostic classification that contradicted much of his scientific work. Kirk was convinced that his science concluded with an emphasis on the requirement that learning-disabled students receive public school remedial instruction, a one-to-one tutoring based on the clinical approach to treatment that he and other leading researchers had devised. New laws had to create public school arrangements in which that kind of focus on intensive treatment would occur. He also believed that the necessary federal laws had to frame childhood learning problems according to the very notions of classification that he had tried to leave behind. Attending to the policy and popular demands for a new diagnostic classification while forwarding a science that measured levels of psychological functioning, Kirk's two decades of articulations of the construct frequently resulted in a rhetorical and conceptual jumble. Causing him much frustration, his many attempts at clarification seemed to only increase the level of ambiguity about the nature of the learning disability.

SCIENCE AND CULTURAL CHANGE

Kirk's goal of maintaining a scientific focus on the psychological profile and the instructional needs of the individual was complicated—perhaps even overwhelmed—by the rushing torrent of political activity that surrounded the learning disability construct in the 1960s and the early 1970s. While Kirk struggled to retain some degree of clarity and conceptual integrity in his understanding of learning disability within the whitewater political rapids of an era of rapid historical transformation, his movement education colleagues Newell Kephart and Marianne Frostig fought back against the speed and technological content of historical change itself. In response to what they viewed as a twentieth-century America spinning too quickly into the anxiety and social decay of modernity, Kephart and Frostig created a sweeping pastoral critique of industrial urbanism that romanticized the natural peace and safety of country living. As Kirk fought to defend a science of learning disability against encroaching political confusion, the movement educators viewed their scientific work as a social tourniquet forestalling further deterioration of a declining culture. They provided neurologically damaged children with a treatment both educational and political, a curriculum addressing the learning delays of child development, and a salve for the technological ravages of modern American history.

CHAPTER SEVEN

Country Movement AND City Children: Agrarianism IN Movement Education

Four-year-old Ethan Oppenheim was an unusual boy. He often played by himself for hours at a time. He generally ignored or seemed disinterested in playing with other children. His speech development was delayed. When he learned a new word, he would use it for a few days and then quickly discard it, never to be spoken again. Attempts to administer standard intelligence tests were unsuccessful due to Ethan's lack of cooperation. Ethan's parents Rosalind and Joe took their son to pediatricians, psychiatrists, neurologists, audiologists, and psychologists. But they found no professional who was prepared to treat their child's puzzling disorder.

In the summer of 1959, after years of unsuccessfully searching for an effective treatment for Ethan's learning and behavior problems, Rosalind and Joe Oppenheim enrolled him in the Glen Haven Achievement Camp run by Newell Kephart in northern Colorado. Many miles from their Chicago home, the Oppenheim's finally found a place of peaceful respite.

> Glen Haven was a thrilling and stimulating experience. Surrounded by the splendors of Colorado's mountains, we found an inner calm. The tensions of the past bitter months fell away in this relaxed atmosphere.... and Ethan bloomed a little—a tentative, fragile flowering, to be sure; but for the first time in over two years, he was rediscovering enjoyment.

The Oppenheims' experience of ease and comfort was precipitated by both the serenity of the natural environment and their confidence in the expertise of the camp director. The effectiveness of Dr. Kephart's unique mode of treatment and the natural beauty of the mountain setting combined to quiet their anxieties and begin the healing process.[1]

It is likely that parents such as the Oppenheims viewed the pastoral milieu of the Glen Haven Achievement Camp as merely an attractive and enjoyable addition to the actual clinical science and treatment practiced by Newell Kephart. Surely the scientific content of Kephart's thinking, a hybrid fusion of psychology and neurology, was enacted in the professional procedures of treatment, not in the blue skies, tall green pine trees, and picturesque rocky peaks. The clean mountain air and the evening chorus of the chirping crickets supplied only an aesthetically pleasing background for the actual scientific work. Or so it would seem.

For Kephart, the mountain location of his center for the treatment of childhood learning disorders was more than a chance to spend summers in the Colorado of his boyhood. It provided an opportunity to take neurologically damaged children to a natural space where the ills of modern life could be properly treated. Layers of historical change and urban development could be stripped away, unleashing the authentic and natural capacities of defective and damaged children. The promotion of growth and development relied on a science clothed in an agrarian social theory, a science that brought the physical experience of old-time country living to the modern child.

Stretched like a long strand of twine, steady and consistent in presence yet often in the background of the movement educator's writings—most notably those of Newell Kephart and Marianne Frostig—was a deep sense of pastoral longing. Their extensive and surprising social theory sounded an alarm of modern, urban-industrial despair and romanticized a rural redemption in the days of old. Historians have captured this tradition in a variety of ways that envisage a range of intellectual and political possibilities. Danbom uses the term "romantic agrarianism" to describe an intellectual direction "following the path trod by Thoreau [to] emphasize the moral, emotional, and spiritual benefits agriculture and rural life convey to the individual."[2] Buell describes a tradition of "pastoral ideology,"[3] the formidable cultural challenge of crafting and recrafting "the notion of nature as refuge from complexity."[4]

Leo Marx articulates a particular American incarnation of "romantic pastoralism" as an effort to craft social stasis within a historical milieu marked by rapid technological change accompanied by a lived experience of uncertainty and liminality.[5] Pastoralism is "that essential habit of mind,"[6] a way of interpreting the world and one's place in it, that facilitates extraordinary mobility "between the imperatives of nature and culture, between the dangers and deprivations of the undeveloped environment [wild nature] and the excessive constraints of civilization."[7] Faced with a vulnerability of self and community in the rapid change of modern life, the pastoral tradition of literature and thought fashioned "the idea of an ordered and happier past set against the disturbance and disorder of the present."[8] It simultaneously offered a hyper-romantic literary vision, an infeasible "poetry of nostalgia for the unrecoverable,"[9] and an imminently practicable prescription for seeking peaceful stability in the midst of an experience of modern alienation.

AGRARIAN THEMES IN MOVEMENT EDUCATION

The romantic agrarianism of the movement educators employed an array of recurring images that mourned the lost virtues of old time, rural living and vilified an urbanized, modern lifestyle as physically and psychologically unhealthy for children. The pastoral ideal served as an idyllic contrast to urban environments viewed as being noxious and delivering a toxic array of insults—physical, cultural, linguistic, and psychological—to the developing bodies and minds of young people. The causes of learning difficulties and often concurrent socioemotional problems in children were traced to a modern lifestyle cultivated in America's cities.

The exemplar case of modernity, the most intensive and damaging concentration of modern lifestyle features, was the urban neighborhood and home. This portrait of the harmful urban setting echoed the popular literature of the 1960s that declared the burgeoning crisis of America's cities. Dramatic book titles such as *Sick Cities* and *Crisis in Our Cities* declared a profound deterioration of major urban areas in terms of virtually all imaginable indicators of well-being: economics, crime, housing, air and water pollution, racial strife, road congestion, politeness, and moral decency.[10]

In the public eye, and in the sober analyses of academics from a variety of disciplines, America's cities were plagued by a host of social and ecological crises.[11] Riots in African American neighborhoods in Philadelphia, Harlem, Watts, Cleveland, Detroit, and Newark between 1964 and 1967 promoted a racialized depiction of the downfall of America's cities. Cities had become virtually unlivable spaces that one author described as "a refuse heap for underprivileged groups...which cannot escape"[12] to the cleanliness and safety of the suburbs.

Popular counterculture books such as *Living the Good Life*[13] and *Small is Beautiful*[14] fueled end-of-days, agrarian escape schemes for readers who dreamed of running away to the country "to share in salvaging what was still usable from the wreckage of the decaying social order."[15] While the actual number of people who fled cities and suburbs for rural retreats (such as communes) was relatively small, the theme of rural flight captured the imagination of anyone seeking "individual liberation from the false consciousness of society and self-fulfillment based on genuine values related to human life."[16]

The mid-1960s popular criticism of urban life is perhaps best captured in a September 1964 *Fortune* magazine article by Richard J. Whalen entitled "New York—A City Destroying Itself." This heated polemic on the moral and spiritual decay of New York City is noteworthy for its extensive analysis of how the environmental decline had caused numerous physiological and psychological symptoms within the population. The city had become "too concentrated with people, cars, and chimneys to provide a healthful environment."[17] The physical congestion of human bodies, buildings, automobiles as well as the overwhelming ugliness of the paved landscaped created a severe constraint on bodily movements required for health. The urban dweller was trapped in his apartment and the office worker was cramped in his cubicle. The sedentary lifestyle of confined physicality was matched by a culture of behavioral and emotional constriction, a social climate "that constantly inhibits emotional spontaneity and physical release of tension."[18] Hemmed in by both the concrete and cultural environment, inhabitants suffered from emotional suffocation.

> The city, in effect, has placed a heavy lid on a cauldron of seething human passions without providing an avenue for their release other than orthopedic difficulties and mental breakdowns.[19]

Without space to exercise one's body and mind, the city was a breeding ground for biological and mental illness. Limitations of the urban physical space restrained human movement in ways that yielded physiological and emotional harm.

Whalen's themes of an urban environment assaulting humanity through physiological and emotional constriction echoed with remarkable fidelity in the scientific and professional writings of movement education.

A NEURO-URBAN DISORDER

In the research of the movement educators, this hyperbolic impression of the American city in moral crisis served as a broad metaphor for a historical interpretation of the development of twentieth-century industrial-technological lifestyle. America had undergone an unfortunate shift from the wholesomeness and simplicity of face-to-face small towns to the anxiety and depersonalization of mechanized metropolises. Country comfort and authenticity had succumbed to a harried modernity in which individuals lost meaningful contact with themselves and their neighbors.

The romantic agrarianism of Kephart and Frostig was motivated by their view that the problematic children they were seeing in their own clinical work—Frostig working in Los Angeles and Kephart in Indiana and Colorado—were individual examples of the damaging effects of metropolitan, technological culture. To their thinking, the modern, urban lifestyle in the post-World War II era had caused a host of problems in the learning and behavior of young children. The public schools had little choice but to respond with programs of instruction of prophylactic and curative purpose.

> Studies of urban living show that it is an added unavoidable responsibility of the school to help counteract the destructive effects of urban living and to help children recover from unhappy experiences caused by the unrest, the anxiety, and the adverse conditions of their lives.[20]

The extensive neurosensory and movement education curricula developed by Kephart and Frostig were contributions to the necessary educational effort to counteract the negative effects of modern life, to "provide a partial substitute for this loss."[21]

PHYSICAL LIMITATION

> Some of the simple yet quite valuable activities of a rural childhood are fast disappearing from the American scene...Not too many years ago, virtually every child used to balance himself walking on a railroad track or on top of a wooden fence; most of today's children have missed this experience.[22]

The detrimental nature of city living was theorized as arising from the physical environment itself, from the ways that the confined physical spaces of pavement, brick, and high-rise steel placed child's bodies into unhealthy environment situations defined by restrictiveness and danger. Kephart understood the young child as learning through experimentation, gradually accumulating adaptive behaviors through the exploratory interactions of the child with the environment. Required for such learning exploration was an environment that allowed for free and open play. What growing children required for healthy learning were "ladders to climb, fences to walk, horses to ride,"[23]—perhaps the common activities of Kephart's childhood in rural Colorado—features of farm life that are nonexistent in the modern, urban setting. His analysis of this childhood need provides an illuminative example of the movement educators' frequent counterpositioning of past and present, rural and urban, preindustrial and postindustrial, safe and dangerous.

> If the children of the past wanted to experiment with locomotion, they climbed on the family horse and he took care of them. The modern automobile is possessed of

no such concern for the safety of our children. If children of the past wanted to see what it was like to run as fast as they could, they ran. But the children of today cannot run far in a modern apartment or even a city lot, and they cannot run out of the yard because of traffic.[24]

The romanticized character of a loyal family horse that genuinely cared for young children was an inviting pastoral symbol that allowed Kephart to gloss over the harsher realities and common hazards experienced by rural children interacting with farm animals and agricultural machinery. Urban life, by contrast to the effusive warmth of the protective pony, was physically restrictive, dangerous, and uncaring. The city itself didn't care about children.

Frostig similarly described urban living, often through focusing on the unfortunate predicament of the city child, as lacking the necessary opportunities for natural physical play, exploration, and learning. Like Kephart, her point of nostalgic, normative reference was the open rural landscape.

> Space is an important cue for movement; open space invites children to move. The sight of a wet, sandy beach sets them skipping; a grassy slope incites them [children] to slide and roll, to romp, to run.[25]

Frostig's naturalistic holism endowed rural geographic features with preternatural capacities supporting healthy child development. There was an essential sympathy between two aspects of nature, the prairies and hillsides of the rural landscape and the natural development of the child. The landscape is a protagonist who "invites" and "incites" specific kinds of movement that are a "necessity for both adequate physical and healthy psychological development."[26] Through "valuable contact with nature,"[27] children develop the neurological and physiological abilities necessary for competent academic learning.

In sharp contrast, Frostig believed that "crowded urban conditions and modern conveniences often permit little opportunity for children to move about freely."[28] The activities and opportunities necessary "to build up the sensorimotor skills which are required by the more complex activities of reading, writing, and arithmetic"[29] are lacking in urban homes and neighborhoods. "The urban child is deprived of the natural exercise needed for him to become aware of his body and the relationship of his body to the environment."[30]

Central to this articulation was the difference between country play and city play, between the kinds of natural movements available to rural children and the kinds of unnatural motor activities engaged in by urban youth. Frostig explained this at length:

> Imagine children playing in the country. For them, the landscape comprises, in effect, the equivalent of a beautifully equipped gymnasium. There are trees to climb,

a slope to roll down, a lawn to run on, a fallen tree for balancing, a ditch to jump over, a branch to swing on, and a rock to throw. Contrast this picture with a city schoolroom.... The children sit for hours, until at last there may be a session of physical education; and even then the children may spend most of that time standing still, waiting their turn for various activities.[31]

This concept relied not only on the movement educators' frequent juxtaposition of agrarian goodness and urban harmfulness. It also derived from a Thoreau-inspired understanding of the correct relationship between the physiology of the child, the entire neurological and perceptual apparatus so fully articulated by Alfred Strauss at the Wayne School, and the surrounding physical environment. Nature, as housed within the child in the form of the neurophysiological body, met in nurturing empathy with nature in the woods, streams, and fields. Nature within the child clashed in destructive antipathy with the man-made artifice of the metropolis.

Although Frostig and Kephart fully adopted Strauss's understanding of the neurophysiology of sensorimotor and perceptual development, they added a new emphasis in theorizing the specific kind of physical (and by extrapolation, social and moral) environment needed to ensure proper child development. That beneficial environment was an agrarian landscape where children could play freely and where the goodness of the soil and trees could pass quite naturally into the bodies of children.

EXPANSION OF CONSTRAINTS

The insidious problem of restriction in urban life consisted of not only physical limitation but also a series of related emotional, social, cognitive, and linguistic constraints. This strand of the movement educators' agrarianism dramatically expanded a theory of how a limited physical space binded bodily movement and hampered learning growth into an extensive assortment of harmful notions detailing how modern, urban environments yield "certain deprivations of experience"[32] that stifle and damage the human condition. The problem of restrictiveness that began with the body migrated into multiple aspects of city life and the damaged urban child in numerous ways.

Kephart believed that the external world perceived by the child becomes the basis for the internal operations of ideation and memory. Through learning in the early years, a child develops an ability to integrate the dominant visual input with other sensory data to fabricate a complex spatioenvironmental scheme, a "space structure" consisting "of the interrelationships between all the objects in our space world."[33] This space structure, a neurologically based achievement of perception, is the basis for all cognitive activity. Kephart utilized a filing cabinet metaphor involving systems of indexing and multiple drawers of categorized concepts to expound his version of cognition. The work of storing and retrieving ideas consisted of file work within an internal, mental space developed as an analog to the external, perceptual space of perception. In this way, not only does good perception lead to good cognition. Open and unconfined external space leads to unrestricted and useful internal space.

> The space structure which the child builds through the developmental processes which we have described determines the universe in which he will live the rest of his life. If his space structure is restricted he will live in a small and restricted universe. If, on the other hand, his space structure is broad and inclusive and permits adequate freedom of operation, he will live in a broad and inclusive universe.[34]

Kephart's rapidly moving theory here translated a concept of limitation from objective space to perceived space to cognitive operations of thought and memory. Early childhood experiences in constricted physical environments yield underdifferentiated perceptual capacities, deficiencies in the child's spatial understanding of the physical world. Because cognition is essentially an outgrowth of perception, these spatial deficiencies become the basis for inadequate forms of conceptualization and memory. The result is that children raised in confined, urban homes and neighborhoods end up living in small and restricted mental universes.

While Kephart often maintained a close focus on neurological impairment, Frostig's arguments were more sweeping and ostensibly less systematic. By her account, the "increasing urbanization of life in the United States"[35] had created an entire generation of American children with "lags in their development," including "the culturally deprived child, the slow-learning child, and the neurologically handicapped child."[36] In this wall-to-wall argument, Frostig blurred diagnostic and etiological lines and expressed great doubt that such professionalized categories mattered very much in the classroom. She theorized that a deficiency of proper bodily movement experiences in childhood caused a wide range of learning, social, and emotional difficulties.[37]

Frostig further theorized that children growing up in the cramped physical spaces of modern life suffered from "an all-pervading anxiety,"[38] a generalized psychophysiological malaise. "The first handicap resulting from lack of movement is a depreciated joy of living."[39] What is lost in an environment of physical constraint "is not only physical but mental and spiritual."[40] In her 1955 doctoral dissertation, she lamented "the decreasing influence of religion upon the character formation of children."[41] While her later publications did not mention religion, she maintained that the cultural decline in the United States had deep psychological and moral dimensions. She viewed the modern era as a "time of anxiety and unrest, or noise and overcrowding in our cities,"[42] a period when "our emotional climate is uncomfortable, including the emotional climate in which millions of children grow up."[43] Just as contact with the goodness of the natural earth seemingly delivered proper health and development to the bodies of children, so too living in the concrete landscape of the cities seemed to infuse children with the cultural toxins of modernity.

Stripped of its extensive historical and political extrapolations, this theory of the impact of environmental restrictions on the learning and well-being of the human organism held closely to Kurt Goldstein's original conclusions. Goldstein had observed that brain-injured soldiers experienced what he called "catastrophic condition"—an experience of severe anxiety—under conditions when the organism was unable to effectively respond to the overwhelming environmental demands.[44] He also theorized the results of the reverse situation. When non-brain-injured persons (such as healthy, developing young children) are placed in environmental conditions marked by restriction, they are then susceptible to that same catastrophic anxiety and suffering. Goldstein's notion of "a state of health . . . . an ordered state"[45] was based on a homeostatic calibration, a balance between environmental requirements and organismic capacities. A situation of extreme, prolonged disproportionality on either side of the organism-environment equation was likely to lead to increased anxiety and diminished health.

The defective neurological and emotional health of modern children, in particular urban children, as viewed within the agrarian thinking of Kephart and Frostig, provided evidence of far-reaching and disastrous changes in the quality of home and neighborhood environments. Over many years, America had gradually traded the beauty, virtue, and freedom of the natural rural setting for blighted urban environments that failed to support the developing organism. Further, American culture had deteriorated with the loss of the rural landscape. In the lives of most children, trees had been replaced by technology and running brooks by household machines. A consciousness closely allied with nature had been supplanted by a mechanized mindset that was inhospitable to nature.

MECHANIZED CULTURE

The agrarianism of the movement educators involved a general state of despair regarding the growth of a technological culture in the United States. Kephart believed that the culture of mechanized thinking and popular machines was harmful to children in three ways. First, since the child is an organism whose learning consists of a process of gradual adaptation to the requirements of the environment, the fast-paced technological lifestyle was increasing the number and complexity of environmental requirements so rapidly that children simply could not keep up. Agrarian society had set a reasonable tempo of change, and children could keep pace in developing the behavioral responses necessary to operate effectively. But the rate and complexity of change in modern civilization had become overwhelming, and children lagged behind developmentally because the physiology of the organism could not adapt to meet the new cultural demands. Second, the machines and devices of the modern home presented an environment that was nonconductive to children's motor experimentation due to the intricacy and frailty of the mechanized objects. From a practical standpoint, one could not allow a young child to play with televisions, telephones, and tape recorders because the devices might break and subsequent repair would be expensive. Third, many of the mundane tasks of physical manipulation that humans had historically accomplished with their bodies had been reassigned to automated machines. This reduced the opportunities for fine and gross motor practice, creating a lack of necessary developmental experiences for young children. The physical basis for all learning and higher cognitive development—basic motor skills—was denied to young children in the mechanized culture.[46]

Frostig agreed in her critique that technology was a sinister foe intruding with a vengeance upon the natural world. "The more people interfere with nature," she expounded later in her career, "the greater are the difficulties that arise."[47] The invasion of the machine into the agrarian landscape was, in her understanding, the source of widespread negative consequences in the learning and well-being of children. This was, at least in part, due to the fact that the machines of modern life took over tasks that once required bodily activity.

> With the growth of automation and the ubiquitous use of mechanical locomotion, physical effort is disappearing from the lives of most people of all ages, with the result that muscular and circulatory weaknesses are prevalent.[48]

The growth of a technological culture in America signaled the demise of developmentally necessary daily activities of physical movement and exertion. Devices of modern convenience—"household machinery"[49]—robbed children of opportunities for physical activity, causing motor and perceptual development lag. As a result, children arrived at school unprepared to handle the curricular demands.

Concomitant with the infringement of a modern technological lifestyle on the maturation of the physiology of the child was the destructive spread of a mechanized consciousness into normative cultural orientations and practices, including schooling. Kephart's comparison between the agrarian horse and the modern automobile pointed to the difference between a living creature that apprehends its rider with recognition and caring and an inanimate instrument that neither has the capacity to know nor care about its human operator. It enacts values of efficiency and depersonalization that Frostig viewed as siphoning the meaning out of schooling and living. In an impersonal and cold culture, children lose the opportunity to discover and express their selves and to become connected to other human beings.

A popular fetish with technological objects brought about a corresponding loss of human value and meaning. Frostig lamented that "the mechanistic outlook and style of living of our age contribute to, if they do not cause, a sense of meaninglessness and chaotic confusion."[50] To the movement educators, the rise of mechanistic culture produced experiences of isolation, powerlessness, and despair. Children underwent a "loss of self-awareness. This loss is felt as lack of identity, so often bemoaned."[51] Suffering from developmental deficits in perceptual and sensorimotor abilities due to a lack of necessary agrarian activities, many children experienced the environment as a series of incomprehensible distortions. The perceptually disordered organism felt lost and ineffective in acting in relation to the environment.[52]

THE URBAN CHILD

The tragic protagonist at the center of the movement educator's narrative of cultural decline was the "the urban child."[53] The entirety of movement education theory concerning the kinds of environments that support or hinder healthy child development was embodied, in melodramatic and pithy fashion, in the unfortunate personage of the child of the city. The movement educators utilized a shorthand discourse of cultural deprivation terms that greatly hinged on a concept of social class and, less clearly, race: "experiential deprivation,"[54] "culturally different or economically deprived child,"[55] "culturally deprived child,"[56] and "socioeconomically deprived."[57] The inner city child was defined by the fact that his "experiences have been restricted"[58] in ways that had stunted his neurosensory development and school readiness.

Kephart and Frostig complemented one another in service to the larger portrait of the culturally deprived child of the inner city. Kephart focused primarily on the way that culturally defined, experiential limitations caused neurologically based, developmental lags among deprived children. Frostig explained how this neurological distortion of development was manifested in a restricted range of linguistic, emotional, and behavioral performances.

Kephart theorized a neuropsychological "hierarchy of readiness skills"[59] that children must develop in a specific sequence. "The development of one stage is essential to the development of the next."[60] Due to the insufficient provision of necessary life experiences that support development and learning, a child may fail to acquire a given skill at the appropriate level. As that child moves ahead to more complex lessons at higher levels of learning, "subsequent stages become confused and disturbed."[61] The disruption of the natural development sequence causes learning difficulties at higher, more complex levels due to the skill lacuna at a foundational level. In this way, a learning disability may be caused by "inadequate presentations of learning experiences,"[62] environmental deficiencies viewed as characteristic of urban, lower-class family life. "It is for this reason," Kephart asserted, "that high proportions of learning disorders are being observed in Head Start and similar programs for the culturally deprived."[63] It was a problem of experiential quantity. The home environment of culturally deprived children "presents learning situations of all types but does not present enough of any of them."[64]

Similarly, Frostig built a theory of cultural deprivation within the notion of an experientially undernourished neurological system, citing two specific manifestations: a "restricted language code"[65] and an emotional/behavioral posture of trepidation. The language restriction concept borrowed from the work of British researcher Basil Bernstein in describing the language of lower-class families and youth as simplified and constrained in comparison to the public school's middle class norms.[66]

> Children from a socioeconomically deprived background, whose experiences have been restricted, and whose language contains few precise descriptive and qualifying words are at a disadvantage when they must start to acquire a knowledge of standard English.[67]

The result was that "a large percentage of economically deprived children suffer from learning disabilities."[68]

The emotional and behavioral plight of the urban child, in Frostig's description, was particularly troubling. Drawing from her educational therapy work in New York and Los Angeles, she came to understand the inner city child as emotionally traumatized by the urban experience. The defining emotions were overwhelming fear and anxiety.

> He is expected to pay attention to the teacher, but often he finds he cannot because paying attention is difficult when one is puzzled and afraid. He is afraid—afraid of the teacher, afraid that he will make a mistake....he may become more and more anxious and talk less and less.[69]

The child's fear and anxiety were due to punitive parenting styles and the "prevalence of crumbling family structures," resulting in the "loss of love" required for healthy emotional development.[70]

A single story from Frostig's experiences with urban youth best captures her interpretation of the emotional state of these children.

> We remember working with inner city children who huddled together for security, leaving no room for movement. Only after we had assuaged their anxiety did they dare stand so that each had sufficient space to move without interfering with another child. At a subsequent session, one of the youngsters shouted happily, "It's easy to find my place now. I just remember where I stood before. That's my place!" The same children were unable to create movement sequences or vary any movement sequence independently. Although they quickly picked up new sequences and rules that were demonstrated in detail by the teacher, these children were unable to decide for themselves what to do.[71]

In this passage, the restrictive urban environment translates into a sense of apprehensive emotional constriction among the children. Insecure within themselves and their physical environment, the children huddle and cower. Even when they finally relax enough to perform, they lack a sense of self-directedness. Frostig concluded that the teachers must focus on teaching the children how to be more "self-reliant" to counteract the deficiencies of culture that had accrued in the damaged neurology of inner city children.[72]

CLASS AND RACE

It was not uncommon for learning disability researchers of the era to draw from the psychological and sociological literatures on the deficits of poor people to theorize learning problems along race and class lines.[73] One study concluded that "poverty creates a milieu for the development of childhood learning disorders."[74] Epidemiologists repeatedly asserted that neurological defects such as minimal brain dysfunction occurred with higher frequency among low-income children.[75] This supported the general conclusion that the "socio-cultural inadequacies of the urban ghetto present an environment [that is] formidable and pathologic."[76]

Daniel Hallahan, a student of William Cruickshank, described low-income children as behaviorally indistinguishable from children with hyperactivity and learning disabilities. He claimed that "the distracting nature of the disadvantaged child's disordered environment"[77] produced a behavioral symptomatology that mirrored that of children with brain injuries. Lower-class children "possess very short attention spans and are easily distracted from the task at hand."[78] They "have an impulsive rather than a reflective cognitive style" marked by a "short attention span, distractibility, figure-ground problems, hyperactivity, and motor disinhibition."[79] This array of deficit symptoms could be traced to "the culture of poverty," including "environmental factors such as overcrowding, maternal and paternal deprivation, undifferentiated noise, inferior health and educational services, and maladaptive, if not utterly pathological, patterns of child-rearing."[80]

Among the views expressed by the movement educators, the social class dimension of their romantic agrarianism was consistent, but the racial character of the problematic urban child was less clear. A vast majority of Kephart's and Frostig's published passages discussing urban schools, neighborhoods, families, and children lacked a racial or ethnic descriptor. Typically, these researchers provided case examples of individual children or families without identifying race or ethnicity.

To the contrary, fellow movement educator Ray Barsch described the child who was *not* "culturally deprived" as the "'plain vanilla' child from average parents in an average neighborhood in an average community." His juxtaposition of "vanilla" with repetitions-for-emphasis of "average" points to a distinctly racial concept of less-than-average. This overt example of racial politics stands out as unusual in the writings of movement education researchers in the field of learning disabilities.

One possibility is that Kephart and Frostig simply assumed that children and families living in poverty in American cities—children and families they generally described in terms of ability deficits—were often African Americans (and, in Frostig's experience in Los Angeles, Latinos). Kephart's 1968 statement that "high proportions of learning disorders are being observed in Head Start and similar programs for the culturally deprived"[81] focused rhetorically on issues of poverty. Yet one must question the unmentioned issue of race. The federal Head Start program of early childhood education for children and families living in poverty began only three years prior to Kephart's published comment. In its initial years of operation, Head Start enrolled a primarily African American student population.[82] Kephart's statement indicates his close attention to students who participated in the early Head Start program. It is difficult to imagine that he was unaware at the time that a majority of the Head Start students were African Americans.

Elsewhere, Kephart provided a definition of cultural deprivation based solely on social class: "The culturally deprived child is here defined as one living in a low socioeconomic environment." He further explained that such a child suffered from "retardation due to a lack of stimulation (books, creative projects, and conversation), and a generally run-down body condition."[83] In this explanation, as with virtually every similar passage in Frostig's work, race is not mentioned. The meaning of the racial information not provided in deficit-based analyses of poor children and families, although provocative in its absence, provides no comfortable or clear conclusion.

AMERICAN ROMANTIC AGRARIANISM

> Beginning in Jefferson's time, the cardinal image of American aspirations was a rural landscape, a well-ordered green garden magnified to continental size. Although it probably shows a farmhouse or a neat white village, the scene usually is dominated by natural objects: in the foreground a pasture, a twisting brook with cattle grazing nearby, then a clump of elms on a rise in the middle distance and beyond that, way off on the western horizon, a line of dark hills. This is the countryside of the Old Republic, a chaste, uncomplicated land of rural virtue.[84]

Where did the agrarian theory of the movement educators come from? By all indications, Kephart and Frostig were thorough and conscientious psychological researchers who typically provided complete academic references for theoretical and empirical sources in their many writings. What is striking about the extensive and often nuanced agrarianism of these two researchers is the complete lack of source material references.

The only hint of an academic source for a pastoral social theory resides in Kephart's 1936 doctoral dissertation on juvenile delinquency at the University of Iowa.[85] In a psychological study examining the disorganized personality of juvenile delinquents, Kephart briefly discussed findings from noted University of Chicago sociologist Clifford Shaw's *Delinquency Areas*, a 1929 study that mapped rates of delinquent activity on a square mile grid of Chicago. Shaw found that the rates of delinquent and criminal activity were highest at the center of the city. Crime then decreased in inverse relation to the geographic distance from the city center. Furthermore, the highest delinquency neighborhoods were areas of physical deterioration and decreasing population. From this, Kephart concluded that a "slum child in Chicago" lived in a community where "stealing is socially accepted."[86] If interpreted out of context, the Shaw study seemed to lend support to two of Kephart's agrarian hypotheses: that the physical condition of the urban surroundings was closely related to deviant behavior, and that the farther one travels from the central city the more peaceable and safe the community.[87]

But one brief source in Kephart's dissertation falls short as an explanation. The omission of references to agrarian writers and thinkers is less than satisfactory evidence for any historical conclusion. Nevertheless, one may posit a series of relatively safe hypotheses on the basis of this absence. It is likely that neither researcher was making a conscious and intentional effort to augment or fortify their neuropsychology with agrarian thought. It is also probable that they simply viewed their many statements about country lifestyles, modern technology, and urban children as objective facts available to any reasonable observer. They were not forwarding scientific hypotheses requiring the formal support of empirical or theoretical sources because these agrarian notions were, from their standpoint, as plain as the nose on one's face. Conscientious scientists need not provide a footnote every time they assume that the earth is round. It is very likely that they believed that they were describing self-evident facts of modern life.

More clear is the fact that Kephart and Frostig were operating within a post-World War II American intellectual context in which a variety of agrarian discourses were active and prominent. Unknowingly, at least to some extent, they borrowed from and participated in a rich and deep American tradition of romantic agrarianism, a multifaceted means of forging a national identity within a modern historical space of contingency and change. Rooted in colonial understandings of America as a nation and American as an identity, agrarianism was continued in numerous versions throughout American history. In order to better understand the ideological positions that Frostig and Kephart espoused, I will provide an overview of that intellectual heritage, stretching from Thomas Jefferson through industrialization to the mid-twentieth-century interpretations available to the movement educators.

Leo Marx traces the eighteenth-century roots of the American literary and political tradition of the pastoral ideal to the writings of J. Hector St. John Crevecoeur and Thomas Jefferson.[88] These colonial authors initiated an American tradition that "grafted Romantic justification to agrarian economics."[89] They located individual and nationalistic virtue at the interface of an economically independent farmer with a rarified moral soil. In this space of interaction, they limned a hero worthy of building a nation that eclipsed all that came before. He was an honest and independent yeoman farmer, a man who had escaped the stifling, class-based culture of Europe and found the opportunity for emancipation working the fresh and rich American earth.

Central to this hero image was an orientation to the aesthetic, moral, and economic meaning of the seemingly endless American landscape. Motifs of the fruitful potency and ethical purity of the virgin territory were allied to the man who labored close to nature and secured an independent livelihood. The notion of a virtuous, politically and morally un-ruined landscape was coupled with an idealized portrait of the farmer who cultivates an economic and spiritual life arising from the good earth. Regular contact with nature was understood to infuse the human soul with decency while yielding crops sufficient to create a life of economic self-sufficiency, thereby allowing the farmer to avoid enslaving entanglements with urban centers of commerce and industry.

In the early years of the Republic, Jefferson advocated an economic and moral stance of "rural virtue,"[90] a national policy maintaining the United States as an agricultural state. America would be the pleasing farm to Britain's ugly factory, shipping harvested materials and resources to the Old Country and receiving manufactured products in return. The admitted economic loss to the United States would easily be offset by the expanded happiness and virtue of the rural lifestyle. Rather than becoming a modern economic man imprisoned by dependence on the oppressive marketplace of barter and trade, the American farmer that Jefferson envisioned was a noble husbandman morally sustained by the satisfactions of economic self-sufficiency and a deeply spiritual and aesthetic connection to the glorious American landscape.

> The yeoman, who owned a small farm and worked it with the aide of his family, was the incarnation of the simple, honest, independent, healthy, happy human being. Because he lived in close communion with beneficent nature, his life was believed to have a wholesomeness and integrity impossible for the depraved populations of cities.[91]

For the Jefferson of 1787, the pastoral ideal was inseparable from a moral vision of American democracy. The vast expanse of open, untilled landscape awaiting American farmers provided an extensive spiritual metaphor for the innocence and endless promise of the young nation.[92]

By the mid-nineteenth century, this optimistic and peaceful rural vision had been disrupted by the mechanized rumble of modern industry, the rapid spread of loud, growling, and powerful machines—railroads and motorized factories— into America's small towns and farms. Marx describes the cultural intrusion of machines as a "counterforce"[93]—a dramatic infringement of the American pastoral ideal by a forceful symbol of modernity that challenged the relatively naive "American archetype of the pastoral design."[94]

A scene from Nathanial Hawthorne's 1844 notebooks provides Marx with a ready example of the initial encroachment of technology into both the natural landscape and the American pastoral imagination. Hawthorne sits in a restful wood known as Sleepy Hollow, in a scene anticipating Thoreau's isolation at Walden, quietly describing the natural vista in his notebook. He writes of a cat-bird mewing, a bird taking flight, and the hum of a mosquito. Then the quietude is broken.

> But, hark there is the whistle of the locomotive,—the long shriek, harsh above all other harshness, for the space of a mile cannot mollify it into harmony. It tells a story of busy men, citizens, from the hot street, who have come to spend a day in a country village,—men of business,—in short, of all unquietness; and no wonder that it gives such a startling shriek, since it brings the noisy world into the midst of our slumbrous peace.[95]

The raw disturbance of the pastoral scene is evocative and unnerving. But Hawthorne's description points not only to the auditory violation of the tranquil, natural space by the screaming engine. The intrusion of the mechanized roar into the bucolic scene, to Hawthorne, invites images of social and historical disruption. Life in the rural village was changing. Business—both as busy-ness invading a place previously free of bustling anxiety and as commerce thrust upon a rural area far from urban centers of pecuniary pursuit—intruded upon the slumber. Modernity as machine and mercantilism arrived in brute force, with "the image of the railroad as counterforce"[96] portending dramatic alterations to the social landscape of American life.

Prior to the year 1800, the agrarian myth was primarily a possession of the educated intellectuals. By the time of Hawthorne's Sleepy Hollow description, "it had become a mass creed, a part of the country's political folklore and its nationalistic ideology."[97] Politicians, newspaper editors, and farmers shared a common agrarian vision of America and saw the farmer as national hero. Agrarianism had entered the ideational fiber of everyday life.

To Ray Williams, the rapid development of industrial production, mechanized farming, and capitalistic agrarian economics brought about an experience of country life that was under the constant threat of urban invasion. The age-old consciousness of contrast between rural and urban life took on heightened proportions under the pressures of modern economic and technological development. The cultural push of modernity struck Americans as "a present experienced as a tension"[98] between a comfortable, rural past and a disruptive and frightening urban future.

> The common image of the country is now an image of the past, and the common image of the city an image of the future.... The pull of the idea of the country is toward old ways, human ways, natural ways. The pull of the idea of the city is towards progress, modernization, development.[99]

The disturbing experience of social change, of a dramatic shift in human lifestyle and relations within the modern era, was envisaged in the image of city life invading the country landscape, in the concrete symbol of the monstrous, inhuman freight train roaring across the grassy prairie or in the metallic din of a new factory ringing throughout the lost serenity of a mountain village.

What Henry David Thoreau added to this American agrarian tradition was a richer articulation of the relationship between the individual and nature. For Thoreau, man was primarily of nature and only through unfortunate contrivance a person of civilization. He begins his essay *Walking* with this point of clarification:

> I wish to speak a word for Nature, for absolute freedom and wildness, as contrasted with a freedom and culture merely civil—to regard man as an inhabitant, or part and parcel of Nature, rather than a member of society.[100]

To be "part and parcel of Nature" is to be at home in an existential and spiritual manner, for natural is synonymous with divinity in Thoreau's vocabulary.[101]

Like his fellow romantic naturalist Goethe, Thoreau felt that nature itself is a timeless abundance of health, as demonstrated in cycles of seasonal rebirth, a sharp contrast to the man-made suffering and disease of civilization. Nature offers opportunities for healing, a regenerating respite from the sickness of society. Participation in the natural environment unites man to "nature as a fostering mother to a poetic child,"[102] a profound form of homecoming, a recovery in body and spirit through a connection with divinity.

As a grit-real counterpoint to Thoreau's idealized pastoral images, American farm life in the final decades of the nineteenth century consisted of arduous labor for little economic reward or security. A series of commodity price depressions in the late 1860s, early 1880s, and the 1890s assailed the economic viability of the farm lifestyle. Steam threshers had appeared in many fields, a sure symbol of the shift from hand labor to a technologically advanced agriculture.[103] Additionally, the main decades of westward expansion had brought tremendous wealth to the railroad companies and the industrialists, but rarely to the farmers.[104] The real money in agriculture was often in land speculation and sale rather than in planting and raising crops for market.[105] Actual life on the farm in the late nineteenth century was not necessarily experienced in the soaring rhetoric of Thoreau.

ROMANTIC AGRARIANISM IN TWENTIETH-CENTURY AMERICA

> For the last couple of years I thought it would be a wonderful idea to have a national boys' camp out in our state. You see, if we could just get the poor kids off of the streets, out of the cities for a few months in the summer, and let them learn something about nature, [about] American ideals.[106]
>
> Senator Jefferson Smith (played by James Stewart) in
> the 1939 film *Mr. Smith Goes to Washington*

Numerous scholars have marked the start of the twentieth century as a dramatic turning point in the history of the romantic agrarian ideal.[107] By the 1890s, the western frontier had closed. There was no more land for expansion and agricultural appropriation. America had become finite. More importantly, the seemingly endless and often mythical vastness of geography—what Thoreau called "primeval, untamed, and forever untameable *Nature*"[108]—that had teased and propelled the American imagination since Thomas Jefferson had been exhausted. The American psyche had cultivated a long and intimate relationship between a virtuous, national identity and an open expanse of what Henry Nash Smith called "the Garden of the World," a relationship that nurtured the development of powerful themes of freedom, self-sufficiency, and equality.[109] Images of westward exploration into virgin territories no longer resourced that national imagination.

Over the course of the twentieth century, the American landscape was irreparably altered by industry, technology, and cosmopolitan growth. Between 1900 and 2000, the American farming population declined from 30 million to 5 million. The utilization of mechanical and chemical technologies reduced the number of man-hours needed to produce 100 bushels of corn from 150 in 1900 to 3 by century's end. The number of farms was reduced by two-thirds as large, technologically advanced agribusinesses replaced smaller, family-owned operations.[110]

Agrarianism, if it were to survive in the twentieth century, needed to take on new forms to cope with a modernity marked by urban and suburban growth, increasing levels of industrial and technological advancement, and a general demise of the traditions of preindustrial, rural life. In this context, after the machine defeated the plow and small villages gave way to big cities and widering suburbs, how would a pastoral ideal survive? Marx responds that it has, in fact, lived on due to "the extraordinary resilience of pastoralism—its capacity for adaptation to new times, new places, new social and political situations."[111] It may well be that romantic agrarianism as a moral and emotional constellation of American images developed over centuries is only further fueled by historical changes experienced as threats and intrusions. What energizes pastoral thought, at least in modern life, is not merely a heightened aesthetic of natural landscapes but a resistance to all that paves, mechanizes, computerizes, and bureaucratizes that green nature out of the lives of Americans. In that vein, David Danbom describes the highly adaptive continuation of romantic agrarianism in twentieth-century America as an intense cultural reaction to the "profound and dehumanizing loss of efficacy, independence, and mastery with industrialization,"[112] the painful experience of disconnection from land, community, and ultimately from the self.

Three specific strands of a twentieth-century agrarian vision have been put forth by scholars: the many pastoral celebrations and reclamations by urban and suburban dwellers in Schmitt's "Arcadian myth,"[113] the various intellectual traditions and social movements of Carlson's "new agrarian mind,"[114] and Holton's countercultural pastoralism.[115] My research has not yielded specific evidence linking Marianne Frostig or Newell C. Kephart directly to cultural and intellectual influences described by Schmitt, Carlson, and Holton. However, these three agrarian strands allow us to place the social theory of the movement educators within a suitable framework of prominent twentieth-century American agrarian thought. They provide us with a sense of the array of agrarian resources available to active intellectuals such as Frostig and Kephart.

In Schmitt's account, the late nineteenth-century demise of family farming and rural lifestyles was countered by the development of a vast popular literature—books, newspapers, magazines—that attempted "to translate nature into urban terms."[116] As many agrarian authors called for a return to the goodness and quietude of nature, metropolitan inhabitants initiated numerous activities and movements designed to bring elements of nature and natural experience into cosmopolitan life. The result was a multifaceted "urban response to nature that seemed most appropriate for an urban age."[117] Schmitt finds this impulse taking a variety of everyday forms in late nineteenth and early twentieth-century American life. A brief sampling will suffice to engender the mundane yet nearly ubiquitous character of these early twentieth-century cultural developments.

- The art and profession of landscape architecture developed as a romantic attempt to replicate the natural greenery of rural life amidst the buildings and pavements of cities and suburban towns. The goodness of the country could be planned, fabricated, and installed in an urban world.
- Extensive efforts were made to appropriate land near urban areas for state and national parks, thereby providing urbanites with genuine experiences of nature often within a day's travel. The social practice of natural retreat, of getting away to clean air and blue sky, was made available as a form of recreation.
- A number of children's nature camps and organizations were founded—including the Woodcraft Indians, the Sons of Daniel Boone, the Campfire Girls, and the Boy Scouts—in order to offer urban youth firsthand experiences camping and hiking in natural settings. Typically, these organizations attempted to train children in the independence-boosting and character-building outdoor crafts of the frontiersman.
- "In an era when native birds provided one of the few remaining links with wild nature,"[118] the modern hobby of birdwatching was organized around the general desire to value a specific feature of nature that had been lost in the shift to cosmopolitan, modern living. Catching sight of a certain species of bird came to symbolize an act of accessing and experiencing— literally, catching—a slice of nature.

The second strand of contemporary agrarianism involved the birth of twentieth-century "new agrarian mind," a multifaceted, not wholly consistent revival of intellectual agrarianism among a group of prominent twentieth-century writers and social movement leaders; including Liberty Hyde Bailey, the leader of the Country Life Movement, a popular agrarian movement that flourished between 1900 and 1920; Carle C. Zimmerman, a Harvard professor who founded the field of rural sociology in the early 1920s; and Father Luigi Liguitti, an Iowa priest who led the National Catholic Rural Life Conference in the 1930s and the 1940s. Appearing in popular magazines and books and on the radio, the new agrarians generally stood for a cluster of social principles:

1. *A radical, anticorporate, profamily economics* (primarily drawn from writings of agrarian economist Louis Borsodi[119]). Granting corporations legal status had created artificial economic and social units that stripped away the economic status of the family. This resulted in unnecessary systems of mass production and distant distribution that pulled apart rural families as their children moved to urban areas for wage labor in factories. An economics based on corporate commercialism and consumerism should be replaced with an economics that frames the family farm as the primary economic and productive unit. Subsistence farming—prioritizing the production of what one's own family needs—should replace commercialized agriculture.

2. *Healthy, stable, and moral family life is necessarily built on a foundation of farming.* Farming is the economic and natural center of good families. As Liguitti phrased, the farm is "an ideal place to raise children, one furnishing ideal home surroundings for mutual love and help."[120] Farming's moral status is based on both the natural virtue of working in close collaboration with the goodness of the soil and the economic virtue of providing self-subsistence without need for commercial exchange.

3. *The "family unit [is] the foundation of society."*[121] A healthy American democracy begins with the moral font of the family. Carlson described the new agrarians as positing "the place of the countryside as the nursery of the nation."[122] Based on the notion that fertility was a natural sign of virtue, the reduced birth rates of urban areas by comparison to rural areas pointed to the moral decline of the modern family,[123] as evidenced in the modern social problems such as weak marriages, sexual promiscuity, and marriages without offspring. Thus, it was only in rural farming communities that one could truly enjoy democratic values: freedom from commercial constraints, independence as demonstrated in subsistence farming, and an egalitarian lifestyle where the citizens were neither poor nor rich.

4. *Modern science and technology, if appropriately utilized, can contribute to the betterment of the family farm and society.* As befits an industrial era, the new agrarians were by no means purely antimodern. They generally adapted to the proliferation of modern, scientific culture by embracing technological advances within a thoughtful, constructive approach that focused on the improvement of agricultural productivity and small-scale industrial operations. Scientific and technological progress, in this view, could be supported within an orientation

that continued to place families and farms at the economic and moral center of society.

The new agrarians, by Carlson's analysis, eventually constituted the intellectual basis for the family values movement of the Reagan Era. Drawing from the new agrarian themes, an idyllic concept of a stable, "traditional" family was mobilized in the 1980s by evangelical Christian commentators such as Jerry Falwell and James Dobson against a range of cultural developments, including single-parent families, unmarried cohabitation, legalized abortion, and the Equal Rights Amendment.[124]

The third strand of twentieth-century agrarian thought was a 1960s resurgence of an American "countercultural pastoral,"[125] a hippie-generation shift toward the country and communes where an individual authenticity might be cultivated far from the corporate cultural monopoly. The envelopment of sexuality within traditional marriage and family was challenged by new sexual freedoms. Conventional notions of progress involving a vast machinery of military, corporate, and technological features were recast as antidemocratic political operations. What had to be opposed and stopped, vaguely but powerfully conceived, was the machine itself. In his 1964 speech to the Berkeley student radicals, Mario Savio advised the free speech protesters to "put your bodies on the machine and make it stop." Leo Marx has described this line as a specific reanimation of Thoreau's words in *Civil Disobedience*: "let your body be a friction to stop the machine."[126] Halt the distortions being clothed as progress and assert the sanctity of humanity and individuality in opposition to the mechanized din of modern civilization.[127]

The 1960s counterculture may be viewed as a middle class response to an experience of alienation within a society that failed to support traditional goals of individualism and democratic community. American society had succumbed to a stale conformism that offered few opportunities for self-expression and personal development. Pervaded by anonymity and anxiety, communities were "too impersonal and corrosively competitive to gratify . . . needs for mutuality and cohesion."[128] The country, as represented in a mythological image of a small town of classless mutuality, as the geographic antithesis of the city, was a symbol of a morally promising retreat from the ills of a failing civilization.

In the 1968 hit song "Going Up the Country," the popular blues-rock group Canned Heat sang of escaping the city, "going to where the water tastes like wine," a rural refuge where a person "can stay drunk all the time."[129] A pastoral image of freedom and fulfillment built of biblical metaphors is contrasted with a city of discord and misery. Through an agrarian flight, "the individual can escape the constraints of society and recapture a lost innocence, that he or she can reclaim a lost freedom in a lost Eden, a paradise almost always associated with nature and almost never with civilization."[130]

By Schiff's interpretation, the countercultural pastoral concept of flight from the city to the country was a reinvigoration of the themes of Thoreau and the early transcendentalists. Canned Heat's redemptive rural retreat retraced Thoreau's purposive withdrawal to Walden Pond.

> Its common core appears to be a total disenchantment with the existing capitalist-pluralist order. The counter-culture shares the early transcendentalist view that capitalist-industrial society, in general, and American society, in particular, is ugly, repressive, and dehumanizing.[131]

The rationale for escaping an urbanized, modern existence to the idealized country rests on an emotional and moral need to trade artifice for authenticity, "the false consciousness of society" for "self-fulfillment based on genuine values related to human life."[132]

MOVEMENT EDUCATION AND AGRARIAN POLITICS

The romantic agrarianism of the movement educators is a complex historical puzzle that defies simple and comprehensive explanations. Any attempt to pull together the disparate and uneven threads of political and cultural history is likely to yield only a tangled jumble of heady confusion. Therefore, in this final portion of this chapter, I will briefly address one scientific issue and one political matter. The first involves a problem of setting boundaries around objects of scientific analysis within holistic forms of psychology. Working in the holistic traditions of clinical and experimental science forged greatly by Gestalt theorists and Goldstein, Kephart and Frostig had tremendous difficulty marking out a clearly delineated terrain for their analysis of learning difficulties. If holism calls a researcher to appreciate the integrated nature of life, of mind and body, of child and environment, where does one draw clear lines of delineation between the object of scientific analysis and the irrelevance residing beyond scrutiny? Kephart and Frostig struggled with this boundary problem.

The second issue, a matter of politics, involves the seemingly contradictory alliance of a conservative romantic agrarianism and a liberal humanistic professional ethos of assisting those in need. The movement educators took a reactionary conservative position in relation to social change in the mid-twentieth century, casting the dramatic and multifaceted growth of modernity as a cultural deterioration involving deficient urban families and children. Their primary solution was a psychoeducational program of individual diagnosis and instruction for children needing assistance, a special education practice ideologically aligned by most scholars with a liberal politics of social assistance for the downtrodden.

HOLISM AND THE BOUNDARY PROBLEM

In a speech given to the Kant Society in Berlin in December 1925, Gestalt theorist Max Wertheimer defined the scientific charge of a holistic psychology:

> There are wholes, the behaviour of which is not determined by that of their individual elements, but where the part-processes are themselves determined by the intrinsic nature of the whole. It is the hope of Gestalt theory to determine the nature of such wholes.[133]

This brief statement neatly captures an essential feature of the clinical science of movement education. Drawing heavily from Goldstein's organismic theory as well as the Gestalt theories, the movement educators viewed children in terms of a series of inherent unities. Psychological domains of activity such as emotion, cognition, and behavior were incorporated under one neurosensory framework. A central nervous system structure was understood to orchestrate and harmonize all mental and bodily functions. Motor development and intellectual development were viewed as integrated aspects within the total growth and maturation of the child. It was the hope of the movement educators, in line with Wertheimer's original scientific charge, to understand the nature of the neurological whole of the moving, thinking, feeling organism.

Later in that same 1925 speech, Wertheimer attempted to define the levels of scientific analysis consistent with a holistic psychology. His description began at the physical center of scientific analysis, the operations of the brain or mind, and then expanded gradually outward in concentric circles. The first level of scientific focus concerned only what is internal to the mind, the traditional psychological investigation of psychic functioning. Gestalt theory added a second concentric ring of analysis, a research "program to treat the organism as a part in a larger field.... in the relation between organism and environment."[134] This was the analytic field inhabited and developed with such intricacy by Goldstein in his examinations of the brain-injured soldiers' adaptation to the immediate environment apprehended by their sensory organs.

Wertheimer's theoretical difficulty, and the larger issue for any holistic psychology, arose in the leap to a third concentric circle, to a social or cultural sphere. It was here where a psychological tradition filled primarily with theoretical and experimental attempts to understand the solitary individual underfunded the holistic desire to define "the character of the whole."[135] Gestalt theory, and holism in general, abhorred the scientific isolation of elements, the piecemeal analysis of bits, slices, and chunks framed in artificial detachment from the entirety of relations and configuration. But what was the whole object of study? What were the proper boundaries of the whole? At what point did analyses of connections and relationships cease?

Certainly, the individual could be understood only within the context of larger social groups. Wertheimer logically asserted: "A man is not only a part of his field, he is also one among other men."[136] A person is a part within many greater wholes: social units such as the family, workforce, or religious group. In Gestalt terms, the social whole consists of but is more than the sum of the individual parts.

> When a group of people work together it rarely occurs, and then only under very special conditions, that they constitute a mere sum of independent egos. Instead the common enterprise often becomes their mutual concern and each works *as* a meaningfully functioning part of the while.[137]

Individuals live and act within social networks involving "balance" and "harmonious and systematic occupation" that greatly determine not only what an individual does but also who he is.[138]

Suddenly, after offering a preliminary outline of a social systems theory, Wertheimer halted.

> Further discussion of this point would carry us into the work of social and cultural science which cannot be followed here.[139]

He stopped his outward journey from individual to cultural at the point where the Gestalt theory, lacking sufficient scientific capacity, ran thin. While the anti-atomistic momentum of the theory required an expansive view that incorporated all possible elements into the structural analysis, a theory of psychology could not, as a practical matter, turn into a science of culture. At some point of Wertheimer's sequence of concentric circle expansion, holism must carve out a defined whole object of study and allow the remainder to drift away without examination.

The holistic psychology of Kephart and Frostig ran into much the same problem. They attempted to unify the broadest variety of theories and factors into a single, comprehensive science capturing the natural whole of the child. As a scientific practice, their holism incorporated a wide variety of neurological and psychological theories within a framework that sutured together experimental psychology, psychometric measurement, and a tradition of clinical phenomenology. Epistemologically, they melded objective forms of quantitative analysis with subjective professional judgment. Within their orientation to the child as an organism, drawing heavily from Goldstein and the Gestalt theorists, they viewed numerous psychic and physiological operations as inseparable. The cognition, affect, and behavior of children were understood as differing exhibitions of a central neurostructural unity. Intellectual process and motor activities—mind and body—were theorized within a single neurological fabric of growth and maturation. The central nervous system was the organizational foundation of all of the child's functions and activities, thereby allowing the movement educators to understand seemingly distinct activities such as balancing on a beam and reading a printed page as intimately related.

While Wertheimer had suddenly paused at the brink of social analysis, the movement educators kept traveling, rejecting the traditional theoretical boundaries of a methodological individualism, writing their own social map as they went. Their Goldstein and Strauss-inspired neuropsychology offered scant intellectual provision for the analysis of historical change and no theoretical orientation to the social situation of urban modernity. Lacking conceptual assets in their professional knowledge base, they reached beyond psychology and education proper for a romantic agrarian social theory. They expanded their neurosensory understanding of the child to incorporate notions of historical and cultural decline appropriated from a broad tradition of American pastoralism. The dominant structural feature of their analysis of the child—the underlying neurological system—became the catch-all explanatory repository for the ill effects of technological modernity. Historical deterioration and cultural decay were discovered in the damaged central nervous systems of academically deficient children.

The movement educators employed two allied theories of deterioration, one cultural and one neurological, one portraying America as a society of declining social stability and moral virtue, and one viewing children as struggling with compromised central nervous systems and associated psychological functions. The frequent conflation of the two theories framed Frostig and Kephart's clinical work with children within a grand theory of a moribund technological civilization. The result was a specific pastoral version of cultural deprivation theory. Although their social theory journey was quite unique among their learning disabilities research colleagues, the political destination of Kephart and Frostig was remarkably similar to that of many others, a science that defined children from low-income families as deficient learners needing intervention.

CONSERVATIVE POLITICS IN A LIBERAL PROFESSIONAL TRADITION

The movement educators lived and worked within a period of post-World War II American history marked by dramatic cultural conflicts and social change—including the Civil Rights Movement, Women's Movement, Disability Rights

Movement, and the Viet Nam War—that was experienced by many Americans as a time of instability and fear. The writings of Kephart and Frostig were laced with a sense of American culture in jeopardy and a heightened need for meaningful response. In an era of social upheaval, they each embraced a conservative stance championing traditional forms of social order as the continuing source of American virtue. It is also clear that they viewed the moral mission of their science and educational practice with children with learning disabilities as inseparable from the social and political challenges of the times. It would not be an overstatement to say that they understood themselves to be attempting to heal a decaying society through the psychoeducational treatment of damaged children.

Staunchly conservative in their response to the social changes of the 1960s and the early 1970s, Kephart and Frostig were also passionate workers within a humanistic psychology of educational assistance, leaders in furthering a professional tradition dedicated to helping children in need. The expansion of educational concern and provision to previously neglected populations is generally considered a form of liberal politics. The twentieth-century professional history of psychology and special education seeking and assisting groups of children with disabilities is often cast as a humanistic liberal effort to support devalued or ignored children and their families.[140]

Viewed in this light, the politics of the movement educators were a seemingly contradictory blend of a class-based theory of cultural deprivation and a liberal, humanistic practice of special education. Frostig and Kephart's science of learning disabilities consisted of an incongruent coupling of a social and historical theory of a deteriorated society needing massive repair with a clinical practice of individual healing. They attempted to address what they understood to be a complex cultural decline that had befallen the United States over decades through psychological practices of individual diagnosis and treatment.

Danbom has insightfully observed that what makes romantic agrarianism so appealing to the American psyche is its "individualistic ideology, stressing the possibility—even the necessity—of individual solutions to social problems."[141] Numerous critics of American special education have made a similar claim about the categorical system of educational services provided to students with learning disabilities and other diagnosed disorders. A variety of social issues involving the cultural diversity of the public school student body, including poverty, social class hierarchy, and racism, have been habitually translated by the special education system into regimens of diagnosis and treatment for problematic individuals.[142] Danbom's comment directs our attention to the possibility that an American ideology of individualism supplies a central philosophical plank to both the pastoral tradition and the early field of learning disabilities. The unification of an agrarian social theory with a developmental neuropsychology of childhood defect in the work of the movement educators in the 1960s made sense only given a distinctly American proclivity to heal society one defective child at a time.

Epilogue: A Science IN Transition

THE INTELLECTUAL ROOTS OF AMERICAN SPECIAL EDUCATION

The nurse's footsteps rang down the dark hallway, growing louder with each echoed clop. Across the long tiled corridor, her shadow stretched like a dark and foreboding arm toward the man and child huddled in the corner. Samuel Kirk put one finger to his lips, and his student playfully gestured a "hush" right back. They held their breath and remained still for a long moment. Then the footsteps and the shadow receded together. The nurse had gone the other way. The psychology graduate student sighed, pulled a book out from under his sweater, and the pair began reading again.

The secretive nature of Kirk's 1929 tutoring experience in an Illinois institution for feebleminded children revealed the transgressive quality of his actions. More than institution rules, he violated the commonsense symbolic complex of mental defect that declared feebleminded children to be largely empty of learning potential. His foolhardy optimism in claiming the possibility of learning potential in a deficient boy was the first plank of the conceptual foundation of modern American special education. The profession would be devoted to seeking human potential in children widely deemed to have little or none.

But Kirk did more than that. After teaching the boy for a number of weeks, he took him to the Institute for Juvenile Research in Chicago for educational testing.

In order to decide if the reading tutoring was working, if it was actually nurturing latent intellectual abilities that had been present in the first place, Kirk asked for a battery of educational tests. This act was symbolic of the second feature of the intellectual foundation of modern special education. While human potential existed in children commonly overlooked and misunderstood, all children did not have latent and hidden capacities ripe for pedagogical cultivation. Harold Skeels' environmental stimulation would prove to be potent medicine, but not all children responded favorably to educational treatment. Central to the professional responsibility of special education was the scientific and authoritative sorting of intellectual potential from mental insufficiency, distinguishing fertile minds from barren.

The science of learning disabilities that developed in the United States between Kirk's 1929 tutoring experience and the enactment of Public Law 94–142 in the late 1970s dramatically widened the scope of children considered educationally capable. That fact is sure. Many students whose learning difficulties and behavioral patterns had been a mystery and a frustration were reframed as children of concealed and obstructed potential, children needing proper educational treatment in order to achieve at an average or even superior level.

But the valuable outcome of convincing educators and parents of the latent learning potential of a significant portion of all children who experienced educational failure did not occur without collateral damage. Two distinct groups of students were construed by learning disability science in a negative light. Children of lower-class families were understood as perhaps the most unfortunate version of the learning disability type, for their dysfunctions were largely born of their parents' limitations and ineptitude. Widespread cultural deprivation theories assumed that low-income families and urban neighborhoods tended to provide insufficient mental stimulation to growing youngsters. Neuropsychology became the unexpected scientific purveyor of a callous social class politics.

As lower class youth were stigmatized through capture by the learning disability construct, children with mental retardation were further reified as the bearers of incurable incompetence by rejection from the new disorder. As learning disability diagnoses culled the greatest intellectual potential from the population of struggling and failing learners, there were human remnants, those left behind, the mentally retarded now doubly identified as lacking promise. In an era when psychologists, physicians, and educators were scrambling to recast thousands of children into a new learning problem category with virtually unlimited upside potential, the diagnostic reconfirmation of mental retardation was a strong educational condemnation. At the cruel underside of human potential discovered was human inadequacy reaffirmed.

Kirk's decision to test his student at the Institute for Juvenile Research also exemplified a third feature of the intellectual basis of American special education.

Through many weeks of close interaction with his student, Kirk had surely developed his own judgment about whether the boy was learning to read. Formed within his own subjectivity, his own thoughts and feelings derived from his many observations and grown within his interpersonal relationship with the child, was an interpretation of what his student was achieving. Perhaps because of his inexperience, perhaps because he was studying to become a psychologist, Kirk did not believe that his own subjective understanding was adequate to determine if the boy was actually learning to read. He turned to a series of objective measures to supplement his own perspective. His final evaluation of learning in this case combined his own subjective appraisal and a group of objective educational tests. The science and practice of American special education in the twentieth century would develop in this gentle tension between subjectivity and objectivity, in a careful balance between opposing epistemological poles of a clinical phenomenology involving interpersonal contact and close observation and a detached precision of objective measurement.

In the mid-1970s, however, that moderate balance of subjectivity and objectivity in the science of learning disabilities was challenged. The very character and quality of the science of learning disabilities fell into doubt. A harsh and convincing critique targeted the scientific foundation of the construct, as well as the two primary traditions of educational treatment that had become widely accepted: movement education and psycholinguistic process training. Suddenly, just as learning disability reached educational legitimacy under federal law, as the construct moved from scattered clinical utilization to public school mass consumption, an unforeseen possibility emerged. By force of law the learning disability construct would enter the public schools, triumphant and provocative, but the very science of clinical treatment that built the construct in the first place might be tossed on the scrap heap.

SNAKE OIL?

The earth-shaking critique of the scientific validity of both movement education and psycholinguistic processing treatment was issued in a series of articles by a group of researchers led by Donald Hammill, a special educator who had studied at the University of Texas. He was, perhaps, demonstrative of a new breed of learning disabilities researcher. He was not a clinical psychologist like Kephart or Kirk, and he was not a physician like Strauss. He was trained as an educational researcher. As Public Law 94–142 was enacted in local districts, the everyday responsibility for the interpretation and utilization of the learning disability construct passed from the original group of clinical researchers to the special educators employed by the public schools as well as to the growing system of university-based teacher educators and researchers. What had developed in the intellectual circles of psychology and neurology would be carried forward by the field of education. Hammill and his colleagues, it seemed, were in charge of the welcoming committee.

After brief stints on the faculty at Wichita State University and Temple University, Donald Hammill left academia in 1972. He founded a publishing company in 1977 that produced journals, tests, and materials in the fields of rehabilitation and special education.[1] Between 1972 and 1974, he wrote two articles reviewing the research on movement education and one reviewing the science of psycholinguistic process training. His ambitious purpose was to question the scientific basis for the two main traditions of learning disability treatment. All three papers were published in prominent journals read by the entire field of learning disabilities. His reviews of the research literature yielded scathing conclusions that sounded an alarm in the new field of learning disabilities.[2]

Movement education, by Hammill's appraisal, was little more than well-marketed snake oil.

> Any interested person who reads the efficacy literature will conclude that the value of perceptual training, especially those programs often used in schools, has not been clearly established. If he concludes that such training lacks solid support, he may begin to question the purchase of attractively packaged materials which some companies offer teachers along with unsubstantiated claims concerning their merits, the practice of providing perceptual-motor training to all school children in the name of readiness training, and the assumption that a lack of perceptual-motor adequacy causes a considerable amount of academic failure.[3]

After reviewing salient studies in the field, he condemned the movement education programs as ineffective in training in processes of visual perception. For example, of eight studies of Frostig's program of perceptual education, "six studies reported no statistical difference between trained and untrained subjects."[4] Only four of sixteen published studies of the Kephart treatment approach resulted in statistically significant gains for the trained students.[5]

Moreover, Hammill found virtually no relationship between perception training and school learning. His examination of literacy research clearly demonstrated that "training in perception does not positively affect reading."[6] In studies of the relationship of visual-motor training to measures of academic functioning, such as school readiness, intelligence, and school achievement, only seven out of twenty-three post-test measures demonstrated training effectiveness. Visual-motor and perceptual training failed both as an intervention for basic psychomotor processes believed to underlie school learning and as a direct preparation for academic success. Swinging with a large hammer, Hammill quickly shattered the central claims of Kephart, Frostig, and the movement educators.

In words that barely concealed his disdain, Hammill chastised the leading perceptual motor training developers, citing them by name—"Frostig, Getman, Kephart, Barsch"—for selling educational programs without valid scientific support.[7] Without hesitation, he tossed aside the decades of clinical activity with children and families engaged in by these prominent figures. He then rebuked the "individuals who have developed and marketed the various visual perception programs and materials" by ironically urging them to "set up efficacy studies utilizing respectable research designs."[8] Not only had the movement educators failed to build a legitimate scientific basis for their theory and treatment, they had committed a grievous ethical error in peddling empirically flawed wares.

Kirk's psycholinguistic processing treatment activities fared only slightly better under Hammill's microscope. On the plus side, Hammill found that the ITPA (Illinois Test of Psycholinguistic Abilities), with the exception of one subtest, was a good measure of psychological abilities underlying communication. That conclusion supported Hammill's later work developing the third version of the ITPA.[9] However, the educational practice of diagnosing and treating the abilities assessed by the ITPA was a professional dead end. He concluded that

> the idea that psycholinguistic constructs, as measured by the ITPA, can be trained by existing techniques remains nonvalidated.... the efficacy of training psycholinguistic functioning has not been conclusively demonstrated.[10]

Kirk's extensive efforts to build the assessment tool assumed that measuring psychological abilities mattered only if those abilities could then, as Alfred Binet had advised, be effectively treated. Hammill claimed that Kirk's ITPA was basically accurate but that all instructional efforts related to that instrument's measurements had proved fruitless. Psycholinguistic abilities appeared to be "impossible or extremely difficult to teach."[11] While Kirk was no charlatan, his attempt to position the ITPA as the central feature of an effective process of educational remediation had, by Hammill's analysis, flopped.

SCIENCE AGAINST SCIENCE

The comprehensive reach and analytic power of Hammill's three articles was readily apparent to any reader. Ostensibly, he had gathered together all pertinent research on sensorimotor or perceptual treatment and psycholinguistic process training, distilled the many studies into summative form, and logically concluded that the two main strands of scientific activity underlying the learning disability construct and its treatment were deeply problematic. But the key to understanding Hammill's analysis was his process of selecting the empirical ingredients, his scheme for the inclusion and exclusion of specific research studies from consideration, that ultimately led to the dramatic deflation of learning disability science. The logic employed within this selection process offered a window into Hammill's philosophical orientation to social science. What read as a direct and resounding critique of the profoundly flawed science of learning disabilities was, in terms of philosophy of science, an objectivist confrontation of the epistemological breadth of the clinical science tradition. Where Hammill differed from Kirk and Kephart was his understanding of what counts as scientific knowledge.

Researchers had examined the theories and treatment practices of Kephart, Frostig, Barsch, Getman, and Kirk for many years prior to Hammill's critique. Numerous studies scrutinized the concepts and measurement instruments employed by the learning disability scientists. Likewise, many studies attempted to replicate the treatment successes that Kirk, Kephart, and the rest had achieved in their own clinical work.[12] A quick reading of this research literature would conclude that research support for the fields of movement education and psycholinguistic process training was mixed, with a fair balance between supporting and nonsupporting studies.

Hammill's interpretation of that research literature relied on the application of a specific set of selection criteria. In his review of studies of visual perception training, he included only those studies that were published after 1955, a strategy that swept the entire catalog of Wayne School research by Strauss, Werner, and Lehtinen into the wastebasket. He ruled out studies of treatment programs that lasted less than 15 weeks. Most importantly, he included "only studies which applied statistical analyses,"[13] a full rejection of the decades of clinical case studies of individual children undergoing various forms of educational treatment.

In Hammill's analysis of the relationship between visual perception training and reading skills, he accepted only those research studies that involved "tests of reading comprehension, rather than word-call or word recognition ability."[14] This criterion set aside investigations of the acquisition of the early reading skills of basic decoding in favor of the more advanced, later skills of comprehension, thereby shifting emphasis away from the early development of young children. These criteria had a dramatic effect on Hammill's final summation and analysis of the relevant literature. In his review of the relationship between reading achievement and visual perception, he winnowed 42 published articles to a final group of 12 acceptable studies. Similarly, in his summary of research on Kephart-based treatment programs, he reduced 42 total studies to a short list of 16 instances of "better research."[15]

The expressed rationale for rejecting the vast majority of research related to the training of visual perception, visual-motor skills, and psycholingustic processes was that he saw "weaknesses in their designs."[16] An examination of the contents strewn across Hammill's cutting room floor offers clues to the epistemological scissors at work. Examples of the subjectivism of the Goldstein-Strauss tradition of scientific observation and expertise-based insight utilized within the course of clinical treatment were deemed invalid. Poorly designed research "used small samples, had no control groups, and/or trained for shorter periods of time."[17] The common practice of closely following a small number of cases over weeks or even months of treatment through clinical observations as well as a battery of psychological and educational measures was construed by Hammill as unscientific. Acceptable research projects used a single, favored research design, the statistical comparison of pre and post-treatment, standardized measures in "an experimental group design" with "at least twenty experimental subjects."[18]

SCIENCE IN THE BALANCE

Working in the broad tradition of American functionalism, featuring the precise psychometrics of Marion Monroe, fortified with a strong dose of Gestalt holism, and embracing the observant phenomenology of Kurt Goldstein, American learning disabilities researchers of the 1950s and 1960s had freely mixed the objectivist and subjectivist tools of science. Learning disabilities researchers took seriously Harvey Carr's vision of a psychological science delicately balanced between extremes of objectivism and subjectivism. It was a pragmatic science with little interest in epistemological arguments favoring one perspective or the other. Rather, in opportunistic style, quantitative measurements and statistical calculations were alloyed with clinical observations of behavior and the phenomenology of individual case studies. Research methods were viewed as an extensive array of useful tools routinely subordinated to the larger mission of understanding and treating learning defects. Undoubtedly, this was a science limited by the constraints of methodological individualism, the practice of interpreting human behavior and social achievements as demonstrations of underlying individual capacities. It sought educational problems and solutions within the mental and physical operations of individual children. But within that individualized focus, the learning disabilities researchers' orientation to scientific activity had been quite eclectic, flexible, and innovative.

Perhaps the clearest articulation of the middle road posture of the learning disability scientists was presented by Marianne Frostig in her 1955 dissertation. She framed her research within the philosophical and practical interplay of objectivism and subjectivism, in the contrast between actuarial science and clinical science.[19] An actuarial approach seeks the objective prediction of human behavior through the application of mathematics to lived events. Large sets of quantitative data are gathered in order to develop probabilities of specific outcomes or occurrences. Frostig explained its strengths and limitations:

> A researcher who works with statistical methods can learn how to predict by the application of his theoretical knowledge, which gives him guidelines for the collection and evaluation of data. He can predict percentages of successes or failures within the sample of which the case is the part, but he is unable to predict to which of the probability groups this particular case belongs.[20]

An actuarial science pursues a prediction based on statistical probabilities involving categories of people or classifications of events. Application of categorical analyses to the distinct case of an individual, Frostig claimed, is problematic given the failure of any system of social classifications to adequately capture individuality.

On the other hand, a clinical science such as the common psychological and medical practice of case study relies on a subjective interpretation of the unique details of a given case. What it lacks in a broad understanding of social probabilities it makes up for in its flexible capacity to track the particular tendencies and performances of an individual on specific tasks in multiple situations. This is achieved because of the researcher's skills of human interaction and interpersonal understanding. "Case study prediction relies on the characteristics of the observer, as well as on characteristics of the subjects and of the situation which are not measureable."[21] The necessary observer characteristics include "sympathy, empathy, recipathy, intuition, and insight."[22]

Where actuarial research employs statistical tables, case studies rely on the observer's judgment, sensitivity, and insight. Frostig concluded that both "actuarial prediction" and case study analysis are of equal importance.[23] Her analysis greatly mirrored a prominent 1941 paper by Paul Wallin, a collaborator with Lewis Terman at Stanford University, on the need for both case studies and actuarial analyses in the prediction of human behavior. Wallin issued strong advice on the need to integrate actuarial and clinical modes into one science.

> The statistician and the case study investigator can make mutual gains if they will quit quarreling with each other and begin borrowing from each other.[24]

Frostig and Wallin's notion of a balance of methods and epistemological perspectives resided at the heart of the science of learning disabilities.

If the architectural house of learning disabilities science stood in the balance of two epistemic piers, an actuarial objectivism and a clinical subjectivism,

Hammill's critique wielded one side of the structure against the other. He hurled a strict objectivism against the blended epistemology of the prior generation of learning disabilities researchers, resulting in the harsh rejection of the subjective elements of clinical knowledge. He issued a thunderous declamation of a purely actuarial science built solely of experimental control and statistical comparison. What read as a fierce critique of the faulty nature of the science behind the learning disability theory and its treatments was a dramatic recalibration of that science from a long tradition of epistemological balance to a strong form of objectivism.

While Hammill's objectivist science clashed resoundingly with the epistemological balance espoused by the learning disabilities researchers, it was not uncommon among educational researchers of the early 1970s. Generally speaking, an objectivist or actuarial orientation featuring complex techniques of inferential statistics ruled the science of education. The comparatively few qualitative or ethnographic educational researchers of the era, according to Norman Denzin and Yvonna Lincoln, took their "cue from statistical colleagues" by employing "the language and rhetoric of positivist and postpositivist discourse."[25] Qualitative or ethnographic methods of educational research that are quite common today did not yet merit inclusion in the standard educational research methods textbooks.[26]

Similarly, educational research design texts published in the 1970s often disregarded the clinical case study method that had been a staple of learning disabilities science. In the rare instances when case study methods were covered in the textbooks, the descriptions were very brief and often emphasized the limitations of the approach. University of Michigan professor M. Clemens Johnson devoted just three pages in his 352-page, research methods textbook to an overview of case studies. He noted that cases had a particular utility in research on "children with learning disabilities, behavioral problems, or physical handicaps."[27] Another methods text warned that case studies were "particularly vulnerable to subjective biases," thereby connoting an objectivist epistemology with accurate representation and subjectivity with error and distortion. The strengths of case studies, in this text, amounted only to their utility providing "background information for planning major investigations," a preliminary function in service to "more generalized statistical" research.[28]

TURNED SOUR

The response from the leading learning disabilities researchers to Donald Hammill's critique was bitter.[29] Certainly, the veteran researchers felt a sense of betrayal. Their many decades of honest contributions to the science of learning disabilities had seemingly been burned with a single match. Kirk complained with uncharacteristic animosity:

> I have been amazed at some individuals that spend most of their time criticizing everyone else without being constructive themselves. We have some iconoclastic individuals who devote their time to telling us that Miss Jones' remedial method is no good or has not been proven or has not solved all the remedial problems. Or that Mr. Jones' test which measures the structure and size of the nose in Timbuktoo is invalid as a measure of the structure and size of the big toe in Bali.[30]

He griped that some researchers seemed to specialize in destruction, tearing down the contributions of others without offering "any constructive solutions."[31]

> Under our system of "publish or perish," what are those in education going to do? The journals are full of articles. New journals are appearing. Some report original research. Others deal with controversies in the field. Many others deal with review articles and critiques of other people's work. As someone said, if you can't do constructive work and you want to make a name, attack those who *are* doing constructive work.[32]

It was not that someone had found weaknesses or flaws in the science that he and his colleagues conducted in the post-World War II decades. What Kirk objected to was the complete deprecation of the work of movement educators and psycholinguistic processing specialists, the total denouncement of the clinical science of educational treatment.

Similarly, Marianne Frostig lamented "the lack of cooperation, and the petty disagreement"[33] that marked the field. Like Kirk, she felt that some researchers were focused "on their own benefits, on power, and on money instead of helping children."[34] By attacking the established traditions of educational science, these critical actors were, to Frostig's mind, convincing many educators that learning disabilities were not amenable to effective treatment.

> One of the trends I have observed worries me, a certain pessimism that can be noticed in this and in other countries, a certain disenchantment with regard to treatment prospects for children with learning difficulties.[35]

To accept the learning disability construct as valid, as a real childhood disorder requiring intensive educational services, while discarding the most prominent and well-researched educational treatment programs was to invite a deep and overwhelming pessimism.

Ray Barsch and Gerald Getman dressed their resentment in sarcastic tones, resistant declarations, and somber intellectuality. They lashed out at the educational science that had vehemently turned on them. Barsch positioned himself as a longtime heretic, an independent thinker who had left behind sheepish conformity to statistical foolishness years ago.

> At one time I entertained aspirations to become an educational scientist. Seduced by tantalizing promise of scientific fulfillment and prospect of entry into the sanctuary of the elite, I carried on a brief fling with the .01 level of confidence, faithfully rehearsing the proper ritualistic incantations to the gods of significance…. By clinical persuasion, I became a conscientious objector…. Freed from the compulsion to affiliation, I have continuously enjoyed the liberties of imagination and the unbridled quest for satisfaction of my curiosity while ignoring any urgency to R. S. V. P. to the scientific committee in charge of affairs.[36]

Barsch's 1976 autobiography boiled with indignation for those researchers and the quantitative science that had attacked his life's work.

Getman stood in cold defiance of the data and findings that contradicted his decades of clinical activity. It was as if someone had told him that his own experiences assisting children with learning difficulties were simply a fictional mirage that could not be trusted.

> I am deeply convinced that if a particular method will allow two or twenty children to acquire a concept that they can utilize and apply in further extension of their knowledge, it is a valid and correct method, even when data can be presented to show this method did not bring the desired results with hundreds of children in controlled and rigidly structured studies in other classrooms. When a method works with a child, averages, means, and standard deviations lose all meaning and relevance.[37]

His stance framed his own direct experience as superior to statistical calculations, asserting the lived validity of his work with children while warning of the detached distortion of psychological measures and positivistic algorithms. "Somehow, cold and controlled statistics and warm, vital children do not come out the same," he declared defiantly, "no matter how much the statistician wishes they would."[38]

A SCIENCE OF TEACHING?

Gerald Getman's comments about the separation of controlled statistics and real life pointed to an important side effect of Hammill's actuarial science. While the researchers of the Kirk and Kephart generation made great efforts to unite science and practice, often through housing scientific activity within practical treatment activities, an actuarial science cleanly split the two. School-based practitioners engaged in diagnostic and instructional tasks, pursuing the messy subjectivity of teaching, while external researchers engineered a controlled objectivity in neatly designed experiments. In the explicit actuarial science proposed by Hammill and his colleagues, the clinical subjectivity of instructional practitioners and the mathematical objectivity of detached researchers were split into two distinct roles. And the latter were deemed the true scientists holding epistemic superiority.

A fundamental reason for the epistemological and methodological stew of the traditional learning disabilities science was the intense devotion of the researchers to the unification of research and treatment, science and practice. Kirk, Kephart, and their colleagues attempted to combine a cold mentality of analytic detachment and a distinctly human interaction within a practical science. What was often called basic research sought a calculated precision through pure design. Variables were controlled and measured at a distance from the actual, lived scene. On the other hand, an applied or clinical form of research took place within the muddy but rich experiential space of daily interaction with children and families. Kirk believed that a balanced integration of both kinds of research was necessary in order to maintain a focus on the improvement of teaching.

> In my experience, the more rigid and basic the experiment, the less it has to do with application in the field.... Advancement will be done when we attack research from all angles. One type of research tends to feed another.[39]

An objectivism practiced at an arm's length from applied, clinical work with children risked a fate of practical irrelevance. Kirk warned that science must be deeply and directly engaged with Getman's "warm, vital children," the actual persons and lived situations.

Viewed in this light, the Hammill critique not only challenged the epistemological orientation and research methods of the science of learning disabilities; it also raised significant questions about how that science would contribute in the coming years to the instructional practices of teachers. After many decades of scientific investigation that supplied the intellectual provisions for the development of the learning disability construct, the paramount issue of how to teach a struggling learner—the same raw question the graduate student Kirk faced in 1929 with his first student—remained. At the essential bottom of the entire learning disability science enterprise endured the challenge of improving actual teaching practices with failing students. Could this learning disability idea and the scientific concepts and practices of the science of learning disabilities actually support the improvement of teaching? This question echoed from the Illinois institution hallway where Kirk first learned to teach to the thousands of new special education classrooms instituted across America after Public Law 94–142.

In a speech at the Council for Exceptional Children, Kirk challenged researchers to closely examine the psychological and social contours of teaching itself.

A survey of the research shows that researchers shy away from the study of the process of teaching. We study characteristics of children. We correlate test results, we evaluate the results of teaching by giving educational tests. But we seem to avoid the study of the process of teaching.[40]

Could this science examine "on a sound and scientific basis, the process of effective teaching?"[41] Could a science nominally organized around a disorder called learning disability contribute to the practical art of pedagogy? After all, what schools and teachers most needed was not a new kind of disordered child, a new category of educational disability with a standard list of learning deficits. They yearned for new and innovative ways of teaching that generated learning and growth in students who seemed, at first or even second glance, to be immune to instruction. They clamored for pedagogical approaches that were effective with the most challenging students. Ultimately, this daily predicament confronted by teachers, families, and children would frame the educational utility of the learning disability construct in the public schools and test the practical legacy of the science of learning disabilities.

Notes

1 INTRODUCTION

1. Samuel A. Kirk, "Autobiography," in *Teaching Children with Learning Disabilities: Personal Perspectives,* ed. James M. Kauffman and Daniel P. Hallahan (Columbus, OH, 1976), 238–269. Samuel A. Kirk, "Lecture—Final Report, Advanced Institute for Leadership Personnel in Learning Disabilities, Department of Special Education, University of Arizona," typescript, 1970, p. 5, Box 10, Samuel A. Kirk Papers (Archives Research Center, University of Illinois, Urbana).
2. Walker Percy, *The Message in the Bottle* (New York, 1975), 47.
3. James Hinshelwood, *Congenital Word-Blindness* (Chicago, 1917).
4. Marion Monroe, *Methods for Diagnosis and Treatment of Cases of Reading Disability Based on the Comparison of the Reading Performance of One Hundred Twenty Normal and One Hundred and Seventy Five Retarded Readers* (Worcester, MA, 1928).
5. Grace M. Fernald and Helen Keller, "The Effect of Kinaesthetic Factors in the Development of Word Recognition in the Case of Non-Readers," *Journal of Educational Research,* 4 (1921), 355–377.
6. Marion Monroe, *Children Who Cannot Read: The Analysis of Reading Disabilities and the Use of Diagnostic Tests in the Instruction of Retarded Readers* (Chicago, 1932), 1.
7. Alfred Binet, *Modern Ideas About Children*, trans. Suzanne Heisler (1911, Menlo Park, CA, 1975), 79.
8. John Dewey, "Mediocrity and Individuality," in *John Dewey: The Middle Works, 1899–1924, Volume 13*, ed. Jo Ann Boydston (Carbondale, IL, 1976), 289–294. John Dewey,

"Individuality, Equality, and Superiority," in *John Dewey: The Middle Works, 1899–1924, Volume 13*, ed. Jo Ann Boydston (Carbondale, IL, 1976), 295–300.

9. Stephen Jay Gould, *The Mismeasure of Man* (New York, 1981). Henry L. Minton, *Lewis M. Terman: Pioneer in Psychological Testing* (New York, 1988). Leila Zenderland, *Measuring Minds: Henry Herbert Goddard and the Origins of American Intelligence Testing* (New York, 1998).

10. Henry Herbert Goddard, *The Kallikak Family: A Study in the Heredity of Feeblemindedness* (New York, 1919).

11. Zenderland, *Measuring Minds*.

12. Goddard, *Kallikak Family*, 116.

13. Goddard, *Kallikak Family*, 116.

14. Goddard, *Kallikak Family*, 60.

15. Goddard, *Kallikak Family*, 117.

16. Henry H. Goddard, *School Training of Defective Children* (Yonkers-On-Hudson, New York, 1920), 75. Goddard, *Kallikak Family*.

17. Goddard, *Kallikak Family*, 55.

18. Edgar A. Doll, "Clinical Methods Applied to Teaching," *Educational Research Bulletin*, 7, 12 (1928), 255.

19. J. David Smith, "Darwin's Last Child: Mental Retardation and the Need for a Romantic Science," *Mental Retardation*, 37, 6 (1999), 504–506. Steven A. Gelb, "Darwin's Use of Intellectual Disability in *The Descent of Man*," *Disability Studies Quarterly*, 28, 2 (2008), n.p.

20. J. E. Wallace Wallin, *Problems of Subnormality* (Yonkers-On-Hudson, New York, 1921). J. E. Wallace Wallin, *The Education of Handicapped Children* (Boston, 1924).

21. Wallin, *Problems of Subnormality*, 333.

22. Wallin, *Education of Handicapped Children*, 263.

23. Wallin, *Education of Handicapped Children*, 309.

24. Wallin, *Education of Handicapped Children*, 309.

25. Wallin, *Education of Handicapped Children*, 306.

26. Wallin, *Education of Handicapped Children*, 309.

27. Wallin, *Education of Handicapped Children*, 318.

28. Wallin, *Education of Handicapped Children*, 309.

29. Wallin, *Education of Handicapped Children*, 309.

30. Wallin, *Education of Handicapped Children*, 319.

31. Public Schools of Trenton, NJ, *A Survey and Program for Special Types of Education* (Trenton, 1929), 16.

32. Meta L. Anderson, *Education of Defectives in the Public Schools* (Yonkers-On-Hudson, New York, 1917). Meta L. Anderson, "Essential Characteristics of the Type of Education Best Adapted to the Needs of the Mental Defective," *The Training School Bulletin*, 25 (1928), 97–107. Henry H. Goddard, *School Training of Defective Children* (Yonkers-On-Hudson, New York, 1920). Nathaniel O. Gould, "How One Michigan Country Cares For Its Mentally Retarded Children," *Nation's Schools*, 10 (1932), 47–52. The Ohio Institute, *Basic Considerations in the Organization of Special Education for Mentally Deficient and Retarded Children* (Columbus, OH, 1925). The Ohio Institute, *Institution for the Feebleminded, a Little Insight into a Child's Life in Our Schools for the Mentally Defective* (Columbus, OH, 1925). Public Schools of Trenton, *Survey and Program*.

33. Committee on Physically and Mentally Handicapped Child, "Problems of Mental Deficiency," in *The Handicapped Child: The White House Conference on Child Health and Protection* (New York, 1933), 345.
34. The Ohio Institute, *Basic Considerations*, 1.
35. The Ohio Institute, *Basic Considerations*, 4.
36. The Ohio Institute, *Basic Considerations*, 5.
37. The Ohio Institute, *Basic Considerations*, 4.
38. Public Schools of Trenton, *Survey and Program*, 23.
39. Public Schools of Trenton, *Survey and Program*, 24.
40. Public Schools of Trenton, *Survey and Program*, 47.
41. Public Schools of Trenton, *Survey and Program*, 24.
42. Public Schools of Trenton, *Survey and Program*, 16.
43. Anderson, *Education of Defectives*, 5.
44. Anderson, *Education of Defectives*, 99.
45. Anderson, *Education of Defectives*, 99.
46. Anderson, *Education of Defectives*, 12.
47. Henry H. Goddard, "Introduction," in *Education of Defectives in the Public Schools* (Yonkers-On-Hudson, New York, 1917), xv.
48. Goddard, "Introduction," xviii.
49. Anderson, *Education of Defectives*, 101.
50. This group of five men was chaired by E. R. Johnstone, the director of the Vineland Training School, and included Edgar Doll as a member.
51. Committee on Physically and Mentally Handicapped Child, "Problems of Mental Deficiency," 146.
52. Anderson, "Essential Characteristics," 97–106.
53. Thorleif G. Hegge, Robert Sears, and Samuel A. Kirk, "Reading Cases in an Institution for Mentally Retarded Children," proceedings and addresses of the American Association for the Study of Feeblemindedness, 37, 1932, 149–212. Thorleif G. Hegge, "Special Reading Disability with Particular Reference to the Mentally Deficient," proceedings of the American Association for the Study of Feeblemindedness, 39 (1934), 297–340.
54. Thorleif G. Hegge, "The Significance of Special Reading Disability in Mentally Handicapped Problem Children," *The American Journal of Psychiatry*, 94 (1937), 77–87.
55. Alfred A. Strauss and Laura Lehtinen, *Psychopathology and the Education of the Brain-injured Child* (New York, 1947). Alfred A. Strauss and Newell C. Kephart, *Psychopathology and the Education of the Brain-Injured Child*, Volume II (New York, 1955).
56. James Hinshelwood, "Word-Blindness and Visual Memory," *The Lancet*, 2 (1895), 1565.
57. Hinshelwood, "Word-Blindness and Visual Memory," 1565.
58. W. Pringle Morgan, "A Case of Congenital Word-Blindness," *The British Medical Journal*, 1871 (1896), 1378.
59. Morgan, "A Case of Congenital Word-Blindness," 1378.
60. Hamilton Cravens, *Before Head Start: The Iowa Station and America's Children* (Chapel Hill, NC, 1993).
61. Newell C. Kephart, untitled paper, typescript, p. 11, Series 1, Box 1, Folder 12, Newell C. Kephart papers (James A. Michener Library, University of Northern Colorado).

62. Beth L. Wellman, "The Effect of Pre-school Attendance Upon the IQ," *Journal of Experimental Education*, 1, 2 (1932), 48–69. Beth L. Wellman, "Growth in Intelligence under Differing School Environments," *Journal of Experimental Education*, 3, 2 (1934), 59–83. Hubert S. Coffey and Beth L. Wellman, "The Role of Cultural Status in Intelligence Changes of Preschool Children," *Journal of Experimental Education*, 5, 2 (1936), 191–202. Beth L. Wellman, "Mental Growth from Preschool to College," *Journal of Experimental Education*, 6, 2 (1937), 127–138. Beth L. Wellman, "Our Changing Concept of Intelligence," *Journal of Consulting Psychology*, 2, 4 (1938), 97–107.

63. Cravens, *Before Head Start*.

64. Cravens, *Before Head Start*.

65. Sam Kirk reported that hearing Skeels tell this story in 1939 had a profound effect on his thinking. Samuel A. Kirk, "Introspection and Prophecy," *Perspectives in Special Education: Personal Orientations*, ed. Burton Blatt and Richard J. Morris (Glenview, IL, 1984), 25–55.

66. Daniel P. Hallahan and Devery R. Mock, "A Brief History of the Field of Learning Disabilities," in *Handbook of Learning Disabilities*, ed. H. Lee Swanson, Karen R. Harris, and Steve Graham (New York, 2003), 16–29. Samuel A. Kirk, "Behavioral Diagnosis and Remediation of Learning Disabilities," in *Proceedings of the Conference on the Exploration into the Problems of the Perceptually Handicapped Child* (Evanston, IL, 1963). Samuel A. Kirk and Winifred D. Kirk, "On Defining Learning Disabilities," *Journal of Learning Disabilities*, 16, 1 (1983), 20–21.

67. United States Department of Education, *Twentieth-Fifth Annual Report to Congress on the Implementation of the Individuals with Disabilities Education Act* (Washington, 2004).

68. James G. Carrier, *Learning Disability: Social Class and the Construction of Inequality in American Education* (New York, 1986). James G. Carrier, "The Politics of Early Learning Disability Theory," in *Learning Disability: Dissenting Essays*, ed. Barry M. Franklin (London, 1987), 47–66.

69. Barry M. Franklin, *From "Backwardness" to "At-Risk": Childhood Learning Difficulties and the Contradictions of School Reform* (Albany, NY, 1994).

70. G. Burrell and Gareth Morgan, *Sociological Paradigms and Organizational Analysis* (London, 1979). Thomas M. Skrtic, *Behind Special Education* (Denver, 1995).

71. Willis F. Overton, "The Arrow of Time and the Cycle of Time: Concepts of Change, Cognition, and Embodiment," *Psychological Inquiry*, 5, 3 (1994), 215–216.

72. Burrell and Morgan, Sociological Paradigms and Organizational Analysis. Overton, "The Arrow of Time and the Cycle of Time: Concepts of Change, Cognition, and Embodiment," 215–237. Skrtic, Behind Special Education.

73. Overton, "The Arrow of Time and the Cycle of Time: Concepts of Change, Cognition, and Embodiment," 216.

74. Richard Shusterman, "Eliot's Pragmatist Philosophy of Practical Wisdom." *The Review of English Studies*, 40, 157 (1989), 74.

75. Harvey A. Carr, *Psychology: A Study of Mental Activity* (New York, 1925), 7.

76. Lars Udehn, "The Changing Face of Methodological Individualism," *Annual Review of Sociology*, 28 (2002), 483.

77. Udehn, "Changing Face of Methodological Individualism," 483.

78. Newell C. Kephart, *Learning Disability: An Educational Adventure* (West Lafayette, IN, 1968). Marguerite P. Ford, "New Directions in Special Education," *Journal of*

School Psychology, 9, 1 (1971), 73–83. Daniel P. Hallahan, "Cognitive Styles—Preschool Implications for the Disadvantaged," *Journal of Learning Disabilities,* 3 (1970), 5–9. Murray M. Kappelmann, E. Kaplan, and R. L. Ganter, "A Study of Learning Disorders among Disadvantaged Children," *Journal of Learning Disabilities,* 2 (1969), 267. Gordon R. Alley, Gerald Solomons, and E. Opitz, "Minimal Cerebral Dysfunction as It Relates to Social Class," *Journal of Learning Disabilities,* 4 (1971), 246–250. Dominic Amante, P. H. Margules, D. M. Hartmann, D. B. Storey, and L. J. Weeber, "The Epidemiological Distribution of CNS Dysfunction," *Journal of Social Issues,* 26, 4 (1970), 105–136. Lester Tarnopol, "Delinquency and Minimal Brain Dysfunction," *Journal of Learning Disabilities,* 3 (1970), 200–207. Samuel A. Kirk and Winifred D. Kirk, *Psycholinguistic Learning Disabilities: Diagnosis and Remediation* (Urbana, IL, 1971). Marianne Frostig and Phyllis Maslow, *Learning Problems in the Classroom: Prevention and Remediation* (New York, 1973). Daniel P. Hallahan and William M. Cruickshank, *Psychoeducational Foundations of Learning Disabilities* (Englewood Cliffs, NJ, 1973).

79. Kirk, "Autobiography," 238–269.
80. Hayden White, "The Historical Text as Literary Artifact," *Clio,* 3, 3 (1974), 277.

2 A BIOLOGICAL HOLISM OF BRAIN INJURY: THE SCIENCE OF KURT GOLDSTEIN

1. Kurt Goldstein, "Notes on the Development of My Concepts," *Journal of Individual Psychology,* 15, 1 (1959), 5–14. Anne Harrington, *Reenchanted Science: Holism in German Culture from Wilhelm II to Hitler* (Princeton, NJ, 1996).
2. Mitchell G. Ash, *Gestalt Psychology in German Culture, 1890–1967: Holism and the Quest for Objectivity* (Cambridge, England, 1995). Kurt Goldstein, "Autobiography," in *A History of Psychology in Autobiography,* Volume 5, ed. Edwin G. Boring and Gardner Lindzey (New York, 1967), 147–167. Harrington, *Reenchanted Science: Holism in German Culture from Wilhelm II to Hitler.*
3. Adhemar Gelb and Kurt Goldstein, "Zur psychologie des optischen Wahrnehmungs –und Erkennungsvorganges," in *Source Book of Gestalt Psychology,* trans. and ed. Willis D. Ellis (1918, Highland, NY, 1997), 315–325.
4. Gelb and Goldstein, "Zur psychologie des optischen Wahrnehmungs–und Erkennungsvorganges," 317.
5. Gelb and Goldstein, "Zur psychologie des optischen Wahrnehmungs–und Erkennungsvorganges," 317.
6. Gelb and Goldstein, "Zur psychologie des optischen Wahrnehmungs–und Erkennungsvorganges," 322.
7. Harrington, *Reenchanted Science: Holism in German Culture from Wilhelm II to Hitler.* Uta Noppeney, "Kurt Goldstein—A Philosophical Scientist," *Journal of the History of the Neurosciences,* 10, 1 (2001), 67–78.
8. Gelb and Goldstein, "Zur psychologie des optischen Wahrnehmungs–und Erkennungsvorganges," 320.
9. Goldstein, "Autobiography," 162.

10. Uta Noppeney, "Kurt Goldstein—A Philosophical Scientist," 67.

11. Goldstein, "Notes on the Development of My Concepts," 5–14.

12. Kurt Goldstein, in Glorida Leviton, *The Relationship Between Rehabilitation and Psychology* (Worcester, 1959), 134.

13. Alfred North Whitehead, *Process and Reality* (New York, 1979), 39.

14. Ulfried Geuter, "The Whole and the Community: Scientific and Political Reasoning in the Holistic Psychology of Felix Krueger," *Science, Technology, and National Socialism*, ed. Manika Renneberg and Mark Walker (New York, 1994), 197–223. Harrington, *Reenchanted Science: Holism in German Culture from Wilhelm II to Hitler*. Anne Harrington, "Unmasking Suffering's Masks: Reflections on Old and New Memories of Nazi Medicine," *Daedalus*, 125 (1996), 181–205. Fritz K. Ringer, *The Decline of the German Mandarins: The German Academic Community, 1890–1933* (Cambridge, MA, 1969).

15. Anne Harrington, "Metaphoric Connections: Holistic Science in the Shadow of the Third Reich," *Social Research*, 62, 2 (Summer, 1995), 357.

16. Ringer, *The Decline of the German Mandarins: The German Academic Community, 1890–1933*, 3. Stephen Cotsgrove, "Styles of Thought: Science, Romanticism, and Modernization," *The British Journal of Sociology*, 29, 3 (1978), 358–371.

17. Harrington, *Reenchanted Science: Holism in German Culture from Wilhelm II to Hitler*. Harrington, "Unmasking Suffering's Masks: Reflections on Old and New Memories of Nazi Medicine," 181–205. Ringer, *The Decline of the German Mandarins: The German Academic Community, 1890–1933*.

18. Harrington, *Reenchanted Science: Holism in German Culture from Wilhelm II to Hitler*, 141.

19. Harrington, *Reenchanted Science: Holism in German Culture from Wilhelm II to Hitler*. Anne Harrington, "Kurt Goldstein's Neurology of Healing: and Wholeness: A Weimar Story," in *Greater than the Parts: Holism in Biomedicine, 1920–1950*, ed. Christopher Lawrence and George Weisz (New York, 1997), 25–45. Goldstein, "Notes on the Development of My Concepts," 5–14. Goldstein, "Autobiography," 147–167.

20. Kurt Goldstein, *The Organism: A Holistic Approach to Biology Derived from Pathological Data in Man* (New York, 1939).

21. Walther Riese and Ebbe C. Hoff, "A History of the Doctrine of Cerebral Localization: Sources, Anticipations, and Basic Reasoning," *Journal of the History of Medicine*, 5 (1950), 51.

22. David Caplan, *Neurolinguistics and Linguistic Aphasiology* (New York, 1987). Gertrude H. Eggert, *Wernicke's Works on Aphasia: A Sourcebook and Review* (The Hague, Netherlands, 1977). Marc Jeannerod, *The Brain Machine: The Development of Neurophysiological Thought* (Cambridge, MA, 1985). Riese and Hoff, "A History of the Doctrine of Cerebral Localization: Sources, Anticipations, and Basic Reasoning," 50–71.

23. Caplan, *Neurolinguistics and Linguistic Aphasiology*. Eggert, *Wernicke's Works on Aphasia: A Sourcebook and Review*. Harrington, *Reenchanted Science: Holism in German Culture from Wilhelm II to Hitler*.

24. Harrington, *Reenchanted Science: Holism in German Culture from Wilhelm II to Hitler*. Harrington, "Kurt Goldstein's Neurology of Healing: and Wholeness: A Weimar Story," 25–45. Caplan, *Neurolinguistics and Linguistic Aphasiology*. Eggert, *Wernicke's Works on Aphasia: A Sourcebook and Review*. Riese and Hoff, "A History of the Doctrine of Cerebral Localization: Sources, Anticipations, and Basic Reasoning," 50–71. Carl Wernicke, "The

Aphasia Symptom Complex: A Psychological Study on an Anatomic Basis," in Gertrude H. Eggert, *Wernicke's Works on Aphasia: A Sourcebook and Review* (1874, The Hague, Netherlands, 1977), 91–145.

25. Wernicke, "The Aphasia Symptom Complex: A Psychological Study on an Anatomic Basis," 91–145.

26. Wernicke, "The Aphasia Symptom Complex: A Psychological Study on an Anatomic Basis," 97.

27. Wernicke, "The Aphasia Symptom Complex: A Psychological Study on an Anatomic Basis," 96.

28. Wernicke, "The Aphasia Symptom Complex: A Psychological Study on an Anatomic Basis," 96.

29. Wernicke, in Eggert, *Wernicke's Works on Aphasia: A Sourcebook and Review*, 26.

30. Wernicke, "The Aphasia Symptom Complex: A Psychological Study on an Anatomic Basis," 99.

31. Wernicke, "The Aphasia Symptom Complex: A Psychological Study on an Anatomic Basis," 98–99.

32. Wernicke, "The Aphasia Symptom Complex: A Psychological Study on an Anatomic Basis," 96.

33. Wernicke, "The Aphasia Symptom Complex: A Psychological Study on an Anatomic Basis," 97.

34. Wernicke, "The Aphasia Symptom Complex: A Psychological Study on an Anatomic Basis," 115.

35. Caplan, *Neurolinguistics and Linguistic Aphasiology*.

36. Harrington, *Reenchanted Science: Holism in German Culture from Wilhelm II to Hitler*. Harrington, "Kurt Goldstein's Neurology of Healing: and Wholeness: A Weimar Story," 25–45.

37. Goldstein, *The Organism: A Holistic Approach to Biology Derived from Pathological Data in Man*. Kurt Goldstein, *Human Nature in the Light of Psychopathology* (Cambridge, MA, 1940). Goldstein, "Notes on the Development of My Concepts," 5–14. Goldstein, "Autobiography," 147–167.

38. Wernicke, "The Aphasia Symptom Complex: A Psychological Study on an Anatomic Basis," 142.

39. Wernicke, "The Aphasia Symptom Complex: A Psychological Study on an Anatomic Basis," 143.

40. Eggert, *Wernicke's Works on Aphasia: A Sourcebook and Review*. Wernicke, "The Aphasia Symptom Complex: A Psychological Study on an Anatomic Basis," 91–145.

41. Goldstein, "Autobiography," 148. Goldstein, "Notes on the Development of My Concepts," 5–14.

42. Caplan, *Neurolinguistics and Linguistic Aphasiology*.

43. Douglas Miller, "Introduction," in Johann Wolfgang von Goethe, *Scientific Studies*, ed. and trans. Douglas Miller (New York, 1988), x–xi. R. H. Stephenson, *Goethe's Conception of Knowledge and Science* (Edinburgh, 1995). Dennis L. Sepper, "Goethe against Newton: Towards Saving the Phenomenon," in *Goethe and the Sciences: A Reappraisal*, ed. Frederick Amrine, Francis J. Zucker, and Harvey Wheeler (Dordecht, Holland, 1987), 175–193. Dennis L. Sepper, *Goethe Contra Newton: Polemics and the Project for a New Science* (New York, 1988).

44. Gunter Altner, "Goethe as Forerunner of Alternative Science," in *Goethe and the Sciences: A Reappraisal,* ed. Frederick Amrine, Francis J. Zucker, and Harvey Wheeler (Dordecht, Holland, 1987), 343.

45. Miller, "Introduction," x–xi.

46. Johann Wolfgang von Goethe, "The Experiment as Mediator between Object and Subject," in *Scientific Studies,* ed. and trans. Douglas Miller (New York, 1988), 15.

47. Sepper, "Goethe against Newton: Towards Saving the Phenomenon," 175–193. Sepper, *Goethe Contra Newton: Polemics and the Project for a New Science.*

48. Hans-Georg Gadamer, 1989, *Truth and Method* (2nd rev. ed., trans. J. Weinsheimer and D. G. Marshall) New York: Crossroad.

49. Johann Wolfgang von Goethe, "Theory of Color: Preface," in *Scientific Studies,* ed. and trans. Douglas Miller (New York, 1988), 159.

50. Johann Wolfgang von Goethe, "Empirical Observation and Science," in *Scientific Studies,* ed. and trans. Douglas Miller (New York, 1988), 24.

51. Goethe, "Empirical Observation and Science," 24–25. Robert J. Richards, *The Romantic Conception of Life: Science and Philosophy in the Age of Goethe* (Chicago: University of Chicago Press). Sepper, "Goethe against Newton: Towards Saving the Phenomenon," 175–193. Sepper, *Goethe Contra Newton: Polemics and the Project for a New Science.* Stephenson, *Goethe's Conception of Knowledge and Science.*

52. Halmar Hegge, "Theory of Science in the Light of Goethe's Science of Nature," in *Goethe and the Sciences: A Reappraisal,* ed. Frederick Amrine, Francis J. Zucker, and Harvey Wheeler (Dordecht, Holland, 1987), 195–218. Sepper, "Goethe against Newton: Towards Saving the Phenomenon," 175–193. Sepper, *Goethe Contra Newton: Polemics and the Project for a New Science.* Goethe, "Empirical Observation and Science," 24–25.

53. Stephenson, *Goethe's Conception of Knowledge and Science,* 8.

54. Sepper, *Goethe Contra Newton: Polemics and the Project for a New Science,* 71.

55. Arthur G. Zajonc, "Facts as Theory: Aspects of Goethe's Philosophy of Science," in *Goethe and the Sciences: A Reappraisal,* ed. Frederick Amrine, Francis J. Zucker, and Harvey Wheeler (Dordecht, Holland, 1987), 219–245. Sepper, "Goethe against Newton: Towards Saving the Phenomenon," 175–193. Sepper, *Goethe Contra Newton: Polemics and the Project for a New Science.*

56. Frederic Will, "Goethe's Aesthetics: The Work of Art and the Work of Nature," *The Philosophical Quarterly,* 6, 22 (1956), 53.

57. Johann Wolfgang von Goethe, "A Study Based on Spinoza," in *Scientific Studies,* ed. and trans. Douglas Miller (New York, 1988), 8.

58. Altner, "Goethe as Forerunner of Alternative Science," 343. Miller, "Introduction," x–xi. Richards, *The Romantic Conception of Life: Science and Philosophy in the Age of Goethe.*

59. Goethe, "The Experiment as Mediator Between Object and Subject," 12.

60. Stephenson, *Goethe's Conception of Knowledge and Science,* 14.

61. Miller, "Introduction," x–xi. Richards, *The Romantic Conception of Life: Science and Philosophy in the Age of Goethe.* Stephenson, *Goethe's Conception of Knowledge and Science.*

62. Johann Wolfgang von Goethe, "Nature," in *Scientific Studies,* ed. and trans. Douglas Miller (New York, 1988), 3.

63. Hegge, "Theory of Science in the Light of Goethe's Science of Nature," 214.

64. Stephenson, *Goethe's Conception of Knowledge and Science*. Will, "Goethe's Aesthetics: The Work of Art and the Work of Nature," 53–65.
65. Hegge, "Theory of Science in the Light of Goethe's Science of Nature," 195–218. Miller, "Introduction," x–xi. Sepper, *Goethe Contra Newton: Polemics and the Project for a New Science*. Stephenson, *Goethe's Conception of Knowledge and Science*.
66. Sepper, *Goethe Contra Newton: Polemics and the Project for a New Science*, 70.
67. Goethe, "The Experiment as Mediator Between Object and Subject," 11–17. Richards, *The Romantic Conception of Life: Science and Philosophy in the Age of Goethe*.
68. Goethe, "The Experiment as Mediator Between Object and Subject," 14.
69. Goethe, "Empirical Observation and Science," 25.
70. Goethe, "Empirical Observation and Science," 25.
71. Ash, *Gestalt Psychology in German Culture, 1890–1967: Holism and the Quest for Objectivity*, 103.
72. See, for example, Wolfgang Kohler, "Physical Gestalten," in *Source Book of Gestalt Psychology*, trans. and ed. Willis D. Ellis (1920, Highland, NY, 1997), 17–54. Kohler started his paper with two introductions, one for philosophers and biologists and one for physicists.
73. Ash, *Gestalt Psychology in German Culture, 1890–1967: Holism and the Quest for Objectivity*. Mitchell G. Ash, "Gestalt Psychology: Origins in Germany and Reception in the United States," in *Points of View in the Modern History of Psychology*, ed. Claude E. Buxton (Orlando, FL, 1985), 295–344. Michael M. Sokal, "The Gestalt Psychologists in Behaviorist America," *The American Historical Review*, 89, 5 (1984), 1240–1263.
74. Christian von Ehrenfels, "On Gestalt Qualities," in *German Essays on Psychology*, ed. Wolfgang Schirmacher and Sven Nebelung (1890, London, 2001), 163–177.
75. Oliver L. Reiser, "Gestalt Psychology and Philosophy of Nature," *The Philosophical Review*, 39, 6 (1930), 556–572.
76. von Ehrenfels, "On Gestalt Qualities," 169.
77. von Ehrenfels, "On Gestalt Qualities," 172.
78. Max Wertheimer, "Laws of Organization in Perceptual Forms," in *Source Book of Gestalt Psychology*, trans. and ed. Willis D. Ellis (1925, Highland, NY, 1997), 2.
79. Wertheimer, "Laws of Organization in Perceptual Forms, 71.
80. Wertheimer, "Laws of Organization in Perceptual Forms, 71.
81. Ash, *Gestalt Psychology in German Culture, 1890–1967: Holism and the Quest for Objectivity*.
82. Clifford Geertz, *Local Knowledge: Further Essays in Interpretive Anthropology* (New York, 1983), 58.
83. Max Wertheimer, "Numbers and Numerical Concepts in Primitive Peoples," in *Source Book of Gestalt Psychology*, trans. and ed. Willis D. Ellis (1912, Highland, NY, 1997), 265–273.
84. Ash, *Gestalt Psychology in German Culture, 1890–1967: Holism and the Quest for Objectivity*, 222.
85. Ash, *Gestalt Psychology in German Culture, 1890–1967: Holism and the Quest for Objectivity*. Max Wertheimer, "Gestalt Theory," in *Source Book of Gestalt Psychology*, trans. and ed. Willis D. Ellis (1925, Highland, NY, 1997), 1–11.
86. Kurt Koffka, "Perception: An Introduction to the Gestalt-Theorie," *The Psychological Bulletin*, 19, 10 (1922), 540.

87. Max Wertheimer, "Experimental Studies of the Seeing of Motion," in *Classics in Psychology*, ed. Thorne Shipley (1912, New York, 1961), 1032–1089.
88. Wertheimer, "Experimental Studies of the Seeing of Motion," 1062.
89. Wertheimer, "Experimental Studies of the Seeing of Motion," 1063.
90. Wertheimer, "Experimental Studies of the Seeing of Motion," 1075.
91. Wertheimer, "Experimental Studies of the Seeing of Motion," 1087.
92. Ash, "Gestalt Psychology: Origins in Germany and Reception in the United States," 295–344. Ash, *Gestalt Psychology in German Culture, 1890–1967: Holism and the Quest for Objectivity*.
93. Ash, *Gestalt Psychology in German Culture, 1890–1967: Holism and the Quest for Objectivity*. Ash, "Gestalt Psychology: Origins in Germany and Reception in the United States," 295–344.
94. Max Wertheimer, "On Gestalt Theory," in *German Essays on Psychology*, ed. Wolfgang Schirmacher and Sven Nebelung (1922, London, 2001), 220.
95. Wertheimer, "On Gestalt Theory," 221.
96. Wertheimer, "On Gestalt Theory," 223.
97. Ash, *Gestalt Psychology in German Culture, 1890–1967: Holism and the Quest for Objectivity*.
98. Kohler, "Physical Gestalten," 23.
99. Ash, *Gestalt Psychology in German Culture, 1890–1967: Holism and the Quest for Objectivity*.
100. Goldstein, "Notes on the Development of My Concepts," 11.
101. Goldstein, "Notes on the Development of My Concepts," 5–14. Harrington, *Reenchanted Science: Holism in German Culture from Wilhelm II to Hitler*, 144.
102. Goldstein, "Notes on the Development of My Concepts," 5–6.
103. Goldstein, "Notes on the Development of My Concepts," 7. Kurt Goldstein, "Preface to German Edition," in *The Organism: A Holistic Approach to Biology Derived from Pathological Data in Man* (New York, 1934).
104. Goldstein, *The Organism: A Holistic Approach to Biology Derived from Pathological Data in Man*, 2.
105. Goldstein, *The Organism: A Holistic Approach to Biology Derived from Pathological Data in Man*, 7.
106. Goldstein, *Human Nature in the Light of Psychopathology*, 10.
107. Goldstein, *Human Nature in the Light of Psychopathology*, 10.
108. Goldstein, *The Organism: A Holistic Approach to Biology Derived from Pathological Data in Man*, 8.
109. Goldstein, *Human Nature in the Light of Psychopathology*, 28.
110. Goldstein, *Human Nature in the Light of Psychopathology*. William James, *Pragmatism* (1907, Indianapolis, 1981). Cornel West, *The American Evasion of Philosophy: A Genealogy of Pragmatism* (Madison, WI, 1989).
111. Christopher Lawrence and George Weisz, "Medical Holism: The Context," in *Greater than the Parts: Holism in Biomedicine, 1920–1950*, ed. Christopher Lawrence and George Weisz (New York, 1998), 2.
112. Harrington, *Reenchanted Science: Holism in German Culture from Wilhelm II to Hitler*, 25.
113. Lawrence and Weisz, "Medical Holism: The Context," 1–22.
114. Wertheimer, "Gestalt Theory," 1–11.

115. Lawrence and Weisz, "Medical Holism: The Context," 2.

116. Lawrence and Weisz, "Medical Holism: The Context," 3.

117. Goldstein, *Human Nature in the Light of Psychopathology*, 12.

118. Goldstein, "Notes on the Development of My Concepts," 13.

119. Geertz, *Local Knowledge: Further Essays in Interpretive Anthropology*.

120. Goldstein, "Autobiography," 151. Goldstein, *The Organism: A Holistic Approach to Biology Derived from Pathological Data in Man*.

121. Goldstein, *The Organism: A Holistic Approach to Biology Derived from Pathological Data in Man*. Goldstein, "Autobiography," 147–167.

122. Kurt Goldstein and Martin Scheerer, *Abstract and Concrete Behavior—An Experimental Study with Special Tests* (Evanston, IL, 1941), 1.

123. Goldstein and Scheerer, *Abstract and Concrete Behavior—An Experimental Study with Special Tests*, 2, italics original.

124. Goldstein, *Human Nature in the Light of Psychopathology*, 39–40.

125. Goldstein, *Human Nature in the Light of Psychopathology*, 40.

126. Goldstein, *Human Nature in the Light of Psychopathology*, 41.

127. Goldstein, *Human Nature in the Light of Psychopathology*, 41.

128. Goldstein and Scheerer, *Abstract and Concrete Behavior—An Experimental Study with Special Tests*, 3.

129. Goldstein, *Human Nature in the Light of Psychopathology*, 59.

130. Goldstein and Scheerer, *Abstract and Concrete Behavior—An Experimental Study with Special Tests*, 4.

131. Goldstein, *Human Nature in the Light of Psychopathology*, 60.

132. Goldstein and Scheerer, *Abstract and Concrete Behavior—An Experimental Study with Special Tests*, 4.

133. Goldstein, *Human Nature in the Light of Psychopathology*, 61.

134. Goldstein, *Human Nature in the Light of Psychopathology*.

135. Kurt Goldstein, "Health as Value," in *New Knowledge in Human Values*, ed. Abraham Maslow (New York, 1959), 178–188.

136. Goldstein, "Notes on the Development of My Concepts," 8.

137. H. Flanders Dunbar, *Emotions and Bodily Changes: A Survey of Literature on Psychosomatic Interrelationships, 1910–1933* (New York, 1935).

138. Goldstein, *The Organism: A Holistic Approach to Biology Derived from Pathological Data in Man*, 35.

139. Goldstein, "Notes on the Development of My Concepts," 5–14. Goldstein, "Autobiography," 147–167. Harrington, *Reenchanted Science: Holism in German Culture from Wilhelm II to Hitler*.

140. Goldstein, *The Organism: A Holistic Approach to Biology Derived from Pathological Data in Man*, 402.

141. Goldstein, *The Organism: A Holistic Approach to Biology Derived from Pathological Data in Man*, 402, italics original.

142. Goldstein, *The Organism: A Holistic Approach to Biology Derived from Pathological Data in Man*, 402.

143. Goldstein, *The Organism: A Holistic Approach to Biology Derived from Pathological Data in Man*, 403.

144. Goldstein, "Notes on the Development of My Concepts," 8.
145. Goldstein, "Notes on the Development of My Concepts," 11.
146. Goldstein, *Human Nature in the Light of Psychopathology*, 194.
147. Abraham Maslow, ed., New Knowledge in Human Values (New York, 1959).
148. Goldstein, *Human Nature in the Light of Psychopathology*, 85–86.
149. Goldstein, *Human Nature in the Light of Psychopathology*, 87.

3   BUILDING THE STRAUSS SYNDROME AT THE WAYNE COUNTY TRAINING SCHOOL

1. Alfred A. Strauss and Heinz Werner, "The Mental Organization of the Brain-Injured Mentally Defective Child," *American Journal of Psychiatry*, 97 (1941), 1194.
2. Laura E. Lehtinen and Alfred A. Strauss, "Arithmetic Fundamentals for the Brain-Crippled Child," *American Journal of Mental Deficiency*, 49 (1944), 149–154. Alfred A. Strauss, "The Education of the Brain-Injured Child," *American Journal of Mental Deficiency*, 56 (1952), 712–718.
3. Strauss also used the term "brain-crippled." See Lehtinen and Strauss, "Arithmetic Fundamentals for the Brain-Crippled Child," 149–154.
4. Strauss and Werner, "The Mental Organization of the Brain-Injured Mentally Defective Child," 1198.
5. William M. Cruickshank and Daniel P. Hallahan, "Alfred A. Strauss: Pioneer in Learning Disabilities," Exceptional Children, 39, 4 (1973), 324.
6. Cruickshank and Hallahan, "Alfred A. Strauss: Pioneer in Learning Disabilities," 321–327.
7. Cruickshank and Hallahan, "Alfred A. Strauss: Pioneer in Learning Disabilities," 321–327.
8. Cruickshank and Hallahan, "Alfred A. Strauss: Pioneer in Learning Disabilities," 323. William M. Cruickshank, Frances A. Bentzen, Frederick H. Ratzeburg, and Mirian T. Tannhauser, *A Teaching Method for Brain-Injured and Hyperactive Children* (Syracuse, NY, 1961). William M. Cruickshank, *The Brain-Injured Child in Home, School, and Community* (Syracuse, NY, 1967).
9. Cruickshank and Hallahan, "Alfred A. Strauss: Pioneer in Learning Disabilities," 321–327. Robert H. Haskell, "The Development of a Research Program in Mental Deficiency over a Fifteen Year Period," *American Journal of Psychiatry*, 101 (1944), 73–81. Samuel A. Kirk, "Autobiography," in *Teaching Children with Learning Disabilities: Personal Perspectives*, ed. James M. Kauffman and Daniel P. Hallahan (Columbus, OH, 1976), 238–269.
10. Kurt Kreppner, "Heinz Werner and the Psychological Institute in Hamburg," in *Heinz Werner and Developmental Science*, ed. Jaan Valsinger (New York, 2005), 55–74. Ulrich Muller, "The Context of the Formation of Heinz Werner's Ideas," in *Heinz Werner and Developmental Science*, ed. Jaan Valsinger (New York, 2005), 25–53. Seymour Wapner and Bernard Kaplan, "Heinz Werner: 1890–1964," *The American Journal of Psychology*, 77, 3 (1964), 513–517. Herman Witkin, "Heinz Werner: 1890–1964," *Child Development*, 36, 2 (1965), 306–328.
11. Cruickshank and Hallahan, "Alfred A. Strauss: Pioneer in Learning Disabilities," 321–327.

12. Wapner and Kaplan, "Heinz Werner: 1890–1964," 513.
13. Wapner and Kaplan, "Heinz Werner: 1890–1964," 513–517. Heinz Werner, *Comparative Psychology of Mental Development* (New York, 1940). Witkin, "Heinz Werner: 1890–1964," 306–328.
14. Witkin, "Heinz Werner: 1890–1964," 312.
15. Alfred A. Strauss and Laura Lehtinen, *Psychopathology and the Education of the Brain-Injured Child* (New York, 1947).
16. Staff, "Laura Lehtinen Rogan," Northwestern Magazine, Summer, 2006, n.p. Staff, "Laura Rogan, 1919–2005," *Freethought Today*, 23, 1, January/February 2006, n.p.
17. Albert Wellek, "The Impact of the German Immigration on American Psychology," *The Journal of the History of the Behavioral Sciences*, 4, 3 (1968), 207–229.
18. Daniel P. Hallahan and William M. Cruickshank, Psychoeducational Foundations of Learning Disabilities (Englewood Cliffs, NJ, 1973).
19. Viktor von Weizsacker, "The Doctor and the Patient," in *The Worlds of Existentialism: A Critical Reader*, ed. Maurice Friedman (1926, New York, 1964), 405.
20. von Weizsacker, "The Doctor and the Patient," 405.
21. Viktor von Weizsacker, "History of Illness," in *The Worlds of Existentialism: A Critical Reader*, ed. Maurice Friedman (1926, New York, 1964), 407.
22. Anne Harrington, *Reenchanted Science: Holism in German Culture from Wilhelm II to Hitler* (Princeton, NJ, 1996). Anne Harrington, "Unmasking Suffering's Masks: Reflections on Old and New Memories of Nazi Medicine," *Daedalus*, 125 (1996), 181–205. Carl Binger, "In Memoriam: Viktor von Weizsacker," *Psychosomatic Medicine*, 19, 4 (1957), 265–266.
23. Kreppner, "Heinz Werner and the Psychological Institute in Hamburg," 55–74. Muller, "The Context of the Formation of Heinz Werner's Ideas," 25–53. Wapner and Kaplan, "Heinz Werner: 1890–1964," 513–517. Witkin, "Heinz Werner: 1890–1964," 306–328.
24. Mitchell G. Ash, *Gestalt Psychology in German Culture, 1890–1967: Holism and the Quest for Objectivity* (Cambridge, England, 1995). Ulfried Geuter, "The Whole and the Community: Scientific and Political Reasoning in the Holistic Psychology of Felix Krueger," in *Science, Technology, and National Socialism*, ed. Manika Renneberg and Mark Walker (New York, 1994), 197–223. Harrington, *Reenchanted Science: Holism in German Culture from Wilhelm II to Hitler. Harrington*, "Unmasking Suffering's Masks: Reflections on Old and New Memories of Nazi Medicine," 181–205.
25. Lous Heshusius, "At the Heart of the Advocacy Dilemma: A Mechanistic Worldview," *Exceptional Children*, 49 (1982), 6–13. Lous Heshusius, "Why Would They and I Want To Do It? A Phenomenological-Theoretical View of Special Education," *Learning Disability Quarterly*, 7 (1984), 363–368. Lous Heshusius, "The Arts, Science, and Study of Exceptionality," *Exceptional Children*, 55 (1988), 60–65. Lous Heshusius, "The Newtonian Mechanistic Paradigm, Special Education, and Contours of Alternatives: An Overview," *Journal of Learning Disabilities*, 22 (1989), 403–415. Mary S. Poplin, "Self-imposed Blindness: The Scientific Method in Education," *Remedial and Special Education*, 8, 6 (1987), 31–37. Mary S. Poplin, "Holistic/Constructivist Principles of the Teaching/Learning Process: Implications for the Field of Learning Disabilities," *Journal of Learning Disabilities*, 21 (1988), 401–416.

26. Geuter, "The Whole and the Community: Scientific and Political Reasoning in the Holistic Psychology of Felix Krueger," 210.

27. See Harrington, *Reenchanted Science: Holism in German Culture from Wilhelm II to Hitler.* Harrington, "Unmasking Suffering's Masks: Reflections on Old and New Memories of Nazi Medicine," 181–205, for discussion of Alexander von Songer, "Erganzungen zu meiner Arbeit 'Rasse und Baukunft,'" *Ziel und Weg: Zeitschrift des Nationalsozialistischen Deutschen Arzle-Bundes*, 5 (1935), 564–569.

28. Harrington, *Reenchanted Science: Holism in German Culture from Wilhelm II to Hitler.* Harrington, "Unmasking Suffering's Masks: Reflections on Old and New Memories of Nazi Medicine," 181–205.

29. Mitchell G. Ash, *Gestalt Psychology in German Culture, 1890–1967: Holism and the Quest for Objectivity*, 343.

30. Gernot Bohme, "Rationalizing Unethical Medical Research: Taking Seriously the Case of Viktor von Weizsacker," in *Dark Medicine: Rationalizing Unethical Medical Research*, ed. William R. Lafleur, Gernot Bohme, and Susumu Shimazono (Bloomington, IN, 2007), 15–29. Harrington, *Reenchanted Science: Holism in German Culture from Wilhelm II to Hitler. Harrington*, "Unmasking Suffering's Masks: Reflections on Old and New Memories of Nazi Medicine," 181–205.

31. Marguerite P. Ford, "New Directions in Special Education," *Journal of School Psychology*, 9, 1 (1971), 73–83. Daniel P. Hallahan, "Cognitive Styles—Preschool Implications for the Disadvantaged," *Journal of Learning Disabilities*, 3 (1970), 5–9. Daniel P. Hallahan and William M. Cruickshank, *Psychoeducational Foundations of Learning Disabilities* (Englewood Cliffs, NJ, 1973). Murray M. Kappelmann, E. Kaplan, and R. L. Ganter, "A Study of Learning Disorders among Disadvantaged Children," *Journal of Learning Disabilities*, 2 (1969), 267. Gordon R. Alley, Gerald Solomons, and E. Opitz, "Minimal Cerebral Dysfunction as It Relates to Social Class," *Journal of Learning Disabilities*, 4 (1971), 246–250. Dominic Amante, P. H. Margules, D. M. Hartmann, D. B. Storey, and L. J. Weeber, "The Epidemiological Distribution of CNS Dysfunction," *Journal of Social Issues*, 26, 4 (1970), 105–136. Lester Tarnopol, "Delinquency and Minimal Brain Dysfunction," *Journal of Learning Disabilities*, 3 (1970), 200–207.

32. Wapner and Kaplan, "Heinz Werner: 1890–1964," 513–517. Witkin, "Heinz Werner: 1890–1964," 306–328.

33. Heinz Werner, "Process and Achievement—A Basic Problem of Education and Developmental Psychology," *Harvard Educational Review*, 7 (1937), 366.

34. Werner, "Process and Achievement—A Basic Problem of Education and Developmental Psychology," 366.

35. Cruickshank and Hallahan, "Alfred A. Strauss: Pioneer in Learning Disabilities," 321–327.

36. Werner, "Process and Achievement—A Basic Problem of Education and Developmental Psychology," 353.

37. Muller, "The Context of the Formation of Heinz Werner's Ideas," 25–53. Werner, *Comparative Psychology of Mental Development.*

38. Werner, *Comparative Psychology of Mental Development.*

39. Werner, *Comparative Psychology of Mental Development*, 41.

40. Werner, *Comparative Psychology of Mental Development*, 41.

41. Werner, *Comparative Psychology of Mental Development*, 55.

42. Werner, "Process and Achievement—A Basic Problem of Education and Developmental Psychology," 360.

43. Werner, "Process and Achievement—A Basic Problem of Education and Developmental Psychology," 362.

44. Werner, "Process and Achievement—A Basic Problem of Education and Developmental Psychology," 353.

45. Alfred A. Strauss and Heinz Werner, "Deficiency in the Finger Schema in Relation to Arithmetic Disability," *American Journal of Orthopsychiatry*, 8 (1938), 719–725. Heinz Werner and Alfred A. Strauss, "Problems and Methods of Functional Analysis in Mentally Deficient Children," *The Journal of Abnormal and Social Psychology*, 34, 1(1939), 37–62. Alfred A. Strauss and Heinz Werner, "Finger Agnosia in Children with Brief Discussion on the Defect and Retardation in Mentally Handicapped Children," *American Journal of Psychiatry*, 95 (1939), 1215–1225.

46. Strauss and Werner, "Deficiency in the Finger Schema in Relation to Arithmetic Disability," 719.

47. Thorleif G. Hegge, "Discussion," in Strauss and Werner, "Deficiency in the Finger Schema in Relation to Arithmetic Disability," 724.

48. Strauss and Werner, "Finger Agnosia in Children with Brief Discussion on the Defect and Retardation in Mentally Handicapped Children," 1215–1225.

49. Strauss and Werner, "Deficiency in the Finger Schema in Relation to Arithmetic Disability," 720.

50. Strauss and Werner, "Finger Agnosia in Children with Brief Discussion on the Defect and Retardation in Mentally Handicapped Children," 1216.

51. Strauss and Werner, "Deficiency in the Finger Schema in Relation to Arithmetic Disability," 719–725. Werner and Strauss, "Problems and Methods of Functional Analysis in Mentally Deficient Children," 37–62.

52. Strauss and Werner, "Deficiency in the Finger Schema in Relation to Arithmetic Disability," 724.

53. In these studies, two groups of ten and eleven boys were compared.

54. Strauss and Werner, "Deficiency in the Finger Schema in Relation to Arithmetic Disability," 719–725. Werner and Strauss, "Problems and Methods of Functional Analysis in Mentally Deficient Children," 37–62.

55. Strauss and Werner, "Finger Agnosia in Children with Brief Discussion on the Defect and Retardation in Mentally Handicapped Children," 1221.

56. Werner and Strauss, "Problems and Methods of Functional Analysis in Mentally Deficient Children," 48.

57. Werner and Strauss, "Problems and Methods of Functional Analysis in Mentally Deficient Children," 37–62. Heinz Werner and Alfred A. Strauss, "Approaches to a Functional Analysis of Mentally Handicapped Problem Children with Illustrations in the Field of Arithmetic Disability," proceedings, *American Association on Mental Deficiency*, 43, 2 (1938), 105–138.

58. Werner and Strauss, "Approaches to a Functional Analysis of Mentally Handicapped Problem Children with Illustrations in the Field of Arithmetic Disability," 105–138. Werner and Strauss, "Problems and Methods of Functional Analysis in Mentally Deficient Children," 37–62.

59. Heinz Werner, "Significance of General Experimental Psychology for the Understanding of Abnormal Behavior and its Correction or Prevention," in *The Relationship Between Rehabilitation and Psychology*, ed. Gloria Leviton (Worcester, 1959), 64.

60. Werner, "Significance of General Experimental Psychology for the Understanding of Abnormal Behavior and its Correction or Prevention," 64.

61. Werner, "Significance of General Experimental Psychology for the Understanding of Abnormal Behavior and its Correction or Prevention," 64.

62. Werner, "Significance of General Experimental Psychology for the Understanding of Abnormal Behavior and its Correction or Prevention," 68.

63. Werner, "Significance of General Experimental Psychology for the Understanding of Abnormal Behavior and its Correction or Prevention," 64.

64. Strauss and Heinz Werner, "Finger Agnosia in Children with Brief Discussion on the Defect and Retardation in Mentally Handicapped Children," 1215–1225.

65. Werner and Strauss, "Problems and Methods of Functional Analysis in Mentally Deficient Children," 41.

66. Werner and Strauss, "Problems and Methods of Functional Analysis in Mentally Deficient Children," 48.

67. Werner and Strauss, "Problems and Methods of Functional Analysis in Mentally Deficient Children," 50.

68. Werner and Strauss, "Problems and Methods of Functional Analysis in Mentally Deficient Children," 58.

69. The clearest explanation of this is offered in Alfred A. Strauss, "Typology in Mental Deficiency," proceedings, *American Association on Mental Deficiency*, 44, 1 (1939), 85–90. For more examples, see Alfred A. Strauss and Newell C. Kephart, "Behavior Differences in Mentally Retarded Children Measured by a New Behavior Rating Scale," *American Journal of Psychiatry*, 96 (1940), 1117–1124.

70. Strauss, "Typology in Mental Deficiency," 86.

71. Strauss, "Typology in Mental Deficiency," 86.

72. Alfred A. Strauss and Newell C. Kephart, "Rate of Mental Growth in a Constant Environment among Higher Grade Moron and Borderline Children," proceedings, *American Association on Mental Deficiency*, 44, 1 (1939), 142.

73. Strauss, "Typology in Mental Deficiency," 85–90. Strauss and Kephart, "Rate of Mental Growth in a Constant Environment among Higher Grade Moron and Borderline Children," 137–142. Heinz Werner and Alfred A. Strauss, "Types of Visuomotor Activity in Their Relation to Low and High Performance Ages," proceedings, *American Association on Mental Deficiency*, 44, 1 (1939), 163–168.

74. Strauss, "Typology in Mental Deficiency," 86.

75. Strauss, "Typology in Mental Deficiency," 86.

76. Strauss, "Typology in Mental Deficiency," 86.

77. Strauss, "Typology in Mental Deficiency," 86.

78. Cruickshank and Hallahan, "Alfred A. Strauss: Pioneer in Learning Disabilities," 321–327. Hallahan and Cruickshank, *Psychoeducational Foundations of Learning Disabilities*.

79. Leo Kanner, "Autistic Disturbances of Affective Contact," *Nervous Child*, 2 (1943), 217–250.

80. Leo Kanner, "Discussion," in Strauss and Werner, "The Mental Organization of the Brain-Injured Mentally Defective Child," 1203.
81. Heinz Werner and Alfred A. Strauss, "Impairment in Thought Processes of Brain-Injured Children," *American Journal of Mental Deficiency*, 47 (1943), 291.
82. Strauss and Werner, "The Mental Organization of the Brain-Injured Mentally Defective Child," 1194.
83. Alfred A. Strauss and Heinz Werner, "Disorders of Conceptual Thinking in the Brain-Injured Child," *Journal of Nervous and Mental Disease*, 96 (1942), 153.
84. Kanner, "Discussion," in Strauss and Werner, "The Mental Organization of the Brain-Injured Mentally Defective Child," 1203.
85. The 1940 American Psychiatric Association meeting took place on May 20–24. Strauss delivered his apparent response paper at the meeting of the American Association on Mental Deficiency on May 25, 1940. Alfred A. Strauss, "The Incidence of Central Nervous System Involvement in Higher Grade Moron Children," *American Journal of Mental Deficiency*, 45 (1941), 548.
86. Strauss, "The Incidence of Central Nervous System Involvement in Higher Grade Moron Children," 548.
87. Strauss, "The Incidence of Central Nervous System Involvement in Higher Grade Moron Children," 548.
88. Strauss, "The Incidence of Central Nervous System Involvement in Higher Grade Moron Children," 549.
89. Also see Chapter 7 of Strauss and Lehtinen, *Psychopathology and the Education of the Brain-Injured Child*.
90. Strauss, "The Incidence of Central Nervous System Involvement in Higher Grade Moron Children," 550.
91. Strauss, "The Incidence of Central Nervous System Involvement in Higher Grade Moron Children," 550.
92. Strauss, "The Incidence of Central Nervous System Involvement in Higher Grade Moron Children," 551.
93. Strauss, "The Incidence of Central Nervous System Involvement in Higher Grade Moron Children," 551.
94. Strauss, "The Incidence of Central Nervous System Involvement in Higher Grade Moron Children," 553.
95. Seymour Sarason, *Psychological Problems in Mental Deficiency* (New York, 1949), 41–42.
96. In the final chapter, I explore this battle of actuarial and clinical orientations to science.
97. Strauss and Kephart, "Rate of Mental Growth in a Constant Environment among Higher Grade Moron and Borderline Children," 137–142. Newell C. Kephart and Alfred A. Strauss, "A Clinical Factor Influencing Variations in IQ," *American Journal of Orthopsychiatry*, 10 (1940), 343–351.
98. Boyd R. McCandless and Alfred A. Strauss, "Objective Criteria Diagnostic of Deviant Personality: An Exploratory Study," *American Journal of Mental Deficiency*. 47 (1943), 445–449.
99. Strauss and Kephart, "Rate of Mental Growth in a Constant Environment among Higher Grade Moron and Borderline Children," 137–142.

100. Kephart and Strauss, "A Clinical Factor Influencing Variations in IQ," 349.
101. Kephart and Strauss, "A Clinical Factor Influencing Variations in IQ," 348.
102. Kephart and Strauss, "A Clinical Factor Influencing Variations in IQ," 348.
103. Kephart and Strauss, "A Clinical Factor Influencing Variations in IQ," 349.
104. Kephart and Strauss, "A Clinical Factor Influencing Variations in IQ," 349.
105. Kephart and Strauss, "A Clinical Factor Influencing Variations in IQ," 343–351.
106. Betty Martinson and Alfred A. Strauss, "Education and Treatment of an Imbecile Boy of the Exogenous Type," *American Journal of Mental Deficiency*, 45 (1940), 278.
107. Martinson and Strauss, "Education and Treatment of an Imbecile Boy of the Exogenous Type," 280.
108. Heinz Werner and Alfred A. Strauss, "Causal Factors in Low Performance," *American Journal of Mental Deficiency*, 45 (1940), 218.
109. Heinz Werner and Alfred A. Strauss, "Pathology of Figure-Background Relation in the Child," *The Journal of Abnormal and Social Psychology*, 36, 2 (1941), 247.
110. Werner and Strauss, "Types of Visuomotor Activity in Their Relation to Low and High Performance Ages," 167.
111. Werner and Strauss, "Types of Visuomotor Activity in Their Relation to Low and High Performance Ages," 164.
112. Werner and Strauss, "Types of Visuomotor Activity in Their Relation to Low and High Performance Ages," 164.
113. Werner and Strauss, "Types of Visuomotor Activity in Their Relation to Low and High Performance Ages," 168.
114. Werner and Strauss, "Pathology of Figure-Background Relation in the Child," 236.
115. Werner and Strauss, "Pathology of Figure-Background Relation in the Child," 236.
116. Werner and Strauss, "Pathology of Figure-Background Relation in the Child," 239.
117. Werner and Strauss, "Pathology of Figure-Background Relation in the Child," 240.
118. Werner and Strauss, "Types of Visuomotor Activity in Their Relation to Low and High Performance Ages," 163–168. Werner and Strauss, "Pathology of Figure-Background Relation in the Child," 236–248.
119. Werner and Strauss, "Pathology of Figure-Background Relation in the Child," 243–244.
120. Werner and Strauss, "Pathology of Figure-Background Relation in the Child," 244.
121. Werner and Strauss, "Pathology of Figure-Background Relation in the Child," 244.
122. Werner and Strauss, "Pathology of Figure-Background Relation in the Child," 245.
123. Werner and Strauss, "Pathology of Figure-Background Relation in the Child," 245.
124. Werner and Strauss, "Pathology of Figure-Background Relation in the Child," 248.
125. Werner and Strauss, "Pathology of Figure-Background Relation in the Child," 247.
126. Werner and Strauss, "Pathology of Figure-Background Relation in the Child," 247.
127. Werner and Strauss, "Pathology of Figure-Background Relation in the Child," 248.
128. Heinz Werner and Mabel Bowers, "Auditory-Motor Organization in Two Clinical Types of Mentally Deficient Children," *The Journal of Genetic Psychology*, 59 (1941), 85–99. Werner and Strauss, "Pathology of Figure-Background Relation in the Child," 236–248.
129. Werner and Bowers, "Auditory-Motor Organization in Two Clinical Types of Mentally Deficient Children," 96.
130. Strauss and Werner, "The Mental Organization of the Brain-Injured Mentally Defective Child," 1198.

131. Strauss and Werner, "The Mental Organization of the Brain-Injured Mentally Defective Child," 1198. Strauss and Kephart, "Behavior Differences in Mentally Retarded Children Measured by a New Behavior Rating Scale," 1117–1124.

132. Lehtinen and Strauss, "Arithmetic Fundamentals for the Brain-Crippled Child," 149–154. Martinson and Strauss, "Education and Treatment of an Imbecile Boy of the Exogenous Type," 274–280. Strauss and Werner, "The Mental Organization of the Brain-Injured Mentally Defective Child," 1194–1203.

133. Heinz Werner and Alfred A. Strauss, "Impairment in Thought Processes of Brain-Injured Children," *American Journal of Mental Deficiency,* 47 (1943), 295.

134. Strauss and Werner, "The Mental Organization of the Brain-Injured Mentally Defective Child," 1195.

135. Werner, "Process and Achievement—A Basic Problem of Education and Developmental Psychology," 353–368. Werner, *Comparative Psychology of Mental Development.*

136. Werner, "Process and Achievement—A Basic Problem of Education and Developmental Psychology," 359.

137. Albert Collins, "From H = log s-super(n) TO CONCEPTUAL FRAMEWORK: A Short History of Information," *History of Psychology,* 10, 1 (2007), 44–72. Howard Gardner, *The Mind's New Science: A History of the Cognitive Revolution* (New York, 1985). Eckart Sheerer, "Towards a History of Cognitive Science," *International Social Science Journal,* 40, 1 (1988), 7–19.

138. Cognitive science slowly gained some ground within circles of the new field of learning disabilities beginning in the late 1960s. See C. Keith Connors, "Information Processing in Children with Learning Disabilities and Brain Damage: Some Experimental Approaches," *International Approach to Learning Disabilities: Third Annual International Conference of the Association for Learning Disabilities* (Tulsa, OK, 1966) 206–221.

139. Werner and Bowers, "Auditory-Motor Organization in Two Clinical Types of Mentally Deficient Children," 96.

140. Strauss and Werner, "Disorders of Conceptual Thinking in the Brain-Injured Child," 155.

141. Strauss and Werner, "Disorders of Conceptual Thinking in the Brain-Injured Child," 158.

142. Strauss and Werner, "Disorders of Conceptual Thinking in the Brain-Injured Child," 158.

143. Strauss and Werner, "Disorders of Conceptual Thinking in the Brain-Injured Child," 158.

144. Strauss and Werner, "Disorders of Conceptual Thinking in the Brain-Injured Child," 159.

145. Strauss and Werner, "Disorders of Conceptual Thinking in the Brain-Injured Child," 161.

146. Strauss and Werner, "Disorders of Conceptual Thinking in the Brain-Injured Child," 161–162.

147. Strauss and Werner, "Disorders of Conceptual Thinking in the Brain-Injured Child," 161.

148. Alfred A. Strauss and Newell C. Kephart, *Psychopathology and the Education of the Brain-Injured Child,* Volume II (New York, 1955).

149. Strauss and Werner, "Disorders of Conceptual Thinking in the Brain-Injured Child," 162.

150. Strauss and Werner, "Disorders of Conceptual Thinking in the Brain-Injured Child," 164.

151. Kurt Goldstein and Martin Scheerer, *Abstract and Concrete Behavior—An Experimental Study with Special Tests* (Evanston IL, 1941), 1.

152. Werner and Strauss, "Impairment in Thought Processes of Brain-Injured Children," 292.

153. Strauss and Werner, "Disorders of Conceptual Thinking in the Brain-Injured Child," 165.

154. Strauss and Werner, "Disorders of Conceptual Thinking in the Brain-Injured Child," 165.

155. Strauss and Werner, "Disorders of Conceptual Thinking in the Brain-Injured Child," 166.
156. Strauss and Werner, "Disorders of Conceptual Thinking in the Brain-Injured Child," 166.
157. Werner and Strauss, "Impairment in Thought Processes of Brain-Injured Children," 292.
158. Werner and Strauss, "Impairment in Thought Processes of Brain-Injured Children," 291.
159. Strauss and Werner, "Disorders of Conceptual Thinking in the Brain-Injured Child," 168.
160. Strauss and Werner, "Disorders of Conceptual Thinking in the Brain-Injured Child," 168.
161. Strauss and Werner, "Disorders of Conceptual Thinking in the Brain-Injured Child," 168.
162. Strauss and Werner, "Disorders of Conceptual Thinking in the Brain-Injured Child," 168.
163. Strauss and Werner, "Disorders of Conceptual Thinking in the Brain-Injured Child," 168.
164. Strauss and Werner, "Disorders of Conceptual Thinking in the Brain-Injured Child," 168.
165. Strauss and Werner, "Disorders of Conceptual Thinking in the Brain-Injured Child," 168.
166. Werner and Strauss, "Impairment in Thought Processes of Brain-Injured Children," 294.
167. Werner and Strauss, "Impairment in Thought Processes of Brain-Injured Children," 294.
168. Werner and Strauss, "Impairment in Thought Processes of Brain-Injured Children," 295.
169. Werner and Strauss, "Impairment in Thought Processes of Brain-Injured Children," 295.
170. Alfred A. Strauss, "Ways of Thinking in Brain-Crippled Deficient Children," *American Journal of Psychiatry*, 100 (1944), 640.
171. Lehtinen and Strauss, "Arithmetic Fundamentals for the Brain-Crippled Child," 150.
172. Strauss and Kephart, "Rate of Mental Growth in a Constant Environment among Higher Grade Moron and Borderline Children," 137–142. Kephart and Strauss, "A Clinical Factor Influencing Variations in IQ," 343–351. Betty Martinson and Alfred A. Strauss, "A Method of Clinical Evaluation of the Responses to the Stanford-Binet Intelligence Test," *American Journal of Mental Deficiency*, 46 (1941), 48–59. Alfred A. Strauss, "Enriching the Interpretation of the Stanford-Binet Test," *Journal of Exceptional Children*, 7 (1941), 260–264.
173. Strauss and Lehtinen, *Psychopathology and the Education of the Brain-Injured Child*, 17.
174. Alfred A. Strauss to Members of the Cove Schools Corporation, November 15, 1947, Box 5, Samuel A. Kirk Papers (Archives Research Center, University of Illinois, Urbana).
175. Alfred A. Strauss to Members of the Cove Schools Corporation, June 30, 1948, Box 5, Samuel A. Kirk Papers (Archives Research Center, University of Illinois, Urbana).
176. Alfred A. Strauss to Members of the Cove Schools Corporation, December 10, 1948, Box 5, Samuel A. Kirk Papers (Archives Research Center, University of Illinois, Urbana).
177. Strauss, "The Education of the Brain-Injured Child," 712.
178. Laura Lehtinen, "Appendix II: Case Histories of Brain-Injured Children Who Score within the Normal Range on Standardized Tests," in Strauss and Kephart, *Psychopathology and the Education of the Brain-Injured Child*, Volume II, 223.

4 "A NEW PERCEPTION OF THINGS":
MOVEMENT EDUCATION AND NEWELL C. KEPHART

1. D. H. Radler and Newell C. Kephart, *Success through Play: How to Prepare Your Child for School Achievement—and Enjoy It* (New York, 1960), 7–8.

2. Radler and Kephart, *Success through Play: How to Prepare Your Child for School Achievement—and Enjoy It*, 8.

3. Radler and Kephart, *Success through Play: How to Prepare Your Child for School Achievement—and Enjoy It*, 8.

4. Radler and Kephart, *Success through Play: How to Prepare Your Child for School Achievement—and Enjoy It*, 8–9.

5. Newell C. Kephart, "Perceptual-Motor Correlates of Learning," in *Conference on Children with Minimal Brain Impairments*, ed. Samuel A. Kirk and Wesley Becker. (Urbana, IL, 1963), 13.

6. Radler and Kephart, *Success through Play: How to Prepare Your Child for School Achievement—and Enjoy It*, 11.

7. Radler and Kephart, *Success through Play: How to Prepare Your Child for School Achievement—and Enjoy It*, xiv.

8. Ray H. Barsch, A. Movigenic Curriculum (Madison, WI, 1965). Ray H. Barsch, *Enriching Perception and Cognition: Techniques for Teachers* (Seattle, 1968). Sean Walmsley, "yoB Cuts Wood with waS; Special Schools Help Children Conquer Language Problem Called Dyslexia Developmental Dyslexia the Major Symptoms Tutorial Program," *The Washington Post*, December 18, 1966. p. E3. John Walker, "Schools Teach 'Sensory Learning,'" *Chicago Tribune*, September 1, p. S5. Robert Reinhold, "Educators Are Divided on Preschool Screening," *The New York Times*, August, 18, 1975, p. 51.

9. Barsch, *A Movigenic Curriculum*. Barsch, *Enriching Perception and Cognition: Techniques for Teachers*.

10. Walmsley, "yoB Cuts Wood with waS; Special Schools Help Children Conquer Language Problem Called Dyslexia Developmental Dyslexia the Major Symptoms Tutorial Program," p. E3.

11. Walker, "Schools Teach 'Sensory Learning,'" p. S5.

12. "When 'Film' is Flim,'" *Newsweek*, July 31, 1967, p. 48.

13. Reinhold, "Educators are Divided on Preschool Screening," p. 51.

14. James M. Kauffman and Daniel P. Hallahan, *Teaching Children with Learning Disabilities: Personal Perspectives* (Columbus, OH, 1976).

15. Wineva Grzynkowicz and Martha Kephart, "Preface," in *Learning Disabilities: The Last Lectures of Newell C. Kephart*, Newell C. Kephart (Romeoville, IL, 1975), n.p.

16. For a representative series of papers in this mode of thought, see Guy Montrose Whipple, *Nature and Nurture: Yearbook of the National Society for the Study of Education* (Bloomington, IL, 1928).

17. Florence L. Goodenough and John E. Anderson, *Experimental Child Study* (New York, 1931), 25.

18. Goodenough and Anderson, *Experimental Child Study*, 24.

19. Goodenough and Anderson, *Experimental Child Study*, 24.

20. Hamilton Cravens, *Before Head Start: The Iowa Station and America's Children* (Chapel Hill, NC, 1993).

21. Beth L. Wellman, "The Meaning of Environment," in *The Thirty-Ninth Yearbook of the National Society for the Study of Education: Intelligence: Its Nature and Nurture, Part 1, Comparative and Critical Exposition*, ed. Guy Montrose Whipple (Bloomington, IL, 1940), 21–40. George D. Stoddard and Beth L. Wellman, "Environment and the IQ,"

in *The Thirty-Ninth Yearbook of the National Society for the Study of Education: Intelligence: Its Nature and Nurture, Part 1, Comparative and Critical Exposition*, ed. Guy Montrose Whipple (Bloomington, IL, 1940), 405–422. Beth L. Wellman, "Iowa Studies on the Effects of Schooling," in *The Thirty-Ninth Yearbook of the National Society for the Study of Education: Intelligence: Its Nature and Nurture, Part 1, Comparative and Critical Exposition*, ed. Guy Montrose Whipple (Bloomington, IL, 1940), 377–399. Harold. M. Skeels, "Mental Development of Children in Foster Homes," *Journal of Consulting Psychology* 2, 2 (1938), 33–43. Harold. M. Skeels, "Some Iowa studies of Mental Growth in Children in Relation to Differentials of the Environment: A Summary," in *The Thirty-Ninth Yearbook of the National Society for the Study of Education: Intelligence: Its Nature and Nurture, Part 1, Comparative and Critical Exposition*, ed. Guy Montrose Whipple (Bloomington, IL, 1940), 281–308. Harold. M. Skeels and Harold B. Dye, "A Study of the Effects of Differential Stimulation on Mentally Retarded Children," proceedings and addresses of the American Association on Mental Deficiency, 44 (1939), 114–136.

22. "IQ Control," *Time*, Monday, November 7, 1938.

23. Quinn McNemar, "A Critical Examination of the University of Iowa Studies of Environmental Influence upon the IQ," *Psychological Bulletin*, 37 (1940), 63–92.

24. Henry L. Minton, Lewis Terman, *Pioneer in Psychological Testing* (New York, 1988), 195.

25. Minton, Terman, *Pioneer in Psychological*, 195.

26. "Nature vs. Nurture," *Time*, Monday, March 11, 1940. Cravens, *Before Head Start: The Iowa Station and America's Children*. Guy Montrose Whipple, *The Thirty-Ninth Yearbook of the National Society for the Study of Education: Intelligence: Its Nature and Nurture, Part I, Comparative and Critical Exposition* (Bloomington, IL, 1940). Guy Montrose Whipple, *The Thirty-Ninth Yearbook of the National Society for the Study of Education: Intelligence: Its Nature and Nurture, Part II, Original Studies and Experiments* (Bloomington, IL, 1940).

27. Ernest R. Hilgard, "Psychology at Iowa before McGeoch and Spence," in *Psychology at Iowa: Centennial Essays*, ed. Joan H. Cantor (Hillsdale, NJ, 1991), 43.

28. Beth L. Wellman, "The Effect of Pre-school Attendance upon the IQ," *Journal of Experimental Education*, 1, 2 (1932), 69.

29. Wellman, "The Effect of Pre-school Attendance upon the IQ," 69.

30. Beth L. Wellman, "Growth in Intelligence under Differing School Environments," *Journal of Experimental Education*, 3, 2 (1934), 59–83. Hubert S. Coffey and Beth L. Wellman, "The Role of Cultural Status in Intelligence Changes of Preschool Children," *Journal of Experimental Education*, 5, 2 (1936), 191–202. Beth L. Wellman, "Mental Growth From Preschool to College," *Journal of Experimental Education*, 6, 2 (1937), 127–138. Beth L. Wellman, "Our Changing Concept of Intelligence," *Journal of Consulting Psychology*, 2, 4 (1938), 97–107.

31. Beth L. Wellman, "Guiding Mental Development," *Childhood Education* (November, 1938), 112.

32. Cravens, *Before Head Start: The Iowa Station and America's Children*.

33. Cravens, *Before Head Start: The Iowa Station and America's Children*, 129.

34. Newell C. Kephart and H. Max Houtchens, "The Effect of the Stimulus Word Used upon Scores in the Association-Motor Test," *American Journal of Psychiatry*, 94 (1937), 393–399. Harold Marshall Williams, Newell C. Kephart, and H. Max Houtchens, "The Reliability

of the Psychoneurotic Inventory with Delinquent Boys," *The Journal of Abnormal and Social Psychology*, 31, 3 (1936), 271–275.

35. Harold M. Skeels, Ruth Updegraff, Beth L. Wellman, and Harold M. Williams, *A Study of Environmental Stimulation: An Orphanage Preschool Project* (Iowa City, 1938).

36. Newell C. Kephart, "An Experimental Study of the Organization of Function in the Delinquent" (Ph.D. diss., State University of Iowa, 1936), Acknowledgements page.

37. Kephart, "An Experimental Study of the Organization of Function in the Delinquent," 3.

38. Kephart, "An Experimental Study of the Organization of Function in the Delinquent," 4.

39. Kephart, "An Experimental Study of the Organization of Function in the Delinquent," 5.

40. Kephart, "An Experimental Study of the Organization of Function in the Delinquent," 31.

41. Kephart, "An Experimental Study of the Organization of Function in the Delinquent," 31.

42. Newell C. Kephart, *Learning Disability: An Educational Adventure* (West Lafayette, IN, 1968), 7. Also see Radler and Kephart, *Success through Play: How to Prepare Your Child for School Achievement—and Enjoy It.*

43. Newell C. Kephart, "The Effect of Highly Specialized Program upon the IQ in High-Grade Mentally Deficient Boys," *The Journal of Psychoasthenics*, 44, 1 (1939), 216–221. Newell C. Kephart and Alfred A. Strauss, "A Clinical Factor Influencing Variations in IQ," *American Journal of Orthopsychiatry*, 10 (1940), 343–351.

44. Newell C. Kephart, "Influencing the Rate of Mental Growth in Retarded Children through Mental Stimulation," in *The Thirty-Ninth Yearbook of the National Society for the Study of Education: Intelligence: Its Nature and Nurture, Part II, Original Studies and Experiments,* ed. Guy Montrose Whipple (Bloomington, IL, 1940). 224.

45. Kephart, "The Effect of Highly Specialized Program upon the IQ in High-Grade Mentally Deficient Boys," 216.

46. Kephart, "The Effect of Highly Specialized Program upon the IQ in High-Grade Mentally Deficient Boys," 216.

47. Alfred A. Strauss and Newell C. Kephart, "Rate of Mental Growth in a Constant Environment among Higher Grade Moron and Borderline Children," proceedings, American Association on Mental Deficiency, 44, 1 (1939), 137–142.

48. Kephart, "The Effect of Highly Specialized Program upon the IQ in High-Grade Mentally Deficient Boys," 216–221. Kephart, "Influencing the Rate of Mental Growth in Retarded Children through Mental Stimulation," 224.

49. Kephart, "The Effect of Highly Specialized Program upon the IQ in High-Grade Mentally Deficient Boys," 217.

50. Kephart, "The Effect of Highly Specialized Program upon the IQ in High-Grade Mentally Deficient Boys," 217.

51. Kephart, "The Effect of Highly Specialized Program upon the IQ in High-Grade Mentally Deficient Boys," 218.

52. Kephart, "The Effect of Highly Specialized Program upon the IQ in High-Grade Mentally Deficient Boys," 218.

53. Kephart, "Influencing the Rate of Mental Growth in Retarded Children through Mental Stimulation," 230. Kephart, "The Effect of Highly Specialized Program upon the IQ in High-Grade Mentally Deficient Boys," 216–221.

54. Strauss and Kephart, *Psychopathology and the Education of the Brain-Injured Child, Volume II* (New York, 1955).

55. Newell C. Kephart, "The Importance of Phoria Measurements in Industrial Vision," *Optometric Weekly*, 38 (1947), 45–50. Newell C. Kephart, "Visual Skills and Labor Turnover," *Journal of Applied Psychology*, 32, 1 (1948), 51–55.

56. Kephart, "The Importance of Phoria Measurements in Industrial Vision," 45.

57. Kephart, "The Importance of Phoria Measurements in Industrial Vision," 45–50.

58. Kephart, "Visual Skills and Labor Turnover," 51–55.

59. Gerald N. Getman and Newell C. Kephart, *Perceptual Development of Retarded Children* (Lafayette, IN, 1956).

60. Arnold Gesell, Frances L. Ilg, Glenna E. Bullis, Vivienne Ilg, and Gerald N. Getman, *Vision: Its Development in Infant and Child* (New York, 1949). Gerald N. Getman, "Autobiography," in *Teaching Children with Learning Disabilities: Personal Perspectives*, ed. James M. Kauffman and Daniel P. Hallahan (Columbus, OH, 1976), 211–237.

61. John Arena, "An Interview with G. N. Getman," *Academic Therapy*, 15, 2 (1979), 231–236. Getman, "Autobiography," 211–237. G. N. Getman, "Four Concepts Held by Modern Optometry: Their Origin...and...Their Future," *Journal of the American Optometric Association*, 49, 6 (1978), 627–631.

62. Arena, "An Interview with G. N. Getman," 231–236.

63. Getman, "Autobiography," 219.

64. Getman, "Autobiography," 211–237.

65. Getman, "Autobiography," 215.

66. A. H. Ismail, Newell Kephart, and C.C. Cowell, *Utilization of Motor Aptitude Tests in Predicting Academic Achievement* (Indianapolis, IN, 1963).

67. Newell C. Kephart, "Visual Skills and Their Relation to School Achievement," *American Journal of Opthalmology*, 36 (1953), 794–799.

68. Newell C. Kephart, "Visual Correction and School Achievement," *American Journal of Optometry*, 28 (1951), 422.

69. Kephart, "Visual Correction and School Achievement," 423.

70. Kephart, "Visual Skills and Their Relation to School Achievement," 794.

71. Kephart, "Visual Skills and Their Relation to School Achievement," 796.

72. Kephart, "Visual Skills and Their Relation to School Achievement," 797–798.

73. "Visual Skills and Their Relation to School Achievement," 794–799.

74. "Visual Skills and Their Relation to School Achievement," 796.

75. "Visual Skills and Their Relation to School Achievement," 796.

76. Robert Glenn Lowder, "Perceptual Ability and School Achievement: An Exploratory Study" (Ph.D. diss., Purdue University, 1956). Dorothy Margaret Simpson, "Perceptual Readiness and Beginning Reading" (Ph.D. diss., Purdue University, 1960). Eugene G. Roach and Newell C. Kephart, *The Purdue Perceptual-Motor Survey* (Columbus, OH; 1966).

77. Kephart, "Perceptual-Motor Correlates of Learning," 17.

78. Ismail, Kephart, and Cowell, *Utilization of Motor Aptitude Tests in Predicting Academic Achievement*.

79. Kephart, Newell C, *Contemporary Authors, Permanent Series*, Volume 2 (Detroit, MI, 1975–1978), 287. Kephart, Newell C., *The National Cyclopedia of American Biography*, 58 (Clifton, NJ, 1984), 484–485.

80. Kephart, *Learning Disability: An Educational Adventure*, 5.
81. Barsch, *A Movigenic Curriculum*, 4.
82. Kephart, *Learning Disability: An Educational Adventure*, 39.
83. Gerald N. Getman and Elmer R. Kane, *The Physiology of Readiness: An Action Program for the Development of Perception for Children* (Minneapolis, MN, 1964), 1.
84. Barsch, *A Movigenic Curriculum*, 5.
85. Kephart, *Learning Disabilities: The Last Lectures of Newell C. Kephart*, 44.
86. Kephart, *Learning Disabilities: The Last Lectures of Newell C. Kephart*, 45.
87. Kephart Center Series Videotape 1, circa 1968–1973. Newell C. Kephart Special Collection, Archival Services, University of Northern Colorado, Greeley, CO.
88. Kephart Center Series Videotape 1, circa 1968–1973. Newell C. Kephart Special Collection, Archival Services, University of Northern Colorado, Greeley, CO.
89. Barsch, *A Movigenic Curriculum*, 4.
90. Kephart, *Learning Disability: An Educational Adventure*, 14.
91. Radler and Kephart, *Success through Play: How to Prepare Your Child for School Achievement—and Enjoy It*, 29.
92. Radler and Kephart, *Success through Play: How to Prepare Your Child for School Achievement—and Enjoy It*, 28.
93. Kephart Center Series Videotape 8, circa 1968–1973. Newell C. Kephart Special Collection, Archival Services, University of Northern Colorado, Greeley, CO.
94. Barsch, *A Movigenic Curriculum*, 6.
95. Radler and Kephart, *Success through Play: How to Prepare Your Child for School Achievement—and Enjoy It*, 33.
96. Radler and Kephart, *Success through Play: How to Prepare Your Child for School Achievement—and Enjoy It*, 33.
97. Radler and Kephart, *Success through Play: How to Prepare Your Child for School Achievement—and Enjoy It*, 24.
98. Kephart, *Learning Disability: An Educational Adventure*, 21.
99. Kephart, *Learning Disability: An Educational Adventure*, 21.
100. Kephart, *Learning Disability: An Educational Adventure*, 13.
101. Kephart Center Series Videotape 1, circa 1968–1973. Newell C. Kephart Special Collection, Archival Services, University of Northern Colorado, Greeley, CO.
102. Kephart, *Learning Disability: An Educational Adventure*, 23.
103. Kephart, *Learning Disability: An Educational Adventure*, 25.
104. Kephart, *Learning Disability: An Educational Adventure*, 26.
105. Kephart Center Series Videotape 2, circa 1968–1973. Newell C. Kephart Special Collection, Archival Services, University of Northern Colorado, Greeley, CO.
106. Kephart Center Series Videotape 2, circa 1968–1973. Newell C. Kephart Special Collection, Archival Services, University of Northern Colorado, Greeley, CO.
107. Of the three most prominent movement educators, only Ray Barsch made a sustained effort to develop instructional materials and practices devoted to the development of auditory perception skills. Ray Barsch, *Fine Tuning: An Auditory-Visual Training Program* (Novato, CA, 1995).
108. Kephart, *Learning Disability: An Educational Adventure*, 26.

109. Kephart, Learning Disabilities: The Last Lectures of Newell C. Kephart, 59. Kephart Center Series Videotape 8, circa 1968–1973. Newell C. Kephart Special Collection, Archival Services, University of Northern Colorado, Greeley, CO. In Kephart, *Learning Disability: An Educational Adventure*, 27, he uses the term "motor-perceptual match" for the same concept.

110. Kephart Center Series Videotape 2, circa 1968–1973. Newell C. Kephart Special Collection, Archival Services, University of Northern Colorado, Greeley, CO.

111. Kephart, "Perceptual-Motor Correlates of Learning," 16.

112. Kephart, "Perceptual-Motor Correlates of Learning," 17.

113. Kephart, *Learning Disability: An Educational Adventure*, 28.

114. Kephart, *Learning Disability: An Educational Adventure*, 28.

115. Kephart, "Perceptual-Motor Correlates of Learning," 18.

116. Kephart, *Learning Disability: An Educational Adventure*, 29.

117. Kephart, *Learning Disabilities: The Last Lectures of Newell C. Kephart*. Strauss and Kephart, *Psychopathology and the Education of the Brain-Injured Child, Volume II*.

118. Kephart, *Learning Disability: An Educational Adventure*, 29.

119. Kephart, *Learning Disabilities: The Last Lectures of Newell C. Kephart*, 62.

120. Kephart, *Learning Disability: An Educational Adventure*, 33.

121. Kephart, *Learning Disabilities: The Last Lectures of Newell C. Kephart*, 23.

122. Barbara B. Godfrey and Newell C. Kephart, *Movement Patterns and Motor Education* (New York, 1969), 12.

123. Kephart, *Learning Disability: An Educational Adventure*, 14.

124. Kephart, *Learning Disability: An Educational Adventure*, 11.

125. Kephart, *Learning Disability: An Educational Adventure*, 11.

126. Kephart, *Learning Disability: An Educational Adventure*, 12.

127. Kephart, *Learning Disability: An Educational Adventure*, 12.

128. Kephart, *Learning Disability: An Educational Adventure*, 12.

129. Samuel A. Kirk, "A Behavioral Approach to Learning Disabilities," in *Conference on Children with Minimal Brain Impairment*, ed. Samuel A. Kirk and Wesley Baker (Urbana, IL, 1963), 41.

130. Marianne Frostig and Phyllis Maslow, *Movement Education: Theory and Practice* (Chicago, 1970). Marianne Frostig and Phyllis Maslow, *Learning Problems in the Classroom: Prevention and Remediation* (New York, 1973).

131. Godfrey and Kephart, *Movement Patterns and Motor Education*, 12.

132. Kephart, *Learning Disability: An Educational Adventure*, 12.

133. Marguerite P. Ford, "New Directions in Special Education," *Journal of School Psychology*, 9, 1 (1971), 73–83. Daniel P. Hallahan, "Cognitive Styles—Preschool Implications for the Disadvantaged," *Journal of Learning Disabilities*, 3 (1970), 5–9. Daniel P. Hallahan and William M. Cruickshank, *Psychoeducational Foundations of Learning Disabilities* (Englewood Cliffs, NJ, 1973). Murray M. Kappelmann, E. Kaplan, and R. L. Ganter, "A Study of Learning Disorders among Disadvantaged Children," *Journal of Learning Disabilities*, 2 (1969), 267. Gordon R. Alley, Gerald Solomons, and E. Opitz, "Minimal Cerebral Dysfunction as It Relates to Social Class," *Journal of Learning Disabilities*, 4 (1971), 246–250. Dominic Amante, P. H. Margules, D. M. Hartmann, D. B. Storey, and L. J. Weeber, "The Epidemiological

Distribution of CNS Dysfunction," *Journal of Social Issues*, 26, 4 (1970), 105–136. Lester Tarnopol, "Delinquency and Minimal Brain Dysfunction," *Journal of Learning Disabilities*, 3 (1970), 200–207.

134. Samuel A. Kirk, *Early Education of the Mentally Retarded: An Experimental Study* (Urbana, IL, 1958).

5 DIAGNOSING AND TREATING PSYCHOLINGUISTIC DEFICIENCIES: THE PRACTICAL SCIENCE OF SAMUEL A. KIRK

1. Samuel A. Kirk, "Experiments in the Early Training of the Mentally Retarded," *American Journal of Mental Deficiency*, 56 (1952), 692.
2. Samuel A. Kirk, "Autobiography," in *Teaching Children with Learning Disabilities: Personal Perspectives*, ed. James M. Kauffman and Daniel P. Hallahan (Columbus, OH, 1976), 238–269.
3 Kirk, "Autobiography," 245.
4. Kirk, "Autobiography," 238–269. Samuel A. Kirk, "Behavioral Diagnosis and Remediation of Learning Disabilities," *Proceedings of the Conference on the Exploration into the Problems of the Perceptually Handicapped Child* (Evanston, IL, 1963), 1–7.
5. Kirk, "Autobiography," 238–269. Samuel A. Kirk, "Introspection and Prophecy," in *Perspectives in Special Education: Personal Orientations*, ed. Burton Blatt and Richard J. Morris (Glenview, IL, 1984), 25–55.
6. Kirk, "Autobiography," 247.
7. Marion Monroe, "The Apparent Weight of Color and Correlated Phenomena" (M.A. thesis, University of Chicago, 1924). Marion Monroe, "The Drawings and Color Preferences of Young Children" (Ph.D. diss, University of Chicago, 1929).
8. Kirk, "Autobiography," 238–269. Samuel A. Kirk, "Lecture—Final Report, Advanced Institute for Leadership Personnel in Learning Disabilities, Department of Special Education, University of Arizona," typescript, 1970, Box 10, Samuel A. Kirk Papers (Archives Research Center, University of Illinois, Urbana). Samuel A. Kirk, "Learning Disabilities: Reopening Pandora's Box," typescript, Dec. 4, 1976, Box 11, Samuel A. Kirk Papers (Archives Research Center, University of Illinois, Urbana). Kirk, "Introspection and Prophecy," 25–55. Monroe, *Methods for Diagnosis and Treatment of Cases of Reading Disability Based on the Comparison of the Reading Performance of One Hundred Twenty Normal and One Hundred and Seventy Five Retarded Readers*. Marion Monroe, *Children Who Cannot Read: The Analysis of Reading Disabilities and the Use of Diagnostic Tests in the Instruction of Retarded Readers* (Chicago, IL, 1932).
9. Kirk, "Autobiography," 238–269.
10. Kirk, "Autobiography," 238–269.
11. Sally, Dick, and Jane History, http://www.tagnwag.com/dick_jane/marion_monroe.html.
12. Susan E. Israel and E. Jennifer Monaghan, *Shaping the Reading Field: The Impact of Early Reading Pioneers, Scientific Research, and Progressive Ideas* (Newark, DE, 2007).
13. Kirk, "Autobiography," 238–269. Kirk, "Introspection and Prophecy," 25–55.

14. Kirk, "Autobiography," 238–269.
15. Fred McKinney, "Functionalism at Chicago—Memories of a Graduate Student: 1929–1931," *Journal of the History of the Behavioral Sciences*, 14, 2 (1978), 142–148. Paul Whitely, "A New Name for an Old Idea? A Student of Harvey Carr Reflects," *Journal of the History of the Behavioral Sciences*, 12 (1976), 260–274.
16. Kirk, "Autobiography," 238–269. Kirk, "Introspection and Prophecy," 25–55.
17. Ludy T. Benjamin, Jr., *A Brief History of Modern Psychology* (Malden, MA, 2007). Forrest A. Kingsbury, "A History of the Department of Psychology at the University of Chicago," *Psychological Bulletin*, 43 (1946), 259–271. McKinney, "Functionalism at Chicago—Memories of a Graduate Student: 1929–1931," 142–148. D. Alfred Owens and Mark Wagner, *Progress in Modern Psychology: The Legacy of American Functionalism* (Westport, CT, 1992). Paul L. Whitely, "A New Name for an Old Idea? A Student of Harvey Carr Reflects," 260–274.
18. Harvey Carr, "Autobiography," in *History of Psychology in Autobiography*, ed. Carl Murchison (New York, 1961), 69–82. Kingsbury, "A History of the Department of Psychology at the University of Chicago," 259–271. Whitely, "A New Name for an Old Idea? A Student of Harvey Carr Reflects," 260–274.
19. William James, *The Principles of Psychology* (New York, 1890).
20. John Dewey, "The Reflex Arc Concept in Psychology," *Psychological Review*, 3 (1896), 357–370.
21. Andrew Backe, "John Dewey and Early Chicago Functionalism," *History of Psychology*, 4, 4 (2001), 323–340. Andrew Backe, "Introduction," in *The Chicago School of Functionalism*, Volume 3, ed. John R. Shook (Bristol, England, 2001), vii–xxi.
22. Charles Sanders Pierce, "How to Make Our Ideas Clear," in *The Collected Papers of Charles Sanders Pierce*, 5, ed. Charles Hartshorne and Paul Weiss (1878, Cambridge, MA, 1931), 402.
23. Richard Rorty, *Objectivity, Relativism, and Truth: Philosophical Papers*, Volume 1 (New York, 1991), 14.
24. Joseph Brent, *Charles Sanders Pierce, a Life* (Bloomington, IN, 1993). William James, *Pragmatism, a New Name for Some Old Ways of Thinking* (New York, 1907). Louis Menand, *The Metaphysical Club: A Story of Ideas in America* (New York, 2001). John R. Shook, "Introduction," in *The Chicago School of Functionalism*, Volume 2 (Bristol, England, 2001), vii–xxiii. Linda Simon, *Genuine Reality: A Life of William James* (Chicago, 1998). Cornel West, *The American Evasion of Philosophy: A Genealogy of Pragmatism* (Madison, WI, 1989).
25. William James, "The Chicago School," *The Psychological Bulletin*, 1, 1 (1904), 1.
26. Edward B. Titchener, "The Postulates of a Structural Psychology," *The Philosophical Review*, 7, 5 (1898), 452. Also see Edward B. Titchener, "Structural and Functional Psychology," *The Philosophical Review*, 8, 3 (1899), 290–299.
27. Kingsbury, "A History of the Department of Psychology at the University of Chicago," 259–271.
28. Benjamin, *A Brief History of Modern*. W. B. Pillsbury, "The Psychology of Edward Bradford Titchener," *The Philosophical Review*, 37, 2 (1928), 95–108. Robert S. Woodworth, *Contemporary Schools of Psychology* (New York, 1931).
29. James Mark Baldwin, "Types of Reaction," *Psychological Review*, 2 (1895), 259–273.

30. James Rowland Angell and Addison W. Moore, "Reaction-Time: A Study of Attention and Habit," *Psychological Review*, 3 (1896), 245–258.
31. Titchener, "The Postulates of a Structural Psychology," 450.
32. Titchener, "The Postulates of a Structural Psychology," 452.
33. Titchener, "Structural and Functional Psychology," 292.
34. Titchener, "Structural and Functional Psychology," 291.
35. James Rowland Angell, *Psychology: An Introductory Study of the Structure and Function of Human Consciousness* (New York, 1904).
36. James Rowland Angell, "The Province of Functional Psychology," *Psychological Review*, 14, 2 (1907), 63.
37. Angell, "The Province of Functional Psychology. Psychological Review," 64.
38. Angell, "The Province of Functional Psychology. Psychological Review," 79.
39. James Rowland Angell, "Autobiography," in *History of Psychology in Autobiography*, ed. Carl Murchison (New York, 1961), 23.
40. Angell, "The Province of Functional Psychology," 86.
41. James Rowland Angell, "The Influence of Darwin on Psychology," *Psychological Review*, 16 (1909), 152–169.
42. Angell, "Autobiography," 23.
43. Harvey A. Carr, *Psychology: A Study of Mental Activity* (New York, 1925), 1.
44. Harvey A. Carr, "The Nature of Mental Process," *Psychological Review*, 24, 3 (1917), 181.
45. Carr, "The Nature of Mental Process," 182.
46. Carr, *Psychology: A Study of Mental Activity*, 7.
47. Carr, "The Nature of Mental Process," 185.
48. Murchison, *The Psychologies of 1925* (Worcester, MA, 1925). Murchison, *The Psychologies of 1930* (Worcester, MA, 1930).
49. Woodworth, *Contemporary Schools of Psychology*.
50. Murchison, *The Psychologies of 1925*.
51. Whitely, "A New Name for an Old Idea? A Student of Harvey Carr Reflects," 261.
52. McKinney, "Functionalism at Chicago—Memories of a Graduate Student: 1929–1931," 142–148.
53. Harvey Carr, "Functionalism," in *The Psychologies of 1930*, ed. Carl Murchison (Worcester, MA, 1930), 59.
54. Carr, "Autobiography," 81.
55. Carr, *Psychology: A Study of Mental Activity*.
56. Carr, "Autobiography," 79.
57. Carr, *Psychology: A Study of Mental Activity*, 13–14.
58. McKinney, "Functionalism at Chicago—Memories of a Graduate Student: 1929–1931," 142–148. Whitely, "A New Name for an Old Idea? A Student of Harvey Carr Reflects," 260–274.
59. W. B. Pillsbury, 1955. Harvey A. Carr: 1873–1954. *The American Journal of Psychology*, 68, 1, p. 149.
60. McKinney, "Functionalism at Chicago—Memories of a Graduate Student: 1929–1931," 145.
61. John B. Watson, "Psychology as the Behaviorist Sees it," *Psychological Review*, 20, 2 (1913), 163.

62. McKinney, "Functionalism at Chicago—Memories of a Graduate Student: 1929–1931," 142–148.

63. Mitchell G. Ash, *Gestalt Psychology in German Culture, 1890–1967: Holism and the Quest for Objectivity* (Cambridge, England, 1995). Michael M. Sokal, "The Gestalt Psychologists in Behaviorist America," *The American Historical Review*, 89, 5 (1984), 1240–1263.

64. Hudson Hoagland, "The Psychologies of 1925," *The Journal of Philosophy*, 24, 13 (1927), 353.

65. Ellsworth Faris, "The Psychologies of 1925," *The American Journal of Sociology*, 32, 2 (1926), 311.

66. R. H. Thouless, "The Psychologies of 1925," *Journal of Philosophical Studies*, 3, 10 (1928), 250.

67. John Macdonald, "The Psychologies of 1930," *The Journal of Philosophy*, 28, 2 (1931), 46.

68. Woodworth, *Contemporary Schools of Psychology*, 327.

69. Macdonald, "The Psychologies of 1930," 49.

70. Woodworth, *Contemporary Schools of Psychology*, 213.

71. Harvey Carr, "Review of Contemporary Schools of Psychology," *Psychological Bulletin*, 29, 6 (1932), 441–442.

72. Carr, "The Nature of Mental Process," 24, 3, 185.

73. Carr, "Autobiography," 69–82. McKinney, "Functionalism at Chicago—Memories of a Graduate Student: 1929–1931," 142–148.

74. Paul D. Chapman, *Schools as Sorters: Lewis M. Terman, Applied Psychology, and the Intelligence Testing Movement, 1890–1930* (New York, 1988). Brian Evans and Bernard Waites, *IQ and Mental Testing: An Unnatural Science and Its Social History* (Atlantic Highlands, NJ, 1981). Daniel J. Kevles, "Testing the Army's Intelligence: Psychologists and the Military in World War I," *The Journal of American History*, 55, 3 (1968), 565–581. Joel H. Spring, "Psychologists and the War: The Meaning of Intelligence in the Alpha and Beta Tests," *History of Education Quarterly*, 12, 1 (1972), 3–15.

75. Chapman, *Schools as Sorters: Lewis M. Terman, Applied Psychology, and the Intelligence Testing Movement, 1890–1930*. Kevles, "Testing the Army's Intelligence: Psychologists and the Military in World War I," 565–581.

76. Carr, *Psychology: A Study of Mental Activity*.

77. http://www.indiana.edu/~intell/lthurstone.shtml. Kingsbury, "A History of the Department of Psychology at the University of Chicago," 259–271. McKinney, "Functionalism at Chicago—Memories of a Graduate Student: 1929–1931," 142–148.

78. Kirk, "Autobiography," 238–269. Kirk, "Introspection and Prophecy," 25–55.

79. Carr, *Psychology: A Study of Mental Activity*, 11.

80. Carr, *Psychology: A Study of Mental Activity*, 327.

81. Carr, *Psychology: A Study of Mental Activity*, 327.

82. Carr, *Psychology: A Study of Mental Activity*, 327.

83. Edwin G. Boring, *A History of Experimental Psychology* (New York, 1950), 559.

84. Carr, "Autobiography," in *History of Psychology in Autobiography*, ed. Carl Murchison (New York, 1961), 69–82. Helen L. Koch, "Harvey A. Carr," *Psychological Review*, 62, 2 (1955), 81–82. McKinney, "Functionalism at Chicago—Memories of a Graduate Student: 1929–1931," 142–148. Pillsbury, 1955. Whitely, "A New Name for an Old Idea? A Student of Harvey Carr Reflects," 260–274.

85. Kirk, "Autobiography," 243.

86. Backe, "Introduction," vii–xxi.

87. Daniel P. Hallahan and Devery R. Mock, "A Brief History of the Field of Learning Disabilities," in *Handbook of Learning Disabilities*, ed. H. Lee Swanson, Karen R. Harris, and Steve Graham (New York, 2003), 16–29.

88. Samuel T. Orton, "Preface," in *Methods for Diagnosis and Treatment of Cases of Reading Disability Based on the Comparison of the Reading Performance of One Hundred Twenty Normal and One Hundred and Seventy Five Retarded Readers, Marion Monroe* (Worcester, MA, 1928).

89. Monroe, *Children Who Cannot Read: The Analysis of Reading Disabilities and the Use of Diagnostic Tests in the Instruction of Retarded Readers*, x.

90. Monroe, *Children Who Cannot Read: The Analysis of Reading Disabilities and the Use of Diagnostic Tests in the Instruction of Retarded Readers*, x.

91. Monroe, *Children Who Cannot Read: The Analysis of Reading Disabilities and the Use of Diagnostic Tests in the Instruction of Retarded Readers*, x.

92. William S. Grey, "Methods of Testing Reading," *The Elementary School Journal*, 16, 6 (1916), 231–246; 281–298. William Scott Gray, *Studies of Elementary School Reading Through Standardized Tests* (Chicago, 1925). William Scott Gray, *Summary of Investigations Related to Reading* (Chicago, 1925).

93. June R. Gilstad, "Commentary: William S. Gray (1885–1960): First IRA President," *Reading Research Quarterly*, 20, 4 (1985), 509–511. William S. Gray, *Oral Reading Paragraphs Test* (Bloomington, IL, 1915). Nancy A. Mavrogenes, "More Commentary on William S. Gray," *Reading Research Quarterly*, 21, 1 (1986), 106–107. Jennifer Stevenson, *William S. Gray: Teacher, Scholar, Leader* (Newark, DE, 1985).

94. Raymond E. Callahan, *Education and the Cult of Efficiency* (Chicago, 1962). Richard L. Venezky, "The History of Reading Research," in *Handbook of Reading Research*, ed. P. David Pearson (Mahway, NJ, 2002), 3–38.

95. W. F. Current and G. M. Rich, "Further Studies on the Reliability of Tests," *Journal of Educational Psychology*, 17 (1926), 476–481. Arthur I. Gates, "An Experimental and Statistical Study of Reading and Reading Tests," *Journal of Educational Psychology*, 12 (1921), 303–314; 378–391.

96. William S. Gray, "The Diagnostic Study of an Individual Case in Reading," *The Elementary School Journal*, 21, 8 (1921), 577–594. William S. Gray, "Diagnostic and Remedial Steps in Reading," *Journal of Educational Research*, 4, 1 (1921), 1–15. William S. Gray, *Remedial Cases in Reading: Their Diagnosis and Treatment* (Chicago, 1922). Gray, *Summary of Investigations Related to Reading*.

97. Gray, *Remedial Cases in Reading: Their Diagnosis and Treatment*, 2.

98. Gray, "Diagnostic and Remedial Steps in Reading," 4.

99. Gray, *Summary of Investigations Related to Reading*, 204.

100. Allan Luke, *Literacy, Textbooks, and Ideology: Postwar Literacy Instruction and the Mythology of Dick and Jane* (Philadelphia, 1988), 75.

101. Gray, *Remedial Cases in Reading: Their Diagnosis and Treatment*, 24. William S. Gray, "Case Studies of Reading Deficiencies in Junior High School," *Journal of Educational Research*, 10, 2 (1924), 136.

102. Gray, "Case Studies of Reading Deficiencies in Junior High School," 136.

103. Gray, *Remedial Cases in Reading: Their Diagnosis and Treatment.* Gray, "Case Studies of Reading Deficiencies in Junior High School," 132–140.
104. Gray, "Case Studies of Reading Deficiencies in Junior High School," 137.
105. Gray, *Remedial Cases in Reading: Their Diagnosis and Treatment,* 24.
106. Gray, "Case Studies of Reading Deficiencies in Junior High School," 137.
107. William S. Gray, "The Diagnostic Study of an Individual Case in Reading," 577–594. William S. Gray, "Diagnostic and Remedial Steps in Reading," 1–15. Gray, *Remedial Cases in Reading: Their Diagnosis and Treatment.* Gray, "Case Studies of Reading Deficiencies in Junior High School," 132–140.
108. Nila Banton Smith, *American Reading Instruction* (Newark, DE, 2002).
109. Gray, "Case Studies of Reading Deficiencies in Junior High School," 137.
110. Monroe, *Methods for Diagnosis and Treatment of Cases of Reading Disability Based on the Comparison of the Reading Performance of One Hundred Twenty Normal and One Hundred and Seventy Five Retarded Readers,* 374.
111. Monroe, *Methods for Diagnosis and Treatment of Cases of Reading Disability Based on the Comparison of the Reading Performance of One Hundred Twenty Normal and One Hundred and Seventy Five Retarded Readers.*
112. Monroe, *Children Who Cannot Read: The Analysis of Reading Disabilities and the Use of Diagnostic Tests in the Instruction of Retarded Readers.*
113. Kirk, "Introspection and Prophecy," 31.
114. Monroe, *Methods for Diagnosis and Treatment of Cases of Reading Disability Based on the Comparison of the Reading Performance of One Hundred Twenty Normal and One Hundred and Seventy Five Retarded Readers,* 387.
115. Monroe, *Methods for Diagnosis and Treatment of Cases of Reading Disability Based on the Comparison of the Reading Performance of One Hundred Twenty Normal and One Hundred and Seventy Five Retarded Readers,* 424.
116. Monroe, *Children Who Cannot Read: The Analysis of Reading Disabilities and the Use of Diagnostic Tests in the Instruction of Retarded Readers,* 1.
117. Hinshelwood, *Congenital Word-Blindness,* 83.
118. Monroe, *Children Who Cannot Read: The Analysis of Reading Disabilities and the Use of Diagnostic Tests in the Instruction of Retarded Readers,* 1.
119. Monroe, *Children Who Cannot Read: The Analysis of Reading Disabilities and the Use of Diagnostic Tests in the Instruction of Retarded Readers,* 1.
120. Monroe, *Methods for Diagnosis and Treatment of Cases of Reading Disability Based on the Comparison of the Reading Performance of One Hundred Twenty Normal and One Hundred and Seventy Five Retarded Readers,* 346.
121. Monroe, *Children Who Cannot Read: The Analysis of Reading Disabilities and the Use of Diagnostic Tests in the Instruction of Retarded Readers,* 14.
122. Monroe, *Children Who Cannot Read: The Analysis of Reading Disabilities and the Use of Diagnostic Tests in the Instruction of Retarded Readers.*
123. Monroe, *Children Who Cannot Read: The Analysis of Reading Disabilities and the Use of Diagnostic Tests in the Instruction of Retarded Readers,* 15.
124. Monroe, *Children Who Cannot Read: The Analysis of Reading Disabilities and the Use of Diagnostic Tests in the Instruction of Retarded Readers,* 15.

125. Monroe, *Children Who Cannot Read: The Analysis of Reading Disabilities and the Use of Diagnostic Tests in the Instruction of Retarded Readers*, 14.

126. Monroe, *Children Who Cannot Read: The Analysis of Reading Disabilities and the Use of Diagnostic Tests in the Instruction of Retarded Readers*, 1.

127. Monroe, *Children Who Cannot Read: The Analysis of Reading Disabilities and the Use of Diagnostic Tests in the Instruction of Retarded Readers*, 10.

128. Monroe, *Methods for Diagnosis and Treatment of Cases of Reading Disability Based on the Comparison of the Reading Performance of One Hundred Twenty Normal and One Hundred and Seventy Five Retarded Readers*, 364.

129. Monroe, *Children Who Cannot Read: The Analysis of Reading Disabilities and the Use of Diagnostic Tests in the Instruction of Retarded Readers*, 34.

130. Monroe, *Children Who Cannot Read: The Analysis of Reading Disabilities and the Use of Diagnostic Tests in the Instruction of Retarded Readers*, 34.

131. Gray, "Diagnostic and Remedial Steps in Reading," 1–15. Gray, *Studies of Elementary School Reading Through Standardized Tests*.

132. Gray, *Summary of Investigations Related to Reading*, 205.

133. Monroe, *Children Who Cannot Read: The Analysis of Reading Disabilities and the Use of Diagnostic Tests in the Instruction of Retarded Readers*, 41.

134. Monroe, *Children Who Cannot Read: The Analysis of Reading Disabilities and the Use of Diagnostic Tests in the Instruction of Retarded Readers*, 41.

135. Monroe, *Children Who Cannot Read: The Analysis of Reading Disabilities and the Use of Diagnostic Tests in the Instruction of Retarded Readers*, 58.

136. Monroe, *Children Who Cannot Read: The Analysis of Reading Disabilities and the Use of Diagnostic Tests in the Instruction of Retarded Readers*, 58.

137. Arthur I. Gates, *The Psychology of Reading and Spelling with Special Reference to Disability* (New York, 1922). Arthur I. Gates, *The Improvement of Reading* (New York, 1927).

138. Zirbes left Teachers College to join the Ohio State University faculty in 1928. Laura Zirbes, "Diagnosis and Remedial Work," in *The Twenty Fourth Yearbook of the National Society for the Study of Education, Part 1: Report of the National Committee on Reading*, ed. Guy Montrose Whipple (Bloomington, IL, 1925), 275–289.

139. Zirbes, "Diagnosis and Remedial Work," 276.

140. Guy Montrose Whipple, *The Twenty-Fourth Yearbook of the National Society for the Study of Education, Part 1: Report of the National Committee on Reading* (Bloomington, IL, 1925).

141. Thorleif G. Hegge, Robert Sears, and Samuel A. Kirk, "Reading Cases in an Institution for Mentally Retarded Children," *Proceedings and Addresses of the American Association for the Study of Feeblemindedness*, 37 (1932), 152.

142. Thorleif G. Hegge, "Special Reading Disability with Particular Reference to the Mentally Deficient," *Proceedings of the American Association for the Study of Feeblemindedness*, 39 (1934), 298.

143. Hegge, "Special Reading Disability with Particular Reference to the Mentally Deficient," 298.

144. Hegge, Sears, and Kirk, "Reading Cases in an Institution for Mentally Retarded Children," 149–212. Hegge, "Special Reading Disability with Particular Reference to the Mentally Deficient," 297–340. Thorleif G. Hegge, "The Significance of Special

Reading Disability in Mentally Handicapped Problem Children," *The American Journal of Psychiatry*, 94 (1937), 77–87.

145. Hegge, Sears, and Kirk, "Reading Cases in an Institution for Mentally Retarded Children," 149–212. Hegge, "Special Reading Disability with Particular Reference to the Mentally Deficient," 297–340. Hegge, "The Significance of Special Reading Disability in Mentally Handicapped Problem Children," 77–87.

146. Thorleif G. Hegge, "Results of Remedial Reading at the Middle Moron Level: A Case Study," *Journal of Juvenile Research*, 19 (1935), 134. Hegge, Sears, and Kirk, "Reading Cases in an Institution for Mentally Retarded Children," 149–212.

147. James Hinshelwood, "Word Blindness and Visual Memory," *The Lancet*, 2 (1895), 1564–1570.

148. W. Pringle Morgan, 1896, "A Case of Congenital Word Blindness," *The British Medical Journal (1871)*, 1378.

149. Hegge, Sears, and Kirk, "Reading Cases in an Institution for Mentally Retarded Children," 148.

150. Samuel A. Kirk, *Manual of Directions for Use with the Hegge-Kirk Remedial Reading Drills* (Ann Arbor, MI, 1936), 5.

151. Hegge, Sears, and Kirk, "Reading Cases in an Institution for Mentally Retarded Children," 64.

152. Hegge, Sears, and Kirk, "Reading Cases in an Institution for Mentally Retarded Children," 172.

153. Hegge, Sears, and Kirk, "Reading Cases in an Institution for Mentally Retarded Children," 164.

154. Hegge, "The Significance of Special Reading Disability in Mentally Handicapped Problem Children," 78.

155. Philip P. Ferguson, *Abandoned to Their Fate: Social Policy and Practice toward Severely Retarded People in America, 1820–1920* (Philadelphia, 1994), 3.

156. Ferguson, *Abandoned to Their Fate: Social Policy and Practice toward Severely Retarded People in America, 1820–1920*, 3. James W. Trent, Jr., *Inventing the Feeble Mind: A History of Mental Retardation in the United States* (Berkeley, CA, 1994).

157. Hegge, "Special Reading Disability with Particular Reference to the Mentally Deficient," 297–340.

158. Hegge, Sears, and Kirk, "Reading Cases in an Institution for Mentally Retarded Children," 149–212. Hegge, "Special Reading Disability with Particular Reference to the Mentally Deficient," 297–340. Samuel A. Kirk, "The Effects of Remedial Reading on the Educational Progress and Personality Adjustment of High-Grade Mentally Deficient Problem Children: Ten Case Studies," *Journal of Juvenile Research*, 18 (1934), 140–162. Hegge, "The Significance of Special Reading Disability in Mentally Handicapped Problem Children," 77–87.

159. Hegge, "Special Reading Disability with Particular Reference to the Mentally Deficient," 297–340.

160. Hegge, Sears, and Kirk, "Reading Cases in an Institution for Mentally Retarded Children," 149–212.

161. Kirk, *Manual of Directions for Use with the Hegge-Kirk Remedial Reading Drills*, 11.

162. Kirk, *Manual of Directions for Use with the Hegge-Kirk Remedial Reading Drills*, 11.

163. Lillian Beatrice Currier, "Phonics or No Phonics?," *The Elementary School Journal*, 23, 6 (1923), 448. Lillian Beatrice Currier and Olive C. Duguid, "Phonics or No Phonics," *The Elementary School Journal*, 17, 4 (1916), 286–287.

164. Currier and Duguid, "Phonics or No Phonics," 286.

165. Currier, "Phonics or No Phonics?," 448.

166. Elmer K. Sexton and John S. Herron, "The Newark Phonics Experiment," *The Elementary School Journal*, 28, 9 (1928), 701.

167. S. C. Garrison and Minnie Taylor Heard, "An Experimental Study of the Value of Phonetics," *Peabody Journal of Education*, 9, 1 (1931), 9–14.

168. Currier and Duguid, "Phonics or No Phonics," 287.

169. Garrison and Heard, "An Experimental Study of the Value of Phonetics," 14.

170. Kirk, *Manual of Directions for Use with the Hegge-Kirk Remedial Reading Drills*. Thorleif G. Hegge, "A Method for Teaching Mentally Deficient Reading Cases," *Proceedings of the American Association on Mental Deficiency*, 40 (1935), 476–483.

171. Kirk, *Manual of Directions for Use with the Hegge-Kirk Remedial Reading Drills*. Samuel A. Kirk, "The Influence of Manual Tracing on the Learning of Simple Words in the Case of Subnormal Boys," *Journal of Educational Psychology*, 24, 7 (1933) , 525–535.

172. Hegge, "A Method for Teaching Mentally Deficient Reading Cases," 477.

173. Kirk, "Autobiography," 238–269. Kirk, "Introspection and Prophecy," 25–55.

174. Samuel A. Kirk, *Teaching Reading to the Slow-Learning Child* (Boston, 1940).

175. Samuel A. Kirk and James J. McCarthy, "The Illinois Test of Psycholinguistic Abilities—An Approach to Differential Diagnosis," *American Journal of Mental Deficiency*, 66 (1961), 399–412. James J. McCarthy and Samuel A. Kirk, *Examiner's Manual: Illinois test of Psycholinguistic Abilities* (Urbana, IL, 1961).

176. Louis L. Thurstone, *Primary Mental Abilities* (Chicago, 1938).

177. Kirk, "Autobiography," 238–269. Samuel A. Kirk, "The Education of Intelligence," *Slow Learning Child*, 20, 2 (1973), 67–83.

178. Kirk, *Teaching Reading to the Slow-Learning Child*, 47.

179. Carr, *Psychology: A Study of Mental Activity*, 1.

180. Marion Monroe, *Reading Aptitude Tests* (Boston, 1935).

181. Samuel A. Kirk, "Reading Aptitudes of Mentally Retarded Children." *Proceedings of the American Association on Mental Deficiency*, 44 (1939), 156–162.

182. Samuel A. Kirk, "A Reading Program for Mentally Retarded Children," *Journal of Exceptional Children*, 6 (1939), 50.

183. Kirk, *Teaching Reading to the Slow-Learning Child*, 47.

184. Marion Monroe, "Diagnosis of Reading Disabilities," in *The Thirty Fourth Yearbook of the National Society for the Study of Education: Educational Diagnosis*, ed. Guy Montrose Whipple (Bloomington, IL, 1935), 218.

185. Kirk, "The Education of Intelligence," 81.

186. Kirk, "The Education of Intelligence," 67–83. Kirk, "Autobiography," 238–269. Kirk, "Introspection and Prophecy," 25–55.

187. Kirk, *Teaching Reading to the Slow-Learning Child*, 21.

188. This was a chapter in Alfred Binet, *Modern Ideas about Children* (Menlo Park, CA, 1975).

189. Kirk, "Introspection and Prophecy," 35.

190. Samuel A. Kirk, "Approaches and Problems in Obtaining Educational Facilities for the Handicapped Child," typescript, April, 1959, Box 2, Samuel A. Kirk Papers (Archives Research Center, University of Illinois, Urbana). Samuel A. Kirk, "The Effects of Educational Treatment," typescript, 1959, Box 2, Samuel A. Kirk Papers (Archives Research Center, University of Illinois, Urbana). Samuel A. Kirk, "Some Factors in the Diagnosis of Mental Retardation, Conference of Community Mental Health Clinics, Allenton Park, IL," typescript, 1960, Box 3, Samuel A. Kirk Papers (Archives Research Center, University of Illinois, Urbana). Samuel A. Kirk, "Diagnostic, Cultural, and Remedial Factors in Mental Retardation, Johns Hopkins Hospital, Baltimore, MD," typescript, April 27, 1964, Box 3, Samuel A. Kirk Papers (Archives Research Center, University of Illinois, Urbana). Samuel A. Kirk, "The Challenge of Individual Differences, Conference on Quality and Equality, Princeton University," typescript, Dec. 2–4, 1964, Box 2, Samuel A. Kirk Papers (Archives Research Center, University of Illinois, Urbana). Samuel A. Kirk, "Educational Aspects of Mental Retardation, Speech in Dublin, Ireland," typescript, March, 1966, Box 3, Samuel A. Kirk Papers (Archives Research Center, University of Illinois, Urbana). Samuel A. Kirk, "The New Emphasis in School Psychology, Speech in Los Angeles, CA," typescript, March, 1966, Box 3, Samuel A. Kirk Papers (Archives Research Center, University of Illinois, Urbana).
191. Kirk, *Teaching Reading to the Slow-Learning Child.*
192. Samuel A. Kirk, "Memorandum Based on the Conference in the President's Office, Nov. 19, 1951, Concerning a Proposal to Establish an Institute for the Study of Exceptional Children," typescript, Nov. 23, 1951, Box 1, Samuel A. Kirk Papers (Archives Research Center, University of Illinois, Urbana). George D. Stoddard to Robert M. Hutchens, Ford Foundation," typescript, June 13, 1951, Box 1, Samuel A. Kirk Papers (Archives Research Center, University of Illinois, Urbana).
193. Kirk, "Autobiography," 238–269. Samuel A. Kirk, "Lecture—Final Report, Advanced Institute for Leadership Personnel in Learning Disabilities, Department of Special Education, University of Arizona," typescript, 1970, p. 5, Box 10, Samuel A. Kirk Papers (Archives Research Center, University of Illinois, Urbana). Kirk, "Introspection and Prophecy," 25–55.
194. Samuel A. Kirk, *Early Education of the Mentally Retarded: An Experimental Study* (Urbana, IL, 1958), 204.
195. Kirk, *Early Education of the Mentally Retarded: An Experimental Study,* 204.
196. Kirk, *Early Education of the Mentally Retarded: An Experimental Study,* 180.
197. Kirk, "The Education of Intelligence", 70.
198. Samuel A. Kirk, "Approaches and Problems in Obtaining Educational Facilities for the Handicapped Child," typescript, April, 1959, Box 2, Samuel A. Kirk Papers (Archives Research Center, University of Illinois, Urbana). Samuel A. Kirk, "The Effects of Educational Treatment," typescript, 1959, Box 2, Samuel A. Kirk Papers (Archives Research Center, University of Illinois, Urbana). Samuel A. Kirk, "Some Factors in the Diagnosis of Mental Retardation, Conference of Community Mental Health Clinics, Allenton Park, IL," typescript, 1960, Box 3, Samuel A. Kirk Papers (Archives Research Center, University of Illinois, Urbana). Samuel A. Kirk, "Diagnostic, Cultural, and Remedial Factors in Mental Retardation, Johns Hopkins Hospital, Baltimore,

MD," typescript, April 27, 1964, Box 3, Samuel A. Kirk Papers (Archives Research Center, University of Illinois, Urbana). Samuel A. Kirk, "The Challenge of Individual Differences, Conference on Quality and Equality, Princeton University," typescript, Dec. 2–4, 1964, Box 2, Samuel A. Kirk Papers (Archives Research Center, University of Illinois, Urbana). Samuel A. Kirk, "Educational Aspects of Mental Retardation, Speech in Dublin, Ireland," typescript, March, 1966, Box 3, Samuel A. Kirk Papers (Archives Research Center, University of Illinois, Urbana). Samuel A. Kirk, "The New Emphasis in School Psychology, Speech in Los Angeles, CA," typescript, March, 1966, Box 3, Samuel A. Kirk Papers (Archives Research Center, University of Illinois, Urbana). Kirk, "The Education of Intelligence," 67–83.

199. Kirk, *Early Education of the Mentally Retarded: An Experimental Study*, 23.
200. For example, see Harold. M. Skeels. "Mental Development of Children in Foster Homes," *Journal of Consulting Psychology* 2, 2 (1938), 33–43. Harold. M. Skeels, "Some Iowa Studies of Mental Growth in Children in Relation to Differentials of the Environment: A Summary," in *The Thirty-Ninth Yearbook of the National Society for the Study of Education: Intelligence: Its Nature and Nurture, Part 1, Comparative and Critical exposition*, ed. Guy Montrose Whipple (Bloomington, IL, 1940), 281–308. Harold. M. Skeels and Harold B. Dye, "A Study of the Effects of Differential Stimulation on Mentally Retarded Children," Proceedings and Addresses of the American Association on Mental Deficiency, 44 (1939), 114–136.
201. Kirk, *Early Education of the Mentally Retarded: An Experimental Study*, 23.
202. Kirk, *Early Education of the Mentally Retarded: An Experimental Study*, 208.
203. Kirk, *Early Education of the Mentally Retarded: An Experimental Study*, 208.
204. Kirk, *Early Education of the Mentally Retarded: An Experimental Study*, 207.
205. Kirk, *Early Education of the Mentally Retarded: An Experimental Study*, 100.
206. Kirk, *Early Education of the Mentally Retarded: An Experimental Study*, 207.
207. Kirk, *Early Education of the Mentally Retarded: An Experimental Study*, 207–208.
208. Samuel A. Kirk, "Remedial Work in the Elementary School," *Journal of the National Education Association*, 48, 7 (1959), 25.
209. Samuel A. Kirk and Winifred D. Kirk, *Psycholinguistic Learning Disabilities: Diagnosis and Remediation* (Urbana, IL, 1971), 122.
210. Marguerite P. Ford, "New Directions in Special Education," *Journal of School Psychology*, 9, 1 (1971), 73–83. Daniel P. Hallahan, "Cognitive Styles—Preschool Implications for the Disadvantaged," Journal of Learning Disabilities, 3 (1970), 5–9. Daniel P. Hallahan and William M. Cruickshank, *Psychoeducational Foundations of Learning Disabilities* (Englewood Cliffs, NJ, 1973). Murray M. Kappelmann, E. Kaplan, and R. L. Ganter, "A Study of Learning Disorders Among Disadvantaged Children," *Journal of Learning Disabilities*, 2 (1969), 267. Gordon R. Alley, Gerald Solomons, and E. Opitz, "Minimal Cerebral Dysfunction as It Relates to Social Class," *Journal of Learning Disabilities*, 4 (1971), 246–250. Dominic Amante, P. H. Margules, D. M. Hartmann, D. B. Storey, and L. J. Weeber, "The Epidemiological Distribution of CNS Dysfunction," *Journal of Social Issues*, 26, 4 (1970), 105–136. Lester Tarnopol, "Delinquency and Minimal Brain Dysfunction," *Journal of Learning Disabilities*, 3 (1970), 200–207.
211. James Carrier, *Learning Disability: Social Class and the Construction of Inequality in American Education* (New York, 1986), 81.

212. Samuel A. Kirk and Winifred D. Kirk, "Use and Abuses of the ITPA," *Journal of Speech and Hearing Disorders*, 43 (1978), 58.
213. Kirk and Kirk, "Use and Abuses of the ITPA," 59.
214. Kirk and Kirk, "Use and Abuses of the ITPA," 59.
215. Daniel P. Hallahan and Cecil D. Mercer, "Learning Disabilities: Historical Perspectives," *The Learning Disabilities Summit: Building a Foundation for the Future*, n.p., http: www. nrcld.org/resources/ldsummit.
216. Kirk and Kirk, "Use and Abuses of the ITPA," 59.
217. Kirk and Kirk, *Psycholinguistic Learning Disabilities: Diagnosis and Remediation*. Kirk and Kirk, "Use and Abuses of the ITPA," 142–148. Kirk and McCarthy, "The Illinois Test of Psycholinguistic Abilities—An Approach to Differential Diagnosis," 399–412.
218. Carrier, *Learning Disability: Social Class and the Construction of Inequality in American Education*, 106.
219. Charles E. Osgood, "Motivational Dynamics of Language Behavior," in *Nebraska Symposium on Motivation*, ed. M. R. Jones (Lincoln, NE, 1957), 348–430. Charles E. Osgood, "A Behavioristic Analysis of Perception and Language as Cognitive Phenomena," in *Contemporary Approaches to Cognition*, ed. Jerome S. Bruner (Cambridge, MA, 1957), 75–118. Joseph M. Wepman, Lyle V. Jones, R. Darrell Bock, Doris Van Pelt, "Studies in Aphasia: Background and Theoretical Formulations," *Journal of Speech and Hearing Disorders*, 323–332.
220. Samuel A. Kirk to Charles E. Osgood, March 5, 1959, Box 7, Samuel A. Kirk Papers (Archives Research Center, University of Illinois, Urbana).
221. Charles E. Osgood to Samuel A. Kirk, April 28, 1959. Box 7, Samuel A. Kirk Papers (Archives Research Center, University of Illinois, Urbana).
222. Osgood, "A Behavioristic Analysis of Perception and Language as Cognitive Phenomena," 81, italics original.
223. Osgood, "A Behavioristic Analysis of Perception and Language as Cognitive Phenomena," 81.
224. Osgood, "A Behavioristic Analysis of Perception and Language as Cognitive Phenomena," 81.
225. Osgood, "A Behavioristic Analysis of Perception and Language as Cognitive Phenomena," 87.
226. Michael J. Reddy, "The Conduit metaphor: A Case of Frame Conflict in Our Language about Language", in *Metaphor and Thought*, ed. Andrew Ortony (Cambridge, England, 1979), 287, italics original.
227. Kirk and Kirk, *Psycholinguistic Learning Disabilities: Diagnosis and Remediation*, 21.
228. Samuel A. Kirk, *The Diagnosis and Remediation of Psycholinguistic Disabilities* (Urbana, IL, 1966), 21.
229. Kirk and Kirk, *Psycholinguistic Learning Disabilities: Diagnosis and Remediation*, 21.
230. Kirk, *The Diagnosis and Remediation of Psycholinguistic Disabilities*, 23. Kirk and Kirk, *Psycholinguistic Learning Disabilities: Diagnosis and Remediation*. Kirk and McCarthy, "The Illinois Test of Psycholinguistic Abilities—An Approach to Differential Diagnosis," 399–412.
231. Osgood, "Motivational Dynamics of Language Behavior," 350.

232. Kirk and McCarthy, "The Illinois Test of Psycholinguistic Abilities—An Approach to Differential Diagnosis," 403.

233. Osgood, "Motivational Dynamics of Language Behavior," 355.

234. Kirk and Kirk, *Psycholinguistic Learning Disabilities: Diagnosis and Remediation*, 11.

6   "ONE DEFINITION DOESN'T INCLUDE EVERYTHING": SAMUEL A. KIRK AND THE LEARNING DISABILITY CONCEPT

1. Samuel A. Kirk to Norris G. Haring, November 2, 1960, Box 2, Samuel A. Kirk Papers (Archives Research Center, University of Illinois, Urbana).

2. Samuel A. Kirk and Winifred D. Kirk, *Psycholinguistic Learning Disabilities: Diagnosis and Remediation* (Urbana, IL, 1971), 11.

3. Samuel A. Kirk to Leonard J. Duhl, National Institute of Mental Health, April 21, 1959, Box 7, Samuel A. Kirk Papers (Archives Research Center, University of Illinois, Urbana). Also see Samuel A. Kirk, "Behavioral Research, Address to the National Association for Retarded Children," typescript, October 30, 1970, Box 11, Samuel A. Kirk Papers (Archives Research Center, University of Illinois, Urbana).

4. Samuel A. Kirk, "Are We Confused?" (version 1), typescript, 1967, pp. 1–2, Box 2, Samuel A. Kirk Papers (Archives Research Center, University of Illinois, Urbana).

5. Samuel A. Kirk, "Lecture—Final Report, Advanced Institute for Leadership Personnel in Learning Disabilities, Department of Special Education, University of Arizona," typescript, 1970, p. 109, Box 10, Samuel A. Kirk Papers (Archives Research Center, University of Illinois, Urbana).

6. Henry H. Goddard, *School Training of Defective Children* (Yonkers-On-Hudson, NY, 1920), 75.

7. J. E. Wallace Wallin, *Problems of Subnormality* (Yonkers-On-Hudson, NY, 1921), 276.

8. Samuel A. Kirk, "Autobiography," in *Teaching Children with Learning Disabilities: Personal Perspectives*, ed. James M. Kauffman and Daniel P. Hallahan (Columbus, OH, 1976), 238–269. Samuel A. Kirk, "Our Current Headaches in Learning Disabilities," in *The Foundations of Special Education: Selected Papers and Speeches of Samuel A. Kirk*, ed. Gail A. Harris and Winifred D. Kirk (Reston, VA, 1993).

9. Kirk, "Our Current Headaches in Learning Disabilities," 115.

10. Samuel A. Kirk and Winifred D. Kirk, "On Defining Learning Disabilities," *Journal of Learning Disabilities*, 16, 1 (1983), 20–21.

11. National Joint Committee on Learning Disabilities, "Learning Disabilities: Issues on Definition. A Position Paper of the National Joint Committee on Learning Disabilities, January 30, 1981," *Learning Disability Quarterly*, 6, 1 (1983), 42.

12. Kirk, "Our Current Headaches in Learning Disabilities," 117.

13. Kirk and Kirk, "On Defining Learning Disabilities," 20–21.

14. Samuel A. Kirk, "Introspection and Prophecy," *Perspectives in Special Education: Personal Orientations*, ed. Burton Blatt and Richard J. Morris (Glenview, IL, 1984), 25–55. Also see Samuel A. Kirk, 1984, "Issues in Learning Disabilities," in *The Foundations of Special*

Education: Selected Papers and Speeches of Samuel A. Kirk, ed. Gail A. Harris and Winifred D. Kirk (Reston, VA, 1993), 125–134.

15. Samuel A. Kirk, "Are We Confused?" (version 2), typescript, 1967, p. 15, Box 2, Samuel A. Kirk Papers (Archives Research Center, University of Illinois, Urbana).

16. Kirk, "Are We Confused?" (version 1), 2.

17. Samuel A. Kirk, The Diagnosis and Remediation of Psycholinguistic Disabilities (Urbana, IL, 1966), 8.

18. Kirk, "Are We Confused?" (version 2), 15.

19. Samuel A. Kirk, 1963. "A Behavioral Approach to Learning Disabilities," in *Conference on Children with Minimal Brain Impairment,* ed. Samuel Kirk and Walter Becker (Urbana, IL, 1963). Samuel A. Kirk, "Behavioral Diagnosis and Remediation of Learning Disabilities," in *Proceedings of the Conference on the Exploration into the Problems of the Perceptually Handicapped Child* (Evanston, IL, 1963), 1–7. Kirk, "Are We Confused?" (version 2). Kirk and Kirk, *Psycholinguistic Learning Disabilities: Diagnosis and Remediation.*

20. See endnotes for Table 1 for a complete list of these 20 documents. These are all of the learning disability concept statements that I was able to gather from published and unpublished sources. Kirk was a very active public speaker, so it is likely that a number of his spoken articulations are not represented here.

21. Samuel A. Kirk, "Learning Disabilities in Children," typescript, March 26, 1960, Box 2, Samuel A. Kirk Papers (Archives Research Center, University of Illinois, Urbana).

22. Samuel A. Kirk and Barbara Bateman, "Diagnosis and Remediation of Learning Disabilities," *Exceptional Children,* 29, 2 (1962), 73.

23. Samuel A. Kirk, "Mental Retardation vs. Learning Disabilities," typescript, 1967, p. 7, Box 3, Samuel A. Kirk Papers (Archives Research Center, University of Illinois, Urbana).

24. Samuel A. Kirk, "Learning Disabilities in Children," typescript, March 26, 1960, Box 2, Samuel A. Kirk Papers (Archives Research Center, University of Illinois, Urbana).

25. Samuel A. Kirk, *Educating Exceptional Children* (Boston, 1962).

26. Samuel A. Kirk and Barbara Bateman, "Diagnosis and Remediation of Learning Disabilities," *Exceptional Children,* 29, 2 (1962), 73–78.

27. Kirk, "A Behavioral Approach to Learning Disabilities."

28. Kirk, "Behavioral Diagnosis and Remediation of Learning Disabilities."

29. Samuel A. Kirk, "The Challenge of Individual Differences," typescript, December, 1964, p. 5, Box 2, Samuel A. Kirk Papers (Archives Research Center, University of Illinois, Urbana).

30. Kirk, *The Diagnosis and Remediation of Psycholinguistic Disabilities.*

31. Kirk, "Are We Confused?" (version 1). Samuel A. Kirk, "Are We Confused?" (version 2).

32. Samuel A. Kirk, "Mental Retardation vs. Learning Disabilities," typescript, 1967, Box 3, Samuel A. Kirk Papers (Archives Research Center, University of Illinois, Urbana).

33. Samuel A. Kirk, "Illinois Test of Psycholinguistic Abilities: Its Origin and Implications," in *Learning Disorders,* Volume 3, ed. Jerome Hellmuth (Seattle, 1968), 395–427.

34. Kirk and Kirk, *Psycholinguistic Learning Disabilities: Diagnosis and Remediation.*

35. Samuel A. Kirk, *Educating Exceptional Children,* 2nd ed. (Boston, 1972).

36. Samuel A. Kirk, "Speech to World Health Organization," Nov. 27, 1972, Box 11, Samuel A. Kirk Papers (Archives Research Center, University of Illinois, Urbana).

37. Kirk, "Autobiography," 238–269.
38. Kirk, "Our Current Headaches in Learning Disabilities," 115–116.
39. Samuel A. Kirk and James J. Gallagher, *Educating Exceptional Children*, 3rd ed. (Boston, 1979).
40. Samuel A. Kirk, "Issues and Problems in Learning Disabilities" typescript, March 22, 1979, Box 11, Samuel A. Kirk Papers (Archives Research Center, University of Illinois, Urbana).
41. Kirk and Kirk, "On Defining Learning Disabilities," 20–21.
42. Samuel A. Kirk and James J. Gallagher, *Educating Exceptional Children*, 4th ed. (Boston, 1983).
43. Samuel A. Kirk and James C. Chalfant, *Academic and Developmental Learning Disabilities* (Denver, 1984).
44. Kirk, "A Behavioral Approach to Learning Disabilities," 41.
45. Kirk, "A Behavioral Approach to Learning Disabilities," 49–50.
46. Bruno Latour and Steve Woolgar. *Laboratory Life: The Social Construction of Scientific Facts* (Beverly Hills, CA, 1979), 84.
47. George Lakoff, "Hedges: A Study in Meaning Criteria and the Logic of Fuzzy Concepts," in Papers from the Eighth Regional Meeting of the Chicago Linguistic Society, ed. Paul M. Peranteau, Judith N. Levi, and Gloria C. Phares (Chicago, 1972), 195.
48. Kirk, *The Diagnosis and Remediation of Psycholinguistic Disabilities*, 2.
49. Kirk, "A Behavioral Approach to Learning Disabilities," 52.
50. Kirk, "Behavioral Diagnosis and Remediation of Learning Disabilities," 3.
51. Kirk, "Autobiography," 238–269.
52. Kirk, "Behavioral Diagnosis and Remediation of Learning Disabilities," 1–7.
53. Kirk, "Autobiography," 255.
54. Kirk, *The Diagnosis and Remediation of Psycholinguistic Disabilities*, 1.
55. Kirk, *The Diagnosis and Remediation of Psycholinguistic Disabilities*, 1.
56. Kirk, *The Diagnosis and Remediation of Psycholinguistic Disabilities*, 2.
57. Samuel A. Kirk, "Mental Retardation vs. Learning Disabilities," typescript, 1967, Box 3, Samuel A. Kirk Papers (Archives Research Center, University of Illinois, Urbana).
58. Kirk, "Mental Retardation vs. Learning Disabilities," 7.
59. Kirk, "Mental Retardation vs. Learning Disabilities," 7.
60. Kirk, "Mental Retardation vs. Learning Disabilities," 7.
61. Kirk, "Mental Retardation vs. Learning Disabilities," 7.
62. Kirk, "Mental Retardation vs. Learning Disabilities," 7.
63. Kirk, "Mental Retardation vs. Learning Disabilities," 7.
64. Samuel A. Kirk and Jeanne McRae McCarthy, "The Beginnings of ACLD," in *Learning Disabilities: Selected ACLD Papers*, ed. Samuel A. Kirk and Jeanne McRae McCarthy (Boston 1975), 3–4.
65. Samuel A. Kirk, "Learning Disabilities: A Historical Note," *Academic Therapy*, 17, 1 (1981), 5–11.
66. Edward C. Frierson, "Autobiography," in *Teaching Children with Learning Disabilities: Personal Perspectives,* ed. James M. Kauffman and Daniel P. Hallahan (Columbus, OH, 1976), 139.
67. Frierson, "Autobiography," 139.

68. Don Murray, "Children of the Empty World," *Saturday Evening Post,* Sept. 13, 1958, pp. 28–29, 77–78, 81. Rosalind C. Oppenheim, "They Said Our Child Was Hopeless," *Saturday Evening Post,* June 17, 1961, pp. 23, 56, 58. Calvin Tompkins, "A Reporter at Large: The Last Skill Acquired," *The New Yorker,* September 14, 1963, pp. 127–128, 130, 132–134, 137–138, 140, 143–144, 146, 148, 150, 152, 154, 156–157. Staff, "When Film is Flim," Newsweek, July 31, 1967.

69. Murray, "Children of the Empty World," 29.

70. Oppenheim, "They Said Our Child Was Hopeless," 23.

71. Staff, "Bobby Joins His World: 5 Millions Brain Damaged Children Can Be Helped," *Look,* November 11, 1966, 84.

72. Staff, "Bobby Joins His World: 5 Millions Brain Damaged Children Can Be Helped," 84–86, 93.

73. Oppenheim, "They Said Our Child Was Hopeless," 23.

74. Murray, "Children of the Empty World," 29.

75. Oppenheim, "They Said Our Child Was Hopeless," 58.

76. Murray, "Children of the Empty World," 29.

77. Murray, "Children of the Empty World," 28.

78. Albert Q. Maisel, "Hope for Brain-Injured Children," *Reader's Digest,* October, 1964, p. 140.

79. Murray, "Children of the Empty World," 81.

80. Public Law 88-164, October 31, 1963. http://history.nih.gov/01Docs/historical/documents/PL88-164.pdf.

81. James J. Gallagher, "The Public Policy Legacy of Samuel A. Kirk," *Learning Disabilities Research and Practice,* 13, 1 (1998), 11–14.

82. Kirk briefly held this position in order to launch the office, and then he returned to the University of Illinois. Kirk, "Autobiography," 238–269. Kirk, "Introspection and Prophecy," 25–55. Gallagher, "The Public Policy Legacy of Samuel A. Kirk," 11–14.

83. Daniel P. Hallahan and Devery Mock, "A Brief History of the Field of Learning Disabilities," in *Handbook of Learning Disabilities,* ed. H. Lee Swanson, Karen R. Harris, and Steve Graham (New York, 2003), 16–29.

84. Hallahan and Mock, "A Brief History of the Field of Learning Disabilities," 16–29. Kirk and Kirk, "On Defining Learning Disabilities," 20–21.

85. Gallagher, "The Public Policy Legacy of Samuel A. Kirk," 11–14.

86. Hallahan and Mock, "A Brief History of the Field of Learning Disabilities," 16–29.

87. Ray H. Barsch, "Autobiography," in *Teaching Children with Learning Disabilities: Personal Perspectives,* ed. James M. Kauffman and Daniel P. Hallahan (Columbus, OH, 1976), 71.

88. Charles Bazerman, "Scientific Writing as a Social Act: A Review of the Literature of the Sociology of Science," in *New Essays in Technical and Scientific Communication: Research, Theory, Practice,* ed. Paqul V. Anderson, R. John Brockmann, and Carolyn R. Miller (Farmingdale, NY, 1983), 171.

89. Frierson, "Autobiography," 140.

90. Fred McKinney, "Functionalism at Chicago—Memories of a Graduate Student: 1929–1931," *Journal of the History of the Behavioral Sciences,* 14, 2 (1978), 142–148. Paul L. Whitely,

"A New Name for An Old Idea? A Student of Harvey Carr Reflects," *Journal of the History of the Behavioral Sciences*, 12 (1976), 260–274.

91. Alfred A. Strauss to Samuel A. Kirk, June 30, 1949, Box 6, Samuel A. Kirk Papers (Archives Research Center, University of Illinois, Urbana). Samuel A. Kirk to Alfred A. Strauss, July 5, 1949, Box 6, Samuel A. Kirk Papers (Archives Research Center, University of Illinois, Urbana).

92. Samuel A. Kirk, "Lecture—Final Report, Advanced Institute for Leadership Personnel in Learning Disabilities, Department of Special Education, University of Arizona," type-script, 1970, Box 10, Samuel A. Kirk Papers (Archives Research Center, University of Illinois, Urbana).

93. Marianne Frostig to Samuel A. Kirk, January 22, 1965, Box 8, Samuel A. Kirk Papers (Archives Research Center, University of Illinois, Urbana). Samuel A. Kirk to Marianne Frostig, February 1, 1965, Box 8, Samuel A. Kirk Papers (Archives Research Center, University of Illinois, Urbana).

94. Jeanne McRae McCarthy, one of Kirk's doctoral students who went on to achieve significant status in the field of learning disabilities, described the field as having a "variegated heritage" involving a variety of perspectives and traditions. Jeanne McRae McCarthy, "Autobiography," in *Teaching Children with Learning Disabilities: Personal Perspectives,* ed. James M. Kauffman and Daniel P. Hallahan (Columbus, OH, 1976), 323.

95. Samuel A. Kirk, "Are We Confused?" (version 2).

96. Gallagher, "The Public Policy Legacy of Samuel A. Kirk," 13.

7 COUNTRY MOVEMENT AND CITY CHILDREN: AGRARIANISM IN MOVEMENT EDUCATION

1. Rosalind C. Oppenheim, "They Said Our Child Was Hopeless," *Saturday Evening Post,* June 17, 1961, pp. 23, 56, 58.

2. David B. Danbom, "Romantic Agrarianism in Twentieth-Century America," *Agricultural History,* 65, 4 (1991), 1.

3. Lawrence Buell, *The Environmental Imagination: Thoreau, Nature Writing, and the Formation of American Culture* (Cambridge, MA, 1995), 31.

4. Buell, *The Environmental Imagination: Thoreau, Nature Writing, and the Formation of American Culture,* 40.

5. Leo Marx, *The Machine in the Garden: Technology and the Pastoral Ideal in America* (New York, 1964), 229.

6. Leo Marx, "Does Pastoralism Have a Future?" in *The Pastoral Landscape,* ed. John Dixon Hunt (Hanover, NH, 1992), 209.

7. Marx, "Does Pastoralism Have a Future," 212.

8. Ray Williams, *The Country and the City* (New York, 1973), 45.

9. David Rosand, "Pastoral Topoi: On the Construction of Meaning in Landscape," in *The Pastoral Landscape,* ed. John Dixon Hunt (Hanover, NH, 1992), 161.

10. Mitchell Gordon, Sick Cities (New York, 1963). Lewis Herber, Crisis in Our Cities (Englewood Cliffs, NJ, 1965). Richard J. Whalen, *A City Destroying Itself: An Angry View of New York* (New York, 1965). York Willbern, *The Withering Away of the City* (Birmingham, AL, 1964).

11. Jeffrey K. Hadden, Louis H. Masotti, and Calvin J. Larson, *Metropolis in Crisis: Social and Political Perspectives* (Itaska, IL, 1967).

12. Willbern, *The Withering Away of the City*, 49.

13. Helen Nearing and Scott Nearing, *Living the Good Life: How to Live Sanely and Simply in a Troubled World* (New York, 1970).

14. E. F. Schumacher, *Small Is Beautiful: A Study of Economics as if People Mattered* (London, 1973).

15. Nearing and Nearing, *Living the Good Life: How to Live Sanely and Simply in a Troubled*, xvi.

16. Martin Schiff, "Neo-transcendentalism in the New Left Counter-culture: A Vision of the Future Looking Back," *Comparative Studies in History and Society*, 15, 2 (1973), 130–142.

17. Whalen, *A City Destroying Itself: An Angry View of New York*, 3.

18. Whalen, *A City Destroying Itself: An Angry View of New York*, 163.

19. Whalen, *A City Destroying Itself: An Angry View of New York*, 164.

20. Marianne Frostig and Phyllis Maslow, *Movement Education: Theory and Practice* (Chicago, 1970), 15.

21. Marianne Frostig and Phyllis Maslow, *Learning Problems in the Classroom: Prevention and Remediation* (New York, 1973), 83.

22. D. H. Radler and Newell C. Kephart, *Success through Play: How to Prepare Your Child for School Achievement—and Enjoy It* (New York, 1960), 76.

23. Newell C. Kephart, *The Slow Learner in the Classroom* (Columbus, OH, 1960), 16.

24. Kephart, *The Slow Learner in the Classroom*, 16.

25. Frostig and Maslow, *Movement Education: Theory and Practice*, 74.

26. Frostig and Maslow, *Movement Education: Theory and Practice*, 83.

27. Frostig and Maslow, *Movement Education: Theory and Practice*, 155.

28. Frostig and Maslow, *Movement Education: Theory and Practice*, 83.

29. Kephart, *The Slow Learner in the Classroom*, 16.

30. Frostig and Maslow, *Learning Problems in the Classroom: Prevention and Remediation*, 160.

31. Frostig and Maslow, *Learning Problems in the Classroom: Prevention and Remediation*, 160.

32. Newell C. Kephart, Learning Disability: An Educational Adventure (West Lafayette, IN, 1968), 13.

33. Newell C. Kephart, *Vision and the Retarded Child* (Duncan, OK, 1956), 14.

34. Kephart, *Vision and the Retarded Child*, 16.

35. Marianne Frostig, "Clinical Approaches to Education" (Ph.D. dissertation, University of Southern California, 1955), 2.

36. Frostig and Maslow, *Movement Education: Theory and Practice*, 84.

37. Marianne Frostig, *Education for Dignity* (New York, 1976).

38. Frostig, *Education for Dignity*, 194.

39. Frostig and Maslow, *Learning Problems in the Classroom: Prevention and Remediation*, 160.

40. Frostig and Maslow, *Movement Education: Theory and Practice*, 38.

41. Frostig, "Clinical Approaches to Education," 2.

42. Frostig and Maslow, *Learning Problems in the Classroom: Prevention and Remediation*, 145.

43. Frostig and Maslow, *Learning Problems in the Classroom: Prevention and Remediation*, 160.
44. Kurt Goldstein, *The Organism: A Holistic Approach to Biology Derived from Pathological Data in Man* (New York, 1939), 35.
45. Kurt Goldstein, "Notes on the Development of My Concepts," *Journal of Individual Psychology*, 15, 1 (1959), 9.
46. Kephart, *The Slow Learner in the Classroom*. Radler and Kephart, *Success through Play: How to Prepare Your Child for School Achievement—and Enjoy It*.
47. Frostig, *Education for Dignity*, 178.
48. Frostig and Maslow, *Movement Education: Theory and Practice*, 17.
49. Frostig and Maslow, *Learning Problems in the Classroom: Prevention and Remediation*, 160.
50. Frostig and Maslow, *Movement Education: Theory and Practice*, 67.
51. Frostig and Maslow, *Movement Education: Theory and Practice*, 19.
52. Frostig and Maslow, *Movement Education: Theory and Practice*. Frostig, *Education for Dignity*.
53. Frostig and Maslow, *Learning Problems in the Classroom: Prevention and Remediation*, 160.
54. Kephart, *Learning Disability: An Educational Adventure*, 14.
55. Frostig and Maslow, *Learning Problems in the Classroom: Prevention and Remediation*, 29.
56. Marylou Ebersole, Newell C. Kephart, and James B. Ebersole, *Steps to Achievement for the Slow Learner* (Columbus, OH, 1968), 12.
57. Frostig, *Education for Dignity*, 29.
58. Frostig and Maslow, *Learning Problems in the Classroom: Prevention and Remediation*, 216.
59. Kephart, *Learning Disability: An Educational Adventure*, 13.
60. Kephart, *Learning Disability: An Educational Adventure*, 13.
61. Kephart, *Learning Disability: An Educational Adventure*, 14.
62. Kephart, *Learning Disability: An Educational Adventure*, 13.
63. Kephart, *Learning Disability: An Educational Adventure*, 13.
64. Kephart, *Learning Disability: An Educational Adventure*, 13.
65. Frostig and Maslow, *Learning Problems in the Classroom: Prevention and Remediation*, 212.
66. Basil Bernstein, *Class, Codes, and Control*, Volume 1 (London, 1971).
67. Frostig and Maslow, *Learning Problems in the Classroom: Prevention and Remediation*, 216.
68. Frostig and Maslow, *Learning Problems in the Classroom: Prevention and Remediation*, 216.
69. Frostig and Maslow, *Learning Problems in the Classroom: Prevention and Remediation*, 28.
70. Frostig and Maslow, *Learning Problems in the Classroom: Prevention and Remediation*. Frostig, *Education for Dignity*, 40.
71. Frostig and Maslow, *Movement Education: Theory and Practice*, 163–4.
72. Frostig and Maslow, *Movement Education: Theory and Practice*, 163.
73. Marguerite P. Ford, "New Directions in Special Education," *Journal of School Psychology*, 9, 1 (1971), 73–83. Daniel P. Hallahan, "Cognitive Styles—Preschool Implications for the Disadvantaged," *Journal of Learning Disabilities*, 3 (1970), 5–9. Daniel P. Hallahan and William M. Cruickshank, Psychoeducational Foundations of Learning Disabilities (Englewood Cliffs, NJ, 1973).
74. Murray M. Kappelmann, E. Kaplan, and R. L. Ganter, "A Study of Learning Disorders among Disadvantaged Children," *Journal of Learning Disabilities*, 2 (1969), 267.
75. Gordon R. Alley, Gerald Solomons, and E. Opitz, "Minimal Cerebral Dysfunction as It Relates to Social Class," *Journal of Learning Disabilities*, 4 (1971), 246–250. Dominic

Amante, P. H. Margules, D. M. Hartmann, D. B. Storey, and L. J. Weeber, "The Epidemiological Distribution of CNS Dysfunction," *Journal of Social Issues*, 26, 4 (1970), 105–136. Lester Tarnopol, "Delinquency and Minimal Brain Dysfunction," *Journal of Learning Disabilities*, 3 (1970), 200–207.

76. Kappelmann, Kaplan, and Ganter, "A Study of Learning Disorders among Disadvantaged Children," 262.
77. Hallahan, "Cognitive Styles—Preschool Implications for the Disadvantaged," 5.
78. Hallahan, "Cognitive Styles—Preschool Implications for the Disadvantaged," 5.
79. Hallahan, "Cognitive Styles—Preschool Implications for the Disadvantaged," 5–6.
80. Hallahan and Cruickshank, *Psychoeducational Foundations of Learning Disabilities*, 41.
81. Kephart, *Learning Disability: An Educational Adventure*, 13.
82. Eliana Garces, Duncan Thomas, and Janet Currie, *Longer Term Effects of Head Start* (Santa Monica, CA, 2000), 2.
83. Ebersole, Kephart, and Ebersole, Steps to Achievement for the Slow Learner, 12–13.
84. Marx, *The Machine in the Garden: Technology and the Pastoral Ideal in America*, 141.
85. Newell C. Kephart, "An Experimental Study of the Organization of Function in the Delinquent. State" (Ph.D. dissertation, University of Iowa, 1936).
86. Kephart, "An Experimental Study of the Organization of Function in the Delinquent. State," 45.
87. Clifford R. Shaw, Frederick M. Zorbaugh, Henry D. McKay, and Leonard S. Cottrell, *Delinquency Areas: A Study of the Geographic Distribution of School Truants, Juvenile Delinquents, and Adult Offenders in Chicago* (Chicago, 1929).
88. J. Hector St. John Crevecoeur, *Letters from an American Farmer* (1782, New York, 1904). Thomas Jefferson, *Notes on the State of Virginia* (1787, New York, 1984). Marx, *The Machine in the Garden: Technology and the Pastoral Ideal in America*.
89. Peter J. Schmitt, *Back to Nature: The Arcadian Myth in Urban America* (Baltimore, MD, 1990), 5.
90. Marx, *The Machine in the Garden: Technology and the Pastoral Ideal in America*, 126.
91. Richard Hofstadter, *The Age of Reform: From Bryan to FDR* (New York, 1961), 24.
92. Jefferson, *Notes on the State of Virginia*.
93. Marx, *The Machine in the Garden: Technology and the Pastoral Ideal in America*, 25.
94. Marx, *The Machine in the Garden: Technology and the Pastoral Ideal in America*, 26.
95. Nathaniel Hawthorne, "Notes for Stories and Essays, 1844," in *Nathaniel Hawthorne and His Wife*, ed. Julian Hawthorne (Boston, 1885), 503.
96. Marx, *The Machine in the Garden: Technology and the Pastoral Ideal in America*, 32.
97. Hofstadter, *The Age of Reform: From Bryan to FDR*, 28.
98. Williams, *The Country and the City*, 297.
99. Williams, *The Country and the City*, 297.
100. Henry David Thoreau, *Walking* (1862, New York, 1910), 1.
101. Buell, *The Environmental Imagination: Thoreau, Nature Writing, and the Formation of American Culture*.
102. Jame McIntosh, *Thoreau as Romantic Naturalist: His Shifting Stance toward Nature* (Ithaca, NY, 1974), 33.
103. Henry Nash Smith, *Virgin Land: The American West as Symbol and Myth* (Cambridge, MA, 1950).

104. Allan Carlson, *The New Agrarian Mind: The Movement toward Decentralist Thought in Twentieth-Century America* (New Brunswick, NJ, 2000).
105. Hofstadter, *The Age of Reform: From Bryan to FDR*.
106. *Mr. Smith Goes to Washington*, dir. Frank Capra (Columbia Pictures Corporation 1939).
107. Carlson, *The New Agrarian Mind: The Movement toward Decentralist Thought in Twentieth-Century American*. Schmitt, *Back to Nature: The Arcadian Myth in Urban America*. Smith, *Virgin Land: The American West as Symbol and Myth*.
108. Henry David Thoreau, 1864. *The Maine Woods*. New York: Literary Classics of the United States, p. 645.
109. Smith, *Virgin Land: The American West as Symbol and Myth*, 123.
110. Carlson, *The New Agrarian Mind: The Movement toward Decentralist Thought in Twentieth-Century American*.
111. Marx, "Does Pastoralism Have a Future", 213.
112. Danbom, "Romantic Agrarianism in Twentieth-Century America," 5.
113. Schmitt, *Back to Nature: The Arcadian Myth in Urban America*.
114. Carlson, *The New Agrarian Mind: The Movement toward Decentralist Thought in Twentieth-Century American*.
115. Rob Holton, "'Real Country and Real People': The Countercultural Pastoral, 1948–1971," in *Beat Culture: The 1950's and Beyond*, ed. Cornelis A. Van Minnen, Jaap Van Der Bent, Mel Van Elteren, and David Amram (Amsterdam, 1999) 93–106.
116. Schmitt, *Back to Nature: The Arcadian Myth in Urban America*, XX.
117. Schmitt, *Back to Nature: The Arcadian Myth in Urban America*, 5.
118. Schmitt, *Back to Nature: The Arcadian Myth in Urban America*, 39.
119. Ralph Borsodi, *The Ugly Civilization* (New York, 1928), Ralph Borsodi, *Flight from the City* (New York, 1933). Ralph Borsodi, *Prosperity and Security: A Study in Realistic Economics* (New York, 1938).
120. Luigi Liguitti, as quoted by Vincent A. Yzermans, *The People I Love* (Collegeville, MN, 1976), 32.
121. Carlson, *The New Agrarian Mind: The Movement toward Decentralist Thought in Twentieth-Century America*, 4.
122. Carlson, *The New Agrarian Mind: The Movement toward Decentralist Thought in Twentieth-Century America*, 4.
123. L. G. Liguitti, "Cities Kill," *Commonweal*, August 2, 1940. pp. 300–302.
124. Joan Aldous and Wilfried Dumon, "Family Policy in the 1980s: Controversy and Consensus," *Journal of Marriage and the Family*, 52, 4 (1990), 1136–1151. Carlson, *The New Agrarian Mind: The Movement toward Decentralist Thought in Twentieth-Century America*. Pamela Johnston Conover, "The Mobilization of the New Right: A Test of Various Explanations," The Western Political Quarterly, 36, 4 (1983), 632–649. Leo P. Ribuffo, "Family Policy Past as Prologue: Jimmy Carter, the White House Conference on Families, and the Mobilization of the New Christian Right," *Review of Policy Research*, 23, 2 (2006), 311–338.
125. Holton, "'Real Country and Real People': The Countercultural Pastoral, 1948–1971," 98.
126. Marx, "Does Pastoralism Have a Future?" 214.
127. Danbom, "Romantic Agrarianism in Twentieth-Century America," 1–12. Holton, "'Real Country and Real People': The Countercultural Pastoral, 1948–1971," 93–106.

Schiff, "Neo-transcendentalism in the New Left Counter-culture: A Vision of the Future Looking Back," 130–142.

128. David Carallo, *A Fiction of the Past: The Sixties in American History* (New York, 1999), 77.

129. Canned Heat, "Going Up the Country," in *Living the Blues* (LP record, Liberty Records, 1968).

130. Danbom, "Romantic Agrarianism in Twentieth-Century America," 10.

131. Schiff, "Neo-transcendentalism in the New Left Counter-culture: A Vision of the Future Looking Back," 132.

132. Schiff, "Neo-transcendentalism in the New Left Counter-culture: A Vision of the Future Looking Back," 138.

133. Max Wertheimer, "Gestalt Theory," in *A Sourcebook of Gestalt Psychology*, ed. Willis D. Ellis (1938, Highland, NY, 1997), 2.

134. Wertheimer, "Gestalt Theory," 6.

135. Wertheimer, "Gestalt Theory," 5.

136. Wertheimer, "Gestalt Theory," 6.

137. Wertheimer, "Gestalt Theory," 6, italics original.

138. Wertheimer, "Gestalt Theory," 6.

139. Wertheimer, "Gestalt Theory," 7.

140. Robert L. Osgood, *The History of Inclusion in the United States* (Washington, DC, 2005). M. A. Winzer, *The History of Special Education: From Isolation to Integration* (Washington, DC, 1993).

141. Danbom, "Romantic Agrarianism in Twentieth-Century America," 10.

142. Ellen A. Brantlinger, *Who Benefits from Special Education?: Remediating (Fixing) Other People's Children* (Mahwah, NJ, 2006). Beth A. Ferri and David J. Connor, *Reading Resistance: Discourses of Exclusion in Desegregation and Inclusion Debates* (New York, 2006).

EPILOGUE: A SCIENCE IN TRANSITION

1. Donald Hammill Foundation, http://www.hammillfoundation.org/about.html#bio anchor001.

2. Esther H. Minskoff, "Research on Psycholinguistic Training: Critique and Guidelines," *Exceptional Children*, 42 (1975), 136–148. Kathryn A. Lund, Georgianna E. Foster, Fred C. McCall-Perez, "The Effectiveness of Psycholinguistic Training, a Reevaluation," *Exceptional Children*, 44 (1978), 310–319. Donald D. Hammill and Stephen C. Larsen, "The Effectiveness of Psycholinguistic Training: A Reaffirmation of Position," *Exceptional Children*, 44 (1978), 402–414. Virginia Sowell, Randall Parker, Mary Poplin, and Stephen Larsen, "The Effects of Psycholinguistic Training on Improving Psycholinguistic Skills," *Learning Disability Quarterly*, 2 (1979), 69–77. Kenneth Kavale, "Functions of the Illinois Text of Psycholinguistic Abilities: Are They Trainable," *Exceptional Children*, 47 (1981), 496–510. Stephen C. Larsen, Randall M. Parker, and Donald D. Hammill, "Effectiveness of Psycholinguistic Training: A Response to Kavale," *Exceptional Children*, 49 (1982), 60–66. Kenneth A. Kavale, "A Meta-analytic Study of the Frostig Test and Training Program," *International Journal of Disability, Development, and Education*,

31 (1984), 134–141. Donald D. Hammill, "A Brief Look at the Learning Disabilities Movement in the United States," *Journal of Learning Disabilities,* 26 (1993), 295–310.

3. Donald Hammill, Libby Goodman, and J. Lee Wiederholt, "Visual-Motor Processes: Can We Train Them?" *Reading Teacher,* 27 (1974), 476.

4. Hammill, Goodman, and Wiederholt, "Visual-Motor Processes: Can We Train Them?" 472.

5. Hammill, Goodman, and Wiederholt, "Visual-Motor Processes: Can We Train Them," 469–478.

6. Donald Hammill, "Training Visual Perceptual Processes," *Journal of Learning Disabilities,* 5 (1972), 556.

7. Hammill, "Training Visual Perceptual Processes," 556.

8. Hammill, "Training Visual Perceptual Processes," 567.

9. Donald D. Hammill, Nancy Mather, and Rhia Roberts, *The Illinois Test of Psycholinguistic Abilities,* 3rd ed. (Austin, TX, 2001).

10. Donald D. Hammill and Stephen C. Larsen, "The Effectiveness of Psycholinguistic Training," *Exceptional Children,* 41, 1 (1974), 11–12.

11. Hammill and Larsen, "The Effectiveness of Psycholinguistic Training," 12.

12. Hammill and Larsen, "The Effectiveness of Psycholinguistic Training, 5–14. Hammill, Goodman, and Wiederholt, "Visual-Motor Processes: Can We Train Them," 469–478. Hammill, "Training Visual Perceptual Processes," 552–559.

13. Hammill, "Training Visual Perceptual Processes," 554.

14. Hammill, "Training Visual Perceptual Processes," 554.

15. Hammill, Goodman, and Wiederholt, "Visual-Motor Processes: Can We Train Them?" 474.

16. Hammill, Goodman, and Wiederholt, "Visual-Motor Processes: Can We Train Them?" 472.

17. Hammill, Goodman, and Wiederholt, "Visual-Motor Processes: Can We Train Them?" 472.

18. Hammill, Goodman, and Wiederholt, "Visual-Motor Processes: Can We Train Them?" 474.

19. Frostig borrowed this framework from Paul Meehl, *Clinical Versus Statistical Prediction: A Theoretical Analysis and Review of the Literature* (Minneapolis, MN, 1954).

20. Marianne Frostig, "Clinical Approaches to Education" (Ph.D. dissertation, University of Southern California, 1955), 24.

21. Frostig, "Clinical Approaches to Education," 25.

22. Frostig, "Clinical Approaches to Education," 25.

23. Frostig, "Clinical Approaches to Education," 26.

24. Paul Wallin, "Supplementary Study A, the Prediction of Individual Behavior from Case Studies," in *The Prediction of Personal Adjustment,* ed. Social Science Research Council (New York, 1941), 249.

25. Norman K. Denzon and Yvonna S. Lincoln, *Handbook of Qualitative Research* (Thousand Oaks, CA, 1994), 8.

26. M. Clemens Johnson, *A Review of Research Methods in Education* (Chicago, 1977). Stephen Isaac and William B. Michael, *Handbook in Research and Evaluation* (San Diego, 1971). William Wiersma, *Research Methods in Education* (Itasca, IL, 1975). Max D. Engelhart, *Methods of Educational Research* (Chicago, 1972).

27. Johnson, *A Review of Research Methods in Education*, 319.
28. Isaac and Michael, *Handbook in Research and Evaluation*, 20.
29. One can only wonder what Newell Kephart would have felt and thought. The first of the three Hammill critique papers had been published before he passed away in 1973. It is unknown whether he read that article on science of training visual processes. Certainly none of the leading learning disabilities researchers, Kephart included, was educated in philosophy. Their understanding of research methods, from the standpoint of philosophy of science, was atheoretical and utilitarian. The group was not prepared to analyze Hammill's critique in terms of questions of epistemology or Thomas Kuhn's recent work on scientific paradigms. Still, of the entire group, it is likely that Kephart would have issued the strongest and most compelling response to the critique. He was not a man who sought out controversy, but he was also not one to back down from serious challenges. What Kephart would have written and how his argument would have been received by the field of learning disabilities are interesting questions.
30. Samuel A. Kirk, "Learning Disabilities: Reopening Pandora's Box—Speech to Orton Society Annual Conference," typescript, December 4, 1976, p. 10, Box 11, Samuel A. Kirk Papers (Archives Research Center, University of Illinois, Urbana).
31. Kirk, "Learning Disabilities: Reopening Pandora's Box—Speech to Orton Society Annual Conference." For more on the failure of research to inform practice, see Samuel A. Kirk, "The Classroom of 1975," typescript, October 29, 1969, Box 11, Samuel A. Kirk Papers (Archives Research Center, University of Illinois, Urbana). "Samuel A. Kirk to Ray Graham," typescript, December 31, 1957, Box 7, Samuel A. Kirk Papers (Archives Research Center, University of Illinois, Urbana).
32. Samuel A. Kirk, "Controversies in Learning Disabilities, ACLD Conference," typescript, February, 1985, p. 2, Box 11, Samuel A. Kirk Papers (Archives Research Center, University of Illinois, Urbana).
33. Marianne Frostig, "Five Questions Regarding My Past and Future and the Past, Present, and Future of Learning Disabilities," 538.
34. Frostig, "Five Questions Regarding My Past and Future and the Past, Present, and Future of Learning Disabilities," 538.
35. Marianne Frostig, "Learning Difficulties: Optimism or Pessimism," *School Psychology Digest*, 5, 1 (1976), 5.
36. Ray H. Barsch, "Autobiography," in *Teaching Children with Learning Disabilities: Personal Perspectives*, ed. James M. Kauffman and Daniel P. Hallahan (Columbus, OH, 1976), 64.
37. Gerald N. Getman, "Autobiography," in *Teaching Children with Learning Disabilities: Personal Perspectives*, ed. James M. Kauffman and Daniel P. Hallahan (Columbus, OH, 1976), 226.
38. John Arena, "An Interview with G. N. Getman," *Academic Therapy*, 15, 2 (1979), 235.
39. "Samuel A. Kirk to Ray Graham," typescript, December 26, 1956, Box 7, Samuel A. Kirk Papers (Archives Research Center, University of Illinois, Urbana).
40. Samuel A. Kirk, "Rearranging Our Prejudices," typescript, p. 5, Box 3, Samuel A. Kirk Papers (Archives Research Center, University of Illinois, Urbana).
41. Kirk, "Rearranging Our Prejudices."

Index

Disability
Studies in
Education

GENERAL EDITORS: SUSAN L. GABEL & SCOT DANFORTH

The book series Disability Studies in Education is dedicated to the publication of monographs and edited volumes that integrate the perspectives, methods, and theories of disability studies with the study of issues and problems of education. The series features books that further define, elaborate upon, and extend knowledge in the field of disability studies in education. Special emphasis is given to work that poses solutions to important problems facing contemporary educational theory, policy, and practice.

To order other books in this series, please contact our Customer Service Department:

(800) 770-LANG (within the U.S.)
(212) 647-7706 (outside the U.S.)
(212) 647-7707 FAX

Or browse by series:

WWW.PETERLANG.COM